CONTENTS

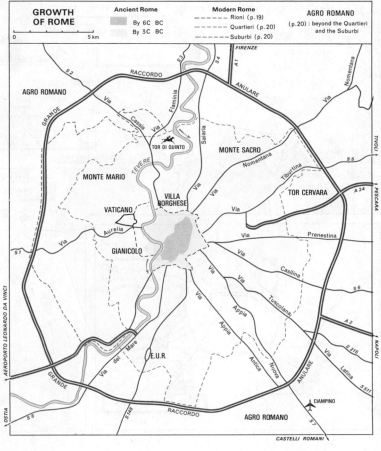

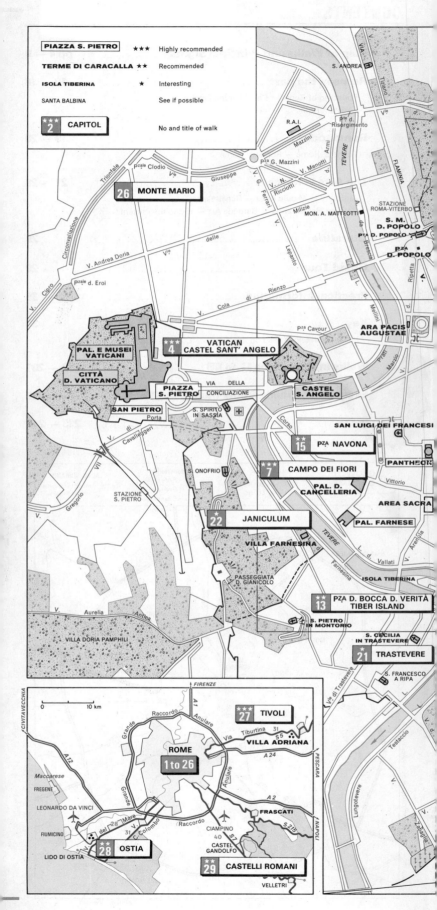

PIAZZA S. PIETRO ★★★ Highly recommended

TERME DI CARACALLA ★★ Recommended

ISOLA TIBERINA ★ Interesting

SANTA BALBINA See if possible

2 CAPITOL No and title of walk

26 MONTE MARIO

4 VATICAN CASTEL SANT' ANGELO

PAL. E MUSEI VATICANI

CITTÀ D. VATICANO

SAN PIETRO

PIAZZA S. PIETRO

VIA DELLA CONCILIAZIONE

S. SPIRITO IN SASSIA

CASTEL S. ANGELO

ARA PACIS AUGUSTAE

SAN LUIGI DEI FRANCESI

15 PZA NAVONA

PANTHEON

7 CAMPO DEI FIORI

PAL. D. CANCELLERIA

AREA SACRA

22 JANICULUM

PAL. FARNESE

VILLA FARNESINA

ISOLA TIBERINA

13 PZA D. BOCCA D. VERITÀ TIBER ISLAND

S. PIETRO IN MONTORIO

S. CECILIA IN TRASTEVERE

21 TRASTEVERE

S. FRANCESCO A RIPA

VILLA DORIA PAMPHILI

0   10 km

FIRENZE

27 TIVOLI

VILLA ADRIANA

ROME **1 to 26**

28 OSTIA

FRASCATI

29 CASTELLI ROMANI

VELLETRI

Maccarese

FREGENE

LEONARDO DA VINCI

FIUMICINO

LIDO DI OSTIA

CIAMPINO

CASTEL GANDOLFO

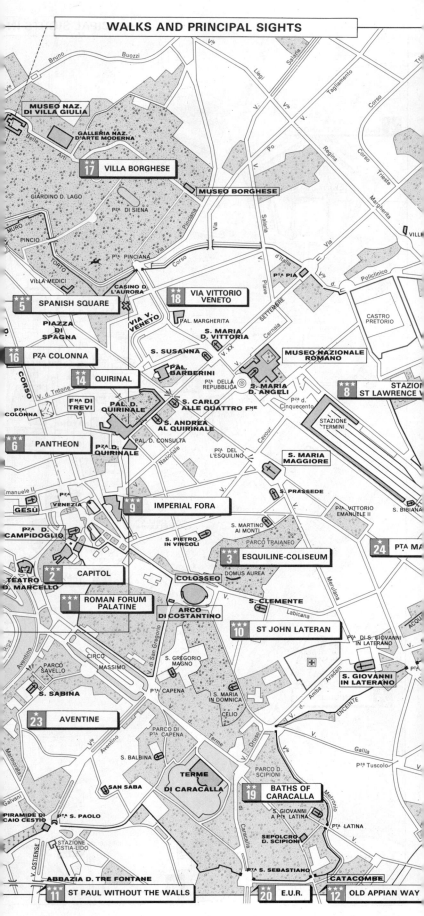

WALKS AND PRINCIPAL SIGHTS

MUSEO NAZ. DI VILLA GIULIA

GALLERIA NAZ. D'ARTE MODERNA

17 ★★ VILLA BORGHESE

GIARDINO D. LAGO

PZA DI SIENA

MUSEO BORGHESE

MURO

PINCIO

VILLA MEDICI

CASINO D. L'AURORA

PZA PINCIANA

PTA PIA

5 ★★★ SPANISH SQUARE

18 ★★ VIA VITTORIO VENETO

PIAZZA DI SPAGNA

VIA V. VENETO

PAL. MARGHERITA

S. MARIA D. VITTORIA

CASTRO PRETORIO

16 ★★ PZA COLONNA

S. SUSANNA

MUSEO NAZIONALE ROMANO

14 ★★ QUIRINAL

PAL. BARBERINI

PZA DELLA REPUBBLICA

S. MARIA D. ANGELI

8 ★★★ STAZIO ST LAWRENCE

PZA COLONNA

V. d. Trtone

FNA DI TREVI

PAL. D. QUIRINALE

S. CARLO ALLE QUATTRO FNE

S. ANDREA AL QUIRINALE

Pza d. Cinquecento

STAZIONE TERMINI

6 ★★★ PANTHEON

PAL. D. CONSULTA

PZA D. QUIRINALE

PZA DEL L'ESQUILINO

S. MARIA MAGGIORE

manuele II

PZA VENEZIA

GESÙ

9 ★★★ IMPERIAL FORA

S. PRASSEDE

PZA VITTORIO EMANUELE II

S. BIBIANA

PZA D. CAMPIDOGLIO

S. MARTINO AI MONTI

PARCO TRAIANEO

24 ★ PTA MA

S. PIETRO IN VINCOLI

3 ★★★ ESQUILINE-COLISEUM

2 ★★★ CAPITOL

COLOSSEO

DOMUS AUREA

TEATRO D. MARCELLO

S. CLEMENTE

Labicana

1 ★★ ROMAN FORUM PALATINE

ARCO DI COSTANTINO

10 ★★★ ST JOHN LATERAN

PZA DI S. GIOVANNI IN LATERANO

CIRCO

S. GREGORIO MAGNO

PARCO SAVELLO

MASSIMO

S. GIOVANNI IN LATERANO

S. SABINA

PTA CAPENA

S. MARIA IN DOMNICA

CELIO

23 ★ AVENTINE

PARCO DI PTA CAPENA

S. BALBINA

Gallia

PZA Tuscolo

S. SABA

TERME DI CARACALLA

PARCO D. SCIPIONI

19 ★★ BATHS OF CARACALLA

S. GIOVANNI A PTA LATINA

PIRAMIDE DI CAIO CESTIO

PTA S. PAOLO

PTA LATINA

STAZIONE OSTIA-LIDO

SEPOLCRO D. SCIPIONI

PTA S. SEBASTIANO

ABBAZIA D. TRE FONTANE

CATACOMBE

11 ★★ ST PAUL WITHOUT THE WALLS

20 ★★ E.U.R.

12 ★★★ OLD APPIAN WAY

5

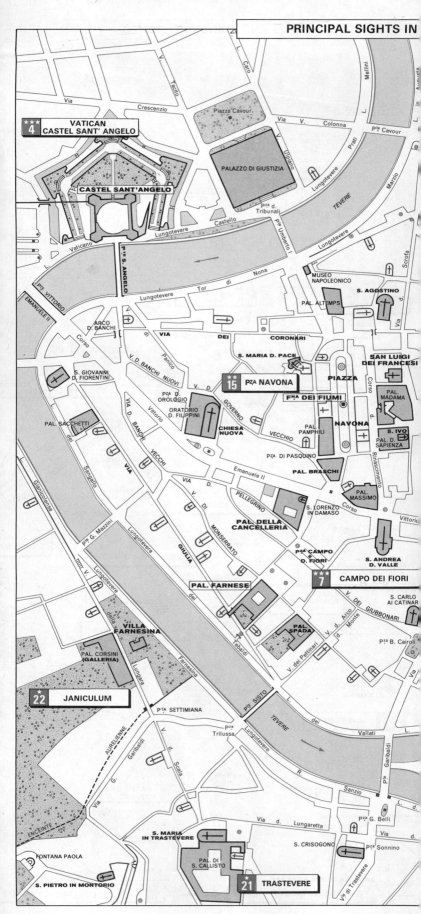

★★★
4 VATICAN
CASTEL SANT' ANGELO

CASTEL SANT'ANGELO

PALAZZO DI GIUSTIZIA

Piazza Cavour

TEVERE

P.te Cavour

Lungotevere

Pza d. Tribunali

Lungotevere

Castello

Lungotevere

Vaticano

di Nona

Tor

MUSEO NAPOLEONICO

S. AGOSTINO

PAL. ALTEMPS

Lungotevere

ARCO D. BANCHI

VIA DEI CORONARI

S. MARIA D. PACE

SAN LUIGI DEI FRANCESI

Corso

S. GIOVANNI D. FIORENTINI

★★
15 P.ZA NAVONA

PIAZZA

PAL. MADAMA

V. D. BANCHI NUOVI

P.ZA D. OROLOGIO

ORATORIO D. FILIPPINI

CHIESA NUOVA

F.NA DEI FIUMI

NAVONA

S. IVO

PAL. SACCHETTI

VECCHIO

PAL. PAMPHILI

PAL. D. SAPIENZA

Emanuele II

P.ZA DI PASQUINO

PAL. BRASCHI

VIA D.

PELLEGRINO

S. LORENZO IN DAMASO

PAL. MASSIMO

Corso

Vittorio

PAL. DELLA CANCELLERIA

GIULIA

MONSERRATO

P.ZA CAMPO D. FIORI

S. ANDREA D. VALLE

★★★
7 CAMPO DEI FIORI

PAL. FARNESE

S. CARLO AI CATINAR

V. DEI GIUBBONARI

VILLA FARNESINA

PAL. SPADA

Arco d. Monte

P.ZA B. Cairoli

Tebaldi

V. del Pettinari

PAL. CORSINI (GALLERIA)

Farnesina

Lungara

★★
22 JANICULUM

P.TA SISTIMIANA

P.TA SISTO

TEVERE

Vallati

ENCEINTE

AURELIENNE

P.ZA Trilussa

Lungotevere

Garibaldi

Sanzio

P.ZA G. Belli

Via d. Lungaretta

S. MARIA IN TRASTEVERE

S. CRISOGONO

P.ZA Sonnino

FONTANA PAOLA

PAL. DI S. CALLISTO

★
21 TRASTEVERE

S. PIETRO IN MONTORIO

PRINCIPAL SIGHTS

(Plans pp 4-5-6 and 8-9)

The index on p 212 gives the page number for the description of the sight.

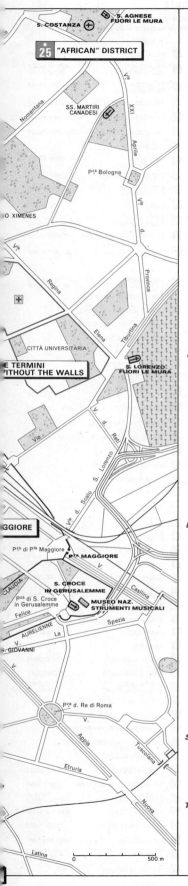

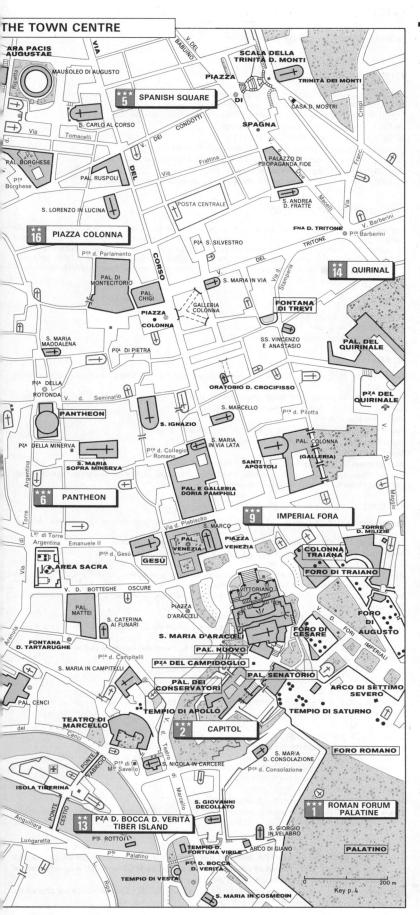

ARA PACIS AUGUSTAE

MAUSOLEO DI AUGUSTO

★★★ 5 SPANISH SQUARE

SCALA DELLA TRINITA D. MONTI

PIAZZA DI

TRINITÀ DEI MONTI

CASA D. MOSTRI

SPAGNA

S. CARLO AL CORSO

V. DEL BABUINO

V. DEI CONDOTTI

Tomacelli

Via

Frattina

PALAZZO DI PROPAGANDA FIDE

PAL. BORGHESE

P.za Borghese

PAL. RUSPOLI

Via

S. ANDREA D. FRATTE

S. LORENZO IN LUCINA

POSTA CENTRALE

FNA D. TRITONE

P.za Barberini

V. Barberini

★★ 16 PIAZZA COLONNA

P.za d. Parlamento

P.za S. SILVESTRO

TRITONE

DEL

Via d. Stamperia

★★ 14 QUIRINAL

PAL. DI MONTECITORIO

PAL. CHIGI

GALLERIA COLONNA

S. MARIA IN VIA

PIAZZA COLONNA

FONTANA DI TREVI

PAL. DEL QUIRINALE

S. MARIA MADDALENA

P.za DI PIETRA

SS. VINCENZO E ANASTASIO

P.za DEL QUIRINALE

P.za DELLA ROTONDA

V. d. Seminario

ORATORIO D. CROCIFISSO

PANTHEON

S. IGNAZIO

S. MARCELLO

P.za d. Pilotta

P.za DELLA MINERVA

S. MARIA SOPRA MINERVA

P.za d. Collegio Romano

S. MARIA IN VIA LATA

PAL. COLONNA

(GALLERIA)

Argentina

★★★ 6 PANTHEON

PAL. E GALLERIA DORIA PAMPHILI

SANTI APOSTOLI

Torre

L.go di Torre Argentina

Emanuele II

Via d. Plebiscito

S. MARCO

★★★ 9 IMPERIAL FORA

TORRE D. MILIZIE

Via

P.za d. Gesù

GESÙ

PAL. VENEZIA

PIAZZA VENEZIA

COLONNA TRAIANA

FORO DI TRAIANO

AREA SACRA

V. D. BOTTEGHE OSCURE

VITTORIANO

FORO DI CESARE

FORO DI AUGUSTO

PAL. MATTEI

S. CATERINA AI FUNARI

PIAZZA D'ARACOELI

V. D. FORI IMPERIALI

FONTANA D. TARTARUGHE

P.za d. Campitelli

S. MARIA D'ARACOELI

PAL. NUOVO

Arenula

S. MARIA IN CAMPITELLI

P.za DEL CAMPIDOGLIO

PAL. SENATORIO

ARCO DI SETTIMIO SEVERO

PAL. CENCI

PAL. DEI CONSERVATORI

TEMPIO DI APOLLO

TEMPIO DI SATURNO

TEATRO DI MARCELLO

Cenci

★★★ 2 CAPITOL

FORO ROMANO

del

P.za di M.te Savello

S. NICOLA IN CARCERE

S. MARIA D. CONSOLAZIONE

P.za d. Consolazione

ISOLA TIBERINA

PONTE FABRICIO

PONTE CESTIO

S. GIOVANNI DECOLLATO

★★★ 1 ROMAN FORUM PALATINE

Anguillara

★★ 13 P.za D. BOCCA D. VERITÀ TIBER ISLAND

P.te ROTTO

S. GIORGIO IN VELABRO

Lungaretta

P.te Palatino

TEMPIO D. FORTUNA VIRILE

ARCO DI GIANO

PALATINO

Via Ripa

P.za D. BOCCA D. VERITÀ

TEMPIO DI VESTA

S. MARIA IN COSMEDIN

0   200 m

Key p. 4

ROME IN THE PAST

(in brown: a few historical landmarks)

THE MONARCHY (753-509 BC)

753	Legendary foundation of Rome on the Palatine by **Romulus**. In fact the union of the Latin and Sabine settlements on the hills **(Septimontium)** took place *c*8C BC.
715-672	Reign of **Numa Pompilius**, a Sabine king. Organisation of religious life.
672-640	Reign of **Tullus Hostilius**, a Sabine king.
640-616	Reign of **Ancus Martius**, a Sabine king.
616-578	Reign of **Tarquin the Elder**, an Etruscan king. Forum laid out *(p 37)*.
578-534	Reign of **Servius Tullius**, an Etruscan king. Name of Rome appears.
534-509	Reign of **Tarquin the Proud**, an Etruscan king.
509?	Rome frees herself from the Etruscan yoke. Establishment of the Republic.

THE REPUBLIC (509-27 BC)

The Republican era is marked by the struggle between the patricians and the plebeians. Faced by the patrician families *(gentes)* who were linked by religious ties and owned the greater part of the best land for cultivation and stock rearing, the plebeians seceded, depriving the town of their labour and the army of their manpower. This period saw the conquest of the Italian peninsula and the Mediterranean basin. The increasing importance of the army promoted the generals who imposed their personality to the detriment of the Senate.

4C BC

A plebeian is elected consul for the first time in 366.
Appius Claudius Caecus (340-273?), censor and consul *(p 21)*.
The magistrature is opened to the Plebeians (300).

3C BC

Andronicus (284-204), a poet of Greek origin who is brought to Rome as a slave, introduces the people to Greek culture.
Rome rules the peninsula from the Straits of Messina to the Arno (265).
Naevius (265?-201?), a poet of Roman history *(p 29)*.
First Punic War (264-241).
Plautus (254-184), poet and adaptor of Greek works; father of operetta.
Ennius (239-169), poet who found his inspiration in Greek works.
Second Punic War (218-201).
Scipio Africanus (235-183), general, politician, conqueror of Spain.
Cato the Censor (234-149), general, politician and writer, defender of Roman civilisation against Greek influence; called for the destruction of Carthage.

2C-1C BC: towards personal power

Tiberius Gracchus (162-133), tribune of the people in whose favour he promulgated agrarian laws. Assassinated.
Caius Gracchus (154-121), Tiberius' brother, tribune of the people, assassinated.
Third Punic War (149-146). Destruction of Carthage.
First Civil War (89-82).
Marius (157-86), general, elected consul by the popular party against the Senate party. Conqueror of Jugurtha the Numidian, of the Teutones and of the Cimbri.
Sulla (138-78), general, consul and supporter of the nobility and the Senate party. Major participant in the civil war with Marius. Proclaimed dictator for life.
Varro (116-27), first Roman encyclopaedist; discovered bacteria.
Crassus (115?-53), general and consul. He put down the revolt led by Spartacus (6 000 prisoners were crucified). Richest man in Rome and Caesar's financier.
Cataline (109?-62), politician. Supporter of the popular party, he master-minded a plot which was uncovered by Cicero *(p 39)*.
Cicero (106-43), consul, writer, orator *(p 29)*. Assassinated *(p 42)*.
Pompey (106-48), general, consul with Crassus.
Second civil war (49-45).
Caesar (101-44), general, consul, ally of Pompey and Crassus **(1st Triumvirate)** *(p 16)*.
Lucretius (98?-55), poet and philosopher.
Catullus (87?-54?), poet.
Sallust (86-35?), historian *(p 29)*.
Brutus (85?-42), politician, defender of the Republic, one of the assassins of Caesar.
Antony (83-30), consul with Caesar, pretender to the succession. Alliance with Octavian and Lepidus **(2nd Triumvirate)**. Married Cleopatra. Defeated by Octavian at Actium in Greece (31).
Virgil (70?-19), poet, author of the Aeneid inspired by Homer.
Horace (65-8), poet.
Agrippa (63-12), general. Admiral of Octavian's fleet at Actium.
Octavian-Augustus (63BC-14AD), general, successor to Caesar *(pp 16-17)*. Promoted a new political regime which resulted in the Empire.

> *Roman historians generally counted the years from the foundation of Rome (Ab Urbe Condita). The system of counting from the birth of Christ (AD) was introduced in 6C by Dionysius Exiguus, a Scythian monk.*
> *According to Varro, Rome was founded in about 753 BC; Caesar's murder therefore took place in the year 710 after the founding of Rome, i.e. 44 BC.*

THE EARLY EMPIRE (1C BC to 3C AD)

The Julio-Claudian Emperors

Augustus (27 BC-14 AD) *(p 16)*	**Livy** (59 BC?-17 AD), historian *(p 29)*.
	Propertius (47?-15 BC?), poet of despair.
	Ovid (43 BC-17 AD), writer of light verse, author of the Metamorphoses, a poem based on Greek fables.
	Drusus (38-9 BC), military leader, adopted son of Augustus, victor in Germany. He was the first Roman to reach the Elbe.
Tiberius (14-37)	**Germanicus** (15 BC-19 AD), general, Drusus' son, campaigned in Germany.
	Jesus condemned to death (29).
Caligula (37-41)	
Claudius (41-54)	
Nero (54-68)	Violent persecution of Christians following the fire in 64.
	Martyrdom of St Peter (first pope) and St Paul.
	Seneca (4 BC?-65 AD), philosopher, politician, tutor to Nero who ordered him to take his own life.
	Succession disputed: reigns of Galba, Otho, Vitellius.

The Flavians

Vespasian (69-79)	**Pliny the Elder** (23-79), author of a natural history in 37 volumes. Died while observing the eruption of Vesuvius at close quarters.
Titus (79-81)	
Domitian (81-96)	Persecution of Christians (95). Pontificate of Clement I (88-97).

The Antonines

Nerva (96-98)	**Martial** (40?-104?), satirical poet.
Trajan (98-117)	**Tacitus** (55?-120?), politician and writer *(p 29)*.
	Pliny the Younger (62-114?), politician and writer *(p 29)*.
	Apollodorus of Damascus (67?-129?), architect to Trajan and Hadrian.
Hadrian (117-138)	**Juvenal** (60?-140?), poet who pilloried society.
Antoninus Pius (138-161)	**Suetonius** (69?-125?), historian who recorded the lives of the Emperors *(p 29)*.
Marcus Aurelius (161-180)	**Apuleius** (125-180?), philosopher, famous for writing the Golden Ass, a Latin romance.
Commodus (180-192)	

The Severans

Septimius-Severus (193-211)	Edict forbidding conversion to Christianity (202).
	Pontificate of Zephyrinus (199-217).
Caracalla (211-217)	**Tertullian** (155?-220?), wrote in defence of Christianity, attacked luke-warm adherents; a model of eloquence.
Elagabalus (218-222)	**Origen** (182?-253?), Christian writer.
Alexander Severus (222-235)	The **end of the Severan dynasty** was followed by a period of anarchy; the majority of the emperors were acclaimed by their soldiers and died by assassination.
	The Empire fragments under the pressure of invasion from the north and east.
Decius (249-251)	Edict against the Christians (250). Pontificate of Fabian (236-250).
Valerian (253-260)	Christian worship forbidden and sacrifice to the gods obligatory. Pontificate of Stephen I (254-257) and of Sixtus II (257-258).
Aurelian (270-275)	Re-unification of the Empire. Rome fortified.

THE LATER EMPIRE (3C - 4C)

Diocletian (284-305) **Maximian** (286-305) **Constantius-Chlorus** (293-306)	Institution of the **tetrarchy** (government by four): Diocletian, assisted by Galerius, ruled the **eastern empire**; Maximian, assisted by Constantius Chlorus, ruled the Western empire. None of them lived in Rome (Diocletian in Nicomedia; Galerius in Sirmium; Maximian in Milan; Constantius Chlorus in Trier).
Galerius (293-311)	Persecution of Christians (303). Pontificate of Marcellinus (296-304). Christians granted freedom of worship by Galerius (311).
Constantine (306-337)	Defeat of Maxentius, Maximian's son (312) by Constantius-Chlorus' son, Constantine who became Emperor in the East. Toleration of Christianity proclaimed (so-called **Edict of Milan** 313). Reunification of the Empire (divided into East and West) (324) and transfer of the capital to Byzantium, re-named Constantinople (330). On his death the Empire was again divided among his three sons.
Julian the Apostate (360-363)	Attempt to foster paganism *(p 39)*.
	St Ambrose (340?-397), Archbishop of Milan, Father of the Church, influenced the policy of the Emperor Theodosius.
	St Jerome (347?-420), adviser to Pope Damasus, Father of the Church, translated the Bible into Latin (the "Vulgate").
Theodosius (379-395)	Paganism outlawed (391). On his death the Empire definitely divided between his two sons: Arcadius in the East; Honorius in the West in Ravenna.
	St Augustine (354-430), converted to Christianity in 386, author of the City of God and the Confessions, the most famous Father of the Church.

THE INVASIONS (5C - 6C)

	Rome captured by Alaric, king of the Visigoths (411).
	Rome sacked by Genseric, king of the Vandals (455).
	Romulus Augustulus deposed by Odoacer, king of the Heruli: **end of the Western Empire** (476).
Justinian (527-565)	Emperor of Byzantium, expelled the Ostrogoths from Rome (536-552). Lombard invasion (568).

11

THE PAPAL CENTURIES (6C - 19C)

Gregory I (590-604)	Disappearance of the Western Empire. The Emperor represented in Ravenna by an exarch. Rome in principle subject to Byzantium, in fact defended and sustained by the Pope in residence.
Stephen II (752-757)	752 - Rome threatened by the Lombards; appeal by Stephen II to Pepin the Short. 756 - Donation of Quiersy-sur-Oise; **birth of the Papal States** *(p 71).* 800 - Charlemagne, conqueror and then king of the Lombards, crowned Emperor of Rome by Leo III. 9C - Disintegration of the Carolingian empire. The papacy passes into the hands of powerful families: the Theophylacti, the Crescenzi (10C), the Counts of Tuscany (early 11C).
John XII (955-964)	962 - Appeal by John XII to Otho I, king of the Saxons, who became king of the Lombards. Crowned Emperor, he founded the **Holy Roman Empire** whose head invested the clergy with their titles.
Stephen IX (1057-1058)	1057 - Stephen IX elected Pope without the Emperor's approval.
Gregory VII (1073-1085)	1075 - Decree by Gregory VII forbidding the clergy to receive their titles from a layman: conflict between the Papacy and the Empire (**Investiture Controversy**). Invasion of Rome by Henry IV (1084). Concordat of Worms (1122): the Emperor renounced investiture by ring and staff.
Callistus II (1119-1124)	
Innocent II (1130-1143)	1130-1155 - Arnold of Brescia's attempt to form a Roman Republic against the Pope.
Eugenius III (1145-1153)	1153 - Treaty of Constance: Frederick Barbarossa protected the Pope. Arnold of Brescia captured and hanged. New conflict between the Pope and the Emperor. Rome fortified with towers (**Roma turrita**) held by different families, some loyal to the Pope and some to the Emperor.
Adrian IV (1154-1159)	
	1309-1377 - **Popes in Avignon.**
	1347 - Rome dominated by Cola di Rienzo *(p 54).*
	1378-1417 - **Great Schism of the West:** two popes, one reigning in Rome and one in Avignon; in 1409 there was a third in Pisa.
Martin V (1417-1431)	1417 - Rome re-instated as capital by Martin V.
Nicholas V (1447-1455)	1453 - Constantinople captured by the Turks. **End of the Eastern Empire.**
Alexander VI (1492-1503)	1494 - En route for Naples, Charles VIII enters Rome, only to be expelled by a coalition including Alexander VI. 1498-1502 - Papacy at war against the Italian States. Conquest of the Romagna by Caesar Borgia, Alexander VI's son, with the assistance of Louis XII installed in the Milan area.
Julius II (1503-1513)	1508-1512 - Julius II at war: to retain the Romagna (supported by Louis XIII); to expel Louis XII ('militant papacy').
Leo X (1513-1521)	1520 - Publication of Luther's 'Great reforming theses', the basis of the **Protestant Reformation.**
Clement VII (1523-1534)	6 May 1527 - Rome put to the sack by the troops of Charles V.
Paul III (1534-1549)	1545-1563 - **Council of Trent** which gave birth to the Catholic or **Counter-Reformation.**
Julius III (1550-1555)	
Marcellus II (1555)	
Paul IV (1555-1559)	
Pius IV (1559-1565)	
Pius V (1566-1572)	1571 - Christian victory against the Turks at Lepanto in Greece which Pope Pius V saw in a vision long before the news reached Rome.
Paul V (1605-1621)	1618-1648 - Thirty Years War, political and religious.
Gregory XV (1621-1623)	
Urban VIII (1623-1644)	
Innocent X (1644-1655)	1791 - The Papacy renounces Avignon and the Comtat-Venaissin which are annexed to France.
Pius VI (1775-1799)	1797 - **Treaty of Tolentino** between Napoleon and the Pope. 1798 - Occupation of Rome by French troops. Roman Republic declared. Pius VI expelled from Rome, died in exile in Valence.
Pius VII (1800-1823)	1800 - Pius VII elected in Venice, reaches Rome. 1801 - Concordat between Pius VII and Napoleon. 1805-1806 - Disagreement between Pius VII and Napoleon (Jerome Bonaparte's divorce, Pius VII's refusal to apply the continental blockade). 1808 - Rome occupied by the French. The Pope confined in the Quirinal. 1809 - The Papal States reunited with the French Empire by decree. Pius VII sent into captivity in Savona (1812) and then in Fontainebleau. 1814 - Pius VII returns to Rome.

THE CAPITAL OF ITALY

Pius IX (1846-1878)	1820-1861 - Struggle for the unification of the Italian States. Proclamation of the kingdom of Italy with Turin as its capital and Victor Emmanuel II as king. The papal state reduced to the outskirts of Rome. 1870 - Rome proclaimed capital of the kingdom. The Law of Guarantees proposed to the Holy See. Refused by the Pope who retired into the Vatican *(p 71).*
Benedict XV (1914-1922)	28-29 October 1922 - Fascist march on Rome.
Pius XI (1922-1939)	1926 - Mussolini Head of Government. 1929 - The Lateran Treaty *(p 71).*
Pius XII (1939-1958)	19 July 1943 - Rome under bombardment. 4 June 1944 - Rome liberated. June 1946 - Republic established after a referendum. Italy divided into 20 regions. Rome the capital of Latio.
John XXIII (1958-1963)	1957 - Treaty of Rome setting up the Common Market.
Paul VI (1963-1978)	1960 - Olympic Games.
John-Paul II (1978)	

FOUNDING OF ROME

Legendary origins: Venus and Mars. — According to the Roman historians and poets (Livy in his Roman History, Virgil in the Aeneid), Aeneas, son of the goddess Venus and the mortal Anchises, fled from Troy when it was captured, landed at the mouth of the Tiber and married Lavinia, the king of Latium's daughter. He defeated Turnus, the chief of the Rutules, with the aid of Evander, the founder of Pallantea on the Palantine, and founded Lavinium (now Pratica di Mare). On Aeneas' death, his son Ascanius (or Iulus) left Lavinia in charge of Lavinium and went off to found Alba Longa *(p 212)*. The last king of this Alban dynasty was Amulius who deposed his brother Numitor and placed the latter's daughter, Rhea Silvia with the Vestals. Her union with the god Mars gave birth to the twins Romulus and Remus whom Amulius tried to eliminate by abandoning them on the Tiber. The river however was in flood and the twins came to rest at the foot of the Palatine where they were nursed by a wolf and brought up by a couple of shepherds, Faustulus and Larentia. When they reached adolescence they reinstated their grand-father Numitor on the throne of Alba and left to found a new town where they had spent their childhood. There they consulted the birds to discover the omens and Romulus marked a furrow round the sacred area on which the new city was to be built. Jesting, Remus stepped over the line; Romulus killed him for violating the sacred precinct *(pomerium)*. These events took place on the Palatine in about 753 BC. Romulus populated his village with outlaws who settled on the Capitol and he provided them with Sabine wives *(p 55)*. An alliance grew up between the two peoples who were ruled by a succession of kings, alternately Sabine and Latin, until the Etruscans arrived.

(After photo by Gabinetto Fotografico Nazionale, Rome)

The She-Wolf

Historical origins. — Livy and Virgil, who chronicled the earliest days of Rome, and Cicero and Dionysius of Halicarnassus, who commented on the periods of the monarchy, were writing in the Augustan age, some seven centuries after the events which they described. Modern historians have therefore been obliged to turn to archaeology and epigraphy to retrace the birth of Rome and identify the legendary aspects of the city's early years. They have distinguished the true facts from the picturesque embellishments inspired by excessive patriotism. They also take into consideration the theory that Livy's account may be based on Indo-European myths which reflect a conception of society being divided into three classes: priests, soldiers and workers.

A favourable site. — The lower Tiber valley was occupied by the Etruscans to the northwest (on the right bank) and by the Latins and Sabines to the south and northeast (on the left bank). The hills on the left bank, shaped by erosion of the volcanic lava flows from the Alban hills *(p 211),* made excellent defensive positions: particularly the Palatine, its steep sides rising from the surrounding marshy ground and its twin peaks giving a clear view of the Tiber. This site was moreover an ideal staging post on the salt road (Via Salaria) between the salt pans at the mouth of the Tiber and the Sabine country. These favourable features no doubt led to the development of Sabine and Latin settlements grouped around the Palatine.

In 6C BC the Etruscans embarked on a campaign for the conquest of Campania; they crossed the Tiber by the bridge provided by the Latin and Sabine settlements, already established as a 'fortress' at the point where the marshy and alluvial plain is relatively easy to cross. It was then that Rome began to develop into a city *(p 37).*

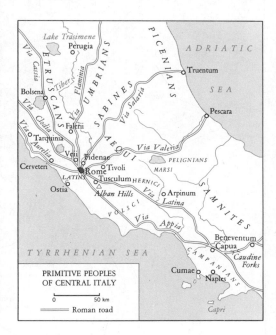

PRIMITIVE PEOPLES
OF CENTRAL ITALY

0   50 km

Roman road

Traces of the origins of Rome are rare.
The oldest include:
— *the items displayed in the Antiquarium in the Roman Forum (11-7C BC) (p 46);*
— *the cemetery in the Roman Forum (8-7C BC) (p 45);*
— *traces of huts on the Palatine (8-7C BC) (p 50);*
— *the Black Stone (Lapis niger) in the Roman Forum (6C BC) (p 42).*

ROME DURING THE EMPIRE

(from 1C BC to 4C AD)

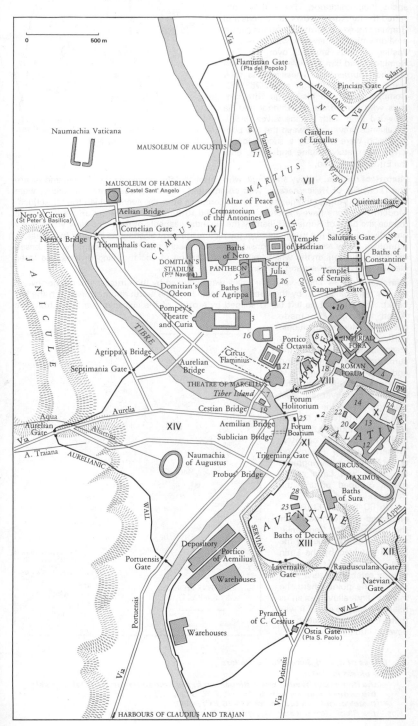

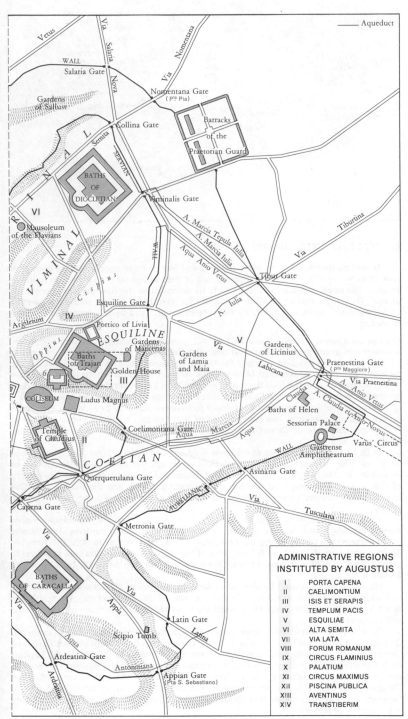

ADMINISTRATIVE REGIONS
INSTITUTED BY AUGUSTUS

I	PORTA CAPENA
II	CAELIMONTIUM
III	ISIS ET SERAPIS
IV	TEMPLUM PACIS
V	ESQUILIAE
VI	ALTA SEMITA
VII	VIA LATA
VIII	FORUM ROMANUM
IX	CIRCUS FLAMINIUS
X	PALATIUM
XI	CIRCUS MAXIMUS
XII	PISCINA PUBLICA
XIII	AVENTINUS
XIV	TRANSTIBERIM

CAPITAL OF THE EMPIRE

It was no doubt desire for extra territory and fear of other peoples strong enough to constitute a threat that drove the Romans out of their village on the Palatine to found an empire. The newly acquired territory had to be defended so the Romans were continually at war. They were also attracted by the desire for gain (booty for the soldiers, new lands to be exploited, taxes to be paid by the subject people) and by the desire for the glory of victory.

Exceptional men. — **Julius Caesar** (101-44 BC), soldier and statesman, orator and writer, a remarkable example of a determined character, began the establishment of the Empire.

He proved his amazing capacity for taking decisions while he was still very young; he was captured by pirates near Miletus in the Aegean; on regaining his liberty he raised a fleet against them and wiped them out. According to a speech he made from the Rostra on the occasion of his aunt Julia's funeral in 68, he was descended from Venus.

While consul in 59 he showed his desire to have his own way by reducing the second consul Bibulus to silence; this was so marked that "certain facetious people... wrote... not of the consulate of Caesar and Bibulus — but — of the consulate of Julius and Caesar" (Suetonius).

In 58 he became Governor of Cisalpine Gaul and of Provincia (later Narbonese Gaul); by 51 he had conquered the whole of Gaul, although the Gauls were thought to be invincible. In January 49 he crossed the Rubicon and marched on Rome against the official powers: Pompey, who had been sole consul since 52, and the Senate fled. Civil war followed. Pompey's army was defeated at Pharsalus in Greece; Pompey was murdered in Egypt.

Early in 44 Caesar was appointed consul and dictator for life; he minted money bearing his effigy, gave his name to the month of his birth (July), pardoned his enemies and weakened the power of the senators by reducing their number to 900. The Republic disintegrated. On 15 March 44 BC (the Ides of March) when the Senate was expected to grant Caesar the title of King of the Orient he was stabbed to death by a group of Senators.

His death was followed by the rise of **Octavian**, the son of Caesar's niece, whom he had adopted as his heir in his will. This young man of 29, who had delicate health and had won no military glory, was to demonstrate great self-control, tenacity of purpose and political genius.

Opposing him was Marc-Antony, consul with Caesar and pretender to the succession. Octavian first weakened his adversary and then became his ally and together with Lepidus, Caesar's cavalry general, they formed the second triumvirate (43 BC). In 13 BC Lepidus died; there remained Antony who was discredited in the eyes of the Romans for repudiating Octavia, Octavian's sister, and marrying Queen Cleopatra of Egypt. Octavian attacked Cleopatra. His victory at Actium in Greece in 31 BC led to Antony's suicide and then to Cleopatra's when she realised that Octavian intended to parade her with the war booty in his victory procession.

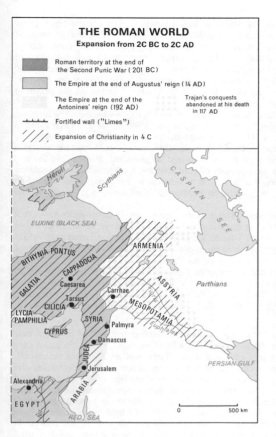

THE ROMAN WORLD
Expansion from 2C BC to 2C AD

Roman territory at the end of the Second Punic War (201 BC)

The Empire at the end of Augustus' reign (14 AD)

The Empire at the end of the Antonines' reign (192 AD)

Trajan's conquests abandoned at his death in 117 AD

Fortified wall ("Limes")

Expansion of Christianity in 4 C

In 27 BC the Senate granted Octavian the title Augustus which invested him with an aura of holiness. A new regime was thus born, the Principate. While maintaining the appearance of Republican government, **Octavian-Augustus** gradually transferred to his own person the political, religious and judicial powers and became the first Roman emperor. His achievements were considerable: he restored peace to the known world, reorganised society which had broken down and divided Rome into 14 districts *(map pp 14-15)*.

The end of his life was saddened by the conduct of his daughter and granddaughter, both called Julia, whom he banned from the family tomb. Suetonius records that on his death bed he asked his friends whether "he had played the farce of life well to the very end". "If the play has pleased you, applaud it and all together show your joy."

After his death he was deified by the Senate and his cult was associated with the cult of Rome and propagated throughout the Empire. In time his reign came to be called the "Augustan era".

Among Augustus' successors there were those who were motivated by cruelty and by hatred of the human race. Such a one was **Tiberius**, son-in-law to Augustus who chose him as his successor against his better judgment following the premature death of his two grandsons Caius and Lucius Caesar. **Caligula** was a psychiatric case: he liked to flatten mountains and raise valleys and hoped for a massacre, a famine or a cataclysm to make his reign memorable in posterity; when the news of his assassination first broke, no one dared rejoice for fear of a trap. After suffering a stroke **Claudius** became very slow witted: "on seeing his funeral, he realised that he was dead" said Seneca. **Nero** was a monster who saw himself as a man of the theatre; "what an artist will perish with me!" he said as he committed suicide.

This succession of disasters came to an end with **Vespasian** who was a good emperor *(p 39)*, concerned for the security of the Empire. His sense of economy led to the installation of public urinals for which the user paid, thus cleansing the streets and providing funds to the exchequer. His son Titus was offended that the State should receive revenue from such a source but the Emperor replied that funds raised in this way had no smell. Titus who was known as the love and delight of the human race reigned only two years while his brother Domitian was responsible for fifteen years of misery.

The reign of the **Antonines** earned the title "golden age" and marked the apogee of the Empire. They included **Trajan**, the "best of Emperors". He was a Spaniard, the first emperor to come from the provinces, intelligent and energetic. He carried out great public works: building a Forum, enlarging the port of Ostia, laying the Via Trajana from Beneventum to Brindisi, constructing a bridge in Alcantara and an aqueduct in Segovia. These projects were largely financed by the gold he amassed from his conquests in Dacia *(p 130)*. He also led campaigns against the Parthians and penetrated as far as the Persian Gulf so that the Empire should profit from the trade between the Far East and the Mediterranean. In 117 he died of exhaustion while returning to Rome. He was succeeded by **Hadrian**, an indefatigable traveller and passionate Hellenist, who toured the Empire from 121 to 125, visited Africa in 128 and journeyed in the Orient from 128 to 134 *(p 202)*. He was almost always away from Rome but he set up a remarkable administrative system which was capable of working in his absence.

CHRISTIAN ROME

As the old order passed away, under attack by barbarians from without and undermined from within by the combined effects of a powerful army, the concentration of authority in the hands of one man, economic misery and moral collapse, a new force — Christianity — emerged. It had first reached Rome in the reign of Augustus. When Paul arrived in about 60 AD there was already a Christian community in existence, although its founder is unknown. There had probably been Christians in Rome since the reign of Claudius (41-54). Suetonius tells how Claudius expelled the Jews who had revolted at the instigation of one Chrestos; Christianity had its roots in Judaism and at first Jews and Christians were confused with one another.

As the Empire crumbled and the world fell into disarray, Christianity preached a new doctrine of brotherly love and the hope of happiness after death. During the last years of 1C and the early years of 2C the Christian church became organised. A collection of texts written at this period by the Apostolic Fathers explains that the Church consisted of deacons who were responsible for providing for the material needs of the community and presbyters whose responsibilities were spiritual and liturgical, with a bishop at the head of each community. Christians met and celebrated the Eucharist in the private house of a convert which was known as a **titulus.**

From the beginning Christians found themselves outside the law because the Emperor was also the chief priest (Pontifex Maximus); to show his loyalty to the State every citizen had to worship the pagan gods. The first violent persecution in Rome was started by Nero in 64 *(p 140).* Trajan recommended that the Christians should not be hounded systematically but that only the most obstinate should be punished. Decius (249-51) and Valerian (253-60), whose reigns were periods of pure anarchy, tried to restore a semblance of unity to the Empire by forcing the Christians to sacrifice to the gods. Under Diocletian (284-305) the repression was extended and reinforced, particularly against the upper classes in society.

It was not until the **Edict of Milan** (313) and the conversion of Constantine (314) that the Church could come out into the open and that Christianity emerged victorious over all attempts to bring back paganism. Theodosius (379-95) was the first Emperor to refuse the title of Pontifex Maximus and in his reign under the influence of Ambrose, Bishop of Milan, Christianity appeared as the state religion.

As the organisation of the Church evolved, there was soon one bishop at the head of several communities and the idea arose that the first bishop of each community had been appointed by an apostle. The bishop of Rome claimed primacy *(p 71).* For nineteen centuries the popes at the head of the Roman church have influenced the history of Christianity.

A reforming pope. — At the end of a period when several popes died of poison if they had not already succumbed to the blows of a cuckolded husband, when the papal tiara was quite shamelessly bought and sold and when Rome had an appalling reputation, **Gregory VII** (1073-85) addressed himself to two scourges which were undermining the Church: the buying and selling of church property and the marriage of the clergy. During the declining years of Charlemagne's empire it had become current practice for a local lord to expropriate an archbishopric, a see, an abbey or a parish so as to protect them and for the clergy to buy them. Once in possession the clergy took wives so as to pass on their property to their children or transformed their houses into virtual courts. In February 1075 Gregory VII issued a series of decrees against these abuses which started the Investiture Controversy. Outnumbered by the Emperor Henry IV's German soldiery, the Pope retreated to the Castel Sant'Angelo and called on the mercenary Robert Guiscard for assistance. Rome suffered terribly from pillaging and massacre and many of the inhabitants were sold into slavery.

A nepotic pope. — **Sixtus IV** (1471-84) was a learned and energetic pope; he wrote a thesis on the blood of Christ and a study of the Immaculate Conception; he made an important contribution to the architectural beauty of Rome: the Sistine Chapel, Santa Maria della Pace, Santa Maria del Popolo.

In order to obtain the bishopric and archbishopric of Imola for his nephews, Jerome and Raphael Riario, he entered into conflict with Lorenzo de' Medici and joined the Pazzi conspiracy which ended in the assassination of Giulio de' Medici, Lorenzo's brother, in Florence cathedral and in the massacre of the conspirators by the furious crowd. Raphael Riario came to possess two archbishoprics, five bishoprics and two abbeys. He was a warrior pope, almost as much as his nephew Giulio della Rovere (future Pope Julius II); he fought against the other Italian states and defeated Mahomet II, who had landed at Otranto and massacred the population.

A wordly pope. — Julius II was succeeded by Giovanni de' Medici, son of Lorenzo the Magnificent, a cultured man. Archbishop at 7, Cardinal at 14, he became pope at 39 taking the name of **Leo X** (1513-21). He was immensely rich and inaugurated his reign by a procession from the Vatican to the Lateran more sumptuous than ever before.

Then he made his cousin Giulio de' Medicis (future Clement VII) archbishop of Florence and presented him with a cardinal's hat. During his reign "the court of Rome was the most brilliant in the world". Stendhal remarked that this pope "had a horror of anything which might upset his pleasant carefree life of self indulgence". Nonetheless Leo X had to face the Lutheran storm. Had not the Holy See suggested to a German archbishop who was in debt that he should preach indulgences, keeping half the proceeds to reimburse his creditors and giving the other half to the re-building of St Peter's? On 15 June 1520 Leo X published a bull against Luther, condemning his ideas and ordering his books to be burned.

A builder pope. — Felix Peretti was born in 1521, the son of poor village folk. He had the face of "a sly old peasant, quite capable of doing someone a bad turn" and was elected pope in 1585. As Pope **Sixtus V** (1585-90) he accomplished an astonishing number of projects in his five years on the throne. With the assistance of Domenico Fontana he set up obelisks in the Piazza dell' Esquilino, the Piazza del Popolo, outside St John Lateran and in St Peter's Square; he built a chapel in the basilica of St Mary Major to contain his tomb, replaced the statue of the Emperor on Trajan's column with one of St Peter, opened up the Via Sistina and set out the crossroads with the Four Fountains and partially achieved his intention of creating broad streets to link the major basilicas and the different districts of Rome. He built an aqueduct *(acqua Felice)* which terminated in a fountain *(p 178)* in the Piazza di San Bernardo, rebuilt the Lateran palace, constructed a building to house the Scala sancta and left his mark on countless churches.

ROME TODAY

Rome may still operate under the emblem of the wolf and use the old republican formula S P Q R. (Senatus Populus que Romanus), the ancient city may still be visible beneath the new street plan, whole districts may still be dressed in their Renaissance or Baroque décor, but it is no longer the marble capital left by Augustus and the emperors nor the ostentatious city of the popes. To fulfil its modern role as capital of a united Italy since 1870, the city has had to double in size, to use concrete, metal and glass, to house its new population of civil servants, to construct administrative buildings and to improve its public transport and traffic flow.

TOURISTS' ROME

From the heights of the Janiculum the tourist looks down on countless domes emerging from a sea of tiled roofs. In the streets madonnas framed by angels keep watch over the human activity; church façades line the pavements: some are sober brick structures, flat and smooth like a blank wall, others are heavily ornate with recesses and scrolls in the style of a Baroque genius. Rome is the **city of churches.** There are said to be about 300. Since 7C the tombs of St Peter and St Paul, the catacombs and the papacy have attracted Christians from all over the world.

St Peter's Square

Nowadays, a solemn council or a holy year attracts the pilgrims in their millions and puts Rome in the fore-front of world events.

A city of palaces. — There is a *palazzo* in every street, its austere façade introducing the visitor to the sober ele-gance of Rome with its ancient frescoes in warm ochre and umber tones.

A city of fountains and obelisks. — The streets with their churches and palaces all emerge eventually into a square with a cooling fountain or commanding obelisk as its focal point. "These fountains", wrote Emile Mâle "provide light by day and music by night". The water pours forth in a variety of forms — the Baroque torrents of the Trevi fountain, the modest trickle from the Facchino's barrel, the delicate tracery of the Turtle fountain — from a multitude of orifices — the depths of a tank, from the mouth of an Egyptian lion, from a dolphin or a monster, or a Triton's shell.

As for obelisks — Egyptian, imperial and papal — they seem to grow in Rome like trees: curiously perched on an elephant's back, contrasting starkly with the façade of the Pantheon, boldly mounted on the fountain of the Four Rivers.

The ruins. — They are usually hemmed in by the modern town and are rarely very extensive but their attraction lies in the role they played in ancient history. The simple chamber of the Mamertine prison and the Forum, stripped of its marble and reduced to a fenced in area dotted with crumbling sections of brick wall, were the cradle of Roman civilisation. A few slender columns hint at the wonders of the ancient world and whet the appetite for further exploration.

> *Monuments, Museums, Churches. — Most museums close at 2 pm and churches are generally closed between 12 noon and 4 pm.*
> *The visitor is very likely to meet the signs "Chiuso per restauri"*
> *and "Chiuso per mancanza di personale"; in both cases the place is closed*
> *(for restoration or for lack of staff).*

ROMANS' ROME

Rome is unusual among capital cities in that it receives double diplomatic missions: one to the Italian government and one to the Holy See. This means that a visiting head of state who has just been received at the Quirinal and wishes to go on and call on the Pope must first return to his own embassy before being collected by the diplomats from the Vatican. In addition many countries maintain permanent representation at the F A O (Food and Agriculture Organisation — a UN agency).

When Rome became the capital of Italy in 1870, the population barely exceeded 200 000. By 1979 it had risen to 2 911 671. The Commune of Rome, which covers about 1 500 km² - c580 sq. miles, is divided into **Rioni** (wards) which have replaced the subdivi-sions of antiquity and are comparable to the wards of our large cities; they cover the area contained within the Aurelianic wall (Mura Aureliane) and extend on to the right (west) bank of the Tiber *(maps pp 3 and 34-35).*

Between the Aurelianic wall and the Orbital Road (Grande Raccordo Anulare) are the **Quartieri** (suburbs) where three quarters of the population live: residential to the north, cheaper and more densely developed to the east, southeast and south, cheaper and less densely developed to the west.

Beyond the western suburbs (quartieri) are the **Suburbi**, undeveloped districts, which become 'quartieri' as they are provided with metalled roads and public services.

Within and beyond the Orbital Road is the **Agro Romano** (the Roman plain), a sparsely populated area which was devastated by malaria until the marshes were drained under Fascism.

Romans at work. — About 70% of the working population is employed in the **services sector**: national or local government, transport, tourism, banking, insurance and commerce.

Agriculture is confined to the Agro Romano and employs about 2% of manpower either in family run small holdings or in larger enterprises owned by companies or mixed-economy operations: the land to the north of Rome is given over to dairy farming and the processing of dairy products, while to the south and west, where the land has been improved, sheep and cows are grazed and cereals are grown.

It was not until 1962 that a plan was drawn up for the provision of industrial estates round Rome. The major sites are to the north of the city, along the Tiber, at San Palomba to the southeast, beside the Via Pontina to the south, near Acilia and Fiumicino airport to the southwest and around Pantano di Grano to the west.

The industrialisation project was followed in 1965 by the formation of an association between the Commune of Rome and a part of the province of Latina. At the head of this Rome-Latina partnership is the building industry, followed by machine tools, publishing, textiles, food processing, carpentry, chemicals and the cinema.

The output of the building, food processing, timber and textile industries is mostly absorbed by the local and regional market, whereas the other products are exported to the rest of Italy (35%) and abroad (20%).

Urban development. — For its first twenty years as the capital of Italy Rome was a building site. The town plans of 1871 and 1883 provided for the construction of housing for the new civil servants round the Piazza Vittorio Emanuele, the Piazza dell'Independenza, at Castro Pretorio and in the Prati; for the demolition of the slum districts of the inner city; for the construction of administrative buildings; for the provision of arterial roads: the Via del Corso and the Via Nazionale, which were opened soon after the inclusion of Rome in the kingdom of Italy, were followed by the Corso Vittorio Emanuele II and the Via XX Settembre; for the establishment of banks and newspapers.

First Quarter of 20C. — More public works were undertaken. In 1902 the Humbert I tunnel was built linking the Quirinal and the business centre. Extensive parks, formerly the private property of the great families, were opened to the public or, like the Villa Ludovisi, sold as building lots for residential development. The Tiber embankment was constructed and the Capitol was cut away to make room for the monument to Victor Emmanuel II. The International Exhibition in 1911 was responsible for the development of the district round the Piazza Mazzini *(p 201)* and a huge museum of modern art in a garden setting was bestowed on the capital. 1920 brought the beginning of the garden suburbs: near to Monte Sacro in the north and at Garbatella in the south.

Mussolini's Rome. — The arrival of Mussolini in 1922 ushered in a policy of grandiose town planning linked to the fascist ideology which favoured a return to ancient grandeur.

Three new streets — Corso del Rinascimento, Via della Botteghe Oscure and Via del Teatro di Marcello — were opened up to allow traffice to penetrate the Campus Martius.

The Via dei Fori Imperiali was opened in 1932 to give a clear view of the Coliseum from Piazza Venezia.

The reconciliation of the Church and State, sealed in the Lateran Treaty in 1929, was marked by the opening of the Via della Conciliazione (1936) to the detriment of the mediaeval district of the Borgo.

As it had been decided that Rome should expand towards the sea, construction began on the new district known as E U R *(p 183)*.

For contemporary architecture see p 28.

Traffic. — There is a remarkable network of bus routes but the underground is limited; there are two lines in operation, one of which runs as far as Ostia, and a third under construction.

Entertainment. — List of events: p 33. The Romans are football fans; the two most popular local teams are *Lazio* and *Roma.* At the weekend the little cafés are crowded: it is time for the *Totocalcio* (football pools). Greyhound racing, also an occasion for betting, is held at the stadium next to the Marconi Bridge near St Paul Without the Walls.

Join us in our never ending task of keeping up to date.

Send us your comments and suggestions please.

Michelin Tyre Public Limited Company
Tourism Department
81 Fulham Road, LONDON SW3 6RD

THE ARTS IN ROME

In the early days Rome was built of very simple materials: **tufa**, a soft brownish stone, volcanic or calcareous in origin; **peperine**, also of volcanic origin, which owes its name to its greyish hue and its granular texture suggestive of grains of pepper (*pepe* in Italian). **Travertine**, a whitish limestone, mostly quarried near Tivoli, is a superior material to the earlier ones and was used only sparingly in the early centuries. **Marble** made rare appearances as a decorative material from 2C BC but became very popular under the Empire. **Brick** was first used in 1C BC; it is usually seen today stripped of its marble facing.

ANTIQUITY (8C BC-4C AD)

ETRUSCAN ART

There are fine pieces of Etruscan art displayed in the Vatican Museum *(p 83)* and in the Villa Giulia *(p 169)*.

Pottery. — The *impasto* technique used for rudimentary clay pots was succeeded in 7C BC by *bucchero* (black terracotta). At first the vases were simply decorated with a stippled design but the shapes grew ever more ornate up to 5C when they were fashioned in the form of human beings or fantastic animals. Many vases were imported from Greece.

Ornamentation. — The work is exquisitely rich: engraved on bronze, in gold filigree or granulation, in finely carved ivory.

Sculpture. — The Etruscans never used marble; they worked in bronze and clay. Their statues are distinguished by an enigmatic smile and large staring eyes.

Architecture. — An Etruscan temple was approached by a flight of steps at the front which led up to a columned portico. The sanctuary itself was a rectangular building, standing on a high podium and containing three shrines *(cellae)* at the rear.

ROMAN ART

Only the remains of a few public works have survived from the period of the kings and the early Republic: the channel of the **Cloaca Maxima** (a sewer dug in 6C BC), the town wall built by King **Servius Tullius** (578-34 BC), the **Old Appian Way** and the **Acqua Appia,** both the work of Appius Claudius Caecus, censor in 312 BC; the Acqua Appia, the oldest aqueduct in Rome, runs almost totally underground for over 16 km - *c*10 miles.

The major artistic influences on the Romans came from the Etruscans, whose works they pillaged, and from the East, whence their victorious generals returned home accompanied by artists and dazzled by the marvels of towns such as Athens or Alexandria.

Architecture. — In their constructions the Romans used the semicircular **arch**. The one built over the Cloaca Maxima in about 2C BC is still admired by archaeologists to this day. Circular rooms were covered by a dome or hemispherical vault; niches set in walls were roofed by half-domes (quarter spheres); the lintel over an opening was surmounted by a rounded arch. There are some impressive examples of vaulting in the Domus Augustana on the Palatine *(p 48)*, in the Pantheon *(p 105)*, in Hadrian's Villa at Tivoli *(p 202)*, in the Baths of Caracalla *(p 180)* and in the Coliseum *(p 67)*. The Romans were past masters at the construction of theatres on level ground rather than set into a hillside as was the Greek practice; for this they had to construct vaults to support the terraces, as in the Theatre of Marcellus *(p 149)*.

They used the Greek architectural **orders** with modifications: in the Tuscan or Roman Doric order the column rests on a base rather than directly on the ground; the Ionic order was seldom used in Rome; the Corinthian order, however, was very popular — the Romans sometimes replaced the curling acanthus leaves on the capital with smooth overhanging leaves and for the flower in the centre of the curved side they substituted various motifs: animals, gods, human figures.

To the three Classical orders they added a fourth, called composite which was distinguished by a capital in which the four scrolls of the Ionic order surmounted the acanthus leaves. The entablature (comprising the architrave, frieze and cornice) was very ornate, richly decorated with pearls, ovoli and ornamental foliage.

The names of two architects have survived: Rabirius, active under Domitian (81-95), and Apollodorus of Damascus who worked for Trajan (98-117) and Hadrian (117-138).

Tuscan order

Ionic order

Corinthian order

Composite order

Sculpture. — It was in this discipline that the Romans were most imitative of Greek art. Such was the enthusiasm for statues that they were erected all over Rome. They were mass produced: bodies were supplied (dressed in togas) ready to receive suitable heads. There were workshops in Rome employing Greeks and local artists but figures were also imported from Greece: a ship loaded with statues, which was wrecked in about 1C BC and found near Madhia in Tunisia, was probably on its way to Rome.

Caesar

The originality of Rome sculpture is to be found in the **portraits.** The taste for likenesses was fostered by the practice in aristocratic families of preserving death masks made of wax and led to a profound search for truth in this medium. Caesar's portraits always show a calm, reflective and energetic character whereas Augustus, with his prominent ears, displays serenity and coldness. There is malice in Vespasian's face set on his thick neck. Trajan must in reality have had a very broad face and his hair style curiously accentuates this peculiarity. The equestrian statue of Marcus Aurelius (p 56) is the sole survivor of a tradition established by Julius Caesar which portrays the emperor as an all-powerful conqueror.

The romans also excelled in **historical low relief sculptures.** The scenes on a sarcophagus or on Trajan's column are models of composition and precision.

The pieces of **decorative sculpture** are worthy of particular attention; practically non-existent in the republican era as the sarcophagus of Scipio Barbatus shows (p 83), decorative sculpture reached its apogee in the Augustan era with the Ara Pacis (p 167).

Finally there was a current in Roman sculpture which gave expression to **popular taste** in the representation in low relief of crafts and scenes from everyday life for the decoration of the tombstones of the working people.

Decadence in sculpture became apparent in 3C: the folds of garments were scored too deep making the figures rigid, the expressions became fixed owing to excessive hollowing out of the pupil of the eye, the hair was carelessly treated.

Materials. — The Romans liked white and coloured marble, dark red spotted porphyry and alabaster. They also worked in bronze (Marcus-Aurelius' statue) (p 56).

Painting. — A study of the frescoes in Pompeii has identified four periods in Roman painting. The 'first style' consists of simple panels imitating marble facing; the 'second style' is marked by architectural features in *trompe-l'œil* to which small illustrated panels were added in the 'third style'; with the 'fourth style' the *trompe-l'œil* became excessive and the decoration overloaded. Examples of Roman painting can be seen in Livia's House and the Griffin House on the Palatine and in the National Roman Museum.

Mosaics. — This technique developed from an attempt to strengthen the floor surface, which was made of a mixture of broken tiles and chalk, by inserting pebbles and then small pieces of marble which could be cut to a uniform size and arranged to form a design.

The simplest method, which was used for floors, consisted of inserting small cubes of marble all cut to the same size into a bed of cement. Larger surfaces (baths) were covered with black figures on a white ground.

Sometimes the cubes were cut in different sizes so as to form curved lines; very small cubes could produce the effect of light and shade. This method was less durable and was reserved for wall panels or for the centre piece of a floor.

Roman workshops also copied the **opus sectile** technique which originated in the east: a stencil of a decorative motif was cut out and applied to a marble base; the outline was traced on to the marble which was then hollowed out within the outline; the hollow itself was filled with small pieces of coloured marble. Examples of this technique can be seen on display at the entrance to the Picture Gallery in the Conservators' Palace (p 60) and in the Ostia museum (p 208).

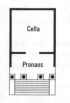
Ancient temple

Monuments. — It requires a powerful effort of imagination to envisage the original construction.

Temples. — Their design was inspired by Greek and Etruscan models and takes several forms ranging from the elemental simplicity of the Temple of Fortuna Virilis to the more complex structure dedicated to Venus and Rome. Every temple contained a place for the statue of the divinity: the **cella.** It was preceded by the **pronaos** behind a colonnade. The whole structure stood on a **podium.**

Triumphal arches. — They consisted of one arch (Titus' Arch) or three arches (Septimius-Severus' and Constantine's Arches) and were built to commemorate the triumph of a victorious general or to raise the statue of a citizen above his peers.

Baths. — Baths proliferated under the Empire when bathing occupied an important place in the Roman day (Baths of Caracalla, p 180).

Basilicas. — The first basilica in Rome was built in 185 BC in the Forum. In antiquity these buildings served no religious function but were used as law courts and meeting places.

Theatres. — The first permanent theatre was built by Pompey; hitherto mobile wooden stages had been used.

Theatrical masks

Circuses. — These were huge oblong arenas where chariot races were held: Circus Maximus *(p 194)* and Maxentius' Circus on the Old Appian Way *(p 147).*

Stadiums. — These too were oblong in shape but were used for athletics: the site of Domitian's stadium is now occupied by the Piazza Navona *(p 163).*

Amphitheatres. — These were a Roman invention, typified by the Coliseum *(p 67)* and held gladiatorial contests which the Romans had inherited from the Etruscans transforming them in the process into an entertainment whereas for the Etruscans they had constituted part of the funeral rites.

Aqueducts. — The impressive arches of these constructions have probably contributed most to the Romans' reputation as builders.

Roads. — In some places considerable stretches of the original paving are still intact. The word **clivus** means a street going up or down hill whereas **vicus** means a side street.

Tombs. — The most ancient were **shaft tombs** (tiled cavities containing an earthenware jar in which stood a cinerary urn shaped like a hut) and **pit tombs** which were used exclusively for interments; the sarcophagus was sometimes made of a hollow tree trunk. The tombs, which were always situated outside the town boundary, were sometimes marked by a simple stone *(stele)* or an altar or consisted of a mausoleum when a family vault was planned. The *columbarium* was a communal grave for the less wealthy and consisted of an underground chamber lined with rows of niches in which the cinerary urns were placed.

Housing. — There were essentially two types of Roman housing: the **Domus,** a detached house, and the **Insula,** a block of apartments several storeys high *(p 207).*

CHRISTIAN ART

The pagan cult of idols and the commandment in the Bible against "graven images" inhibited the spontaneous development of a new style of art among the early Christian communities.

At first Christian art borrowed from the pagan repertoire those subjects which could be used as symbols of Christianity: the vine, the dove, the anchor etc. *(p 144).*

Painting. — The earliest Christian paintings appeared on the walls of the catacombs as a result of people following the pagan tradition and decorating the tombs of their relatives. The oldest date from 2C.

Sculpture. — The evolution of Roman sculpture, both in the round and in relief, can be traced in the Museum of Christian Art in the Vatican *(p 93):* from the use of symbols to the representation of the leading figures in Christianity (Jesus, St Peter, St Paul) and scenes from the Bible.

Architecture. — The chief Christian building was the **basilica** (not to be confused with the pagan basilicas which had nothing to do with religion: *see above*). The first buildings of this type were erected by Constantine over the tombs of Peter and Paul the Apostles (St Peter's in the Vatican: *p 73;* St Paul Without the Walls: *p 140*) and next to the imperial palace (St John Lateran: *p 133*).

MIDDLE AGES (5C-14C)

Supplanted by Constantinople as the capital of the Empire and invaded by barbarians, by 6C Rome was a ruined city with barely 20 000 inhabitants. In 10C it became the battleground in the struggle between the Pope and the German Emperor. Until 15C only simple constructions were built.

Architecture. — Civil architecture consisted mainly of fortresses built by the noble families on strategic sites (Crescenzi House, *p 152;* Militia Tower, *p 131).*

Churches. — They were constructed of material taken from ancient monuments which provided a great choice of capitals, friezes and columns such as can be seen in St Mary Major, Santa Sabina etc. As such material grew scarcer, items from different sources were combined in one church (columns in San Giorgio in Velabro, Santa Maria in Cosmedin etc.).

The **basilical plan** of the early churches was retained during the mediaeval period *(see plans of Santa Maria d'Aracoeli, p 55; Santa Maria in Cosmedin, p 151; San Clemente, p 138).* It consisted of a rectangular building divided down its length into a nave flanked by two or four aisles separated by rows of columns; one of the shorter sides contained the entrance, the other the apse (with quarter-sphere vault). Between the apse and the nave and at right angles to them ran the transept. The nave extended above the side aisles and was lit by high windows. It was covered by a pitched roof, left open or masked by a flat ceiling in the interior. The main entrance was sometimes preceded by a square court surrounded by a portico *(atrium)* or by a simple portico supported on columns which served as a narthex (the area reserved for those who had not yet been baptised).

The façade was often flanked by a bell tower *(campanile).* In Rome these towers are decorated with horizontal cornices dividing them into several storeys, with white mini columns standing out against the brick work and ceramic insets in brilliant colours.

By 6C a rail had been introduced separating the congregation from the clergy and creating the chancel **(presbyterium)** on either side of the bishop's throne **(cathedra)** which stood in the apse. In front were the choristers in the **schola cantorum.** Beneath the high altar there was often a crypt containing the relics of a martyr **(martyrium);** the **confessio** also contained the relics of a martyr but could only be seen through a small window. The high altar was covered by a baldaquin or canopy **(ciborium)** *(illustration p 141).*

Sculpture - painting and mosaic. — The period from 12 to 14C is dominated by the **Cosmati**, who were descended from one Cosma and formed a guild of marble workers to which the Vasselletto family was related. The Cosmati workshops used fragments of ancient materials to create beautiful floors with decorative motifs of multicoloured marble and the furniture of a mediaeval church: episcopal throne, *ambones* (lecterns), paschal candlesticks. The early works, composed entirely of white marble, are very simple. Later they added porphyry and serpentine marble (green) cut in geometric shapes (roundels, lozenges etc.); they produced very lively effects with incrustations of enamels — blue, red and gold — on the friezes and wreathed columns of cloisters.

Arnolfo di Cambio moved to Rome from Florence in about 1276 (baldaquins in St Paul Without the Walls, *p 141;* and in Santa Cecilia, *p 187;* statue of Charles of Anjou, *p 57).*

Frescoes and mosaics were the chief forms of mediaeval decoration. The Romans had a taste for anecdotes and bright colours.

In the latter half of 5C but particularly in 6C the influence of Byzantine mosaics was introduced to Rome by the entourage of Justinian's general, Narses, who occupied Rome in 552, and also by eastern monks who took refuge in Rome in 7C *(p 195).* The mosaics of this period show figures with enigmatic expressions, often richly dressed, in conventional poses, which express the mysticism of the Eastern church through symbolism.

Through the good relations enjoyed by the Papacy with Pepin the Short and then Charlemagne Carolingian art brought a less rigid style to Roman mosaics, e.g. works dating from the reign of Paschal I (817-24) (Santa Prassede, *p 65;* Santa Maria in Domnica, *p 138).* From 11 to 13C the Roman workshops produced sumptuous work (apse in San Clemente, *p 137).* **Pietro Cavallini**, the greatest artist in this period, must have worked in Rome at the end of 13C and early in 14C. He was both painter and mosaicist and a master of the different influences; his very pure art is best known through the mosaic of the life of the Virgin in Santa Maria in Trastevere *(p 189)* and by the fresco of the Last Judgment in Santa Cecilia *(p 188).* **Jacopo Torriti** et **Rusuti** were disciples of his.

RENAISSANCE (15C-16C)

The Renaissance made less impact on Rome than on Florence. At the beginning of 15C Rome was exhausted by the struggles of the Middle Ages and had nothing to show of artistic merit. By the end of the century the city was an important archaeological centre and was famous for its abundant artistic activity commissioned by Popes and prelates. It was **Martin V** (1417-31) the first pope after the Great Schism who inaugurated this brilliant period. It came to an end in 1527 when Rome was sacked by the troops of Charles V.

Architecture. — The inspiration for Roman Renaissance buildings is to be found in Classical monuments: in the Coliseum — its superimposed orders and engaged columns are imitated in the court of the Farnese Palace; in Maxentius' Basilica — the vaulting inspired the dome of St Peter's in the Vatican; in the Pantheon — the curved and triangular pediments in the interior have been reproduced many times.

Churches. — They are austere in appearance. The nave is covered by rib vaulting and flanked by apsidal side chapels; the arms of the transept end in rounded chapels. The first domes began to appear (Santa Maria del Popolo, Sant'Agostino). The screen-like façade is composed of two stages one above the other linked by scrolls. Broad flat surfaces predominate; shallow pilasters are preferred to columns. The first hints of the Counter-Reformation and the Baroque can be seen in the use of broken lines, of recesses and columns progressively more and more accentuated.

Sixtus IV (1471-84) was responsible for the majority of the Renaissance churches: Sant'Agostino, Santa Maria del

(After photo by Gab. Fot. Naz., Rome)

Façade of Santa Maria del Popolo

Popolo and San Pietro in Montorio were built in his reign; he founded Santa Maria della Pace and made great alterations to the Church of the Holy Apostles.

Palaces. — The *palazzi* were large private houses built in the district between the Via del Corso and the Tiber, in the streets which were used by the pilgrims and by the papal processions which proceeded on feast days from the Vatican to the Lateran: Via del Governo Vecchio, Via dei Banchi Nuovi, Via dei Banchi Vecchi, Via di Monserrato, Via Giulia etc. They supplanted the mediaeval fortresses; the Palazzo Venezia which was begun in 1452 has retained its crenellations. From the outside the *palazzi* are gaunt and austere (barred windows on the ground floor). The inside was designed to accommodate an elegant and cultivated life style, associated with men of letters and artists in a setting of ancient sculptures and paintings.

Sculpture and painting. — The personalities of Michelangelo and Raphael predominated. After working in Rome from 1496 to 1501 **Michelangelo** returned in 1505 to design a tomb for Julius II. **Raphael** had lived in Urbino, his home town, Perugia and Florence before coming to Rome in 1508; he was presented to Julius II by Bramante.

In **decorative sculpture** delicate ornamental foliage and floral motifs are often picked out in gold (door frames, balustrades etc.). Funeral art flourished under **Andrea Bregno** and **Andrea Sansovino** who combined a taste for decoration with a taste for ancient architecture.

Mino da Fiesole who was usually based in Tuscany made several visits to Rome; he became famous for his very simple representations of the Virgin and Child in low relief sculpture.

Rome attracts the masters. — The Renaissance style reached Rome after being developed elsewhere and all the artists came from outside the city: the Umbrians with their gentle touch, the Tuscans with their elegant and intellectual art and the Lombards with their rich decoration.

- **Gentile da Fabriano** and **Pisanello** were summoned to Rome in 1427 by Martin V and Eugenius IV to decorate the nave of St John Lateran (destroyed 17-18C).
- **Masolino** who came from Florence painted St Catherine's Chapel in St Clement's Basilica between 1428 and 1430.
- From 1447 to 1451 **Fra Angelico**, also from Florence, decorated Nicolas V's Chapel *(p 86)*.
- For the painting of the Sistine Chapel walls Sixtus IV called on **Pinturicchio, Perugino** and **Signorelli** from Umbria and on **Botticelli, Ghirlandaio, Cosimo Rosselli** and his son **Piero di Cosimo** from Florence. He also commissioned **Melozzo da Forli** to paint the Ascension in the apse of the Church of the Holy Apostles (fine fragments in the Vatican Picture Gallery and in the Quirinal Palace).
- In about 1485 **Pinturicchio** painted the life of St Bernard in Santa Maria d'Aracoeli and a Nativity in Santa Maria del Popolo; between 1492 and 1494 he decorated the Borgia Apartment in the Vatican for Alexander VI *(p 87)*.
- From 1489 to 1493 **Filippino Lippi** was at work on the Carafa Chapel in Santa Maria Sopra Minerva.
- **Bramante** who arrived in 1499 designed the *tempietto* (1502) *(p 192)*, built the cloisters at Santa Maria della Pace (1504) and extended the choir of Santa Maria del Popolo (1505-09).
- From 1508 to 1512 **Michelangelo** was at work painting the ceiling of the Sistine Chapel for Julius II. In 1513 he began the pope's tomb. The Last Judgment was painted between 1535 to 1541 and he worked on the dome of St Peter's from 1547 until his death in 1564. His last work was the Porta Pia (1561-4).
- From 1508 to 1511 **Baldassarre Peruzzi** built the Villa Farnesina for Agostino Chigi.
- In 1508 **Raphael** began to paint the *Stanze* in the Vatican *(p 84)*. In 1510 he designed the plan for the Chigi Chapel in Santa Maria del Popolo. From 1511 he worked on the decoration of the Villa Farnesina for Agostino Chigi. In 1512 he painted Isaiah in Saint'Agostino and the Sybils in Santa Maria della Pace in 1514.
- **Sodoma** arrived in Rome from Milan in 1508 to paint the ceiling of the Signature Room in the Vatican for Julius II; he worked on the Farnesina in about 1509.
- Early in 16C **Jacopo Sansovino** built San Giovanni dei Fiorentini for Leo X.
- In 1515 **Antonio da Sangallo the Younger** began to build the Farnese Palace; Michelangelo took over in 1546.

COUNTER-REFORMATION (16C-17C)

The Counter-Reformation, which covered the period from the reign of Paul III (1534-49) to the reign of Urban VIII (1623-44), was marked by the sack of Rome in 1527 and by the rise of Protestantism. The Counter-Reformation movement sought to put down the heretics, restore the primacy of Rome and to rally the faithful to the church. The Society of Jesus, which was formed in 1540, proved to be a most efficacious instrument in the struggle. Hence-forward the influential power of art was put at the service of the Faith.

The initial period of struggle was followed by several successes — the battle of Lepanto (1571), the conversion of Henri IV of France (1593) and the Jubilee (1600) — all expressed in an artistic style which presaged the Baroque.

Architecture

Churches. — The style is sometimes called 'Jesuit' owing to the comprehensive contribution made by the Society of Jesus. The architecture combines an austere solemnity with a rich marble décor: the Church was to appear majestic and powerful. Since they were designed to assemble the faithful together, the churches of the Counter-Reformation are vast. The Gesù Church is a typical example *(p 109)*. The nave is broad and uncluttered so that every member of the congregation could see the altar and hear the preaching. On the façade, the plain surfaces of the Renaissance are replaced with recesses and projections and engaged columns are gradually substituted for the flat pilasters.

(After photo by Gab. Fot. Naz., Rome)

Façade of the Gesù Church

Civil architecture. — The most flourishing period was the early years of the Counter-Reformation during the reigns of Paul III, Julius III, Paul IV and Pius IV who continued to live like Renaissance princes.

The Borghese family illustrates the era of the Church triumphant: Paul V acquired the Borghese Palace and built the Pauline fountain; his nephew, Cardinal Scipione Borghese led a cultivated life as is evident from the splendours of the Palazzo Pallavicini and the 'Palazzina' Borghese, which now houses the Borghese Gallery.

Sculpture and painting

In the spirit of the Counter-Reformation painting had to exalt the themes rejected by the Protestants: the Virgin, the primacy of St Peter, the doctrine of the Eucharist, the cult of the saints and their intercession for the souls in Purgatory.

The work of the Counter-Reformation artists followed in the wake of Michelangelo and Raphael and continued to be in the 'manner' of these two giants; hence the term **Mannerist** which is applied to 16C sculpture and painting.

In sculpture there is the work of two of Michelangelo's close followers: **Ammanati** (1511-92) and **Guglielmo della Porta** (1500?-77). The end of the period is marked by the presence in Rome of **Pietro Bernini** (1562-1629), the father of Gian Lorenzo *(see below)*.

Among the painters are **Daniele da Volterra**, who worked with Michelangelo, **Giovanni da Udine, Sermoneta, Francesco Penni, Giulio Romano**, who formed part of the 'Roman School' round Raphael. The style of the next generation — **Federico and Taddeo Zuccari, Pomarancio, Cesare Nebbia, Cavaliere d'Arpino** etc. — is a direct development of Raphael's art. **Barocci** whose soft and emotional style never lapsed into affectation deserves a special place.

In their attempts to imitate the attitudes and expressions painted by Michelangelo and Raphael the Mannerist painters were often guilty of excess. Their colours are pallid as if faded by the light. Decoration also tends to be excessive: fresco paintings are framed with stucco and gilding or elaborate combinations of marble. Large areas are often divided into smaller panels which are easier to paint.

Reaction. — Reaction was introduced by the '**Bologna group**' and Caravaggio who heralded the first signs of the Baroque. The Bologna group was led by the **Carracci** who ran an academy in Bologna from 1585 to 1595: Ludovico (1555-1619), founder of the academy, his cousins Agostino (1557-1602) and Annibale (1560-1609) who were brothers. After them came Guido Reni (1575-1642), Domenichino (1581-1641) and Guercino (1591-1666). Without abandoning idealism they tried to achieve more verity of expression.

Michelangelo Merisi (1573-1610), known as **Caravaggio** after the name of his home village near Bergamo, arrived in Rome in 1588 and began to work with Cavaliere d'Arpino. But he was quarrelsome and had to flee from the city in 1605, first to Naples, then to Malta and finally to Sicily. His painting was quite unconventional; his powerful figures are illuminated by a harsh light which causes contrasting heavy shadow. His wayward behaviour did not allow him to have pupils but his influence had repercussions throughout Europe and many artists were said to paint in the style of Caravaggio.

BAROQUE ART (17C-18C)

17C and early 18C art is known as Baroque (from the Portuguese *barroco* an uneven stone) on account of the ornate and undisciplined appearance of the style. Baroque art was used to express the triumph of the Roman Church against heresy and had a great vogue in the papal capital starting in the reign of Urban VIII (1623-44).

The leading artists

Two men dominated Roman Baroque: **Gian Lorenzo Bernini** and Francesco Borromini.

Bernini (1598-1680) was born in Naples. From the very first Cardinal Scipione Borghese recognised his talent and commissioned him to do the sculptures for his villa which are now exhibited in the Borghese Gallery *(p 175)*: at 17 he produced his first work, Jupiter and the goat Amalthea. On the election of Urban VIII he was appointed official artist to the papal court and to the Barberini family. On Maderno's death in 1629, the Pope made him architect in charge of the rebuilding of St Peter's.

During the reign of Innocent X (1644-55) he sculpted the extraordinary Ecstasy of St Teresa *(p 178)* and the Fountain of the Four Rivers *(p 163)*. In the reign of Alexander VII (1655-67) he built Sant'Andrea al Quirinale, the colonnade enclosing St Peter's Square, redesigned St Peter's Chair and built the Scala Regia in the Vatican Palace *(p 79)*.

In 1664 he was invited to Paris by Colbert and Louis XIV to extend the façade of the Cour Carrée in the Louvre but his final design was never carried out.

Bernini was not only an architect and sculptor, but also a theatrical scene designer, poet and painter. He probably painted some hundred pictures of which only a few have survived. He produced a great deal of work; he rose rapidly and was very successful.

(After photo by Gab. Fot. Naz., Rome)

Bernini: the Ecstasy of St Theresa

His genius was recognised in his lifetime and he received many decorations; his contemporaries saw in him another Michelangelo. He was welcome in the most brilliant circles; he put on plays for his friends, designing the stage sets, writing the words and playing a role. He was fleetingly by eclipsed Borromini when Innocent X succeeded Urban VIII but soon returned to favour with his Fountain of the Four Rivers.

Borromini's career (1599-1667) followed a quite different course. He was the son of Giovanni Domenico Castelli, an architect from the Visconti family in Milan. As a young man he was a stone mason and acquired great technical experience. In 1621 he was in Rome where he worked as Carlo Maderno's assistant on St Peter's, Sant'Andrea della Valle and the Barberini Palace. In 1625 he received the title of *maestro* and in 1628 he took his mother's name of Borromini. Anxious and introverted he shunned the world; he based his art on rigour and sobriety excluding marble decorations and paintings. In Borromini's art the Baroque style is expressed by the lines of the architecture which he cut and curved with a sure hand.

(After photo by Gab. Fot. Naz., Rome)

Façade of San Carlo alle Quattro Fontane

San Carlo alle Quattro Fontane, which was his first full scale work (1638), probably shows his genius at its best. At the same period he designed the façade of the Oratory *(p 160)* which is typical of his original and balanced style. These projects earned him the protection of Fr Spada who became Innocent X's adviser. The Pope raised him to the first rank and appointed him to renovate St John Lateran. The façade of San Carlo alle Quattro Fontane was designed in the year in which he died.

Borromini lived in constant anxiety and never knew the fame enjoyed by his rival. One night in a fit of anguish and anger against his servant he took his own life.

There were other architects working in Rome at that period. **Carlo Maderno**, the designer of the façades of St Peter's and Santa Suzanna, and **Giacomo della Porta**, probably the most active architect around 1580, were both great admirers of Michelangelo and are often included among the Mannerists. **Flaminio Ponzio** worked for the Borghese (façade of the Borghese Palace, Pauline Fountain). **Giovanni Battista Soria** designed the façades of Santa Maria della Vittoria and St Gregory the Great. The well-proportioned architecture of **Pietro da Cortona** is most attractive (Sts Luke and Martina, the façades of Santa Maria della Pace and Santa Maria in Via Lata, the dome of San Carlo al Corso). The name of **Carlo Rainaldi** deserves to be remembered for his work in Santa Maria in Campitelli (1655-65) and for his arrangement of the 'twin' churches in the Piazza del Popolo.

Roman Baroque

Baroque art seeks to convey an effect of movement and contrast. Water with its undulations and powers of reflection was an essential element. Dazzling effects were created with expensive materials such as marble and precious stones. Stucco (chalk, plaster and marble dust mixed with water) was frequently employed for its plastic qualities. Allegories were taken from Cesare Ripa's dictionary which appeared in 1594 and explained how to express an abstract idea.

Architecture. — Even the plan of the buildings was contrived so as to express movement (San Carlo alle Quattro Fontane, Sant'Andrea al Quirinale). Façades are embellished with disengaged columns, bold projections, curved contours and recesses.

Sculpture. — Sculpture is dominated by flowing garments and figures expressing abstract qualities. The altarpieces are decorated with pictures of sculpted marble and wreathed columns; the latter, a feature of ancient Roman art, were very popular with Bernini (baldaquin in St Peter's). Church interiors are full of cherubs perched on pediments and cornices.

In addition to the sculptors associated as pupils with Bernini (Antonio Raggi, Ercole Ferrata, Francesco Mochi etc.) mention must be made of **Alessandro Algardi** (1592-1654), who produced some remarkable portraits and marble pictures.

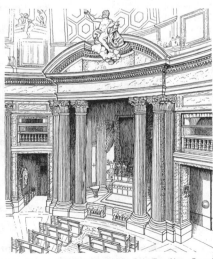

(After photo by Gab. Fot. Naz., Rome)

Sant' Andrea al Quirinale: the high altar

Painting. — Baroque painters sought to achieve effects of perspective and *trompe-l'œil* with spiralling or diagonal compositions. They included **Pietro da Cortona**, architect but also interior decorator, Giovanni Battista Gaulli, known as **Baciccia** and protégé of Bernini, and **Lanfranco** (1582-1647).

Andrea Pozzo, a Jesuit, who was a painter and studied the theory of architecture, had a passion for studies in *trompe-l'œil*. His book *Prospettiva de' pittori e architetti* appeared in 1693 and circulated throughout Europe.

(After photo by Gab. Fot. Naz., Rome)

St Ignatius': section of ceiling by A Pozzo

Rome attracted artists of all nationalities. Nicolas Poussin died there in 1665, Claude Lorrain in 1682. Rubens made several visits; he admired Michelangelo, the Carracci and Caravaggio and completed the paintings in the apse of the New Church. Velazquez painted a fine portrait of Innocent X *(p 103)*.

FROM 18C TO THE PRESENT

Neo-Classicism. — This trend developed from the middle of 18C until the early 19C and was marked by a return to Greek and Roman architecture which had recently been discovered with great enthusiasm during the excavations of Herculaneum, Pompeii and Paestum. Following on the heels of the Baroque craze, neo-Classicism was characterised by simplicity and symmetry, even a touch of frigidity. This was the period when Winckelmann, who was Librarian at the Vatican and in charge of Roman antiquities, published his works on Classical art, when Francesco Milizia launched his violent criticism of the Baroque style and of superfluous decoration and praised the simplicity and nobility of ancient monuments.

Piranesi (1720-78), engraver and architect, took up permanent residence in Rome in 1754. He produced some 2 000 engravings including the series "Views of Rome" which was published in 1750 and constitutes an incomparable collection full of charm and melancholy. It was he who designed the attractive Piazza dei Cavalieri di Malta.

Antonio Canova (1757-1821) was the dominant talent at this period and Napoleon's favourite sculptor. The calm regularity of his work enchanted his contemporaries.

In architecture mention should be made of the name of **Giuseppe Valadier** who laid out the Piazza del Popolo (1816-20). In painting it is the foreigners, such as the German Mengs and the French at the Villa Medici who stand out. David in particular came to Rome twice, in 1774 and 1784 when he painted the Oath of the Horatii.

From 1870 to Fascism. — After 1870 Rome simply copied previous styles and was prone to excess as in the monument to Victor Emmanuel II. The Fascist period saw the excavation of the Theatre of Marcellus and of the Area Sacra in the Largo Argentina but it was also responsible for the creation of the Via dei Fori Imperiali which entailed the covering up of a large part of the Imperial Fora. The central station (Stazione Termini) and the E U R district were begun and the sports complex in the Foro Italico was built.

Artists and contemporary trends. — In painting and sculpture the National Gallery of Modern Art *(p 173)* is the best place to trace the evolution of modern artistic trends.

In Holy Year 1950 the Via Cristoforo Colombo was opened and the Stazione Termini was completed ready to receive the pilgrims. In 1960 the Flaminio Stadium, the Palazzetto dello Sport in the Via Flaminia, and the Palazzo dello Sport in E U R were built for the Olympic Games. The Olympic Village (Via Flaminia) for the athletes was built on the site of some old army barracks. The Corso di Francia relieved congestion in the north of the city; designed as an overpass its bold sweep is not unartistic. The Via Olimpica to the west links the Foro Italico with E U R. The Leonardo da Vinci International Airport at Fiumicino was opened in 1961 to supplement the capacity of Ciampino.

The Orbital Road (Grande Raccordo Anulare), some 70 km - 44 miles long, was finished in 1970. Successful modern buildings in Rome include the RAI building *(p 201)*, the British Embassy *(p 122)*, some of the E U R buildings *(p 183)*, the Audience Hall by Pier Luigi Nervi (1971) and the Christian and Pagan Museums (1970) in the Vatican *(p 91)*, several hotels, the Jolly, its gold tinted glass panels reflecting the greenery of the Villa Borghese and the Hilton which was the subject of violent protests when it rose on the Monte Mario.

LITERATURE

Since the poet **Naevius** wrote the first national epic poem in 3C to describe the first Punic war, Rome has never ceased to be a source of inspiration for writers.

Latin literature. — **Cicero** (106-43 BC), a star performer in the law courts, denounced profiteers and conspirators in his orations (the Verrines, Pro Murena, Pro Milone, the Catalines, the Philippics).

Caesar (101-44 BC) wrote an account of the Gallic wars and of the civil war in which he described his own contribution to the grandeur of Rome.

Sallust (86-35? BC), who lived in a house where the Via Vittorio Veneto now runs, gave an explanation of the significant events in Roman history.

Livy, who died in 17BC, devoted 42 rolls of papyrus to a history of Rome from the founding to 9 BC. The style is pleasant and the surviving books are an agreeable read.

Tacitus (55?-120?), advocate and civil servant, was a self-appointed historian of the reigns of the Emperors from Tiberius to Nero and from Galba to Domitian.

Pliny the Younger (62?-114), civil servant under Domitian and Trajan and governor of Bithynia, painted a picture of Roman high society in his letters.

Suetonius (69?-125?), one of the imperial secretaries under Hadrian, left a fascinating work on the Lives of the twelve Caesars full of details about the public and private lives of the emperors from Julius Caesar to Domitian.

Besides the great histories there is the Satyricon, which is attributed to **Petronius** and describes some aspects of the bawdy side of Roman life.

Rome in contemporary literature. — Two Italian poets — Giosuè **Carducci** (1835-1907) *(Odi Barbare, Levia Gravia)* and Giovanni **Pascoli** (1855-1912) *(Inno a Roma)* — have expressed the grandeur of the eternal city.

Gabriele d'**Annunzio** (1863-1938) chose Rome as the setting for his novel *Il Piacere* (The Child of Pleasure).

Alberto **Moravia** (1907) used it as a background to the development of his bourgeois characters: Gli Indifferenti (The Time of Indifference); *Racconti romani* (Roman Tales).

Giuseppe **Ungaretti** (1888-1970) spent many years in Rome where he taught modern literature. He used to meditate on Keats' and Shelley's tombs in the Protestant Cemetery.

Despite his complaints about the noise of the Carnival, **Goethe** admitted that he came alive the day he arrived in Rome (*Italianische Reise* — Italian Journey).

Alexis **Curvers**, who is sometimes irreverent but always devoted, has written some of the most beautiful pages on Rome *(Tempo di Roma)*.

Among those writers who loved Rome mention must be made of the poets who celebrated the eternal city in Roman dialect, finding their inspiration in the events of daily life and the common sense of the people: Cesare Pascarella (1858-1940), Giuseppe Gioachino Belli (1791-1863), Trilussa (1871-1950) are worthy of particular mention.

THE GRAND TOUR

A continental tour of one or two years culminating in a visit to Rome was a peculiarly British custom which lasted 300 years reaching its height in 18C when the Grand Tour formed part of a gentleman's education. A young man would set out with a tutor, known as a 'bear leader', to superintend his studies, protect him from bad company and show him the sights. On arriving in Rome, preferably at Eastertime, these early tourists would set out 'equipped with all things needful to measure the dimensions of the antiquities they would be shown'. It was important to engage a good guide such as Winckelmann, a German archaeologist, who was superintendent of antiquities in Rome, or Gavin Hamilton who became well known as a dealer and antiquary. The tour had great influence at home on manners and architectural style and the formation of art collections. **Lord Burlington**, the arbiter of good taste in early 18C, made two tours which led to his patronage of **William Kent** and the introduction of the **Palladian** style into England.

Many English artists studied in Rome: **Richard Wilson** (1752-6); **Sir Joshua Reynolds** (1750-2); **Sir George Romney** (1773-5) whose portraits show the influence of the Classical style in their backgrounds and draperies; **John Flaxman**, the sculptor (1787-94), nicknamed the English Michelangelo, who encouraged **John Gibson** to become a pupil of Canova. **Benjamin West** (1760-3) and **John Copley** (1774) from America visited Rome before settling in London.

In 19C instead of the established tour of the most famous cities, works of art and monuments, with its accent on antiquities, visitors preferred to settle in less well known towns, taking an interest in Italian life and customs and even in the nationalist movement. **Charles Dickens** visited Rome in 1845 while writing a travel book *Pictures of Italy.*

Rome provided poetic inspiration: in May 1817 **Byron** toured the ruins gathering material for the Fourth Canto of *Childe Harold;* **Shelley** composed *Prometheus Unbound (p 180)* and *The Cenci* while lodging in the Corso in 1819; in 1860 **Robert** and **Elizabeth Barrett Browning** made a visit to Rome which inspired his greatest work *The Ring and the Book,* a poem based on a 17C Roman murder trial.

Rome still attracted many artists: **Eastlake** made invaluable purchases of early Italian art for the National Gallery in London; **Turner** visited Rome twice (1819, 1828) and used quotations from *Childe Harold* as titles for his paintings. From America came **William Page** (1849-60) who painted portraits of Robert and Elizabeth Browning; he had trained under **Samuel Morse**, an artist who studied in Europe in 1832 and invented the electric telegraph.

Many American writers visited Rome: **Washington Irving** (1804-6), **Fenimore Cooper** (1820-7), **Longfellow** (1828), **Hermann Melville** (1856-7), **Nathaniel Hawthorne** (1858-9) and **Mark Twain** (1867) while collecting material for *Innocents Abroad.* Most famous of all was **Henry James** who first visited Italy in 1869; his first important novel was set in Rome.

The journey

Being only 28 km - 17 miles from the sea, Rome has a relatively mild climate all the year round but May, June, September and early October are the best months for a visit owing to the gentle light in May and June and the long evenings.

By rail. — International trains arrive at the Stazione Termini (EX).

By air. — International flights arrive at Leonardo da Vinci Airport near Fiumicino, 26 km - 16 miles from Rome: a bus *(1 500 L)* takes passengers into Rome (Via Giolitti (DEX) near the station); and also at Ciampino Airport (SE of Rome): a bus takes passengers to the nearest underground station.

The plan on p 176 shows the offices of the major air lines in Rome.

By road. — *Use Michelin map no 988 and the Michelin Green Guide to Italy.* For details concerning the car (breakdowns, agents etc.) consult the current Michelin Red Guide Italia (hotels and restaurants).

Customs and exchange control. — A current passport or a national identity card are required.

Each traveller can import a maximum of 200 000 L (approx. £80); the rate of exchange in August 1984 was 2 305 L = £1.

Useful addresses. — Tourist information is available from the Italian State Tourist Office, 1 Princes Street, London W1, Tel: 408 1254; 626 Fifth Avenue, New York 20 NY, Tel: 24 54822; and in Rome from the EPT (Ente Provinciale per il Turismo), via Parigi, 11, Tel: 461-851 (DV 27).

Travelling and sightseeing in Rome

By taxi. — Taxis can be reserved by ringing 3570, 3875 or 4994.

By bus, tram and underground. — It is essential to buy a public transport plan on sale in bookshops or the plan published by ATAC (Azienda Tramvie e Autobus del Comune di Roma), on sale at bus ticket kiosks. Bus and tram stops are indicated by the sign *Fermata; Fermata di richiesta* is a request stop. The entrance door *(Salita)* is at the back of the bus and the exit *(Uscita)* in the middle.

The ticket *(biglietto or scontrino)* costs 400 L and is valid for one journey and must be purchased in advance and punched at the turnstile on the underground and in the machine in the bus. Tickets are supplied by automatic machines accepting 50 L and 100 L pieces or from bus ticket kiosks at the bus stations or from tobacconists.

By car. — It is difficult and ill-advised to try to drive into the town centre as many streets are limited to pedestrians, taxis and buses or authorised vehicles. Foreigners run the risk of taking a wrong turn; they should be patient and observant and not try the goodwill of the traffic police *(vigili)*. Car parks are often improvised; the attendant is responsible for moving the cars when they are in the way; for this he requires the keys and a tip.

On foot. — This is the best way of seeing Rome.

Monuments, museums and churches. — *See p 19.*

It is advisable to carry a pair of binoculars for looking at the mosaics and paintings which are often high up.

Guided tours. — Travel agencies supply information about guided tours for foreigners. Such information is also available from ATAC, Piazza dei Cinquecento (in front of the railway station).

Staying in Rome

Lodgings. — The Michelin Red Guide Italia lists a wide range of hotels, from the most luxurious to the simple but acceptable.

For information on Youth Hostels apply to the Associazione Italiana Alberghi per la gioventù, 61 Lungotevere Maresciallo Cadorna (near to the Foro Italico, BU). For information about camping apply to the EPT *(see above)*.

Restaurants and cafés. — When deciding where to eat, consult the Michelin Red Guide Italia.

In Rome one can sample the famous *fettucine* — narrow ribbons of pasta, *gnocchi alla Romana* — pasta made with milk and eggs and cooked in the oven with butter and cheese, *saltimbocca* — veal scallops with ham and sage cooked in a butter and marsala sauce. Lamb *(abbacchio)* is delicious, baked in the oven or grilled in cutlets *(abacchio alla scottadito)* or 'chasseur' *(alla cacciatora)* with an anchovy sauce.

The fruit and vegetables are the crowning glory of the Roman table. Cheeses *(caciocavallo, pecorino etc.)* are often served accompanied by broad beans.

These dishes can be accompanied with wines from the Castelli district (Frascati).

Since most cafés have a terrace and as opportunities for sitting down in Rome are rare, the main cafés are marked on the map on pp 34-35. It is customary to pay on ordering rather than on leaving.

For additional information about the papacy, its history and organisation, refer to the introductory paragraphs about the Vatican (p 71).

Post and telephone. — Letters sent poste restante can be addressed to the Central Post Office, Piazza San Silvestro (CV). Post offices are usually open from 8.30 am to 2 pm. Letters to the United Kingdom cost 500 L, postcards 350 L; to the USA: 770 L and 620 L; to Australia: 930 L and 780 L.

Coin operated telephones are available in the post offices whereas coin and token operated telephones are available in other public places. To telephone or telegraph abroad, apply to the Central Post Office *(offices open day and night)* or to the SIP, Via Santa Mari in Via *(open until 10 pm)* (CX).

Church Services. — In English: Anglican — All Saints' Church, Via del Babuino 153 B (CV); St Paul's Church, Via Nazionale (DX); Baptist — Rome Baptist Church, Piazza S Lorenzo in Lucina 35 (CV); Methodist — Piazza Ponte Sant'Angelo (BX); Presbyterian: St Andrew's Church, Via Venti Settembre 7 (DV); Roman Catholic — San Silvestro, Piazza San Silvestro 1 (CV 39); Sta Susanna, Via Venti Settembre 14 (DV); St Patrick's Church, Via Boncampagni 31 (DV).

On Sundays Roman Catholic mass is celebrated in Latin at St Peter's in the Vatican, St John Lateran, St Mary Major, San Silvestro (next to Central Post Office — CV 39) and at St Stanislas, Via delle Botteghe Oscure 15 (CX 9).

Shopping. — Luxury articles (model clothes, famous jewellers etc.) are to be found in the Via Vittorio Veneto (CDV) and in the district bordered by Piazza del Popolo, the Via del Babuino, the Via del Tritone and the Via del Corso (Via Frattina, Via Borgognona, Via dei Condotti etc.) (CV).

The Via del Babuino is full of antique shops and the neighbouring street, Via Margutta, with art galleries.

In the Via dei Coronari (BX) antique shops alternate which junk shops. Every Sunday there is a flea market at the Porta Portese (BY) in Trastevere.

The best of the picturesque local markets in the town centre are in the Piazza Campo dei Fiori (BX), just off the Via dei Giubbonari (BX 22) — one of the busiest shopping streets in the town; the Via Sannio (EY) for garments; the Piazza Borghese (CV) for second-hand books and prints.

"Everyone soon or late comes round by Rome." So wrote Robert Browing in The Ring and the Book in 1868. Rome, however, is a city of contrasts, both vibrant and luxurious, sordid and dilapidated, and does not yield its charms easily. Not all her visitors have been impressed. "It appears to me that nothing romantic or poetical can coexist with what is Roman... The Romans were a blunt, flat people" wrote Walter Savage Landor in 1809. A more recent comment by Andy Warhol in 1975 is hardly flattering: "Rome, Italy, is an example of what happens when the buildings in a city last too long."

Those who are disappointed with their first experience of Rome should consider how Pope Gregory XIV addressed departing visitors; if they had spent less than three weeks in Rome, he bid them 'Farewell' but if they had stayed several months he would wish them 'Until next time'.

SIGHTSEEING PROGRAMMES

THREE DAYS IN ROME

To find where the places are situated, consult the general plans on pp 4-9 and the local plans attached to each walk.

First day

Morning. — Piazza Venezia ★ and Palazzo Venezia ★ *(p 125)* — Victor Emmanuel II Monument *(p 53)* — Santa Maria d'Aracoeli ★★ *(p 54)* — Capitol Square ★★★ *(p 55)*: Conservators' Palace Museum ★★★ *(p 57)* and Capitoline Museum ★★ *(p 60)*.

Afternoon. — Roman Forum ★★★ *(p 37)* and Palatine ★★★ *(p 46)*: including only the starred sights and finishing at the Temple of Venus and Rome ★ — Coliseum ★★★ *(p 67)* — Constantine's Arch ★★★ *(p 68)* — Imperial Fora ★★★ *(p 127)* (Trajan's Column ★★★ and Trajan's Market ★★★).

Evening. — Dinner at a *trattoria* in Trastevere: going via Tiber Island if possible.

Second day

Morning. — Castel Sant'Angelo ★★★ *(p 93)* — Vatican Museums ★★★ *(p 79)* — St Peter's Square ★★★ *(p 74)* — St Peter's Basilica ★★★ *(p 73)*.

Afternoon. — Farnese Palace ★★★ *(p 113)*; Gesù Church ★★★ *(p 109)* — Pantheon ★★★ *(p 105)* — San Luigi dei Francesi ★★ *(p 106)* — Piazza Navona ★★ *(p 163)*.

Evening. — Dinner in a trattoria near the Pantheon or in the Piazza Navona.

Third day

Morning. — St John Lateran ★★★ *(p 133)* — Baths of Caracalla ★★ *(p 180)* — Catacombs ★★★ *(p 143)*: one of the group of three only *(St Sebastian's or St Callistus' or Domitilla's)* — St Paul Without the Walls ★★★ *(p 140)*.

Afternoon. — St Mary Major ★★★ *(p 62)* — Trevi Fountain ★★★ *(p 158)* — Via dei Condotti *(p 99)* — Spanish Square ★★ *(p 99)* — Piazza del Popolo ★★ *(p 96)* — Santa Maria del Popolo ★★ *(p 97)* — Pincio: view ★★★ *(p 100)*.

Evening. — Dinner in the Via Vittorio Veneto.

EIGHT DAYS IN ROME

To find the position of the places mentioned, consult the general plans on pp 4-9 and the local plan attached to each walk. We recommend that one evening be spent taking dinner in a trattoria in Trastevere which still has a pleasant village atmosphere, another evening dining near the Pantheon or in the Piazza Navona, and another taking a stroll and then dining in the Via Vittorio Veneto which is very lively at night.

First day

Morning. — Piazza Venezia★ and Palazzo Venezia★ *(p 125)* — Victor Emmanuel II Monument *(p 53)* — Santa Maria d'Aracoeli★★ *(p 54)* — Capitol Square★★★ *(p 55)*: Conservators' Palace Museum★★★ *(p 57)* and Capitoline Museum★★ *(p 60)*.

Afternoon. — Roman Forum★★★ *(p 37)* and Palatine★★★ *(p 46)* — Coliseum★★★ *(p 67)* — Constantine's Arch★★★ *(p 68)*.

Second day

Renaissance and Baroque Rome:

Morning. — Gesù Church★★★ *(p 109)* — Walk no 6 in the Pantheon district★★★ *(p 101)*.

Afternoon. — Walk no 15 near the Piazza Navona★★ *(p 159)* — Farnese Palace★★★ *(p 113)*.

Third day

Morning. — Castel Sant'Angelo★★★ *(p 93)* — Vatican Museums★★★ *(p 79)* — Vatican Gardens★★★ *(special visiting times: see p 69)*.

Afternoon. — St Peter's Square★★★ *(p 74)* — St Peter's Basilica★★★ *(p 73)* — Janiculum: view★★★ from the Garibaldi Monument *(p 192)*.

Fourth day

Morning. — Imperial Fora★★★ *(p 127)* — St Peter in Chains★ (Moses★★★) *(p 132)* — St Clement's Basilica★★ *(p 137)* — St John Lateran★★★ *(p 133)*.

Afternoon. — Baths of Caracalla★★ *(p 180)* — St Sebastian's Gate★ *(p 182)* — Old Appian Way★★★ *(p 143)* as far as Cecilia Metella's tomb — St Paul Without the Walls★★★ *(p 140)*.

Fifth day

Morning. — San Pietro in Montorio★ and view★★★ *(p 191-2)* — Piazza★ and Basilica of St Mary in Trastevere★ *(p 188)* — Tiber Island★ *(p 152)* — Marcellus' Theatre★★ *(p 149)* — Temple of Apollo★★ *(p 149)*.

Afternoon. — Piazza Bocca della Verita★ *(p 151)*; Santa Maria in Cosmedin★ *(p 151)*; Temple of Vesta★ *(p 151)*; Temple of Fortuna Virilis★ *(p 152)*; Crescenzi House *(p 152)* — Circus Maximus *(p 194)* — Santa Sabina★★ *(p 194)* — St Paul's Gate★ *(p 196)* — Caius Cestius' Pyramid★ *(p 196)*.

Sixth day

Tivoli★★★. — *31 km - 19 miles from Rome — p 202*. Tour of Hadrian's Villa★★★ in the morning; of the Villa d'Este★★★ and the Villa Gregoriana★ in the afternoon.

Seventh day

Morning. — St Mary Major★★★ *(p 62)* — National Roman Museum★★★ *(p 118)*: starred works only — Santa Maria dei Angeli★★ *(p 121)* — Santa Maria della Vittoria★★ *(p 178)* — Barberini Palace★★ *(p 153)* and the picture gallery★★ (starred works).

Afternoon. — Trevi Fountain★★★ *(p 158)* — Spanish Square★★ *(p 99)* — Trinità dei Monti★ *(p 99)* — Pincio: view★★★ *(p 100)* — Piazza del Popolo★★ *(p 96)* — Porta del Popolo★ *(p 96)* — Santa Maria del Popolo★★ *(p 97)*.

Eighth day

Morning. — Borghese Gallery★★★ *(p 175)* — Villa Giulia Etruscan Museum★★★ *(p 169)*.

Afternoon. — Altar of Peace★★ *(p 167)* — Augustus' Mausoleum *(p 167)* — Via dei Condotti *(p 99)* — Stroll in the pedestrian precinct which contains many smart boutiques and lies in the triangle formed by the Via del Corso, the Via del Tritone and the Via del Babuino.

*The current **Michelin Guide Italia** offers a selection of pleasant quiet and well situated hotels.*

Each entry includes the facilities provided (gardens, tennis courts, swimming pool and equipped beach) and annual closure dates.

Also included is a selection of establishments recommended for their cuisine: — well prepared meals at a moderate price, stars for good cooking.

TOURIST CALENDAR OF EVENTS

A more detailed calendar of events can be obtained from the Ufficio Informazioni Pellegrini e Turisti (in the Vatican) and from the EPT (plan pp 34-35).

21 January. — At the patronal festival of St Agnes Without the Walls two lambs are blessed and then given to the Benedictines at St Cecilia who use the wool to weave the *pallium* which the Pope gives to each archbishop.

Good Friday. — Stations of the Cross at night between the Coliseum and the Palatine.

Easter. — At noon in St Peter's Square the Pope gives his benediction *Urbi et Orbi.*

May. — International equestrian competition, Piazza di Siena (Villa Borghese).

May and October. — Open air art exhibition, Via Margutta.
　　In May: Antique Fair, Via dei Coronari.
　　Municipal Rose Gardens in flower (Roseto di Roma, Via di Valle Murcia).

June. — Rome Industrial and Commercial Fair, Via Christoforo Colombo.

28 and 29 June. — Services at St Peter's in the Vatican on the feast of St Peter and St Paul, the grandest of the Roman religious festivals.

July-August. — Music in Maxentius' Basilica and the Baths of Caracalla.

5 August. — Commemoration in St Mary Major of the miraculous fall of snow which led to the construction of the basilica *(p 63):* white flower petals are released in a shower in the Pauline Chapel.

8 December. — Celebration of the Immaculate Conception in Spanish Square in the presence of the Pope.

December. — At **Christmas** the Holy Child is put on show in Santa Maria d'Aracoeli *(p 55).* Beautiful Christmas cribs are set up in the following churches: Sts Cosmas and Damian, Santa Maria in Via, Sant'Alassio on the Aventine, the Holy Apostles, San Marcello, the Gesù, Santa Maria d'Aracoeli, Santa Maria del Popolo and St Mary Major (13C crib). In the Via Giulia there is a display of 50 cribs. Midnight mass at St Mary Major and Santa Maria d'Aracoeli are particularly solemn services. In St Peter's Square benediction *Urbi et Orbi.*

　　In December and January the Piazza Navona is covered with market stalls *(bancarelle)* selling presents for Epiphany which are delivered by Befana, the Italian equivalent of Father Christmas.

FURTHER READING

General, Tourism

H. V. MORTON: **A Traveller in Rome** (Methuen).
H. V. MORTON: **The Waters of Rome** (Methuen).
G. MASSON: **The Companion Guide to Rome** (Collins).
F. COARELLI: **Guida archeologica di Roma** (Mondadori — in Italian).
E. AMFITHEATROF: **The Enchanted Ground — Americans in Italy 1760-1980** (Little, Brown & Co., Boston and Toronto).

History, civilisation

M. GRANT: **The Etruscans** (Weidenfeld & Nicolson).
D. DUDLEY: **Roman Society** (Pelican).
K. CHRIST: **The Romans** (Chatto & Windus, The Hogarth Press — translated from German).
U. E. PAOLI: **Rome — Its People, Life and Customs** (Longman — translated from Italian).
J. RICHARDS: **The Popes and the Papacy in the Early Middle Ages** (Routledge & Kegan Paul).
P. PARTNER: **Renaissance Rome — A Portrait of a Society** (University of California Press).
E. R. CHAMBERLIN: **The World of the Italian Renaissance** (George Allen & Unwin).
A. G. DICKENS: **The Counter Reformation** (Thames & Hudson).
D. BEALES: **The Risorgimento and the Unification of Italy** (Longman).
H. HEARDER: **Italy in the Age of the Risorgimento** (Longman History of Italy).
P. C. KENT: **The Pope and the Duce** (Macmillan).
A. RHODES: **The Power of Rome in the Twentieth Century** (Sidgwick & Jackson).

Art

Sir M. WHEELER: **Roman Art and Architecture** (Thames & Hudson).
M. HENIG: **A Handbook of Roman Art** (Phaidon).
J. B. WARD-PERKINS: **Roman Imperial Architecture** (Pelican History of Art).
VASARI: **Lives of the Artists** (Penguin Classics).
B. BERENSON: **The Italian Painters of the Renaissance** (Phaidon).
A. BLUNT: **Guide to Roman Baroque** (Granada).
P. PORTOGHESI: **Architettura del Rinascimento a Roma** (Electa, Milano — in Italian).
P. PORTOGHESI: **Roma Barocca** (Besteti, Roma — in Italian).

Literature: See p 29.

Specialist guides

Guide to the Vatican Museums; Guide to the Vatican City (Monumenti, Musei e Gallerie Pontificie).

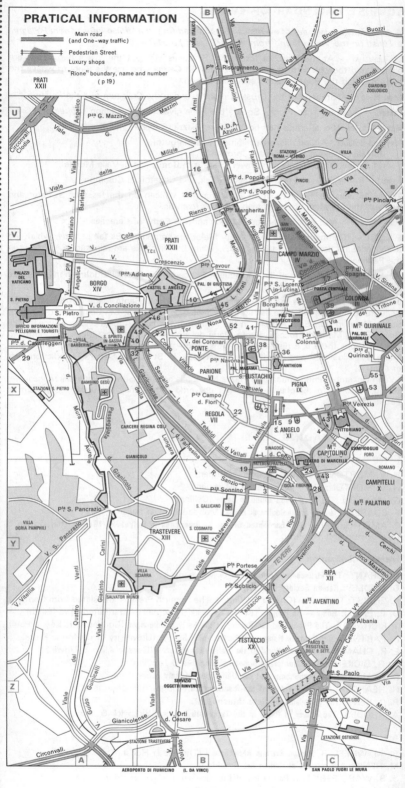

PRATICAL INFORMATION

→ Main road
(and One-way traffic)

Pedestrian Street

Luxury shops

"Rione" boundary, name and number
(p 19)

PRATI
XXII

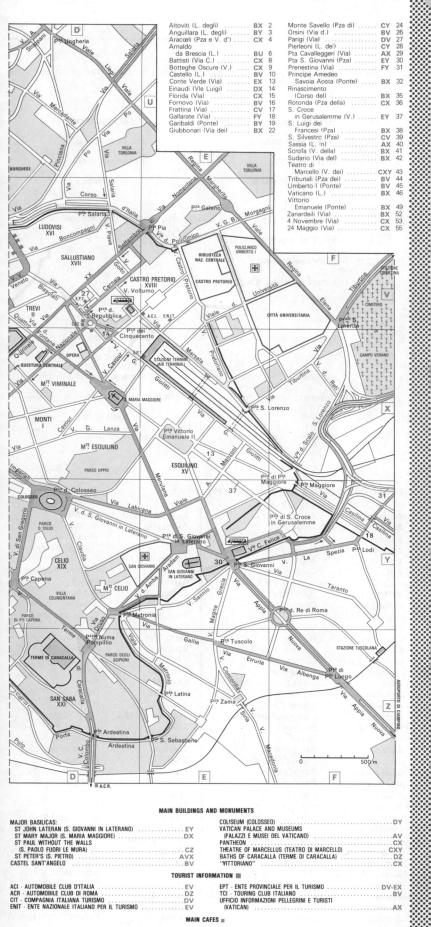

MAIN BUILDINGS AND MONUMENTS

MAJOR BASILICAS:	
ST JOHN LATERAN (S. GIOVANNI IN LATERANO)	EY
ST MARY MAJOR (S. MARIA MAGGIORE)	DX
ST PAUL WITHOUT THE WALLS	
(S. PAOLO FUORI LE MURA)	CZ
ST PETER'S (S. PIETRO)	AVX
CASTEL SANT'ANGELO	BV
COLISEUM (COLOSSEO)	DY
VATICAN PALACE AND MUSEUMS	
(PALAZZI E MUSEI DEL VATICANO)	AV
PANTHEON	CX
THEATRE OF MARCELLUS (TEATRO DI MARCELLO)	CXY
BATHS OF CARACALLA (TERME DI CARACALLA)	DZ
"VITTORIANO"	CX

TOURIST INFORMATION ■

ACI - AUTOMOBILE CLUB D'ITALIA	EV
ACR - AUTOMOBILE CLUB DI ROMA	DZ
CIT - COMPAGNIA ITALIANA TURISMO	DV
ENIT - ENTE NAZIONALE ITALIANO PER IL TURISMO	EV
EPT - ENTE PROVINCIALE PER IL TURISMO	DV-EX
TCI - TOURING CLUB ITALIANO	BV
UFFICIO INFORMAZIONI PELLEGRINI E TURISTI	
(VATICAN)	AX

MAIN CAFES ■

KEY

The Sights are shown by name and by a black box or black outline on the local plans attached to the walks in which they are described.

★★★ **Highly recommended**   COLOSSEO

★★ **Recommended**   S. CLEMENTE

★ **Interesting**   PORTA MAGGIORE

See if possible   VILLA MEDICI

▢ Colour shading showing a sight described (museum, church...)

▧ Start of sightseeing tour

⟶ Sightseeing route

A Letter locating a sight

⛪ Church   Fountain, monument   ⊙ ■

▦ Park or garden   Dual carriageway   ≡≡ ≡≡

⛢ Cemetery   Stepped street   ▥▥▥▥

✚ Hospital   Subway, tunnel   ⨑===[

✉ Covered market   Path in park or garden   ─┼─┼─

⬭ Stadium   Railway line   ─────

⋞ ⁘ Viewpoint, ruins   Underground station   Ⓜ

ITALIAN WORDS USED ON THE PLANS

Accademia	Art academy	**Ospedale (Osp.)**	Hospital
Acquedotto, Acqua	Aqueduct	**Palazzetto**	Small palace
Ambasciata	Embassy	**Palazzina**	Villa, small palace
Anagrafe	Register office		
Arco	Arch	**Palazzo (Pal.)**	Palace, private house
Atrio	Courtyard, entrance hall		
		Parco	Park
Battistero	Baptistry	**Passeggiata**	Walk
Camposanto	Cemetery	**Piazza (Pza)**	Square
Cappella	Chapel	**Piazzale (Pzale)**	Large square
Carcere	Gaol, prison	**Ponte (Pte)**	Bridge
Casa, Casina	House	**Porta (Pta)**	Town gate
Casino	Casino, pavilion	**Questura**	Police station
Castello, Castel	Castle	**San (S.)**	Saint
Cimitero	Cemetery	**Sant' (S.)**	Saint
Clivo	Street on an incline	**Santa (S.)**	Saint
Convento	Convent	**Santi (SS.)**	Saints
Corso (Cso)	Street	**Santo (S.)**	Holy
Cortile	Court, courtyard	**Santissimo/i (SS.)**	Most holy
Fontana (Fna)	Fountain	**Scala**	Stairway
Foro	Forum	**Scuola**	School
Galleria	Art gallery, shopping arcade	**Sepolcro**	Tomb, sepulchre
		Stazione	Station
Galoppatoio	Racecourse	**Teatro**	Theatre
Giardino/i	Garden/s	**Tempio**	Temple
Isola	Island	**Tevere**	Tiber
Istituto	Institute	**Torre**	Tower
Largo (Lgo)	Small square	**Ufficio informazioni**	Information Bureau
Lungotevere (L.;			
Lung.; Lungotev.)	Embankment	**Ufficio postale, Posta**	Post Office
Mausoleo	Mausoleum	**Via (V.)**	Street
Ministero	Ministry	**Viale (Vle)**	Avenue
Monte (M.; Mte)	Hill	**Vico**	Side street
Monumento	Monument	**Vicolo (Vic.)**	Alley
Museo	Museum	**Villa**	Villa, park
Obelisco	Obelisk	**Villino**	Country cottage
Oratorio	Oratory		

Allow 3 1/2 hours for visiting the Forum and 3 1/2 hours for the Palatine. There are three entrances to the Forum — in Via della Salara Vecchia (north side), Via Sacra (east side) and Via del Foro (south side) (plan pp 40-41) — but it is best to start in Via del Campidoglio which gives an excellent view of the whole site from above. Parts of the ruins may be closed to visitors owing to lack of staff or restoration work.

■ ROMAN FORUM ★★★ (Foro Romano)

This site, where a few columns stand among ruined walls and crumbling foundations, bears traces of the twelve centuries of history which forged the Roman civilisation.

HISTORICAL NOTES

In about 750 BC the site of the Forum was a marshy valley, subject to flooding by the Tiber and by streams from the seven surrounding hills: the Palatine, the Coelian, the Esquiline, the Velia which linked the Palatine to the Esquiline, the Viminal, the Quirinal and the Capitoline *(map pp 14-15)*. Small villages composed of rough shacks grew up on the hillsides. Their inhabitants, the Latins and the Sabines *(map p 13)*, were principally engaged in agriculture but would take up arms in defence of their homesteads when threatened with invasion by their neighbours. The valley, which lay roughly at the centre of the circle of hills and which later became the Forum, was used as a burial ground and as a meeting place where their leaders made decisions affecting the community and where the people exchanged goods and gathered for worship.

Two centuries later the marshy valley had completely changed in appearance and become a real square at the centre of a town: the cemetery had been abandoned and covered with houses; the west side of the Forum had been paved. The people responsible for this transformation were the **Etruscans**. Originally from the right bank of the Tiber, they extended their dominion as far as Cumae on the borders of Magna Graecia (southern Italy). They settled on the site of Rome, built a citadel on the Capitol, unified the villages and organised the social life of the community. From 616 to 509 BC Rome was governed by kings of Etruscan origin. The city was enclosed by fortifications; the stagnant water in the Forum was drained into the Tiber through a channel which was to become the Great Sewer *Cloaca maxima*.

The Forum during the Republic. — The last Etruscan king, Tarquin the Superb, was thrown out in 509 BC and the Consulate was instituted. The Republican era had begun: from being a rural town Rome began to develop into the capital of an empire. The forum, barely 2 ha-5 acres in extent was the focal point of events which ushered in the new era.

The Republican period was first and foremost a time of territorial expansion: from early in 5C BC Rome was at war with her neighbours. Victories were celebrated in the Forum: a temple was built in honour of the Dioscuri *(p 44)* who came to the assistance of the Romans at Lake Regillus. In 260 during the first Punic war a column was raised to Caius Duilius who gained the first Roman naval victory at Milazzo in Sicily. All victorious generals processed in triumph through the Forum.

Commercial centre. — The Roman conquests brought with them immense riches: the contents of confiscated enemy treasuries, indemnities paid by the conquered nations and the tribute paid by the provinces. By 3C BC Rome was an important financial centre. Money changing, loans and credit were arranged in the Forum. The shops which had formerly housed small traders were taken over by the bankers.

Political centre. — The five centuries of the Roman Republic which preceded the Empire were full of activity. The men who decided the destiny of Rome met in the **Comitium**, an area in the northwest corner of the Forum where the popular assemblies *(comices)* were held.

Right in the corner stood the Senate House *(Curia)*. It was also called the 'Hostilia' because, so it was said, it had been created by Tullius Hostilius, a Sabine king who ruled from 672 to 640 BC. The Curia was the seat of the highest level of Republican government, the Senate. 200 Senators, appointed for life, decided foreign policy, directed military operations, drew up peace treaties and enacted measures for public safety. Opposite the Curia were the Rostra where the tribunes held forth. People came to listen to the pitiless logic and measured accents of Tiberius and Gaius Gracchus. Next to it stood the *Graecostasis,* a platform where foreign ambassadors waited. In 185 BC the **Basilica Porcia**, the first building of this sort in Rome was erected on one side of the Comitium by Porcius Cato, thus enabling the citizens to assemble under cover.

Religious centre. — In 497 BC the Temple of Saturn *(p 43)* was built in the Forum; other religious buildings already existed from the regal period. Troubled times were approaching and religious belief was waning. The practice of offering the spirits of the dead a combat which ended in the death of one of the participants degenerated into an entertainment: by 264 BC gladiatorial combats were being held in the Forum.

Troubled Times. — For a hundred years the Republican regime tore itself to pieces in a civil war. In 52 BC the tribune Clodius was killed by Milo, his body being carried to the Comitium and cremated; the fire spread, destroying the Curia and the Basilica Porcia.

Caesar had already decided that the Forum was too small and intended to enlarge it. In 44 BC he moved the Rostra and realigned the Curia.

Scarcely anything of the Republican Forum survives. The early buildings were of tufa, peperine *(p 21)* or wood. The emperors faced them with marble, then built others larger and more magnificent. Augustus could boast that he had inherited a town built of brick and left a city built of marble.

The Forum during the Empire. — On 16 January 27 BC the Senate granted Octavian the title Augustus (protected by the gods in every act); a new regime was born under the sign of grandeur. Taking up Caesar's project, Augustus, and then Vespasian, Domitian and Trajan, enlarged the old Forum and built the Imperial Fora *(p 127)*. In the Augustan era the original Forum lost some of its uses: the huge popular assemblies and the reviews of the troops were moved to the Campus Martius.

The Forum became the chosen site for erecting monuments: commemorative arches, basilicas and temples dedicated to emperors deified after their death. Even in 2C BC confusion reigned according to Plautus, a satirist who died in 184 BC. Every sort of citizen could be found there: "vicious or virtuous, honest or dishonest. If you want to meet a perjurer, go to the Comitium; for a liar and a braggart, try the Temple of Venus Cloacina; for wealthy married wasters, near the Basilica. There too you will find well perfumed prostitutes and men ready to do a deal, while the fish market is frequented by members of the eating clubs. Wealthy and reputable citizens stroll in the lower Forum; the middle Forum near the Canal is favoured by the merely showy set... Behind the Temple of Castor are those whom you would do well not to trust too lightly; in the Tuscan district those who are willing to sell themselves."

In 3C building came to a halt: not only for lack of space but also because of the spread of a new religion which entailed the worship of one god. At first it was preached by a handful of nobodies and then from 60 AD by a certain Paul of Tarsus. The emperors resisted but in 391 AD Theodosius finally closed the pagan temples.

The Forum's downfall began in 410 when Alaric the Goth swept in from the Danube with his savage hordes and set fire to the Curia and the Basilica Aemilia. There followed an earthquake in 442, the depredations of Genseric's Vandals in 455, the armies of Theodoric in 500 and of Belisarius in 537, after which the Forum was dead. Rome's prestige no longer lay in grandiose monuments but, as the resting place of St Peter the Apostle, the city was celebrated throughout the Christian world.

The Forum from the Middle Ages to the Renaissance. — With the church organised, the Bishop of Rome, the Pope, was recognised as the head of Christianity. Gradually the imperial buildings were converted into places of Christian worship. Some still survive, a curious juxtaposition of traditions; many have disappeared such as the two oratories in the portico of the Basilica Aemilia or the Church of Sts Sergius and Bacchus which existed between the Temples of Saturn and Concord until 16C or the Church of Santa Maria in Cannapara in the Basilica Julia. In 9C the buildings began to crumble away; the earth built up round them and the ruins were buried.

In 12C the quarrel between the Pope and the Holy Roman Emperor *(p 12)* brought civil war between the noble Roman families. The ancient structures were turned into fortresses; towers rose between the Temple of Antoninus and Faustina and Caesar's Forum. The old buildings were stripped of their decoration which was used to embellish churches and palaces; the statues and columns were baked in lime kilns to produce chalk.

The deserted Forum became a sewage farm. By 15C the pillars of the Temple of Vespasian were half underground and the podium of the Temple of the Dioscuri was completely buried; both were surrounded by fields. The Forum had become the *campo vaccino,* a cows' field. Near the Temple of the Dioscuri the marble basin of a fountain was being used as a drinking trough for animals; it is now in the Piazza del Quirinale. When Charles V visited Rome in 1536, Pope Paul III laid out a broad avenue from the Arch of Titus to the Arch of Septimius Severus.

Excavations. — The names of many famous archaeologists, both Italians and foreigners, are connected with the history of the excavation of the Roman Forum: Carlo Fea who began investigations in 1803, Antonio Nibby, Bunsen and Canina, Pietro Rosa after 1870, Giuseppe Fiorelli, Rodolfo Lanciani, H Jordan, C Hülsen and particularly Giacomo Boni who carried out methodical excavations from 1898 onwards, reaching the oldest levels which were essential to an understanding of early Rome.

TOUR

From Via del Campidoglio look down on the west end of the Forum where excavations are in progress.

Clivus Capitolinus. — There are some fine sections of paving to be seen. This was the road used by religious processions and military triumphs proceeding from the Forum to the Temple of Jupiter on the Capitol. The present Via del Campidoglio follows the original route.

Tabularium. — This building filled the depression between the Citadel and the Capitol, the two peaks of the Capitoline Hill. Its façade formed the west side of the Forum. It was built in 78 BC to house the state records, including some bronze tablets on which were inscribed the old Roman laws, hence the name Tabularium. Only the podium and six of the nine pillars of the original portico remain; the use of peperine, a very simple building material, and of the Doric order, a plain architectural style, typify the austerity of Republican architecture. In 12C the ruins of the Tabularium became the base of the Senatorial Palace *(p 56)*.

Portico of the Di Consentes ★. — The twelve columns with Corinthian capitals were reconstructed in 1858. The portico was built by Domitian in honour of the twelve great gods in the Roman pantheon who met in council to assist Jupiter. Their statues stood in the portico, two by two: Jupiter and Juno, Neptune and Minerva, Mars and Venus, Apollo and Diana, Vulcan and Vesta, Mercury and Ceres.

It was restored in 367 by the Prefect of Rome, Vettius Agorius Praetextatus, who had been a friend of Julian the Apostate and shared his great sympathy for the pagan religions; it was certainly the last gesture made to paganism in Rome where thirty seven popes had already acceded to the throne of St Peter.

Temple of Vespasian ★★. — Three very elegant columns, excavated by Valadier in 1811, are still standing; they formed a corner of the earlier part of the temple. Above the architrave is a detailed decorative frieze: a cornice with dentil, ovolo and palm leaf moulding above a band decorated with bucranes and sacrificial instruments. The temple was approached by steps from the Clivus Capitolinus.

Vespasian became emperor in 69 AD following the struggles which arose among the pretenders to Nero's succession. He therefore established the principle of a hereditary monarchy founded on primogeniture. He announced to the Senate that "his sons would succeed him or there would be no successor". His elder son Titus therefore succeeded him and began to build a temple in honour of his father who had been deified on his death: in practice if an emperor had ruled well the Senate would issue a decree raising him to the rank of the gods; all that was needed was a witness who had seen an eagle carry off the dead man's soul during the cremation ceremony.

Titus died before the temple was finished; it was Domitian, his brother and successor as emperor, who completed the building and dedicated it to Vespasian and Titus. Their two statues stood on a pedestal in the *cella*.

Temple of Concord. — The Romans always attributed a divine character to the mysterious forces which influenced events; thus they worshipped as gods such abstract ideas as concord, justice, liberty and abundance. Most of these divinities were represented by the statue of a female figure: the attributes of concord were two linked hands and a dove.

There had been a temple of Concord in the Forum since 367 BC; it commemorated the re-establishment of peace between the patricians and the plebeians who had been at odds since the beginning of 5C BC. Some two and a half centuries later, when the assassination of the people's tribune, Caius Gracchus, had restored peace at home, Concord was again held in honour and the temple rebuilt.

The plan of the building is quite unusual: the *cella* extends laterally beyond the width of the *pronaos* which was reached by steps from the Clivus Capitolinus.

Walk up Via del Campidoglio to Piazza del Campidoglio and then round into Via di San Pietro in Carcere in order to descend the steps in the northwest corner of the Forum.

Mamertine Prison ★. — This is the name given to two rooms, one above the other, hollowed out of the Capitoline Hill beneath the Church of San Giuseppe dei Falegnami (St Joseph of the Carpenters).

The Mamertine was used as a prison where many enemies of the Roman state were incarcerated. On the right of the entrance is a list of names of well known people who perished here. In 104 BC Jugurtha died of starvation while his conqueror Marius led his victory parade through the Forum. Vercingetorix was beheaded here in 46 BC after Caesar's triumph. However, after the victory of Aemilius Paullus against Perseus of Macedonia at Pydna in 168 BC, worthy enemy chiefs often escaped death; Jugurtha and Vercingetorix had not been considered worthy of such clemency. It was here on 5 December 65 BC that Cataline's fellow conspirators were strangled after Cicero had given his fourth Cataline speech.

In the Middle Ages a legend arose that St Peter had been imprisoned here; hence the name San Pietro in Carcere (St Peter in prison). On the left of the entrance is a list of Christian martyrs who died in the prison. At the head of the staircase linking the two rooms is a hollowed-out stone said to bear the imprint of the Apostle's head as he was jostled by his gaolers.

The lower chamber *(Tullianum)* was built at the end of 4C BC out of huge blocks of tufa arranged in a vault and was used as a cistern or a tomb. Legend tells how Peter and Paul made water miraculously spring from the earth so that they could baptise their gaolers. The spring and the pillar to which the prisoners were chained can still be seen.

Church of Sts Luke and Martina ★ (SS. Luca e Martina). — On the site of the Senate archive *(Secretarium Senatus,* an annex of the Curia) a church was built in about 7C and dedicated to Martina who had been martyred under Septimius Severus. From 1588 it was also associated with St Luke since in that year Pope Sixtus V gave the church to the members of St Luke's Academy, a guild of painters who recognized the Evangelist as their patron saint; according to a 6C legend he had painted a portrait of the Virgin Mary.

In 1634 a terracotta sarcophagus was found containing the remains of St Martina. Cardinal Francesco Barberini commissioned Pietro da Cortona to build a new shrine above the old one. Da Cortona, who was a contemporary of Bernini and Borromini, leading exponents of the Baroque style, designed a beautiful façade ★. Its shallow convex curve is reminiscent of the style of Borromini; so too is the interior, which is designed on the Greek cross plan and decorated all over with pale stuccoes in beige and grey revealing a search for complicated forms.

Take Via della Curia to the right of the church and turn right into Via della Salara Vecchia to reach the entrance to the Forum.

Open 9 am to one hour before sunset. Sunday and holidays, 9 am to 1 pm. Closed Tuesday, 1 January, Easter, 1 May, 1st Sunday in June, 15 August, Christmas. 4 000 L.

Beyond the ticket office the path leads down into the Forum; immediately on the right are the ruins of the Basilica Aemilia.

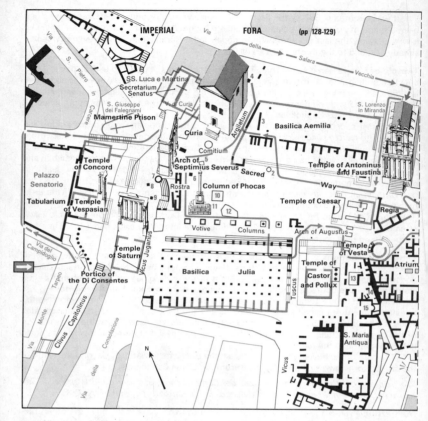

Basilica Aemilia. — This was the second basilica to be built in Rome (in 179 BC) after the Basilica Porcia had been built not far away in 185 BC *(p 37)*. Like all the monuments in the Forum it was frequently restored and reconstructed. The present remains are those of the 1C rebuilding.

It was named after the Aemilia family *(gens Aemilia)* who were responsible for its maintenance. Like all the ancient basilicas it served no religious purpose. The huge covered hall was used for business transactions and for sheltering from the heat or cold; judges and litigants retreated here to hold their hearings out of the hubbub of the more public places.

Along the south side of the basilica there was a line of shops opening into a portico; the party-walls can still be seen (some have been reconstructed). The shops sold jewellery and perfume.

Behind the shops was the main hall divided into three by two rows of coloured marble columns with a finely carved entablature of white marble; fragments of the architrave and columns are displayed against the rear wall.

In the southeast corner of the Basilica Aemilia stands a Latin **inscription** (1) dedicated to Augustus' adopted grandsons, Caius and Lucius, who died before reaching manhood.

Sacred Way ★★★. — This was the most famous street in ancient Rome. From the earliest days of the Forum, the Temple of Vesta and the Regia flanked the Sacred Way along which victorious generals rode in triumphal procession; dressed like Jupiter and standing in a four-horse chariot, they proceeded to the Capitoline Hill to give thanks to Jupiter, the Great and Good, for his protection during the campaign.

Sanctuary of Venus Cloacina (2). — A travertine circle on the ground marks the site of the sanctuary dedicated to the goddess who protected the main sewer; traces of the steps leading down to it are still visible. Here in 5C BC Verginius, a humble plebeian officer, took his daughter's life to save her from the lust of Appius Claudius, a decemvir; Livy tells how the latter was prepared to abuse his power in his desire to make Virginia his slave; he provoked a riot amoung the people and the abdication of the decemvirs.

Go to the northwest corner of the Basilica Aemilia.

Beneath a protective roof are the bases of three columns and other fragments belonging to the Basilica built in the Republican period (3).

Argiletum. — This street, one of the busiest in Rome, separated the Basilica Aemilia from the Curia and led to Suburra, a slum district *(p 131)*. There remain some fine sections of travertine paving. During the reign of the kings there was said to be an arch over the Argiletum, flanked by a shrine containing the two-faced statue of the god Janus. Legend tells how during the war against the Sabines Janus had produced a jet of hot water from the ground which stopped the enemy dead in their attack on the Capitol. The shrine was therefore always left open in time of war so that Janus could come to the aid of the Romans.

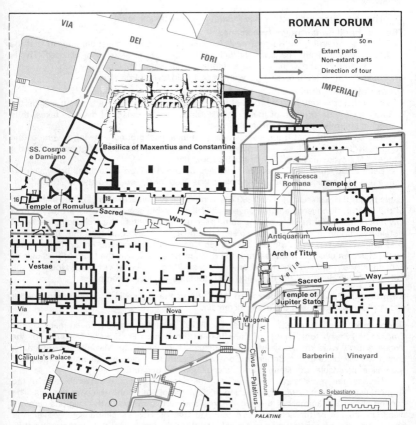

ROMAN FORUM

0   50 m

Extant parts
Non-extant parts
Direction of tour

VIA
DEI
FORI
IMPERIALI

SS. Cosma
e Damiano

Basilica of Maxentius and Constantine

S. Francesca
Romana   Temple of

16   17   18
Temple of Romulus   Sacred   Way   Venus and Rome

Antiquarium

Arch of Titus

Vestae   Vellia   Sacred   Way

Via   Nova   Temple of
Jupiter Stator

Pta Mugonia

Barberini   Vineyard

Caligula's Palace

Clivus – Palatinus
V. di S. Bonaventura

S. Sebastiano

PALATINE

PALATINE

Curia ★★. — The brick building visible today is not the one in which the Senate met in the Republican period when it was in charge of Roman policy. The first Curia was more or less on the site of the chancel and left transept of St Luke's Church but facing in a different direction. In 1C BC Caesar moved it and enlarged it and Diocletian rebuilt it in 3C.

Diocletian's Curia was restored in 1937 after the removal of St Adrian's Church which had occupied the building since 7C.

It was less austere than it is today: the façade, faced with marble and stucco, was surmounted by a tympanum covered in travertine; the bronze door, which was sheltered by a portico, was removed to St John Lateran by Alexander VII in 17C.

The Curia was a *templum,* a consecrated place where an augur could communicate to the people the wishes of the gods as they had been revealed to him by certains signs: the flight of birds, the manner of feeding of the sacred chickens and any unusual events. Every sitting of the Senate began with the president taking the auguries to see whether they were favourable or not. The Senators did not have fixed seats. Once the agenda had been read each Senator in turn — according to the order fixed by the list in the *album* — was called upon to give his opinion.

For a considerable period the Senate had immense power but once imperial government had been introduced it became practically impossible for the Senators to oppose the decisions of the Emperor who appointed them to office. At the very most, after an Emperor's death, they could condemn him and thus oppose his deification.

The mystery of the Statue of Victory. — At the far end of the Curia there are traces of a pedestal on which stood the statue of Victory: it was a golden statue placed there in 29 BC by Octavian who defeated the armies of Antony and Cleopatra at Actium in Greece in 31 BC and became the ruler of the Roman empire. For over three centuries the emperors worshipped the statue, burning incense on the altar. At their funerals the statue was carried at the head of the cortege which culminated in the apotheosis and deification of the Emperor. In his Epistle to the Romans St Paul had already asserted that the one God of the Christians should have dominion over the living and the dead. In 380 AD the Edict of Thessalonica was issued stipulating that all people ''should rally to the faith transmitted to the Romans by the Apostle Peter...''. From then on the statue of Victory constituted an offence to Christianity, the new state religion; in 382 the Emperor Gratian had the statue removed. Symmachus, Prefect of Rome, protested but in vain; the statue never reappeared.

Trajan's Plutei ★★★. — The Curia houses two sculpted panels found in the Forum and probably commissioned by Trajan or his successor Hadrian to decorate the Rostra.

On the back of the two panels are represented the three animals which were sacrificed during the purification ceremony: a pig, a sheep and a bull; in Latin: *sus, ovis* and *taurus,* hence the name of the sacrifice: *suovetaurilia.* The anatomy of the animals is represented in a very realistic manner; each detail has been carefully executed, particularly the fleeces of the sheep.

The sculptures on the other side illustrate imperial beneficence.

The righthand panel shows two scenes:

— Trajan, standing on the Rostra *(see below)* with his lictors, has just announced that the interest due on loans made to smallholders will be used to assist poor children. This is the institution of the *Alimenta* which Hadrian continued to implement.

— The Emperor, seated, receiving a woman and child, symbolizing Italy.

On the lefthand panel:

— The Emperor is watching a group of men piling up documents. He is about to give the order for the destruction of these records which contain details of overdue taxes, thus freeing a number of citizens from their debts.

The sculptor has set these scenes against a local background showing several of the Forum buildings. The edges of the panels are decorated with the sacred figtree *(p 43)* and a statue of Marsyas, his flayed skin about his shoulders.

Behind the Curia *(walk round the building by the Argiletum)* is a small brick altar (4) with a recess for relics proving that the place was used for Christian worship in 7C to 8C.

Lapis Niger (Black stone) (5). — In 1899 Giacomo Boni, who was in charge of the excavation of the Forum, discovered an area paved with black marble slabs (currently protected by a low fence). Beneath the slabs among some piled up blocks of tufa the archaeologists found a stele bearing an inscription whose meaning is obscure. They concluded they had uncovered a monument dating from 6C BC. When Caesar re-arranged the Forum he had protected this area because it was sacred; the Romans believed it was the tomb of Romulus or Faustulus (the shepherd who had seen the wolf suckling the twins) or Hostus Hostilius, the father of Tullus Hostilius, the third king after Romulus and Numa Pompilius.

Comitium. — *p 37.* It extended from the Curia to the Lapis Niger. It once contained a circular fountain; traces of the base still remain.

Decennalia Caesarum (6). — In 286 Diocletian decentralised the government of the Empire; he himself took charge of the affairs of the Eastern Empire and Maximian of the Western. Both were known by the title Augustus. Seven years later Maximian entrusted the administration of Gaul and Britain to Constantius and Diocletian put Galerius in charge of the Balkan peninsula. Constantius and Galerius bore the title of Caesar.

The first ten years' reign *(decennalia)* of the two Caesars and the twenty years of the Augusti were celebrated with the erection of a column of which only the base remains. The carving shows the animals of the *suovetaurilia* and certain events in the religious ceremonies. The quality of the sculpture is inferior to that of Trajan's period *(see above)*; the background figures are flattened and simply indicated by a deep line; the costumes are stiff, the fold lines being too deeply chiselled.

Rostra ★. — After 338 BC the orators' platform was always called the Rostra. In that year the Romans had attacked Antium (modern Anzio), then notorious for its pirates, and captured the prows *(rostra)* of the enemy ships which they fixed to the orators' platform. In the Republican period the Rostra resounded with the speeches of all the great exponents of the oratorical art. In those days the platform stood between the Lapis Niger and the present Curia. The remains which can be seen today are those of the Rostra moved in 44 BC by Julius Caesar. After his assassination, Octavian, Antony and Lepidus formed the second triumvirate (late October 43 BC). The period of proscriptions began; Cicero was one of the most famous victims. A declared enemy of Antony, whose illegal acts and imperial ambitions he had denounced in his Philippics, he was sacrificed for reasons of state by Octavian and murdered in his house in Gaeta in December 43 BC by agents of the triumvirate. His hands and head were exposed on the Rostra.

The construction known as the Rostra was a raised platform reached by a curving staircase at the rear (Capitoline side). When the emperors were all-powerful, the great assemblies of the people, roused by the speeches of their tribunes, had no power of decision. The platform therefore was used only for dignified official ceremonies. Before the erection of the two commemorative columns, the crowd could congregate in front of the Rostra. It became very noisy on the days when food was distributed; the numbers of the poor grew incessantly and when Caesar came to power there were about 300 000 citizens on the lists for the distribution of free corn.

Arch of Septimius Severus ★★. — It was built in 203 and is surmounted by statues of Septimius Severus, his two sons (Caracalla and Geta) and the figure of Victory. The Emperor had just won a series of victories over the Parthians (197 to 202) and had organized a new province, Mesopotamia, *(map pp 16-17)*. The heroes' names appeared in the dedicatory text; Geta's was obliterated after Caracalla had him murdered so as to be the sole successor.

In 3C architecture became more complicated: four detached Corinthian columns stand before the façade forming a false portico. Decoration is abundant. At the base of the columns are prisoners in chains.

(After photo by Gab. Fot. Naz., Rome)

**Arch of Septimius Severus:
prisoner in chains**

The panels on the façade are divided by thick ribs into horizontal bands. The figures are too small and although this style of presentation serves well for triumphal columns *(pp 130 and 163)* here it only causes confusion.

Umbilicus Urbis (7). — The remains of a 3C circular temple which marked the symbolic centre of the city.

Altar of Vulcan (8). — This venerable hollow in the tufa goes back to the time of the kings. Under the Republic the day of 23 August was devoted to the Volcanalia festival: little fishes or other animals symbolising human lives that people wished to preserve were offered to the god of Fire.

Golden Milestone (9). — A marble column covered with gilded bronze was set up by Augustus to mark the point from which mileages were measured. The distances between the capital and the major cities of the Empire were written on it.

Temple of Saturn ★★★. — From 497 onwards a temple dedicated to Saturn stood on this site. This god was supposed to have taught the Romans to cultivate the earth; hence his prestige with this peasant people. The temple was restored several times under the Republic and then rebuilt in 4C after a fire. The eight columns of the *pronaos* which remain date from this period, whereas the travertine podium goes back to 1C BC.

The Saturnalia. — This celebrated festival took place in December in the Temple of Saturn. The general licence which accompanied it was intended to help the sun rise again in the sky. During the Saturnalia all distinctions between masters and slaves were suspended; the latter in particular were entitled to free speech.

State Treasury. — The treasure was lodged in the temple basement. This place may have been chosen because the cult of Saturn was associated with that of Ops the goddess of Abundance. The Senate administered the treasure, assisted by the Censors and the Quaestors. Late in 49 during the civil war Caesar did not hesitate to draw on the funds.

Vicus Jugarius. — This important street ran between the temple of Saturn and the Basilica Julia and led to the vegetable market (Forum Holitorium: *p 148*).

Phocas' Column ★. — In 608 AD the Eastern Emperor Phocas gave the Pantheon to Pope Boniface IV and it was turned into a church. In gratitude a statue of the donor was set up on a column in the Forum. The column had to be taken from an already existing building because by then there were no artists capable of producing fine sculpture. This was the last monument to be erected on the old public place.

The sacred **fig tree,** symbol of the tree beneath which the cradle of Romulus and Remus had been found, the **vine** and the **olive tree (10),** symbols of the prosperity which Rome owed to agriculture, have been replanted. Here also stood the very popular statue of Marsyas, brought from Greece in 2C BC. It represented a Silenus looking, as they all did, like an old satyr, very ugly and often drunk, wearing a skin over his shoulders. He wore a Phrygian cap, symbol of liberty, so that newly freed slaves would come and touch the statue.

The large **inscription (11),** reconstructed in bronze letters, bears the name of Naevius and commemorates the relaying of the paving carried out by this magistrate in 15 BC.

Curtian Lake (12). — This name refers to a circular area paved with stone within a shallow surround, protected by a roof and a railing. During the early Republic it was a cleft full of water that could not be drained away. The oracle was consulted and pronounced that the opening would close when Rome threw her dearest treasure into it. A valuable young soldier called Curtius rode into it fully armed and the abyss closed up leaving a small pool of water. The adjacent low relief sculpture illustrating the legend was executed in 1C BC *(p 59)*; it does not reveal whether this legend should be given more credit than another which says that Curtius was a Sabine soldier who was nearly sucked down into the marshy ground of the Forum during the legendary war between Romulus and Tatius.

Votive Columns. — There were seven, probably erected during Diocletian's reign (284-305 AD) to commemorate army generals. Two have been partly reconstructed.

Basilica Julia ★★. — In 170 BC the Censor Sempronius Gracchus, father of the tribunes Tiberius and Caius, built a basilica on this site which was called "Sempronia". In 55 BC Julius Caesar, who was Consul, replaced it with another basilica, larger and more elegant, which started the trend for gigantic buildings in the Forum: 109 m - 358 ft long, 40 m - 131 ft wide and divided into five aisles, it was paved with precious marble in the centre and white marble in the side aisles. Close observation of some of the paving stones will reveal geometric designs which were marked out by idlers for their games.

There was a portico on the northeast side and shops on the opposite side.

Julius Caesar was murdered in 44 BC before the basilica was finished; it bears his name nonetheless, although it was Augustus who completed it.

In about 8C the Church of Santa Maria in Cannapara was established in the west corner (traces of brick walls).

Vicus Tuscus. — This street curved round the foot of the Palatine to join the cattle market near the Tiber (Forum Boarium: *p 148*). Many Etruscan merchants had shops there, hence its name (the Romans called the Etruscans *Tusci*).

Temple of Caesar. — Almost nothing is left of this building which started the cult of Emperor worship. On the evening of the Ides of March 44 BC the body of Caesar, who had been stabbed to death in the Curia of Pompey *(p 108)* was carried to the Forum and cremated before the Rostra.

A column and altar were set up nearby but were immediately pulled down by Caesar's enemies. They were replaced by a temple consecrated by Octavian in 29 BC to the 'god' Julius Caesar.

The podium was extended forward to form a raised terrace containing a semi-circular recess at ground level in which stood a round altar (traces visible). In the *cella* stood a statue of Caesar, a star on his head. Suetonius explains why he was always represented in this way: "after his apotheosis, during the first days of the games given in his honour by his successor Augustus, a comet appeared at about the eleventh hour and burned for seven days; it was thought to be Caesar's soul being admitted to heaven...".

When Octavian defeated the fleets of Antony and Cleopatra at Actium in Greece on 2 September 31 BC, he took the prows *(rostra)* of the enemy ships and fixed them to the terrace of Caesar's temple; the terrace became known as the Caesar's Rostra and later Emperors often spoke from there.

Arch of Augustus. — Two commemorative arches were erected by Augustus between the temples of Caesar and Castor: the first was built in 29 BC after his victory at Actium in Greece; ten years later as the first became dilapidated, a second was built to celebrate Augustus' recovery of the Roman standards which had been captured by the Parthians at the battle of Carrhae in Mesopotamia in 53 BC.

Only the foundations have been discovered (the bases of two pillars are visible).

Temple of Castor and Pollux ★★★ (the Dioscuri). — The chief remains are three columns supporting an architrave fragment, which form one of the most famous sights of the Roman Forum. The founding of the temple goes back to the beginning of 5C BC; it has remained on its original site.

Its whole history is surrounded by legends. Early in 5C BC Rome took the offensive against her poorer envious neighbours: the conflict came to a head on the shores of Lake Regillus in about 496 BC. During the battle the Romans saw two divine knights fighting on their side; these were Castor and Pollux, sons of Jupiter and Leda. They subsequently made their way to Rome to announce the victory to the people gathered in the Forum; their thirsty horses drank at Juturna's spring. A temple dedicated to the Dioscuri, Castor and Pollux, was built on the site of this apparition by the son of the dictator Postumius who had directed the battle against the Latins.

The three beautiful columns, which had been pulled down in 1811, date from a reconstruction undertaken in the Augustan era and belong to the long lefthand side of the sanctuary.

The very high podium which raises the columns high into the sky, the magnitude of the Corinthian capitals and the use of very white marble combine to make a most majestic effect. The remains of the temple of Castor and Pollux show what magnificence Augustus sought to bestow on the city to replace the damage caused in the civil war.

It is said that the Emperor Caligula (37-41 AD), whose excesses led to his being presumed insane, built a bridge from the Temple of Castor and Pollux (the ante-chamber to his palace on the Palatine) to the Temple of Jupiter on the Capitol so that he could go and converse with the god whom he considered his equal or even sometimes take his place.

Juturna's sacred precinct (13). — Juturna was a nymph who reigned over all the springs in Latium and was made immortal by Jupiter who loved her. Her shrine contained a spring which played a part in the legend of the Dioscuri. In the basin stands an altar, probably 2C, with low relief sculptures representing Castor and Pollux and a woman bearing a long torch *(on the front and back)* and Leda and the swan, and Jupiter *(on the sides)*. The adjacent **aedicule** (14), partially reconstructed, the round well and the altar were also part of the sacred precinct. The well is inscribed with the name of Barbatius Pollio who put up a dedication to Juturna probably in the reign of Augustus; low relief figures on the altar.

Santa Maria Antiqua. — *Closed for restoration.*

Oratory of the Forty Martyrs (15). — The original purpose of the building is unknown; in 7C it was decorated with paintings and dedicated to the forty martyrs of Sebastea in Armenia who were exposed in chains on a frozen pond.

Temple of Vesta and House of the Vestal Virgins ★★★. — In the days when fire was still a precious commodity, the village on the Palatine where Romulus lived must have included a round hut, similar to all the other huts, where the communal fire was kept alight. This process was organised around Vesta, the goddess of fire.

The institution of the cult in Rome goes back to Romulus or to Numa Pompilius (715-672 BC). A group of priestesses, known as the Vestal Virgins, at first four in number but later increased to six, officiated in the cult of Vesta.

When the first temple was built, probably late in 6C BC, it conserved the circular form of the earlier hut. It was destroyed by fire and rebuilt several times, always in circular form, until the time of Septimius Severus. Only the central foundation and a few marble fragments survived to be used in the 1930 reconstruction. It was an enclosed shrine, surrounded by a portico supported on twenty fluted Corinthian columns; the frieze showed the instruments of sacrifice in low relief. The *cella* housed an altar where the fire was kept burning constantly. There was also a secret place where certain objects which were supposed to have made Rome's fortune, were jealously guarded; they included the famous Palladium, a statuette in wood or bone of the goddess Pallas, which was able to protect the city which possessed it. It had fallen from the sky on the city of Troy, possibly pushed by Zeus on Olympus. The Romans thought it had come into their possession through Aeneas who had stolen it from Troy and brought it to Italy.

Next to the temple was the house of the Vestal Virgins: the **Atrium Vestae**. It was a large two storey building enclosing a rectangular courtyard with a portico, containing two pools of water and a garden. The Vestal Virgins were chosen from the patrician families and entered into service at the age of ten and stayed for at least thirty years: ten as pupils, ten performing their duties and ten teaching. Most of the Vestals spent their whole lives in the house. Discipline was strict: a virgin who let the fire go out, a portent of disaster for Rome, was severely punished and one who broke her vow of chastity was buried alive. From 3C statues were erected to the Vestals in recognition of their service. Some of these statues with an inscription on the base have been placed in the courtyard of the house.

Regia. — Religious observance in Rome centred on the Regia and the Temple of Vesta. The Regia was held to have been the residence of King Numa Pompilius, who succeeded Romulus and organised the state religion. Later it was the residence of the Pontifex Maximus, the head of the college of priests. During the regal period it was the kings who kept the religious records. Under the Republic the Pontifex Maximus took charge of the national religion and became so influential that the Emperors appointed themselves to the position.

The legend of the shields. — One day King Numa received a shield *(ancile)* from heaven which was thought to foretell victory for the Romans. He entrusted it for safekeeping to the priests of the cult of Mars and to prevent it from being stolen he had eleven copies made; all were kept in the Regia. The workman who made the shields asked as his reward to be remembered in the chanting that accompanied the procession of the shields.

The Regia and the House of the Vestals mark the limit of the Forum at the time of the kings and the Republic. The section extending to the Arch of Titus was added later.

Temple of Antoninus and Faustina ★★.

— The Emperor Antoninus Pius who succeeded Hadrian in 138 AD belonged to a rich family originally from Nîmes in the south of France. He was well known for his kindness and reigned for 23 years in peace and moderation. On the death of his wife, Faustina, in 141 AD he raised her to the ranks of the goddesses in spite of her scandalous behaviour. A huge temple to her was erected in the Forum.

When Antoninus himself died in 161 AD the Senate decided to dedicate the temple to both husband and wife.

The beautiful monolithic columns of the *pronaos* still stand on their high podium. The frieze of griffins and candelabra on the entablature is a masterpiece of fine craftsmanship.

In 11C the Church of San Lorenzo in Miranda was established in the ruins. When Charles V visited Rome in 1536 the façade of the church was set back to reveal the colonnade. In 1602 the church was rebuilt.

Excavations beside the temple of Antoninus and Faustina have uncovered a **cemetery** (16) dating from the time of Romulus (8 - 7C BC).

(After photo by Gab. Fot. Naz., Rome)

Temple of Antoninus and Faustina

Temple of Romulus. — The Romulus to whom the temple is thought to be dedicated was not the founder of Rome but the son of the Emperor Maxentius who died in 307.

Dating from the early 4C the construction is circular and flanked by two rooms with apses: it may have been built in honour of Constantine to celebrate his victory over Maxentius in 312 or in honour of the divine city of Rome. In 6C when the room behind the temple became a church *(p 52)* the temple itself became a vestibule to the church.

The doorway between two porphyry columns in the concave façade is closed by the original 4C bronze doors; the lock still works.

On the left of the Temple of Romulus are traces of six small **rooms** (17) on either side of a corridor: they may have belonged to a brothel in the Republican era.

The remains of a mediaeval arcaded building (18) high above the Sacred Way indicate how much the ground level in the Forum had risen by the Middle Ages.

Higher up the slope quite in harmony with the ancient monuments below is the church of Santa Francesca Romana with its Romanesque belfry and three parapet statues.

Basilica of Maxentius and Constantine ★★★. — *This building is well known for its summer symphony concerts.*

Maxentius was proclaimed Emperor by the people after the abdication of Maximian, his father, and Diocletian in 305. Almost immediately he began to build a basilica, the last to be erected in Rome. Built of brick beneath a groined vault, it was different from the other two basilicas, Aemilia and Julia. It was rectangular and divided into three by huge pillars flanked by columns; one long side ran parallel to the Sacred Way while the other followed the line of the present Via dei Fori Imperiali; one of the short sides constituted the main façade (facing east towards the Coliseum) while the other projected in an apse.

The imperial throne, however, was coveted by Constantine, son of the Emperor Constantius, who had reigned jointly with Maximian and Diocletian. He defeated Maxentius at the battle of the Milvian bridge *(p 201)* in 312 and completed the basilica with modifications. He moved the entrance to the façade overlooking the Sacred Way and graced it with a portico of four porphyry columns *(still visible)*; an apse was added to the opposite façade.

This grandiose building housed some colossal statues; fragments of the statue of Constantine, which stood in the west apse, can still be seen in the courtyard of the Palazzo dei Conservatori *(p 57)*. The gilded bronze tiles were used in 7C to roof St Peter's Basilica.

Forum Antiquarium. — The exhibits in this museum, which is housed in a former convent attached to the church of Santa Francesca Romana, are mostly connected with the Roman Forum: the earliest traces of ancient Rome taken from tombs dating from 1 000 to 600 BC or found in the Forum or on the Palatine (hut shaped urns and hollow tree trunks used as coffins); marble fragments from the frieze which decorated the Temple of Caesar; fine porphyry statue found behind the Curia (2C) draped with an elegant toga *(in the cloisters)*.

Marble fragments from the frieze of the Basilica Aemilia: it showed scenes from Roman history and extended for 185 m - 167 ft round the nave; it dates from 1C BC or early 2C AD.

Statues of the Vestals (2C) and a statue of King Numa Pompilius in a toga (2C).

Arch of Titus ★★. — The arch stands on the Velia, a spur of the Palatine jutting out towards the Esquiline, and appears in all the views of the Forum.

Titus, the eldest son of Vespasian, suceeded his father as Emperor but his reign was brief — from 79 to 81 AD. In 70 he had captured Jerusalem, thus bringing to a successful conclusion a campaign his father had been pursuing since 66. After his death an arch was erected to commemorate his success. The fall of Jerusalem was among the most tragic events in Jewish history. The city was destroyed and the temple, the spiritual bond between Jews of the diaspora, was burned down. In its place Hadrian built a sanctuary to Jupiter and the city was called Aelia Capitolina (Hadrian's family name was Aelius). The single archway of the Arch of Titus was restored by Luigi Valadier in 1821.

At the centre of the panelled vault is a low relief sculpture representing the apotheosis of Titus: his soul is carried up to heaven by an eagle; this event made him eligible for deification.

The frieze *(above the arch on the side facing the Coliseum)* is indistinct: in a sacrificial procession a recumbent figure represents the Jordan, symbolising the defeat of Palestine.

The two low reliefs under the vault are among the masterpieces of Roman sculpture: on one side, Titus rides in his chariot in triumph, crowned with victory; on the other, the triumphal procession exhibiting the booty pillaged from the temple in Jerusalem *(p 129)*: the seven branch candlestick which Moses had made and placed in the Tabernacle as commanded by God on Mount Sinai, the table for the shewbread which was placed in the temple each week in the name of the twelve tribes of Israel, the silver trumpets which announced the festivals.

It was on the Velia that Nero built the vestibule to his Golden House *(p 66)*.

Temple of Jupiter Stator. — On 8 November 63 BC Cicero delivered his first Cataline oration here before the assembled Senate. Feeling ran high among his audience who were impressed by the security measures which had been thought necessary.

Bear right up the hill (Clivus Palatinus) to the Palatine.

■ PALATINE ★★★

Of the seven hills of Rome, it is the Palatine which captures the visitor's imagination. As the cradle of the Eternal City it is a prime archaeological site. Since the Renaissance it has offered pleasant walks among flower beds and shady trees.

Byron wrote of the beauty of the Palatine and its overgrown ruins:

> *"Cypress and ivy, weed and wallflower grown*
> *Matted and mass'd together, hillocks heap'd*
> *On what were chambers, arch crush'd, column strown*
> *In fragments, choked up vaults, and frescos steep'd*
> *In subterranean damps, ..."*

HISTORY AND LEGEND

It was inconvenient for political reasons that Romulus and Remus, twin sons of the Vestal Rhea Silvia and the god Mars, should survive *(p 13)*. They were therefore abandoned on the banks of the Tiber but the river was in spate and their cradle came to rest on the Palatine. They survived thanks to a she-wolf which suckled them in the Lupercal cave. The shepherd Faustulus who witnessed this unusual event took charge of the twins and brought them up.

In the middle of 8C BC Romulus ploughed a deep furrow round the Palatine lifting his ploughshare in three places: this was the beginning of Rome, a symbolic enclosure with three gateways: the Porta Mugonia, the Porta Romana and the Porta Scalae Caci *(plan pp 48-49)*. This is obviously a legendary account... but in 1949 traces of huts thought to date from 8 and 7C BC were excavated on the legendary site of Romulus' house.

During the Republic the Palatine was a quiet residential area. Cicero lived on the hill as did Antony, the Triumvir, and Agrippa, Octavian's friend before becoming his son-in-law. Foreigners came to visit the shepherd's hut and the wolf's cave in the southwest face of the hill.

In 63 BC "on the ninth day before the Kalends of October, a little before daybreak" Octavian was born. When he became the Emperor Augustus the Palatine began to alter. He enlarged his house and then rebuilt it after it was destroyed by fire in 3 BC. Tiberius who succeeded him, Caligula, Claudius and Nero all lived on the Palatine but it was **Domitian**, the last Flavian emperor (81-96 AD), who transformed the hill by turning it into the imperial palace and giving it the appearance that has been revealed by the archaeologists. The hollow which divided it into two peaks (Germalus and Palatium) was filled with new buildings, the ruins of which now occupy the central section of the plateau; they are the **Domus Flavia** and the **Domus Augustana**; the **Stadium** also dates from this period. In 191 a fire seriously damaged the buildings on the Palatine. The Emperor Septimius Severus was not content with simply undertaking repairs. He enlarged the imperial palace to the south and built a monumental façade, the Septizonium, parallel with the Old Appian Way so that travellers arriving in Rome by this route would be immediately impressed by the grandeur of the capital. This section of the palace remained standing until Pope Sixtus V demolished it to provide building materials at the end of 16C.

The Palatine began to go into decline in 3C when Diocletian, Galerius, Maximian and Constantius deserted Rome and built new imperial residences in Nicomedia, Sirmium, Milan and Trier respectively. In 330 Constantine moved the imperial capital to Constantinople, formerly Byzantium, and the Palatine was abandoned.

The Christians generally ignored the Palatine plateau and built only on the slopes: in 4C a sanctuary was dedicated to St Anastasius on the south side; on the north face the Church of St Sebastian was established in what had been a temple to the Sun; it had been built by the Emperor Elagabalus (218-222), a native of Emesa (modern Homs) in Syria, who dreamed of a religion which would combine the various oriental cults and appointed himself high priest to the Sun god.

In 11 and 12C Rome became the prize in the struggles between the Pope and the Emperor and was studded with fortresses and towers; hence the description *Roma turrita*. The Frangipani family, who supported the Emperor, fortified the whole of the southeast face of the Palatine. When the Renaissance came the buildings on the Palatine (from which the word 'palace' is derived) were in ruins. The wealthy Roman families built country houses on the site, surrounded by vineyards and gardens: the Barberini near to St Sebastian, the Farnese on the northwest part of the hill between Tiberius' and Caligula's palaces. In 16C the Mattei had built a villa on the site of the Domus Augustana; three centuries later an Englishman, Charles Mills, converted it into a sort of romantic Gothic castle. This extraordinary building was demolished at the end of 19C at the instigation of P Rosa, the archaeologist in charge of the excavations.

Excavations. — They began in 1724 at the suggestion of Francis I of Parma, who had inherited the Farnese Villa. The Domus Flavia was the first building to see the light of day. About fifty years later a Frenchman, the Abbé Rancoureuil, excavated the Domus Augustana and the buildings overlooking the Circus Maximus. In 1860, under Napoleon III, archaeologists discovered Tiberius' palace, Livia's house and the Temple of Apollo which was first attributed to Jupiter. The identification of the buildings on the Palatine has provoked passionate argument between archaeologists and historians. Many of the constructions have never been discovered but excavations on the Palatine continue, particularly in the area of the Temple of Apollo.

Very little of the ruined buildings remains standing and it requires a big effort of the imagination to evoke the splendour of the ancient palaces on the Palatine.

TOUR

Clivus Palatinus. — This road approximately follows the depression between the two peaks: the Palatium to the left, the Germalus to the right.

Walk stright up the path (south) leaving on the right the steps which go up to the Farnese Gardens.

The rectangular ditch (1) marks the site of Domitian's arch. The sections of high brick wall facing down the hill belonged to the portico of the Domus Flavia. The path emerges at the top of the hill in the centre of the artificial plateau which was created when Domitian filled in the depression between the Palatium and the Germalus.

Domus Flavia ★. — This was the centre of official imperial activity. Although the buildings have been rased to the ground it is still possible to envisage them. There were three rooms behind the portico:

— the **Lararium** — the shrine of the household gods, the Lares — was the Emperor's private chapel;

— the **Throne Room** was enormous, over 30 m - 98 ft wide by 40 m - 131 ft long, with huge statues standing in the recesses in the walls;

— the **Basilica**, where the Emperor dispensed justice, had an apse at one end and a row of columns down each of the long sides. Outside the west wall are traces of the west portico of the Domus.

Behind these three rooms is a courtyard, the **Peristyle**, originally surrounded by a portico (traces of the columns remain). Suetonius wrote that Domitian was so hated by everyone for his injustice and cruelty that he had the walls of the portico faced with phengite (a very shiny stone) so that he could "see by reflection what was going on behind his back". The octagonal basin at the centre of the court, which is now planted with flowers, was probably a fountain.

Beyond the peristyle is the **Triclinium,** the dining room, which was certainly the most beautiful room in the palace; part of the coloured marble floor has been preserved. It was supported on little brick pillars to allow the passage of warm air produced by an underground stove to heat the room.

The *triclinium* was flanked to right and left by two small leisure rooms, *nymphaea.* The one on the right is well preserved. Beneath it to the right are the remains (2) of a beautiful coloured marble floor which belonged to one of the rooms in Nero's Domus Transitoria which he built on the Palatine before embarking on his stunning Golden House *(p 66).*

The extant building in the far corner of the *nymphaeum* dates from the Farnese era.

The traces of walls and columns and apses on the terrace behind the Triclinium may mark the site of the libraries of the imperial palace.

Underground rooms★. — *To visit, apply to the keeper of the Antiquarium.*

These rooms are all that remained of houses from the Republican era and of Nero's constructions when they were buried under Domitian's building projects.

— Beneath the Basilica, a rectangular room: the paintings with which it was decorated are conserved in a room (3) east of the Antiquarium; they probably date from the Augustan era and depict the cult of Isis.

— Beneath the Lararium, the **Griffin House,** sometimes also erroneously called ''Catalina's house'': it was built in 2C BC (walls composed of irregular sized stones mixed with mortar), altered in 1C BC (walls composed of regular stone blocks arranged in a diamond pattern) and then altered again by Nero; many of the paintings have been removed to the Antiquarium for safekeeping; one room contains a stucco relief of two griffins face to face.

— Beneath the peristyle: a circular chamber containing a well which communicates with another room by a passage. The discovery of this complex early this century caused quite a stir among archaeologists who thought they had found the *Mundus.* At the time of the founding of Rome the *Mundus* was a well into which a handful of earth was thrown by each new immigrant who, through this symbolic gesture, became a citizen of the new city. In fact it is probably only a silo for water or grain.

Domus Augustana★★. — This is not Augustus' own private house but the official imperial residence.

The rooms are arranged round two peristyles (one very much lower than the other). At the centre of the upper peristyle (4), marked by an umbrella pine, is the base of a construction which was reached by a bridge from the edge of the surrounding basin. Around the sides are various living rooms.

PALATINE

0   50 m

⬛ Extant parts
▬ non-extant parts
➔ Sightseeing route

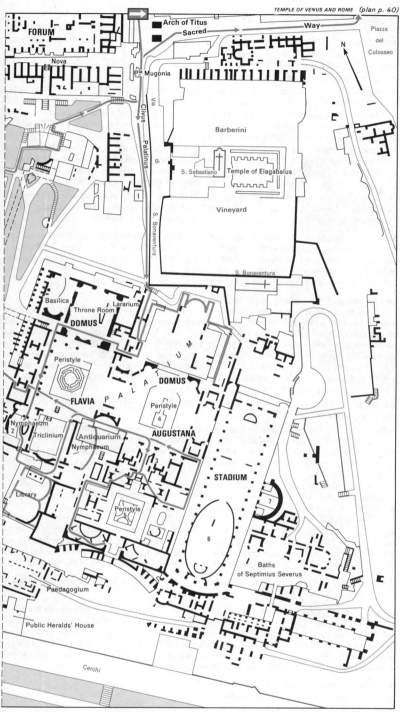

TEMPLE OF VENUS AND ROME (plan p. 40)

The rooms on the south side of the upper peristyle overlook the lower peristyle. The central basin (5) which is composed of a pattern of compartments was designed to collect rain water. The palace itself faces the Circus Maximus from behind a concave façade.

Even in ruins the Domus Augustana gives an impression of grandeur and luxury owing to its sophisticated design, its soaring walls and the daring of some of the vaulting.

Stadium ★. — This was one of Domitian's projects. It looks like a gigantic trough, some 145 m - 159 yds long, surrounded by a two storey portico. Some say it was designed to stage private games and spectacles for the Emperor; others say it was a garden or an athletics ground. The small oval track (6) at the southern end dates from 6C and is the work of Theodoric, the Ostrogoth, who occupied the Palatine at that period. The huge recess (7) in the centre of the long east side may have been reserved for the Emperor.

On the east side of the Stadium are the ruins of a bathhouse attributed to Septimius Severus but probably built by Maxentius.

Antiquarium. — *Same opening hours as the Forum Antiquarium.*

This museum is housed in a building which once belonged to the Convent of the Visitation, between the Domus Augustana and the Domus Flavia and contains articles and fragments found on the Palatine, although many pieces of sculpture have been removed to the National Roman Museum *(p 118).*

In the room to the left of the entrance hall:

— the paintings (3C) which come from the Public Herald's House *(not open)* which is situated beside the present Via dei Cerchi: note the expressions on the faces;

— a fine painting *(left of the door)* from the Augustan era of Apollo with his lyre: beside him is the "Omphalos", a sacred stone laced with ribbons, which fell from the sky to land at Delphi and was thought by the Greeks to be the centre of the earth;

— a very moving exhibit *(left arm of the room)*, which was found in the Paedagogium (the Imperial Pages' School): an immature hand has drawn Christ on the cross with an ass's head and a figure at the foot of the cross; written in Greek beneath is "Alexamenos adores his god"; perhaps it was drawn by a Roman to mock a Christian colleague.

In the inner section of the entrance hall: an altar to an unknown god; a money lender, C. Sestius Calvinus, dedicated it in 1C BC without knowing whether to a god or a goddess.

In the room on the left: incomplete statue of Diana, very gracefully dressed.

Temple of Apollo. — For many years this temple was thought to be dedicated to Jupiter but it is probably the one mentioned by Suetonius: Augustus built a temple to Apollo "in a corner of his house on the Palatine which had been struck by lightening and which, according to the omens, Apollo was claiming for himself".

The temple is fenced off; the podium and a column of the *pronaos* are recognisable.

Livia's House ★★. — *Apply to the keeper to visit the interior.*

This house which is named after Augustus' wife was probably where the Emperor himself lived. The diamond pattern on the walls and the style of the décor date the building to the end of the Republic. The wall paintings which had already deteriorated somewhat were detached and erected just in front of the walls to which they belonged; this means they can be appreciated in their original setting. The names given to the various rooms do not necessarily correspond to their use. On either side of the centre room (*tablinum* - study) are two narrow rooms (wings) where wax images of the family ancestors were kept or which, in more modest houses, were used as storerooms.

Left wing. — The lower part of the wall is decorated to look like marble; above are panels showing people and griffins face to face.

Tablinum. — On the righthand wall: a central panel, surrounded by architectural motifs, shows Io, Argos' daughter; Zeus fell in love with her and turned her into a heifer to protect her from the fury of his wife, Hera, who was nevertheless suspicious and set Argus, who had a hundred eyes, to watch over the animal. The painting shows Hermes who was sent by Zeus to rescue Io.

On the lefthand wall: lead pipes engraved with the name IVLIAE AV (Julia Augusta). The archaeologists who discovered this inscription in 1869 thought that it referred to Augustus' wife, the Empress, and attributed the house to Livia.

The rear wall depicts Galatea fleeing from Polyphemus.

Right wing. — The decorations on the lefthand wall, although damaged by the opening of the door, are still fresh: simulated columns flanking beautiful garlands of fruit and leaves from which hang baskets, and sticks, horned animal heads, lyres and other representations of nature. Above on a yellow ground is a frieze showing people at work in the open air.

Cisterns (8). — They date from 6C BC; one is shaped like a beehive while the other is uncovered.

Cacus' Steps (Scala Caci). — This was one of the three original approaches to the Palatine. The steps are named after a local hero, Cacus, who is linked in legend to Hercules. When Hercules was returning to the Argos with the cattle stolen from Geryon, he halted on the banks of the Tiber and Cacus, an evil three headed monster who breathed fire from his three mouths, took the opportunity to steal three animals; he made them walk backwards to avoid detection but Hercules was not fooled and he killed Cacus.

Huts in Romulus' village (9). — Together with the Forum cemetery *(p 45)*, these huts are some of the earliest traces of the city (8 - 7C BC). The modern roof which covers them creates a real reliquary. Three huts have been discovered, both oval and rectangular and sunk in the ground. The ring of holes held the posts which supported the walls and the roof. The gap in the south side (facing the Tiber) marks the doorway and is flanked by smaller post holes which indicate the possibility of a porch. The ditch surrounding each emplacement was probably to drain off the rain water from the roof.

(After document by Istituto Archeologico Germanico, Rome)

A hut on the Palatine during the time of Romulus

Temple of Cybele. — Cybele, the great goddess of Phrygia (also called the Mother of the gods, the Great Mother or Magna Mater) was the personification of the powers of nature. Her cult was introduced into Rome late in 3C or early in 2C BC. In 204 BC at the height of the Second Punic War a hail of stones fell on Rome. The priests appealed to the gods and the Senate was obliged to send for the **"black stone"**, symbol of the goddess Cybele, from Pessinus in Asia Minor *(p 60)*. The temple on the Palatine was inaugurated in 191 and then rebuilt by Augustus after several fires. Today only the base of the *cella* walls remains in the shade of a group of holm oaks.

The goddess' statue (2C) has been placed under an arch (**10**) of Tiberius' palace.

Each year from 4 to 20 April a festival took place in front of the temple: the Megalesia which consisted of theatrical presentations and circus acts and had been founded in 204 in honour of Cybele. Terence's comedy "Andria" was played for the first time during the festival in 168 BC; but on that occasion the audience preferred the tightrope walkers, perhaps because Terence did not have Plautus' biting wit "nor his coarse jokes, his broad humour, his puns, his quips..."

Domus Tiberiana. — The arches facing Cybele's temple belonged to the rear façade of Tiberius' palace. Only a few traces of this huge rectangular building are visible since Cardinal Farnese's gardens cover the greater part of it.

The main façade of the palace faced the Forum. Caligula extended the building as far as the Via Nova; Trajan and Hadrian added the ranges overlooking the Clivus Victoriae.

Cryptoporticus. — This is a network of passages, partially underground, which probably linked the various imperial buildings which occupied the hill. It dates from Nero's reign although the arm linking up with Domitian's Domus Flavia must have been added later.

The stuccoes which decorated the vaulting in the section of the passage near Livia's house have been removed to the Antiquarium and replaced by copies.

The oval basin (**11**) on the left of the steps leading up to the Farnese gardens was a fish tank in the southeast corner of Tiberius' palace.

Farnese Gardens. — The gardens were laid out in the middle of 16C by Cardinal Alexander Farnese, Paul III's nephew. The entrance, set in a semicircle at the level of the Forum (which was higher then than now), gave access to a series of terraces rising up the north face of the Palatine. On the flat top of the hill, over the ruins of Tiberius's palace, stretched the Farnese's magnificent botanical garden, one of the richest in the world at that time.

The northwest corner of the gardens gives an excellent **view★★** of the Forum, the Tabularium, the Senatorial Palace, the monument to Victor Emmanuel II, the domes of the Church of Sts Luke and Martina and of the two churches next to Trajan's Column, the Militia Tower etc.

In the northeast corner of the gardens are two buildings (reconstructed) which formed a complex comprising two aviaries above a nymphaeum. From the terrace there is a pleasant **view★★**, particularly at sunset, of the Basilica of Maxentius, the belfry of Santa Francesca Romana and the upper storeys of the Coliseum.

Below the aviaries there used to be a monumental gate marking the entrance to the gardens. It was begun by Vignola and completed by Girolamo Rainaldi but taken down in 1882. It now stands on the east side of the Via di S. Gregorio *(plan p 137)*.

Leave the Palatine by Clivus Palatinus, turning right into Via Sacra at Titus' Arch to visit the other monuments which belong to the Forum but are accessible only from outside the gates. Plan pp 40-41.

Temple of Venus and Rome★. — The temple was built between 121 and 136 AD by Hadrian, completed by Antoninus Pius and restored by Maxentius, on the site of the vestibule to Nero's Golden House. It was the largest temple in Rome, 110 m - 361 ft by 53 m - 174 ft, and designed in the Greek style with steps on all sides (the majority of Roman temples had only one flight of steps leading up to the *pronaos*). It was surrounded by a colonnade and uniquely comprised two *cellae* with apses back to back. One was dedicated to the goddess Rome and faced the Forum; the other was dedicated to Venus and faced the Coliseum.

The plans for the temple were drawn by Hadrian who was keen on architecture. He also designed two gigantic seated figures to be set in niches which were disproportionately small. Trajan's brilliant architect, Apollodorus of Damascus, commented that "if the figures tried to stand they would bump their heads on the vault". He had already poured scorn on the Emperor's rather peculiar taste for painting pumpkins. It was too much; Hadrian had the architect silenced once and for all.

The part of the temple which faces the Forum has been incorporated in the church of Santa Francesca Romana and the adjoining convent of Olivetan monks. An idea of the temple's appearance is given by a few columns which were re-erected in 1935; the position of the missing parts is marked by bushes of privet, box and oleander.

Santa Francesca Romana. — In 8C an oratory dedicated to Sts Peter and Paul was built in the western half of the Temple of Venus and Rome by Pope Paul I. In the following century it was replaced with the church of Santa Maria Antiqua in the Forum and was called Santa Maria Nova. The church was placed under the patronage of Santa Francesca Romana (St Frances of Rome) when she was canonised in 1608.

The 12C Romanesque **bell tower★** is one of the most elegant in Rome.

The façade by Carlo Lombardi (1615) is characteristic of the Counter-Reformation. The use of a single order of flat pilasters resting on a high portico lends it a certain solemnity. Inside there is a beautiful 17C coffered ceiling.

Apsidal mosaic. — The Virgin and Child are enthroned between Sts Peter and Andrew, James and John. The mosaic dates from c1160 at a period when mosaic art was marked by a certain eclecticism: the vivid colours of the ancient art together with the rigidity of the figures typical of Byzantine art.

Right transept. — Two stones are preserved behind a grating; they are supposed to bear the print of St Peter's knees; he prayed at length to God to prevent Simon Magus from flying; Simon crashed to earth near the church.

There is also a monument (16C) to Gregory XI, the last French pope, who brought the Holy See back to Rome from Avignon in 1377. The central low relief shows St Peter entering Rome; the flanking statues are Faith and Prudence.

Crypt. — Opposite the remains of St Frances of Rome is a marble low relief showing the saint and an angel (17C work by one of Bernini's pupils).

Sacristy. — Beautiful painting of Santa Maria Nova showing a Virgin and Child which art historians date to 5 or 8C.

Take Via dei Fori Imperiali.

Sts Cosmas and Damian (SS Cosma e Damiano). — The church was dedicated in 526 by Pope Felix IV to two saints of Arabian origin, Cosmas and Damian, twin brothers whose help was invoked to cure illness. The church was established in Romulus' temple *(p 45)* and in an adjacent room which had been the library of Vespasian's Forum; it was the first Christian church to occupy a pagan building in the Roman Forum. When the relics of the two saints were discovered in 16C the popes began to alter the original church. In 17C Clement VIII reduced the width of the nave by creating side chapels which cut off the outer edges of the mosaic on the chancel arch. The floor was raised and a doorway was opened in the west wall and a plaster arcade was added in front of the apse.

Ceiling ★. — Beautiful 17C coffered ceiling showing the triumph of Sts Cosmas and Damian *(centre)* and *(at each end)* the coat of arms with its bees of Cardinal Francesco Barberini, who promoted the greater part of the 17C alterations.

Mosaics ★. — Those on the chancel arch date from the late 7C and show the Lamb of God surrounded by seven candelabra and four angels. The angels on the left and right, symbolizing the Evangelists, St Luke and St John, have survived the 17C alterations. The lamb and the throne were restored in 1936.

The mosaics in the apse date from 6C. In the centre is the figure of Christ against a sunset sky. At his sides are the apostles Peter and Paul presenting Sts Cosmas and Damian, dressed in brown. On the left is Pope Felix IV offering a model of his church while on the right is St Theodore dressed in a handsome chlamys (short mantle) like a Byzantine courtier. Below, partially screened by the Baroque altar (1637) is the Pascal Lamb surrounded by twelve beautiful angels representing the apostles.

Southeast chapel. — *Facing the entrance.* Above the altar is a curious fresco showing the living Christ on the cross, a work in the Byzantine style, repainted in 17C.

Neapolitan Crib ★. — *Closed for restoration.* The entrance is on the right of the side door into the church. This 18C creation has been housed in Romulus' temple since 1939. The background is modelled on the ancient ruins which were beginning to be excavated in 18C; the costumes are reproduced in great detail; the scenes are those of everyday life.

Distance: 1 km — 1/2 mile. Time: about 3 1/2 hours. Start: Piazza Venezia.

The Capitoline, the smallest of the seven hills of Rome, is also the most famous *(p 55)*. Nowadays it is the seat of the local authority which administers Rome.

It was in 1764, as Edward Gibbon later wrote, "on the fifteenth of October in the gloom of the evening, as I sat musing on the Capitol, while the barefoot fryars were chanting their litanies in the temple of Jupiter, that I conceived the first thought of my history... the decline and fall of the Roman Empire".

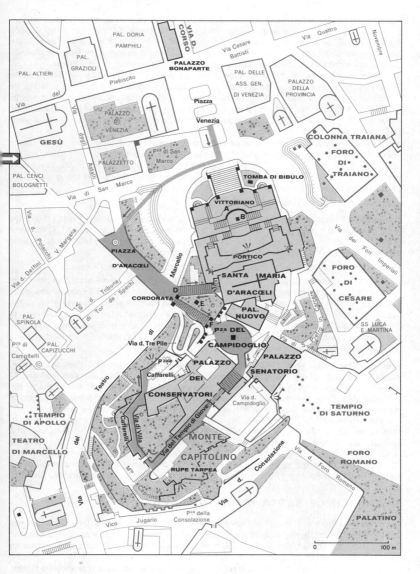

■ MONUMENT TO VICTOR EMMANUEL II (Vittoriano)

This huge monument by **Giuseppe Sacconi**, which was begun in 1885 and inaugurated in 1911, was erected in honour of King Victor Emmanuel II who achieved the unification of Italy in 1870 with Rome as the capital city. The dazzling white marble clashes with the warm tones of the Roman townscape and the grandiloquent style strikes a jarring note.

A very broad flight of steps, flanked by two allegorical groups in bronze gilt representing Thought and Action, leads up to the Altar to the Nation; the steps divide before meeting at an equestrian statue of Victor Emmanuel; they then divide again and lead up to the concave portico which is surmounted by two bronze quadrigas bearing statues of winged victory. The foot of the stairway is flanked by two fountains representing the Tyrrhenian Sea *(right)* and the Adriatic *(left)*.

Caius Publicius Bibulus' Tomb (tomba di Bibulo). — The travertine and brick wall remains of the tomb of Bibulus, who died 2 000 years ago, are of major archaeological interest: as burials were forbidden within the precincts of the city, the position of this tomb shows that in 1C BC the city boundary skirted the Capitoline hill and the Via Flaminia, the trunk road to the north began at this point.

Altar to the Nation (A). — At the foot of the statue of Rome is the tomb of the unknown soldier constantly guarded by two sentries. Since 1921 the tomb has contained the remains of a soldier who died in the 1915-18 war.

Equestrian statue of Victor Emmanuel II (B). — Enrico Chiaradia's statue was unveiled on 4 June 1911 in the presence of the king and some veteran Garibaldi troops before a crowd gathered in Piazza Venezia. A contemporary chronicler recorded that 50 tonnes of bronze had been used to cast the monument in a foundry in Trastevere and that His Majesty's moustaches were 1 m - 3 ft long.

Portico. — *Temporarily closed.* There is a unique **view** ★★ of the city from the portico.

From the west terrace in the foreground are Santa Maria d'Aracoeli and the Capitol. Beyond the Tiber rise the Janiculum, the dome of St Peter's, the Vatican and Castel Sant'Angelo. Then again on this side of the river are the domes for which Rome is famous: Sant'Andrea della Valle, the Gesù Church and the shallow curve of the Pantheon.

From the centre of the terrace: immediately below is Piazza Venezia linked to Piazza del Populo by the straight line of Via del Corso. At the beginning of this street on the left is the **Palazzo Bonaparte** *(p 101);* built in 1660 it later came into the possession of Napoleon's mother who lived there after her son's fall from power taking great pleasure, so it is said, in watching what was going on in the street below from behind the shutters of the first floor balcony. She died there in 1836.

From the east terrace: the whole extent of the Imperial Fora (built by Caesar, Augustus, Trajan etc.). In the distance, slightly to the left of the Coliseum, are the statues on the pediment of St John Lateran. To the right of the Coliseum is the Basilica of Maxentius, the bell tower and façade of Santa Francesca Romana; in the foreground is the dome of the Church of Sts Luke and Martina.

Walk round to Piazza d'Aracoeli.

Fountain in Piazza d'Aracoeli. — It is a modest work by Giacomo della Porta (1589), the great designer of the fountains of Rome. At least he produced the design. In 17C the arms of the Chigi family were added and a hundred years later the base with two flights of steps designed by della Porta was replaced by the present circular basin.

From Piazza d'Aracoeli climb the steps to the church of Santa Maria d'Aracoeli.

The broad plain façade of the church standing at the top of the steps is one of the famous sights of tourist Rome. Here from the earliest days of the city's existence stood the Citadel *(Arx)* which protected the northern flank of the Palatine which already enjoyed the natural protection of the Tiber to the west. During the Republic a temple was built here to Juno Moneta (Counsellor). According to the legend it was here that the Virgin and Child appeared to the Emperor Augustus after he had asked the Tiburtine Sibyl whether there would one day be a greater man than himself.

Aracoeli Steps (D). — In 1346 the plague ravaged Italy; Rome miraculously was spared and built the steps as a thank offering. The first person to climb them was **Cola di Rienzo.** At this time the Pope was in Avignon; Rome was in a state of anarchy at the hands of the noble families. Cola gave himself the task of restoring the grandeur of Rome. He stood at the top of the steps dressed like an Emperor and roused the people with his speeches.

Petrarch himself had begged the Pope to restore the capital to its former splendour. In 1354 he set out to lend his support to Cola di Rienzo but before he reached the Capitol he learned that the 'tribune of Rome' had been killed in a riot by a servant of the Colonna family.

From the top of the steps there is a fine view of the domes of St Peter's in the background, of the Synagogue to the left and of Sant' Andrea della Valle and the Gesù Church.

■ CHURCH OF SANTA MARIA D'ARACOELI ★★

Following the arrival in 552 of General Narses from Greece, several Greek monasteries were established in Rome. One of them occupied an oratory which was turned into the Church of Santa Maria d'Aracoeli in 1250 by Franciscan monks. The name comes from an altar *(ara)* dedicated to the goddess of the sky or from the citadel *(arx)* *(p 55).*

The severity of the brick façade is relieved by the Renaissance doorway and two Gothic rose windows. The shallow concave band at the top was originally covered with mosaic.

The interior is built on the basilical plan and contains several works of art. The side chapels and the aisle ceilings were added in 16 and 17C when the chancel and the upper part of the nave were remodelled according to contemporary taste.

Floor and Ceiling. — The floor is one of the best preserved examples of work by the Cosmati, Romans who worked in marble from 12 to 14C *(p 24).* The ceiling was an ex-voto offering by Marcantonio Colonna who fought with the troops of the Holy League when the Christians defeated the Turks at Lepanto in Greece on 7 October 1571.

Cardinal d'Albret's tomb (1). — This is one of Andrea Bregno's best works. The fine work of the motifs, particularly on the sarcophagus, and the use of architectural elements (pilasters, arcades) are characteristic of his art.

Giovanni Crivelli's tombstone (2). — It is attributed to Donatello whose signature used to be legible, so it is said, but was worn away when the stone lay on the ground.

Chapel of St Bernardino of Siena (3). — The decorative **frescoes** ★ were painted by **Pinturicchio** in about 1485 and illustrate the life and death of Bernardino. The funeral scene *(left wall)* shows some well composed portraits against an accomplished landscape.

The huge statue of Gregory XIII (4) complements that of Paul III (5); both are Counter-Reformation works.

In the passage leading to the side door there is a tomb (6) designed by Michelangelo of a young man, Cecchino Bracci.

Mosaic of the Virgin and Child (7). — This mosaic is over the side door on the outside of the church.

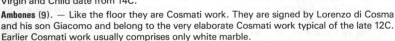

It comes from the Cosmati workshop *(p 24)* and reveals the influence of Pietro Cavallini, the greatest Roman artist in the Middle Ages; his style is characterised by balanced composition, rich in Byzantine influence and knowledge of classical models.

Although the Piazza del Campidoglio (Capitoline Square) can be reached from the side door of the church (down the steps), to receive the full effect of the architecture, it is best to approach up the "Cordonata" from the bottom of the hill.

Savelli family tomb. — An antique sarcophagus was used for the tomb of Luca Savelli (8). The mosaics and the Virgin and Child date from 14C.

Ambones (9). — Like the floor they are Cosmati work. They are signed by Lorenzo di Cosma and his son Giacomo and belong to the very elaborate Cosmati work typical of the late 12C. Earlier Cosmati work usually comprises only white marble.

St Helen's Chapel (10). — This is an elegant 17C domed construction. Beneath the porphyry urn is a 12C altar decorated with Romanesque sculptures and mosaic insets and commemorating the appearance of the Virgin to Augustus *(p 54)*.

Cardinal Matteo d'Acquasparta's Monument (11). — This is a typical Italian Gothic tomb (vertical composition with angels drawing curtains round the death bed). The painting of the Virgin and Child is related to the art of Pietro Cavallini. Cardinal d'Acquasparta, vicar general of the Franciscans, who died in 1302, is mentioned by Dante in his Divine Comedy as a man who broke the severity of the rule.

In the left transept is an enormous statue (12) of Leo X (16C).

Holy Child Chapel (Cappella del Santo Bambino) (13). — Legend has endowed this little statue with miraculous powers of healing. Numerous letters are received from all over the world.

Third Chapel on the left (14). — In 15C it was decorated with frescoes by Benozzo Gozzoli, Fra Angelico's assistant; only St Antony of Padua remains above the altar.

In the pre-Christmas period young children gather in the **second chapel on the left** (15) to recite or improvise verses *(sermoni)* before the Santo Bambino.

Go down the Aracoeli steps and turn left into the 'Cordonata'.

The 'Cordonata'. — Michelangelo's design for this ramp was not faithfully executed. The two lions guarding the entrance are Egyptian (restored in 1955); they were found on the Campus Martius and placed here in 1582; in 1588 Giacomo della Porta converted them into fountains which on feast days sometimes flowed with red and white wine.

A **statue (E)** of Cola di Rienzo was put up in 19C on the spot where he was killed.

■ CAPITOL SQUARE ★★★ (Piazza del Campidoglio)

The visitor who is only passing through Rome should pause a moment in Capitol Square, a haven of peace where charm and majesty mingle in harmony. To see it as it was in antiquity one must envisage the monuments and temples facing the Forum. There were two high points: the **Capitolium** (site of the Conservators' Palace) and the **Arx**, the citadel (site of Santa Maria d'Aracoeli) separated by a saddle (Capitol Square and the Senatorial Palace).

In the Middle Ages Capitol Square was known simply as 'Monte Caprino' (Goat Hill) where goats grazed among the ruins. Change came in 16C. On the occasion of Charles V's visit in 1536, Pope Paul III decided that Rome, which had been sacked 9 years earlier by the same Charles V, should be restored to its former elegance and he commissioned **Michelangelo** to draw up plans for the Capitol. The design was executed over the next hundred years or so and altered in certain respects. The square is lined by three buildings (the Senatorial Palace, the New Palace and the Convervators' Palace) and is shaped like a trapezium to accommodate the position of the Conservator's Palace which had already been built. Michelangelo turned the square round to face the modern city rather than the ancient Forum. The balustrade with its overlarge statues was not part of Michelangelo's design.

HISTORICAL NOTES

The Rape of the Sabines and Tarpeia. — In order to avenge the rape of his womenfolk, perpetrated by Romulus *(p 13)*, Titus Tatius, chief of the Sabines, seized the citadel on the Capitol through the treachery of Tarpeia, the keeper's daughter. He and his men encountered the Latins under Romulus in the Forum but the Sabine women interposed themselves between their brothers and their new husbands who were thus reconciled.

Jupiter Capitolinus. — In 6C BC the Etruscan king, Tarquin the Proud, had already built a temple on the Capitol to Jupiter the Great and Good, which the Romans considered was second only to the sky as the god's abode.

During a Triumph, the general who was being honoured would approach the temple dressed in purple and gold, bearing an ivory sceptre surmounted by an eagle, the symbol of Jupiter. The temple was built on the Etruscan plan and divided into three sanctuaries; the central one was dedicated to Jupiter and the other two to Juno and Minerva. These three deities comprised the Capitoline Triad. A treasure was kept beneath Jupiter's statue. In Juno's sanctuary the Romans placed a silver goose in memory of the **'geese of the Capitol'** whose cries alerted the Romans, secure in their Citadel when the Gauls attacked Rome (390-388 BC). The Temple of Jupiter was rebuilt by Augustus after being destroyed by fire; it was rebuilt for the last time by Domitian.

'It is only a step from the Capitol to the Tarpeian rock'. — The bluff on the southwest edge of the Capitol overlooking the present Via della Consolazione is generally agreed to be the Tarpeian Rock (rupe Tarpea — from the name of the traitor Tarpeia) from which traitors were hurled to their death under the Republic (not far from the Temple of Jupiter).

TOUR

Equestrian statue of Marcus Aurelius ★★. — Michelangelo transferred it here from the square outside St John Latran in 1538; he greatly admired it and restored it himself. Cast in bronze and once gilded it is a fine example of late 2C Roman realism. It has survived intact because it was thought to represent Constantine, the first Christian Emperor. Had they known, the mediaeval Christians would never have tolerated the survival of the effigy of the Emperor who persecuted St Blandina, St Pothinus and St Justin.

The statue stands, as if on a carpet, at the centre of a beautiful geometric design, conceived by Michelangelo but executed only recently.

Statues of the Dioscuri ★ (F). — The two knights *(p 44)* are shown standing beside their horses.

The statues are Roman and date from the late Empire; they were found in 16C on the Campus Martius and restored (the head of one of them is modern).

"Marius' Trophies". — This is the name given to the 1C BC sculptures which commemorate Domitian's conquest of the German people. Until 16C they adorned a fountain in Piazza Vittorio Emanuele II.

The Roman custom of piling up the arms of the vanquished goes back to their origins when at the end of a battle they would stack up breastplates, helmets and shields against a tree.

Milestones. — *Next to the statues of Constantine and Constantine II.* One was the first and the other the seventh milestone on the Appian Way.

Senatorial Palace ★★★ (Palazzo Senatorio). — *Not open, occupied by the offices of the local authority.*

In 1143 under the influence of Arnold of Brescia who inveighed against the corruption of the clergy in his speeches, the Roman people deprived the Pope of his temporal power and set up the Roman Commune. Senators were created to lead the government; the palace was contructed like a castle on the ruins of the Tabularium *(p 38)* to house the meetings of the magistrates.

Michelangelo kept the walls of this old building but designed a new façade. His plans were carried out from 1582 to 1605 by Giacomo della Porta and then by Girolamo Rainaldi.

The municipal tower was built by Martino Longhi the Elder from 1578 to 1582.

The double staircase is the only part of the building to be completed during Michelangelo's lifetime. The fountain which was added in 1588 on Sixtus V's initiative was not part of the original design. The goddess of Rome, in porphyry and marble, seems lost in her recess, perched on a pedestal which is disproportionately high. The flanking statues come from Constantine's baths on the Quirinal and represent the Nile and the Tiber. The latter statue *(right)* originally represented the Tigris but the tiger's head was replaced with a wolf's head and it became the Tiber.

Some blocks of stone from the old **Arx Capitolina** (citadel) can be seen in a little garden on the left of the Senatorial Palace.

Conservator's Palace and New Palace ★★★ (Palazzo dei Conservatori e Palazzo Nuovo). — The Conservators' Palace, which was built in 15C to house the meetings of the Conservators, magistrates who governed the town with the Senators, was altered in 1568 by Giacomo della Porta at Michelangelo's request.

Although not built until 1654 the New Palace, which was the work of Girolamo and Carlo Rainaldi, was identical with the Conservators' Palace as Michelangelo had intended. At this time Via delle Tre Pile was opened and the development of the Capitol was complete. The two flanking palaces with their porticos at ground level and façades decorated with a single order of flat pilasters form an elegant pair.

They house two museums; the collections on display were started by Sixtus IV in 1471, enlarged by Pius V in 1566 and opened to the public in 1734 by Clement XII; they rank among the most important in Rome.

Roman historians generally counted the years as from the foundation of Rome (Ab Urbe Condita). The system of counting from the birth of Christ (AD) was introduced in 6C by Dionysius Exiguus, a Scythian monk.

■ CONSERVATORS' PALACE MUSEUM ★★★ *plan p 59*

Open 9 am to 2 pm; also 5 to 8 pm Tuesdays and Thursdays. Closed Mondays, 1 January, 1 May, 15 August and Christmas. 1 000 L.

In the internal courtyard are the Gothic arches of the 15C palace *(right)* and a few pieces of a colossal statue of Constantine which used to be in Constantine's Basilica in the Forum. The statue of a seated figure was a good 10 m - 33 ft high and was probably an acrolith statue where only the parts of the body uncovered by clothing were made of stone and the rest was of wood covered in bronze. On the left are low relief sculptures of figures representing the Roman provinces which come from the Temple of Hadrian in Piazza di Pietra *(p 106)*.

From the entrance hall take the stairs to the upper floor.

On the first landing are some **low relief sculptures:** three of them belonged to an arch erected in 176 to commemorate Marcus Aurelius' victories over the Germans and the Sarmatians. They show Victory (1), Clemency (2) and imperial Piety (3). The place beside Marcus Aurelius in the triumphal chariot is empty; it may have been occupied by his son Commodus, whose figure was then effaced when the Senate condemned this terrible Emperor. The low relief of Marcus Aurelius at a sacrificial ceremony is in traditional style: the solemnity of the scene is stressed by the definite lines of the background; the crowd seems to be contained in an enclosure. This work is also remarkable for containing a reproduction of the Temple of Jupiter Capitolinus *(back left)* of which almost nothing remains *(p 55)*.

Statue of Charles of Anjou (4). — The seated figure is attributed to **Arnolfo di Cambio** who came to Rome in the late 13C, entered the service of the king of Sicily and sculpted this effigy, both austere and majestic, a rare example of Gothic sculpture in the round at a period when the arts of mosaic and painting were dominant.

Horatii and Curatii Room (1). — The marble statue of Urbain VIII (5) was sculpted by Bernini and his pupils. The Romans scolded the Pope for his expenses and were very indignant when he wanted to set up a statue of himself on the Capitol during his lifetime. The statue of Innocent X (6) which is in bronze is a masterly piece on which Algardi worked from 1645 to 1650; he was one of the greatest Baroque sculptors.

The wall frescoes which give the room its name are by Cavaliere d'Arpino *(p 26)*; treated like tapestries in pastel shades they belong to the works which Caravaggio confronted with his 'luminism'.

Captains' Room (2). — It is named after the 16 and 17C statues of papal generals (Marcantonio Colonna, Alessandro Farnese etc.) which are displayed there.

The fine coffered **ceiling** ★ with historical scenes painted in the panels comes from a 16C palace, now demolished.

The late 16C pictures hanging on the walls illustrate legendary episodes in the history of Republican Rome: Brutus condemning his sons to death (7); the battle of lake Regillus (8); Horatius Cocles defending the bridge (9); Mucius Scaevola and Porsenna (10).

Triumph Room (3). — Fine 16C gilded wooden ceiling. Painted 15C frieze illustrating the triumph of Emilius Paulus over Perseus, king of Macedon in 168 BC.

— In the centre of the room is the famous **'Spinario'** ★★★ (11), an original Greek work or a very good 1C BC copy. In the Hellenistic period the child became a favourite subject among artists. The frailty and spontaneous grace of youth was refreshing after the classical period with its admiration of solidity and reason. The charming pose of this boy who is removing a thorn from his foot and the studied treatment of his hair and face make this an admirable work.

— The bronze vase (12) comes from the spoils of war taken from Mithradates, king of Pontus who was finally defeated by Pompey in 63 BC.

— The bust of **Junius Brutus** ★★ (13): the head which dates from 3C BC was placed on a bust during the Renaissance. It was thought to be a portrait of the founder of the ancient republic whose legendary severity and integrity seemed to find expression in this head. In fact it probably belonged to an equestrian statue.

— The *camillus* (14): this was the name given to the young servers who assisted the priests in the religious ceremonies. Work of Roman art from the Augustan era (1C).

Wolf Room (4). — Here is the famous bronze statue of the **She-wolf** ★★★ (15), the emblem of Rome. The twins were added at the Renaissance by Antonio del Pollaiuolo. It is said that in antiquity the wolf stood on the Capitol and was struck by lightening in 65 BC. Sometimes one is shown the marks of the lightening on the rear paws. The statue dates from the 6 or 5C BC and could be the work of a Greek or Etruscan artist. The anatomical accuracy is treated in a remarkably stylised manner.

— On the walls are fragments of the 'Fasti Consulares' and the 'Fasti Triumphales': they come from the Arch of Augustus in the Forum and are lists of the successive consuls down to 13 AD and of triumphant generals from Romulus to 12 AD.

Goose Room (5). — Two small bronze geese (16) give this room its name. The handsome mastiff in flecked green marble (17) derives from a 4C BC Greek original.

Both the ceiling and the frieze, which is illustrated with views of Rome prior to 1550, are 16C work.

Room 18. — The statue of a charioteer about to get into his chariot (18) is a Roman imitation of a Greek bronze from the classical period (470-460 BC). The room also contains a tomb stone showing a **young girl with a dove** ★ (19): this is a Greek work, dating from the early 5C BC, probably by an artist from southern Italy. The lion's head (20) is also original Greek from the early 5C BC which has retained traces of orientalism.

Room 17. — The torso of an amazon (21) is a Greek work from 510 BC, an example from the 'severe' period of transition between archaic and classical art and characterized by the disappearance of rigid forms in favour of a certain naturalism.

Magistrates' Room (16). — Two magistrates (22) are portrayed giving the starting signal for the races (late 4C AD). The fairly heavy treatment is characteristic of the late Empire.

Tapestry Room (8). — The fine 16C coffered ceiling is painted and gilded. The huge tapestries were woven in a Roman workshop in 18C; one of them (23) shows the wolf and the twins, the subject of a picture by Rubens hanging in the gallery upstairs (p 60).

Following the Punic Wars Room (9) and the former chapel (10), there is a corridor (11), once occupied by the archives and now hung with several small works by **Vanvitelli** (p 155) showing 18C views of Rome. The Tiber near to Castel Sant' Angelo has not yet been chanelled between embankments and Rome has a countrified appearance.

Three rooms of Fasti Moderni. — The first (12) contains the list of Roman magistrates from 1640. In the second (13) is a bust of the Empress Faustina (24) (2C), wife of Antoninus Pius; together they shared a temple in the Forum (p 45).

Lamiani Gardens Gallery ★★ (15). — These sculptures were found in the gardens of Elius Lamia, 3C Consul, on the Esquiline. The young girl seated (25) is a very sophisticated Greek work from the Hellenistic period (late 2C BC). The headless statue of an old countrywoman (26) is a remarkably realistic Hellenistic work.

— The Centaur's head (27) is either an original Greek work from the Pergamum school or at least a good copy probably made in Pergamum, a city in Asia Minor and one of the centres of Hellenistic art.
— The Esquiline Venus (28): this is the name given to the statue of a young girl attending to her hair (a fragment of her hand can be seen in her hair). The work is attributed to the school of Paxiteles (1C BC), a Greek sculptor from southern Italy who mostly produced imitations of Greek works from the Classical era.
— The bust of Commodus as Hercules (29): Commodus' father, Marcus Aurelius had included him in the government of the Empire but was apprehensive of his tendency to excess. The bust of the Emperor himself as Hercules is a late 2C work. At this period Roman art had attained such technical skill that it could fashion marble as if the stone were a plastic medium.

Two rooms of Christian Monuments (19-20). — Fragments of inscriptions, 3 and 4C sarcophagi and various fragments of Christian sculpture are to be found here.

Chimney Room (21). — It contains the remains of a chimney (30) made of antique fragments from the Conservators' Palace. There is also a fine **collection of antefixa ★ (31)**, which were sometimes richly painted and ornamented the ridge of the Etruscan temples in Capua in 6 and 5C BC, demonstrating Etruscan taste for the fantastic.

First Castellani Room (22). — It is named after the donor of the collection of 7C and 6C BC vases which it contains: Italic vases influenced by Greek geometric art; Etruscan vases inspired by the Corinthian workshop; black *bucchero* vases, a great Etruscan speciality. A 4C chariot (32), for carrying the effigies of the gods in procession, has been reconstructed.

Second Castellani Room (23). — The peperine low reliefs (33) belonged to a 6C BC Etruscan funeral couch. The display case contains a fine vase (34): on one side Ulysses and his companions blinding Polyphemus who is collapsing; on the other are two galleys about to engage in battle. The artist (an Etruscan or Greek of 7C BC) has signed it 'Aristonothos' (above Polyphemus' head).

Bronze Room (24). — The huge head (35) and hand (36) belonged to a standing figure of the Emperor Constantine (4C). The dancing god (37) holding a horn *(rhyton)* and a cup, is an elegant statue of Lares, protector of the domestic hearth (1C).

Here too is the sphere (38) which topped the Vatican obelisk until it was moved to the centre of St Peter's Square (1585). It is scored by the bullets fired by French soldiers in the sack of Rome in 1527.

Maecenas' Gardens Room (25). — Here are displayed the items found in the gardens which Maecenas laid out on the Esquiline in 25 BC. Hercules in combat (39) is a Roman work inspired by a statue sculpted by a colleague of Lysippus.

— 'Marsyas' (40) is interesting: he had dared to challenge Apollo in a musical competition and was bound to a tree before being flayed. The sculpture is a good 2-1C BC Roman copy of a Hellenistic work.
— The low relief of a **maenad dancing ★ (41)** is a Roman copy of a Greek work by Callimachus who was one of the most brilliant exponents of Greek art in the late 5C BC. The serenity of the first Classical period has passed. In his tragedies Euripides has described the extreme violence of which the Maenads (Bacchantes or Furies) were capable: in a bacchic trance they tore to pieces Pentheus, king of Thebes, because he opposed the introduction into his kingdom of the cult of Dionysius.

(After photo by Gab. Fot. Naz., Rome)

Maenad dancing

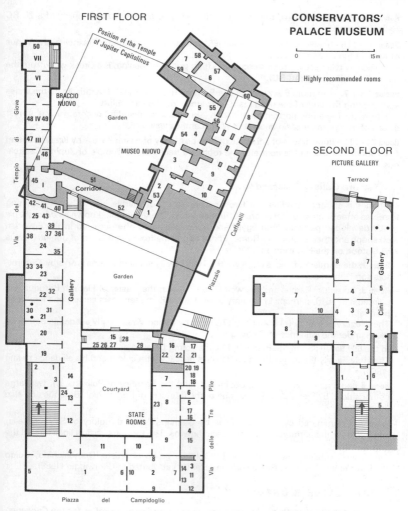

FIRST FLOOR

Position of the Temple of Jupiter Capitolinus

0 ——————— 15m

Highly recommended rooms

SECOND FLOOR

PICTURE GALLERY

— The head of an Amazon (**42**) is a very fine replica of a statue by Kresilas (5C BC); he had been in competition with Phidias and Polyclitus for the Amazon of Ephesus.
— The great vase shaped like a horn *(rhyton)* (**43**) was made in 1C for a fountain. At this period in Rome many artists copied the neo-Attic style in vogue in Athens where the Classicism of 5C BC was much admired.

'New Wing' (Braccio nuovo). — *Open: restoration in progress.*

Room I. — The low relief shows Curtius (**45**) plunging into the lake in the Forum *(p 43)*.

Rooms II and III. — A plan of the Temple of Jupiter Capitolinus (**46**) is on display *(p 55)* and the southern limit of the sanctuary is shown on the ground; a few traces of the foundations are also visible.

The figure holding the busts of his ancestors (**47**) in the series of 1C portraits shows the great mastery of the Roman artists in portraiture.

Room IV. — The statue of Apollo (**48**) is an original Greek work dating from the first half of 5C BC. The sculptor may have been Pythagoras of Samos, a Greek who established himself in Rhegium (Reggio di Calabria) in about 470 BC. Probably brought to Rome as the spoils of war, it was altered and set up in the Temple of Apollo Sosianus.

The statue of Aristogiton (**49**) is the best extant replica of one of the statues in the bronze group of the Tyrannocides sculpted in 477-476 BC.

Room VII. — The frieze ★ (**50**) showing a triumphal procession decorated the interior of the *cella* of the Temple of Apollo Sosianus.

"New Museum" (Museo nuovo) *Closed for restoration.*

In the passage is part of a wall (**51**) from the Temple of Jupiter (6C BC).
The urn (**52**) which contained the ashes of Agrippina the Elder (14 BC to 33 AD), mother of Caligula, was used in the Middle Ages as a grain measure.
The "new museum" was set out in 1925 in the rooms of the Caffarelli Palace.

Room 2. — In a cabinet (**53**) displaying many heads is one of a child, a Greek work in the 'severe' style (early 5C BC), and one of a goddess, the work of an artist in Magna Graecia (southern Italy) in the late 5C BC.

Room 4. – Polyhymnia ★ (54), the muse of lyric poetry, is a good Roman replica of a 2C BC Hellenistic work.

Room 5. — The headless statue of Venus (55) is a copy of a statue by Praxiteles, the Venus of Arles in the Louvre in Paris.

The low relief sculpture of Aesculapius (56), god of medecine, is a Greek work from the first Hellenistic period (4C BC).

Rooms 6 and 7. — In room 6 is the stele of a Roman shoemaker (57), identifiable by the shoes surmounting the bust of the dead man; an example of popular sculpture.

In room 7 is a fine portrait of Domitian (58) and some beautiful decorative sculptures: pieces of friezes and a basin decorated with acanthus leaves (59).

Room 8. — The huge statue of Athena (60) may be a copy of a Greek work by Kresilas dating from about 430 BC. In the centre of the room are traces of the Temple of Jupiter Capitolinus.

Picture Gallery ★ *(second floor)*

On the entrance landing are two fine panels (1) of marble intarsia work depicting tigresses attacking cattle; these are 4C Roman work. The technique, known as *opus sectile (p 22)* developed particularly in Egypt and the panels were often created in the Egyptian workshops and then brought to Rome. These two come from the Basilica of Junius Bassus which stood on the Esquiline until 17C.

— **Room 2:** the Baptism of Jesus (2), a youthful work by Titian, and several works by Tintoretto's son Domenico.

— **Room 3:** Romulus, Remus and the wolf (3) by Rubens, the master of Flemish Baroque. He painted it in 1618, perhaps in memory of his stay in Rome ten years earlier, and kept it till his death.

The allegory of Vanity (4) is an early 17C work by Simon Vouet, fairly academic before he came under the influence of Caravaggio.

— In the **Cini Gallery:** John the Baptist (5) by the young Caravaggio.

The Holy Family (6) shows Pompeo Batoni's delicacy with colour and his elegance of line (18C).

— **Room 6** contains the Rape of the Sabines (7) and the Sacrifice of Polixena (8), two large compositions by Pietro da Cortona, one of the founders of Roman high Baroque and also an architect.

— **Room 7** is dominated by a huge canvas by Guercino (9) to the glory of St Petronella, admirable for the harmony of the blues and browns. The tortuous vertical lines foretell the Baroque style.

This room contains other works by the Bologna group of artists (Domenichino, Guido Reni, A Carracci) and the Gipsy Fortune-teller (10) attributed to Caravaggio (1589).

■ CAPITOLINE MUSEUM ★★

Housed in the New Palace. Same opening times and same ticket as for the Conservators' Palace Museum.

The fountain in the courtyard is dominated by the recumbent statue of an antique god christened **'Marforio'**. The huge peaceful figure seems a little bored with watching the water in the basin.

In the Middle Ages the statue was one of the group of 'talking statues' and received satirical comments directed against the people in power.

For a long time Marforio was to be found next to the Church of Sts Luke and Martina and the cost of moving him (1595) was so great the government raised the price of wine. Marforio thereupon 'wrote' to Pasquino, another talking statue *(p 160)*, that the Romans were having to do without wine so that he could preside over a fountain.

Egyptian collection. — *In the courtyard on the right.* Egyptian sculptures from the sanctuaries in the Campus Martius. The granite monkey heads (4C BC) decorated the Temple of Isis as did the basalt sphinx (6C BC).

Ground floor rooms. — The rooms on the left of the entrance are devoted to the oriental cults of Mithras and Cybele.

There are several representations of the god Mithras killing the bull while the forces of evil (dog, scorpion and serpent) try to prevent the sacrifice taking place.

An altar bears a dedication to the Vestal Claudia who used her girdle to refloat a ship which had gone aground in the Tiber; the ship was carrying the "black stone" representing the goddess Cybele from Pessinus *(p 51)*; the goddess had been judged immoral and the Augurs declared that only a young virgin could bring the ship to shore.

In the rooms on the right of the entrance *(re-opening shortly)*: a Roman sarcophagus showing the battle between the Greeks and Galatians (2C). The decoration derives from models copied from the artists of the Hellenistic period of the Pergamum school who generally represented barbarians as Galatians (Gauls who occupied Galatia in Asia Minor).

The next room contains a fine sarcophagus decorated with low reliefs of the life of Achilles and surmounted by the dead husband and wife (3C).

Atrium. — The huge statue of Mars is a reproduction of the one which stood in the Temple of Mars Ultor in Augustus' Forum *(p 129).*

Take the stairs to the first floor.

Doves' Room (1). — It takes it name from the **mosaic ★★** (1), an extremely fine piece of work, which decorated the floor of a room in Hadrian's villa at Tivoli. It is probably a copy of a 2C BC Greek mosaic from Pergamum.

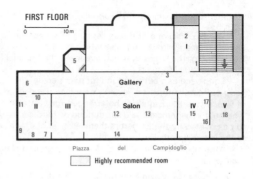

FIRST FLOOR

Piazza   del   Campidoglio

☐ Highly recommended room

— The statue of a young girl holding a dove in her arms and warding off a serpent (2) is a Roman copy of a 2C BC Hellenistic sculpture. During restoration the serpent was substituted for the original animal (a dog or a cat).

Gallery. — The old woman in her cups (3) may be a replica of a Hellenistic work from 3C BC when artists often portrayed human nature with great realism.

— Roman woman as Venus (4): from the Augustan period a taste for disguise developed. The face of the statue is the portrait of a woman from the Flavian period (second half of 1C), her body is a copy of a 4C BC Greek model.

Capitoline Venus ★★ (5). — The Greek original which inspired the Roman copy of this Venus was a Hellenistic work derived from the Venus of Cnidus sculpted by Praxiteles, the master of feminine divinities in the Classical period. The Capitoline Venus, who is shown leaving her bath, is distinguished from the Classical style by the double gesture of modesty.

— The stone well surround (2C) supporting a great bowl (6) is decorated with a procession of the 12 Di Consentes who had a portico in the Forum (p 38).

Emperors' Room ★★ (II). — Rarely have so many famous portraits been assembled in one place. Every emperor is represented; among them in particular are:

— Two portraits of Octavian-Augustus: one (7) shows him at the time of the battle of Actium (upper row) and the other (8), crowned with myrtle, shows the cold will and determination of the Emperor.

— The bust of the youthful Commodus (9) demonstrates the sculptor's great skill in working marble and a search for the effects of light and shade.

— Plotina (10 - upper row), Trajan's wife, is represented by a sad and solemn portrait. On Trajan's death it was she who told the Senators that in his last moments he had named Hadrian as his successor. There was always some doubt about the truth of this declaration; although Trajan had always shown affection for Hadrian, he had never adopted him officially.

— The portrait of a woman with her hair piled high in curls (11 - on a column) dates from the late 1C and is one of the most beautiful works in the collection.

Philosophers' Room (III). — It contains over 80 busts.

Salon. — Here are two statues of Centaurs, one laughing because he is young (12) and the other weeping because he is old (13). They are Roman works from Hadrian's reign (117-138), reproductions in sombre marble of Hellenistic originals in bronze. The **wounded Amazon ★** (14) is a fine Roman copy of a statue sculpted by Kresilas for the Amazon of Ephesus in competition with Phidias and Polyclitus.

Faun Room (IV). — Here is a 'Satyr' (15) from the same period as the two Centaurs.

— Among the Roman inscriptions is the *Lex de imperio Vespasiani* (16) engraved on bronze. With this decree the Senate conferred full powers on Vespasian on 22 December 69. Cola di Rienzo (p 54) commented on the text to the assembled crowds.

— The statue of a child wringing a goose's neck (17) is a 2C Roman sculpture inspired by a bronze by the Greek Boethos; in the Hellenistic period a child and an animal were often sculpted together in a spontaneous attitude.

Gladiator Room (V). — It is known by this name because the magnificent sculpture (18) in the middle of the room was long thought to be a gladiator. It is in fact a Gaul from Galatia (p 60), a Roman imitation of a work in bronze from the Pergamum school (late 3C, early 2C BC). It was probably part of a group of sculptures commemorating the victory of Attalus I, king of Pergamum, against the invading Gauls. All the nobility and suffering of the body in its agony are sensitively expressed; the **Dying Gaul ★★★** ranks among the most beautiful pieces of antique art.

Return to Piazza del Campidoglio and take the steps on the left of the Conservators' Palace which lead up to the southern peak of the Capitoline Hill (the ancient Roman Capitol).

The area has been laid out as a pleasant garden overlooking the steep drop from the Tarpeian Rock. Take Via del Tempio di Giove which leads down past several stone blocks which formed a corner of the Temple of Jupiter (pp 55 and 59). Turn right into Via di Villa Caffarelli which opens into Piazzale Caffarelli: from here there is a pleasant **view ★** of Rome from the Janiculum to the northern districts.

For your next walk consult the maps on pp 4 to 9.

Distance: 3 km - 2 miles. Time: about 4 hours. Start: Piazza di Santa Maria Maggiore.

The **Esquiline,** one of the seven hills of Rome, has been inhabited since 8C BC. It is an uneven plateau with three peaks which the Romans named the **Oppius,** now covered by the Parco Oppio, the **Fagutalis,** which overlooks the Imperial Fora, and the **Cispius,** now crowned by Santa Maria Maggiore.

Long used as a burial ground for poor people, the Esquiline was one of the most sinister parts of Rome. Augustus gave it a new face. He divided the city into fourteen districts, one of which was the Esquiline; he arranged for part of it to be given to his friend Maecenas who built a magnificent villa surrounded by gardens. In the course of time the district came to be coveted by the Emperors themselves and after a series of confiscations it was added to the imperial domain.

After the fire in 64 AD had cleared the ground Nero built his Golden House *(p 66)* on the Oppius.

Piazza di Santa Maria Maggiore. — The fluted column which stands at the centre is the sole survivor of the eight columns which graced the Basilica of Maxentius in the Forum. It was brought here in 1614 on the initiative of Pope Paul V and set up on its base by the architect Carlo Maderno and crowned with a statue of the Virgin.

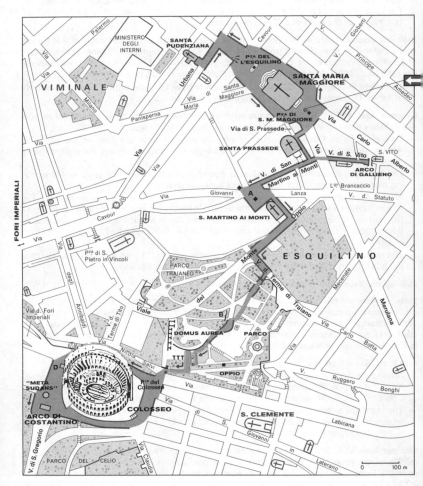

■ BASILICA OF ST MARY MAJOR ★★★ (Santa Maria Maggiore)

It is one of the four Roman basilicas which bear the title 'major' (the others are St John Lateran, St Paul Without the Walls and St Peter's in the Vatican) and enjoys the privilege of extraterritoriality conferred by the Lateran Treaty in 1929 *(p 71).*

The basilica was built by Sixtus III (432-40) in honour of Mary one year after the Council of Ephesus at which Nestorius, the Patriarch of Constantinople, had claimed that Mary was not the Mother of God.

Subsequent popes have left their mark; in their desire to contribute to the glory of the Virgin they made numerous alterations. The portico was rebuilt in 12C by Eugenius III, in 16C by Gregory XIII and again in 18C by Benedict XIV. The campanile, the highest in Rome, was added in 1377 by Gregory XI. In the 17 and 18C under Clement X and Clement XI the apse was remodelled. The main façade was given its present appearance in 18C under Benedict XIV by Ferdinando Fuga (1743-50).

Main Façade

The portico and loggia are sandwiched between two identical wings although more than a century elapsed between the construction of the one on the right (1605) and the one on the left (1721-43). Like the majority of architects in the first half of the 18C, **Ferdinando Fuga** had a taste for Classical forms but also adopted certain elements from the Baroque art of Borromini. The façade is enlivened by sculptures, the broken lines of the pediments and the interplay of the openings in the portico and the arcade of the loggia.

In the portico stands a statue of Philip IV of Spain (1), a benefactor of the basilica; it is by a pupil of Algardi (1692). The loggia from which the Pope used to give his blessing *Urbi et Orbi* was added to the original facade which still retains its early 14C mosaic decoration.

Loggia Mosaics ★. — *Open 9 to 11 am; apply to the Sacristy.* The upper part — Christ, angels, the evangelistic symbols, the Virgin and the saints — is the work of **Filippo Rusuti** (late 13C), who took over from Pietro Cavallini.

Below are four scenes illustrating the **legend of the basilica** which was built here late in 4C by Pope Liberius: the Virgin appeared in a dream to a Giovanni Patrizio, a rich man, and to Pope Liberius inviting them to build a church in her honour; the site for the sanctuary would be marked by a fall of snow on the morrow. When the Pope and Patrizio consulted one another they were astonished to find that in spite of the time of year (5 August 356) there had been a snow fall on the Esquiline. The Pope drew up a plan of the church; Patrizio financed the construction. The graceful lines, richly apparelled figures and fine deep perspectives link these scenes with the Florentine style of Cimabue and Giotto. The mosaics were extensively restored in the 19C.

Interior ★★★

It too has undergone many alterations: at the end of 13C Nicolas IV (1288-92) extended the chancel and in the middle of 15C Cardinal Guillaume d'Estouteville, archpriest of the Basilica, covered the aisles with vaulting in keeping with Renaissance taste. Despite that the interior of this basilica with its almost perfect proportions and two rows of Ionic columns is a remarkable example of early Christian architecture; brilliant with colour, it is at its most spectacular on Sundays and feast days.

Mosaiques ★★★. — Those in the nave, on the chancel arch and in the apse are beyond compare.

Mosaics in the nave. — Dating from 5C they consist of a series of panels above the entablature which is decorated with a fine frieze of interlacing. They are some of the oldest Christian mosaics in Rome, together with those in Sta Pudenziana *(p 65)*, St Constance' *(p 200)* and the Lateran Baptistry *(p 135)*. They are examples of an art which has rediscovered a taste for vivid narrative after accepting the rigidity of the late Empire.

The scenes are taken from the Old Testament with Abraham, Jacob, Moses and Joshua in the leading roles. On the lefthand side of the nave, beginning at the chancel end, are incidents from Genesis:

2) Melchizedek comes to meet Abraham

3) Abraham's dream near the Mamré oak

4) The separation of Abraham and Lot

Next comes the arch opened up in the 17C during the construction of the Pauline chapel which entailed the destruction of the mosaics at this point. Then:

5) Isaac blesses Jacob. Esau returns from hunting.

The next panel is a painting.

6) Rachel tells Laban of the arrival of Jacob, his nephew. Laban and Jacob embrace.

7) Jacob agrees to serve Laban for 7 years and to receive Rachel as his wife.

8) Jacob reproaches Laban for giving him Lea, his elder daughter, in marriage. Jacob marries Rachel.

9) Jacob asks Laban for the speckled and spotted sheep. The division of the flock.

10) God tells Jacob to leave. Jacob announces his departure to the women.

Next between two painted panels:

11) The meeting of the two brothers, Jacob and Esau.

12) Hamor and his son Shechem ask Jacob for the hand of his daughter Dinah, whose brothers are angry.

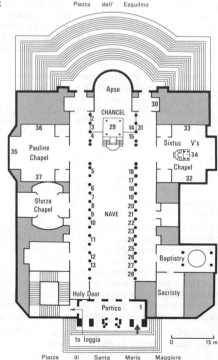

Piazza dell' Esquilino

Piazza di Santa Maria Maggiore

13) Dinah's brothers insist that the men among Hamor's people be circumcised. Hamor and Shechem explain the situation to their people.

The last three panels on this side are painted.

On the righthand side of the nave, starting at the chancel end, there is first a painted panel and then:

14) Pharaoh's daughter receives Moses. He discusses with the Egyptian doctors.

15) Moses marries Zipporah. God appears in the burning bush.

Then comes the arch opened up during the construction of Sixtus V's Chapel which takes the place of the mosaics (1741-50).

16) The passage of the Red Sea.

17) Moses and the people of Israel. The miracle of quails.

18) The salt sea of Mara. The people of Israel reproach Moses who, after praying to God, touches the water with a rod sent by God and makes it fresh. The meeting of Moses and Amalek.

19) The battle against the people of Amalek and Moses praying on the hillside.

20) The return of the chiefs of the tribes who had gone to explore the promised land. The stoning of Moses, Joshua and Caleb.

21) The tablets of Law are handed down. The death of Moses. The transport of the Arc.

22) The passage of the Jordan. Joshua sends spies to Jericho.

23) The angel of God (the captain of the Lord's host) appears to Joshua. The harlot Rahab helps the spies to scale the walls of Jericho. The return of the spies.

24) The besieging of Jericho. The procession of the Arc to the sound of trumpets.

25) The taking of Ai. Joshua before God and among the soldiers.

26) Joshua fights the Amorites. Hail of stones on Israel's enemies.

27) The sun and moon stand still upon Gibeon.

28) Joshua punishes the rebel kings.

The last three panels are paintings.

Mosaic on the chancel arch. — It dates from 5C and has the liveliness of the first Christian mosaics. It is divided into four horizontal bands. Probably later than the mosaics in the nave, it shows Byzantine influence:

— In the Annunciation scene *(top row left)* where Mary is dressed like an oriental empress;
— In the Epiphany scene *(second row left)*, presented as a sumptuous court reception, where the Child Jesus is sitting on a throne decorated with precious stones. The cities of Jerusalem and Bethlehem *(two lower rows)* with sheep representing the Apostles appear in almost every mosaic from this date.

Apsidal mosaic. — It is a dazzling composition of pieces taken from a 5C mosaic transformed at the end of the 13C by **Jacopo Torriti** when Nicolas IV rebuilt the apse. All the figures are the work of Torriti since the earlier mosaic consisted only of birds, foliage and scrolls. The central theme of the composition is the Crowning of the Virgin, surrounded by groups of angels and a procession of saints. Kneeling before them are Nicolas IV and Cardinal Colonna.

The four 15C sculptured panels lower down come from the altar of Sixtus IV. The imposing baldaquin (29), supported on porphyry columns wreathed in fronds of bronze, is by Fuga. Unfortunately it hides some of the mosaic.

Beneath the baldaquin is the Confessio where Pope Pius IX (1846-78) is shown at prayer, resplendent in bronze gilt, marble and frescoes (19C); fragments thought to belong to Jesus's crib are venerated here.

Ceiling ★. — The coffers were decorated with the first gold to come from Peru which was offered to Pope Alexander VI, a Spaniard (1492-1503), by Ferdinand and Isabella of Spain. The Pope continued the work begun by Calixtus III (1455-58) in constructing this ceiling which is decorated with the arms of the Borgia family to which the two Popes belonged. The roses at the centre of the coffers are 1 m - 3 1/4 ft in diameter. Vasari, a 16C art historian and author of *'Lives of Italian Artists'*, attributes this work to Giuliano da Sangallo (1445-1516).

Floor. — It is 12C Cosmati work radically restored by Ferdinando Fuga in 18C.

Right aisle. — The tomb of Cardinal Consalvo Rodriguez (30) (late 13C) is typically Gothic (a recumbent figure under a trilobed arch, flanked by angels beneath a mosaic of the Virgin). In the floor is the simple tombstone (31) of the family of Bernini, the master of the Baroque style.

Sixtus V's Chapel. — It is named after Sixtus V who during his five year reign (1585-90) turned Rome into a huge building site with his restorations, conversions and new constructions. His favourite architect was Domenico Fontana, to whom he therefore entrusted the design of this chapel. It is almost a church in itself. Designed on the Greek cross plan beneath a dome painted with frescoes, it is resplendent with gilding, stucco and marble. In the right and left arms of the cross are the monumental tombs of Popes Sixtus V (32) and Pius V (33) decorated with low relief sculptures illustrating the great events of their reigns.

Beneath the high altar (34) in 1590 Domenico Fontana set up the Oratory of the Crib which had held the relics of the grotto in Bethlehem since 7C.

Baptistry. — It is the work of the Baroque architect Flaminio Ponzio. The beautiful porphyry font was decorated in 19C by Giuseppe Valadier. The high relief of the Assumption on the altar is by Pietro Bernini, father of Gian Lorenzo.

Left aisle. — It contains in particular two beautiful chapels.

Sforza Chapel. — Its highly original architectural style is by Giacomo della Porta, probably from designs by Michelangelo.

Pauline Chapel. — It is also called the Borghese Chapel after the family name of Pope Paul V who commissioned it in 1611 from Flaminio Ponzio. It is identical in plan to Sixtus V's Chapel but with even more sumptuous decoration. In 1612 Cigoli painted the dome without first sub-dividing it with ribs; he was the first to follow this course and the result was not perfect. When, some ten years later, Lanfranco (who also worked on the Pauline Chapel) painted the dome of Sant'Andrea delle Valle using the same process, he achieved a masterpiece. The main altar (35) is incomparably rich, like a jewel, set with jasper, lapis-lazuli, agate and amethyst. The altarpiece is of a Virgin and Child in the Byzantine style. She may have been painted in 12C after a 9C Byzantine original. She is greatly venerated among the faithful and has

(After photo by Gab. Fot. Naz., Rome)
Pauline Chapel (detail)

even been attributed to St Luke *(p 39)*. She is surrounded by a 'glory' of angels in gilded bronze, a feature very popular with Baroque artists. Above the alterpiece is a sculpted panel by Stefano Maderno illustrating the legend of the tracing of the basilica's plan *(p 63)*. As in Sixtus V's Chapel the right and left arms of the cross contain papal tombs: Clement VIII (36) and Paul V (37).

Leave the church by the door at the end of the aisle to the right of the choir.

Piazza dell' Esquilino. — From here there is a fine **view★★** of the apse of Santa Maria Maggiore. When the Pauline and Sistine chapels were added beneath their domes they looked like two separate buildings. Clement IX (1667-9) therefore commissioned Bernini to integrate them with the basilica by altering the apsidal end of the church. Bernini conceived a grandiose design but the excessive cost prevented it from being carried into effect. The following pope, Clement X, therefore gave the work to Carlo Rainaldi.

The Egyptian obelisk at the centre of the square comes from the mausoleum of Augustus. Sixtus V ordered it to be moved and set up by Domenico Fontana, a specialist in such matters.

From Santa Maria Maggiore to the Coliseum

At the bottom of the Piazza dell' Esquilino turn left into Via Urbana.

Santa Pudenziana. — *If the church is closed, ring at the door on the left.*

The church is one of the oldest in Rome. Legend tells how Senator Pudens, who lived in a house on this site, welcomed Peter under his roof. In 2C a bath house stood on the site. Late in 4C a church *(ecclesia pudentiana)* was established in the baths. The similarity between the girl's name Pudentiana and the adjective derived from Pudens turned Pudentiana into the daughter of Pudens.

Pudentiana, like her sister Praxedes, was not martyred but both are shown with the martyrs whose bodies they prepared for burial.

The façade was repaired in 19C. The bell tower dates from 12C as does the elegant doorway, with its fluted columns and its sculpted frieze inset with five medallions. The interior shows the signs of many changes: in 8C the aisles were added. In 1589 the dome was built and the chancel altered so that several figures in the fine 4C **mosaic★** were lost. It is one of the oldest examples of a Christian mosaic in Rome (together with those in the nave of St Mary Major *p 63*, in St Constance' *p 200* and the baptistry of St John Lateran *p 135*). The way in which Christ is represented, the brilliant colours and the lively figures show the persistence of Roman qualities in Christian mosaic art before it was influenced by the Orient and its traditional forms.

The Caetani chapel in the left aisle, richly decorated with marble and stucco, was built by Francesco da Volterra during the Counter-Reformation (late 16C) and completed by Carlo Maderno early in 17C.

Return to Piazza di Santa Maria Maggiore and then take Via Merulana before turning right into Via di S. Prassede.

Santa Prassede★. — *The usual entrance is in the right aisle.*

The brick façade with the main doors giving on to a small courtyard can be seen through the entrance arch *(closed)* which opens into Via di San Martino ai Monti beneath a loggia supported on two columns.

The church is an old *titulus,* i.e. a private house where Christian services were held in antiquity. The present building was put up by Pascal I in 822.

It was built to the basilical plan, the nave and aisles separated by two rows of columns directly supporting the architrave. It was altered in 13C by the addition of three transverse arches in the nave, decorated with frescoes in 17C and given a coffered ceiling in 19C.

Chancel mosaics ★. — They date from 9C, the reign of Pascal I, and show the influence of Byzantine traditionalism and then of Carolingian art. Colour is paramount and no longer used in half tones. In this respect it is interesting to compare the apsidal mosaic here with the one in the Church of Sts Cosmas and Damian *(p 52)* which is three centuries earlier and inspired the iconography of the later one: against a background of sky quite lacking in depth the figure of Christ is flanked by Sts Peter and Paul presenting Praxedes and Pudentiana. The other two figures are St Zenon and Pope Pascal I offering his church (his square halo showing that he was alive at the time). The two palms represent the Old and New Testaments and the Phoenix on the one on the left is the symbol of the Resurrection.

The chancel arch shows *(upper part)* the arrival of the Elect in the Celestial City of Jerusalem with groups of the Blessed *(lower part)* (spoiled in 16C by the balconies).

St Zenon's Chapel ★★. — *Right aisle.* The chapel was built between 817 and 824 by Pope Pascal I. The doorway is made up of various elements taken from earlier buildings: two black granite columns, the entablature, the column bases decorated with an interlaced pattern, the marble urn in the arch over the entrance. Above this are several portrait medallions arranged in two arcs, one centred on Christ surrounded by the Apostles and the other on the Virgin and Child surrounded by various saints. The two portraits in the rectangular panels at the bottom of the arrangement are much later than 9C.

The interior is fascinating, covered in mosaics against a gold background *(time switch)*: on the central vault Christ, in strict Byzantine style, is supported by four angels; above the opening to the left of the altar is the Virgin accompanied by two saints and the mother of Pascal I, Theodora Episcopa, with a blue halo; the mosaic above the opening to the right of the altar was spoiled in 13C when an oratory was built to house a fragment of the scourging column. This relic was greatly venerated by pilgrims.

Return to Via Merulana and turn left into Via di S. Vito.

Arch of Gallienus (Arco di Gallieno). — It was erected in 262 in honour of the Emperor Gallienus (253-68) who was assassinated by some Illyrian officers. It stands on the site of the Esquiline Gate (Porta Esquilina) in the Servian wall *(plan pp 14-15)*. Traces of this wall, which was probably started in 6C BC and several times repaired, can be seen in Via Carlo Alberto (next to the Church of SS Vito, Modesto e Crescenzia).

Return to Via Merulana and cross over into Via di San Martino ai Monti opposite.

The street leads into an open space between the two **Cappocci towers** (**A**) which, despite extensive restoration, still evoke the power of the noble families in the Middle Ages.

The apse of the Church of San Martino ai Monti dates from 9C *(see below)*.

San Martino ai Monti. — This venerable church was founded in 5C and dedicated to St Martin by Pope Symmachus (498-514) next to a *titulus* existing in 3C in the house of Equitius *(the underground remains can be visited: ask in the Sacristy)*. As Pope Sylvester (314-35) was revered in the *Titulus Equitii,* when Pope Sergius II rebuilt the church in 9C, he dedicated it to both St Martin and St Sylvester.

The church was completely transformed in 17C. The interior was divided into a nave and two aisles by two rows of columns which date from the time of Symmachus (set on their bases in 17C). In the aisles Gaspard Dughet, Poussin's brother-in-law, painted frescoes of Roman landscapes and the story of the Prophet Elijah. At either end of the left aisle are views of the interiors of the old basilicas of St Peter in the Vatican and of St John Lateran (before the intervention of Borromini) by Filippo Gagliardi (17C).

The walk now enters the **Parco Oppio** (the Oppian Hill of antiquity) and skirts the ruins of **Trajan's Baths**, of which a plan is displayed on the outer curve of an apse (**B**).

Golden House (Domus Aurea). — *Closed for restoration owing to a landslip.* This is the palace built by Nero after the fire in 64 AD. The vestibule was on the Velia (where the Arch of Titus stands) and contained the famous statue of Nero *(p 67)* while the rooms were on the Oppian Hill. In the intervening depression, now occupied by the Coliseum, was a lake and all around were gardens and vineyards creating a truly rural environment. Inside the house 'the dining room ceilings were composed of movable ivory tiles pierced with holes so that flowers or perfume could be sprinkled on the guests below; the main dining room was circular and turned continually on its axis, day and night, like the world'.

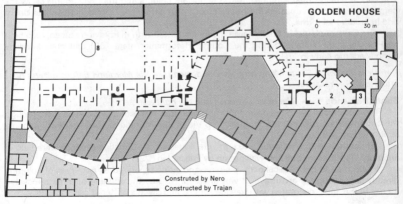

Nero committed suicide in 68 AD; the Senate condemned him. The lake was drained and the Coliseum was erected on the site. Then the upper part of the house was razed and what remained was used as foundations for the Baths of Titus and Trajan. The Golden House was not discovered until the Renaissance. Raphael and some of his fellow artists were very enthusiastic about the paintings which they found: geometric designs, foliated scrolls, decorated with faces and animals. As the rooms decorated in this way were underground like caves or grottoes, the decorative motifs were called **grotesques**.

The fine brick façade belongs to Trajan's Baths. The tour begins in one of the slanting passages built in front of Nero's house as foundations for Trajan's Baths and continues through a series of fairly obscure rooms.

In a room **(1)** are traces of houses destroyed by the fire in 64. Another **(2)** which is octagonal and lit by a dome, leads into five other rooms and shows the daring design of the house. In a third room **(3)** the statue of Laocoon, now in the Vatican *(p 82)*, was found in 1506. Another room **(4)** contains rare and attractive traces of paintings including landscapes. On the ceiling of the corridor **(5)** are scratched the names of artists who entered the rooms through the ceiling. Two other rooms **(6** and **7)** exemplify the ingenious design of the house: one overlooks an internal garden **(8)** where the base of a pool is visible, the other looks out on the external garden, now filled with the slanting passages of Trajan's Baths.

■ COLISEUM ★★★

In 72 AD Vespasian, the first of the Flavians, undertook to devote to public entertainment some of the excessive space occupied by the Golden House. On the site of Nero's lake he built the largest Roman amphitheatre in the world where fabulous spectacles took place.

The Flavian amphitheatre may have got the name Coliseum (**Colosseo** in Italian) because of the huge **statue of Nero**, the 'Colosseum', which stood near by, or perhaps because of the colossal dimensions of the building itself; 527 m - 1 730 ft round and 57 m - 187 ft high, it makes an unforgettable impression of massiveness.

The position of the statue of Nero is marked on the ground (D). The Emperor's head was surrounded by rays like the sun. According to Suetonius, the statue was over 35 m - 120 ft high.

TOUR

The whole construction consists of three floors of arcades supported on engaged columns, Doric on the ground floor, Ionic on the first and Corinthian on the second, surmounted by a wall divided into sections by regularly spaced engaged pilasters which alternate with small recesses. In Domitian's time the flat wall spaces were decorated with bronze shields. The projections supported wooden poles, inserted through holes in the upper cornice; the poles carried a linen awning which could be extended over the amphitheatre to protect the spectators from sun or rain. The job of putting up the awning, which was made more difficult by the wind, was entrusted to the sailors of Misenus' fleet.

The huge blocks of travertine, which were never covered in marble, were originally held together with metal tenons which were removed in the Middle Ages although the sockets are still visible. The blocks of stone were brought from the quarries at Albulae, near Tivoli, along specially built roads, 6 m - 20 ft wide.

The entrances were numbered and the spectators went into the amphitheatre by the entrance whose number appeared on their ticket *(tessera)*. They made their way to their seats by a warren of vaulted passages and stairs decorated with stuccowork.

Interior. — *The terraces are open from 9 am to one hour before sunset (9 am to 1 pm Sundays); closed 1 January, 25 April, 1 May, 1st Sunday in June, 15 August, 25 December. 2 000 L.* The construction is a rounded oval with axes measuring 188 m - 617 ft and 156 m - 512 ft. At either end of the shorter axis were the seats reserved for the Emperor and his suite (north) and the Prefect of Rome and the magistrates (south).

The *cavea,* the terraces for the spectators, began 4 m - 13 ft above the arena. First came the *podium,* a terrace protected by a balustrade and reserved for the marble seats of the important spectators. Then came three series of terraces, separated from one another by passages and divided by sloping corridors *(vomitaria)* down which the multitude poured out after the show. Places were allotted according to social station. At the top under a colonnade sat the women while the slaves stood on the terrace supported by the colonnade. In all there were probably about 45 000 seats and space for 5 000 standing.

The gladiators entered through doors at either end of the longer axis. Marching in ranks like soldiers they made a tour of the arena dressed in purple and gold and then halted before the Emperor. With right arm raised they pronounced the formula: *Ave, Imperator, morituri te salutant* (Hail, Emperor, those who are about to die salute thee).

The surface which formed the floor of the arena where the spectacles took place disappeared during the excavations revealing the underground warren where the wild animals waited before being brought to the surface by a system of ramps and lifts for the greater pleasure of the assembled crowd. "This degraded people clammers with covetous anxiety for only two things in the world, bread and circuses" said Juvenal at the end of 1C.

Circuses. — Originally they held a religious significance for the Romans and constituted a rite intended to maintain good relations between the City and the gods. For many years the spectators attended head uncovered as at a sacrifice. Caesar was blamed for reading his post in the amphitheatre and Suetonius, the Emperors' biographer, reproached Tiberius warmly for disliking the spectacles.

The Coliseum, though still incomplete, was inaugurated in 80 AD by Titus, Vespasian's son. The spectacle which he organised on this occasion lasted 100 days. The racing and the duels between gladiators were followed by bouts between men and wild animals. 5 000 animals died. Even naval engagements were re-enacted in the flooded arena. In 249 to celebrate the millennium of the founding of Rome 1 000 pairs of gladiators met in combat; 32 elephants, a dozen tigers, over 50 lions, 6 hippos etc, sent by the imperial provinces, were killed.

The spectacles usually lasted from dawn to dusk. Some were very cruel and caused the arena to be covered in blood. Others, such as the presentation of wild animals, were like modern circus acts.

The last days of the Coliseum. — Gladiatorial duels were forbidden in 404 by the Emperor Honorius. Wild animal fights disappeared in 6C. In 13C the Frangipani family turned the Coliseum into a fortress which then passed to the Annibaldi. It was however in 15C that the building suffered its greatest losses: it literally became a quarry and the huge blocks of travertine were taken for the construction of the Palazzo Venezia, the Palazzo della Cancelleria and St Peter's Basilica. Benedict XIV put an end to the quarrying in 18C by consecrating the building to the Christian martyrs who were thought to have perished there. The stations of the cross were set up round the arena. Stendhal wrote of his embarrassment at the 'pious murmuring of the faithful who observe the stations of the Cross in groups of 15 or 20'. Today a cross still stands at the eastern entrance in memory of those Christians who may have met their deaths here, condemned like other criminals to fight unarmed against wild animals or armed men.

According to custom one should stand before the Coliseum, massive in its unperturbability, and in Byron's well known words quote the prophecy made early in 8C by the Venerable Bede, an English monk and historian:

> *"While stands the Coliseum, Rome shall stand;*
> *When falls the Coliseum, Rome shall fall;*
> *And when Rome falls, the world."*

■ CONSTANTINE'S ARCH ★★★

At the height of the tourist season it is sometimes difficult to come close to the arch. Such is its fame that anyone merely passing through Rome comes to see it. This magnificent construction with its three arches was built in 315 by the Senate and the Roman People three years after Constantine's victory over his rival Maxentius at the Milvian bridge *(pp 46, 201)*. Like the Coliseum it was incorporated into the mediaeval fortifications. It was first restored in 18C and put into its present state in 1804. The proportions are harmonious. The abundant decoration was not all 4C work. Many of the sculptures were taken from 2C monuments (by Trajan, Hadrian and Marcus Aurelius) and re-employed.

North face. — The statues of four Dacian prisoners on the upper storey belonged to a monument erected in honour of Trajan (98-117). The way in which they are set up on a huge base above the entablature is characteristic of 4C taste. The four low reliefs between the statues date from 2C; together with those displayed in the museum in the Conservators' Palace *(p 57),* they belonged to monuments set up in honour of the Emperor Marcus Aurelius (although his head has been replaced by a head of Constantine). From left to right they represent: Marcus Aurelius being greeted by a personification of the Via Flaminia on his return to Rome in 174 after fighting in Germany; his triumph; distribution of bread and money to the people; interrogation of a royal prisoner.

The four medallions come from a monument to Hadrian (117-138). The subjects are hunting, a sport of oriental origin to which Hadrian was particularly partial, and sacrifices: *(from left to right)* wild boar hunting and a sacrifice to Apollo; lion hunting and a sacrifice to Hercules, who is wearing a lion skin.

The other sculptures, which date from 4C, illustrate the reign of Constantine.

South face *(facing down Via S. Gregorio).* — The design is identical to that on the north face. At the top are four low reliefs belonging to the same series as those in the museum in the Conservators' Palace and on the other side of the arch: on the left, two incidents in the wars of Marcus Aurelius; on the right, the Emperor addresses his army beside a sacrificial ceremony (below are the animals being led to the sacrifice).

The four medallions (which are damaged) show *(from left to right):* the hunt moving off and a sacrifice to Silvanus, god of the forest; bear hunting and a sacrifice to Diana, goddess and huntress par excellence.

The "Meta Sudans". — Only the site now remains of this fountain which was built by Titus and repaired by Constantine. It took the form of a cone of porous stone oozing water. What remained of it was demolished in 1936.

The 29 walks described in this guide cover historic sites and districts,

the art treasures in the museums.

Make your choice using the maps on pp 4 to 9.

Programmes for a 3-day and an 8-day stay

are laid out on pp 31 and 32.

Distance: 4 km - 2 1/2 miles. Start: Corso Vittorio Emanuele II.

Tour of the Vatican and Castel Sant' Angelo. — In view of the current opening times for the monuments described in this walk, the following programmes are suggested:

1 *For tourists with only one day available:*

Morning: Castel Sant' Angelo *(p 93)*: open 9 am to 1 pm (12 noon Sunday and holidays). It is planned to stay open until 7 pm in summer. Closed Monday, 1 January, Easter, 1 May, 15 August, Christmas. 2 000 L. Duration: 2 hours. Vatican Museums: *the most highly recommended sections only (Pio-Clementino Museum, the Raphael Stanze, the Sistine Chapel, the Picture Gallery). During the greater part of the year they close at 2 pm (ticket office open until 1 pm; details p 80). Duration: 3 hours.*

Lunch after visiting the museums.

Afternoon: St Peter's Basilica: *Duration: 2 hours.* It is not possible to include a tour of the Necropolis beneath St Peter's Basilica in this programme.

2 *Tourists with more time can cover the whole walk in three days:*

First day - Morning: Victor Emmanuel II Bridge; Via della Conciliazione; Castel Sant' Angelo *(see opening times above).*
Afternoon: Law Courts; the "Passetto"; Santo Spirito in Sassia; St Peter's Basilica.

Second day - Vatican Museums *(there is a restaurant in the museum).*

Third day - Vatican City and its gardens and the Necropolis beneath St Peter's Basilica in accordance with the following opening times:
Vatican City and Gardens: *guided tour only at 10 am; buy a ticket in advance from the Tourist Information Office (Ufficio Informazioni Pellegrini e Turisti) (plan p 70). On certain days the tour also includes either the Sistine Chapel or St Peter's Basilica. 4 000 or 7 000 L.*
Necropolis beneath St Peter's Basilica: *guided tour; write in advance to or fill in an application form at the Ufficio Scavi (open 9 am to 12 noon and 2 to 5 pm; closed Sunday and holidays; plan p 70). 3 000 L.*

Vatican bus service. — The bus runs between St Peter's Square and the Vatican Museums. It leaves from the Tourist Information Office or from the Museum Post Office every half hour from 9 am to 2 pm. 1 000 L.

Historical notes. — The **Ager Vaticanus** lay outside the boundary of ancient Rome and was not well known in antiquity. Under the Empire Caligula built a circus there. Nero improved it and used it for the massacre of the first Roman martyrs who may have included St Peter. Hadrian built his mausoleum, the present Castel Sant' Angelo, in the gardens belonging to the Domitii.

The history of the Vatican took on a new significance when the Emperor Constantine built a basilica there over St Peter's tomb, which is now St Peter's Basilica.

Today the Vatican enjoys immense prestige as the seat of the Papacy; St Peter's Basilica attracts Christians from all over the world. The papal palace houses some of the most precious art treasures in the world.

The "Leonine City". — On 23 August 846 the Saracens invaded Rome, pillaging the Basilicas of St Peter and St Paul. In the following year therefore Leo IV energetically set to work to raise a defensive wall round the Vatican district, which was known as the Borgo. The wall was restored in 15C by Nicholas V, reinforced with bastions by Sangallo the Younger under Paul III in 16C and extended by Pius IV in 1564 to Santo Spirito Gate.

Victor Emmanuel II Bridge

There was a bridge here in 60 AD, built by Nero, which collapsed in 4C. The present construction, which is decorated with allegorical groups and winged Victories, was begun soon after the unification of the Italian state and completed in 1911, thus linking Rome and the Vatican.

Cross the bridge to the right (north) bank and turn right.

On the left is the imposing brick building of the **Santo Spirito hospital** which was founded by Innocent III and rebuilt in 15C by Sixtus IV.

The **Church of the Sanctissima Annunciata** (Most Holy Annunciation), although small, is graced by an attractive façade full of movement (18C).

Via della Conciliazione

The decision to create this wide thoroughfare was taken in 1936 and the road was opened in 1950, Jubilee Year. The façades of the buildings flanking the southern end bear the arms of Pius XII *(right)* and of Rome *(left).* Two rows of street lamps in the shape of obelisks line the broad road which leads directly to St Peter's Basilica.

Church of Santo Spirito in Sassia

The church was built in 8C for Anglo-Saxon pilgrims. It was sacked in 1527 and rebuilt by the architect, Sangallo the Younger who died before it was finished. The façade, in the Renaissance style, with flat pilasters and an oculus, was constructed according to Sangallo's design under Sixtus V (1585-90) whose coat of arms appears above the door.

The interior, beneath a beautiful coffered ceiling, is richly decorated with paintings in the Mannerist style (divided into small panels, overworked). Fine 16C organ.

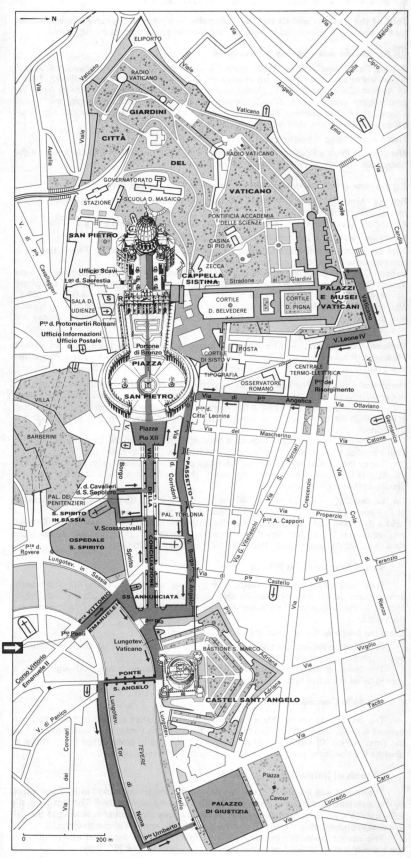

■ THE VATICAN STATE

Once in St Peter's Square the visitor has left Italy and is in the Vatican State. The Vatican City, which lies to the north of the Janiculum Hill and is bounded on three sides by the wall overlooking the Viale Vaticano and on the east by the curved colonnade in St Peter's Square, is the largest part of the papal state. It comprises St Peter's Basilica, the Vatican palaces and the beautiful gardens surrounding the various administrative offices of the papal state.

From the Papal States to the Vatican State

From the first days of Christianity, the bishop was Christ's representative on earth. The Bishop of Rome maintained that his see in the traditional capital of the Empire had been founded by the Apostles, Peter and Paul, and therefore claimed first place in the ecclesiastical hierarchy. The expression "the Apostolic See" appeared for the first time in 4C during the reign of Pope Damasus. Gradually the name "Pope", derived from the vulgar Latin *papa* meaning father, which had been used for all bishops, was reserved for the Bishop of Rome alone.

The gift of Quiersy-sur-Oise. — In 752, the Lombards occupied Ravenna and the imperial territory between the river Po, the Apennines and the Adriatic. In Rome the king of the Lombards Astolphe demanded a tribute of one gold piece per head. When the intervention of Constantine V, the Emperor in Byzantium (to whom Rome was in principle subject) proved useless, Pope Stephen II approached the Carolingian dynasty. In 756 at Quiersy-sur-Oise Pepin the Short, king of the Franks, undertook to restore the occupied territory not to the Emperor in Byzantium but to the "Republic of the Holy Church of God", that is to the Pope. This led to the creation of the Papal States and to the temporal power of the Pope.

The Lateran Treaty. — The unification of Italy (1820-70) would have been incomplete without the inclusion of the Papal States in the new kingdom. On 20 September 1870 the troops of King Victor Emmanuel II entered Rome and proclaimed the city the capital of the kingdom. On 2 May 1871 the Italian Parliament passed the **Law of the Guarantees** to show that it did not wish to subjugate the Papacy. The Pope was to retain the Vatican City and to receive an annual allowance. Pius IX excommunicated the authors of the Act and shut himself up in the Vatican declaring that he was a prisoner. His successors maintained this stance and the Roman Question was not resolved until 1929 when the **Lateran Treaty** was signed on 11 February by Cardinal Gaspari, representing the Holy See and Mussolini, the head of the Italian government.

The terms included a political agreement which recognised the Pope as sovereign of the Vatican State which comprised the Vatican City itself and a number of other properties which enjoy the privilege of extraterritoriality: the four major basilicas (St John Lateran, St Peter's in the Vatican, St Paul Without the Walls, St Mary Major), the Roman Curia, colleges and seminaries and the Villa at Castel Gandolfo; in all 44 ha - 109 acres and just under a thousand inhabitants. The Treaty also included a financial indemnity and a religious settlement granting the Church a privileged position in Italy in respect of schooling and marriage. The republican constitution of 1947 established a new relationship between the Roman church and the Italian state on the basis of the Lateran Treaty. Another agreement modifying the 1929 Lateran Treaty was signed on 18 February 1984 by the President of the Council and the Vatican Secretary of State.

Although the smallest state in physical size, the Vatican spreads the spiritual influence of the Roman church throughout the world through the person of the Pope.

The Pope, supreme head of the Roman church

The Pope is also called the Roman Pontiff, the Sovereign Pontiff, the Vicar of Christ, Holy Father, His Holiness. Sometimes he calls himself *Servus servorum Dei,* the Servant of the Servants of God. In his mission as Pastor to the church founded by Jesus Christ, he is assisted by the Sacred College of Cardinals and by the Roman Curia.

The College of Cardinals. — In 1586 Sixtus V fixed their number at 70; it was increased to 85 by John XXIII in 1960. In 1970 there were 145 cardinals; 128 in 1984. A cardinal's dress consists of a scarlet cape (a short hooded cloak) worn over a linen rochet (a surplice with narrow sleeves). The cardinals are the Pope's closest advisers; it is they, assembled in "conclave", who elect the Pope.

The conclave. — This is the name of the secret meeting at which a new pope is elected. This method of election was established by **Gregory X** (1271-6) whose own election lasted nearly three years. He imposed very strict regulations involving confinement and secrecy and requiring the election to be held within 10 days of the death of the previous pope in a palace from which the cardinals would not be released until the new pope had been elected. He added that if after three days no vote had been held the cardinals would be reduced to one meal a day for five days and then to bread and water. Nowadays the cardinals meet in conclave in the Sistine Chapel and absolute secrecy is maintained. A vote is held twice a day and after each inconclusive vote the papers are burned so as to produce dark smoke. A majority of two thirds plus one is required for an election to be valid ; then a plume of clear smoke appears above the Vatican. The senior cardinal appears at the window in the façade of St Peter's from which papal blessings are given and announces the election in the Latin formula: *Annuntio vobis gaudium magnum: habemus papam.* (I announce to you with great joy: we have a pope...). The new pope then gives his first blessing to the world.

The Roman Curia. — The Curia consists of a group of bodies, the dicasteries, which, together with the Pope, administer the Holy See. Each dicastery has a cardinal at its head. Since the reform instituted in 1967 by Paul VI, the Curia has consisted of two supreme bodies presided over by the Cardinal Secretary of State: the **Secretariat of State** which carries into effect the decisions taken by the Pope; in the Pope's immediate entourage the Secretary of State periodically assembles the cardinals who are heads of dicasteries into a sort of cabinet under his presidency; the **Council for the Public Affairs of the Church** which deals with diplomatic relations with foreign governments.

Questions of doctrine, the organisation of the churches and the administration of the papal household are dealt with by congregations (the equivalent of civil ministries), secretariats, councils, commissions, committees and offices.

There are also three courts contained in the Curia. The Tribunal of the Apostolic Signatura is a final court of appeal for ecclesiastical disputes and an administrative tribunal concerned with protecting the law. The Roman Rota is a court of appeal and of first instance which deals in particular with the annulment of marriages. The Apostolic Penitentiary judges matters of conscience.

The Councils. — Within the Roman church there are two rites (oriental and Latin); all the constituent churches belong to one or the other and are grouped into dioceses under the direction of **bishops.** The spiritual authority of a bishop is symbolised by his crozier, his pectoral cross, his ring and his mitre. His dress is no different from that of a cardinal except that it is purple. The episcopal college, consisting of about 4 000 bishops spread throughout the world, is presided over by the pope who calls them together in an **Oecumenical Council** to discuss the life of the Church. There have been 21 councils in 20 centuries, the last being the Second Vatican Council (the First which took place in St Peter's Basilica was held in 1869-70). The Second assembled in 1962 under John XXIII and was closed three years later by Paul VI.

Holy Year. — According to the Law of Moses one year in fifty should be devoted to God and to rest. Boniface VIII revived this tradition in 1300 when he proclaimed the first Jubilee or Holy Year. Clement VI (1342-52) fixed the frequency of Jubilees at every 50 years; Paul II (1464-71) reduced it to 25 years. The most recent Holy Years were 1950, 1975 and exceptionally 1983, announced by Pope Jean-Paul II. The beginning of a Holy Year is marked with great solemnity by the opening of the Holy Door in each of the four major basilicas. Pilgrims who visit Rome during Holy Year and visit certain basilicas are granted exceptional grace.

Papal Audiences. — *When the Pope is resident in Rome he gives a weekly public audience (Wednesday). To attend, apply in advance to the Prefettura della Casa Pontificia (Portone di bronzo, plan p 70) between 9 am and 1 pm. It is sometimes helpful but not essential to obtain a letter of recommendation from a parish priest.*

The audiences are held in St Peter's Square in summer and in winter either in St Peter's Basilica or in the huge modern hall designed by Pier Luigi Nervi under Paul VI. During the ceremony the Pope gives his blessing and preaches on the great questions of the Church and humanity. His homily is delivered in Italian and then translated into English, French, German, Spanish and Polish. Official groups of pilgrims are greeted by name in the appropriate language.

The Pope, head of State

The Pope is the Sovereign of the Vatican State and in this capacity wields the full range of legislative, executive and judicial power. He is assisted in the internal administration of the Vatican by a **Pontifical Commission** composed of cardinals and a lay member. Beneath the commission is the **Administration (Governatorato)** which since 1969 has been assisted by a **Council of State** and is composed of offices and directorates employing lay staff.

The Vatican State has a yellow and white flag, bearing the tiara and the crossed keys, and a hymn, the 'pontifical march' composed by Gounod.

The armed regiments were disbanded by Paul VI in 1970; only the Swiss Guards have been retained, dressed in their picturesque yellow, red and blue uniforms which are supposed to have been designed by Michelangelo.

The Vatican issues its own stamps, mints its own coins which are valid currency in Italy, operates a post office and has a railway station linked to the national rail network.

Cultural, scientific and artistic activity. — The **Apostolic Vatican Library** ranks very high; it was founded by papal bull in 1475 and contains over 60 000 volumes of manuscripts, 100 000 autographs, 800 000 prints, 100 000 engravings and maps and a collection of coins including an important section consisting of Roman money from the Republican era.

The **Secret Archives,** composed of documents dating from 13C, have been open to the public for consultation since 1881 and are of worldwide importance in historical research.

The **Pontifical Academy of Science** was founded in 1936 by Pius XI and consists of 70 academicians chosen by the Pope among scholars throughout the world.

The **Fabric of St Peter** is the body of architects and specialists in charge of the conservation of St Peter's Basilica. The mosaic workshop is annexed to it.

The Vatican has a printing works which produces texts in almost all languages; there is also an daily newspaper, the Osservatore Romano, and a weekly paper, the Osservatore della Domenica which is published in several languages. The Vatican Radio transmits programmes in forty different languages. Press conferences take place in the press room of the Holy See.

■ ST PETER'S BASILICA ★★★ (San Pietro)

The history of Christianity from the earliest days of the church is reflected in the basilica which is the largest of all Christian sanctuaries.

HISTORICAL NOTES

The building of St Peter's Basilica is linked to the martyrdom of Peter, which took place *c*64 AD. After a huge fire which destroyed the greater part of Rome and for which the Emperor Nero held the Christians responsible, he ordered many of them to be executed. Simon, called Peter by Jesus, was probably among the condemned. According to the law, he was simply a Jewish fisherman, a native of Capernaum in Galilee, who therefore suffered the appalling punishment of crucifixion in Nero's Circus at the foot of the Vatican Hill. In order to distinguish his own death from Jesus', Peter humbly begged to be crucified upside down.

Constantine's Basilica *(plan p 76).* — After his conversion to Christianity, Constantine built a sanctuary in 324 over the tomb of Peter, who had been chosen by Christ as his chief Apostle. In 326 Pope Sylvester I consecrated the building which was completed some 25 years later. The basilica had a nave, four aisles and a narrow transept; the apsidal wall stood just behind the present papal altar. The entrance was through an *atrium* at the centre of which stood a fountain decorated with the beautiful pine cone *(la Pigna)* which can now be seen in a courtyard of the Vatican Palace. The façade gleamed with mosaics. The *confessio* (a crypt containing the tomb of a martyr) was not completely underground; an opening at floor level gave access to the tomb. At the end of 6C Pope Gregory the Great raised the chancel; beneath it the confessio took the form of a corridor following the curve of the apse and contained a chapel called *ad caput (p 78)*.

For more than a century the basilica was pillaged by barbarians: Alaric in 410 and Totila in 546. In 846 it was raided by the Saracens. Its prestige however remained intact. Imperial coronations were held there in solemn state. On Christmas Day 800 AD Leo III crowned Charlemagne King of the Romans. 75 years later it was the turn of his grandson, Charles the Bald, during the pontificate of John VIII, the first soldier pope and the first to be assassinated. Arnoul, the last of the Carolingians, became Pope Formosus on 22 February 896.

John XII, who lived like a Mohommedan prince, surrounded by slaves and eunuchs, crowned Otho I on 2 February 962 and then conspired against him. His intrigues brought the papacy under the control of the German Emperor for over a century.

After a thousand years, despite frequent restoration and embellishment, St Peter's Basilica was in a parlous state.

1452, Nicholas V intervenes. — B Rossellino was appointed by the Pope to restore the basilica. While retaining the dimensions of Constantine's building, Rossellino proposed a cruciform plan with a dome and a new choir. The Pope died in 1455 and the project was abandoned. For the next 50 years his successors were content to shore up the existing building.

1503, Julius II, an energetic pope. — His plan for renovation was radical. His architects were Bramante, who had arrived in Rome in 1499, and Giuliano da Sangallo. The chosen design was Bramante's: a Greek cruciform plan with jutting apses beneath cupolas and over the crossing a central dome similar to the Pantheon dome. On 18 April 1506 the first stone was laid at the base of a pillar; a temporary chancel had been provided and a large part of the apse and transept demolished, causing Bramante to be nicknamed the 'Destructive Maestro'. Sometimes a young man came to watch the work. His name was Michelangelo. Julius II had commissioned him to design his tomb which was to be placed at the heart of the new basilica. Michelangelo admired Bramante's plan but disapproved of his administration. Having at first been regarded as an intruder, he came to be hated by Bramante. Believing himself to be in danger, Michelangelo retreated to Florence but returned to Rome after violently denouncing the Pope and Rome where, so he wrote, "they turn chalices into swords and helmets".

Julius II died in 1513 and Bramante in 1514. For the next 30 years the design of the building was the subject of interminable discussion. Raphael and Giuliano da Sangallo suggested going back to a Latin cruciform plan. Baldassare Peruzzi drew up another plan based on Bramante's design. Antonio da Sangallo, Giuliano's neplew, wanted to keep the Greek cross plan while adding a bay in the form of a porch with two towers flanking the façade and altering the dome; he died in 1546.

From Michelangelo to Bernini. — In 1547 **Paul III** appointed Michelangelo, then 72 and chief architect to the Vatican, to put an end to all the discussion. "To deviate from Bramante's design is to deviate from the truth", declared the Master. He therefore returned to the Greek cruciform plan, simplified so as to accentuate its circular base; the circle, the sign of infinity, glorifying the Resurrection. The dome was no longer the shallow dome of the Pantheon but reached high into the sky. His intransigence in carrying out his ideas exasperated his detractors.

The number of masterpieces in the Vatican is so great that a very rigorous selection of the outstanding items has had to be made;
for a more detailed description of the exhibits consult the Guide to the Vatican City and the Guide to the Vatican Museums published by the Monumenti, Musei e Gallerie Pontificie.

He worked on St Peter's, surrounded by intrigues, refusing any payment, doing all for the glory of God and the honour of St Peter. When he died in 1564, the apse and transepts were complete and the dome had risen as far as the top of the drum. It was completed in 1593 by Giacomo della Porta assisted by Domenico Fontana, who may have been inspired to raise the dome even higher by one of the Master's alternative designs.

In 1606 **Paul V** (1605-21) finally settled for the Latin cruciform plan; it was more suitable for high ceremony and preaching, and thus more in accordance with the preoccupations of the Counter-Reformation. The new basilica was to cover all the area occupied by the original church, whereas Michelangelo's plan had not extended so far east. The façade was entrusted to Carlo Maderno. The new basilica was consecrated by Urban VIII.

The final phase in St Peter's architectural history was directed by Bernini who took over on Maderna's death in 1629. He turned what would have been a fine example of Renaissance architecture into a sumptuous Baroque monument.

In all, from Bramante to Bernini, the building of St Peter's encompassed 120 years, the reigns of 20 popes and the work of 10 architects.

EXTERIOR

St Peter's Square ★★★ **(Piazza San Pietro).** — The square, which was intended to isolate the basilica without creating a barrier in front of it, acts in fact as a sort of vestibule. The gentle curves of the colonnades like two arcs of a circle framing the rectangular space are a gesture of welcome extended to the pilgrims of the world.

The square was begun by **Bernini** in 1656 under Pope Alexander VII and completed in 1667. By flanking the façade with a broader and lower colonnade, the architect aimed to minimise the width and accentuate the height of the basilica. To create the effect of surprise so dear to Baroque artists, the colonnade was designed to enclose the square and mask the façade so that the basilica was hidden from view until the visitor stood in the entrance between the arms of the colonnade. Bernini's intention was not fully realised: the triumphal arch planned to link the two arms was not built and the Via della Conciliazione gives a distant view of the basilica. Two belfries were planned, one at each end of the façade, but the foundations proved to weak to carry the additional weight.

At its widest point the square measures 196 m - 643 ft across. The **colonnade** is formed by rows of columns, four deep, surmounted by statues and the arms of Alexander VII: a remarkably sober and solemn composition.

At the centre of the square stands an **obelisk**, a granite monolith, carved in 1C BC in Heliopolis for Caius Cornelius Gallus, the Roman Prefect in Egypt. It was brought to Rome in 37 AD by Caligula who had it set up in his circus (left of the basilica). It was still there when **Sixtus V** decided to erect it in St Peter's Square. It was the first obelisk to be moved by this pope who was responsible for re-siting several others. His official architect was **Domenico Fontana**. The work took four months and gave birth to an appropriate legend. The obelisk was to be re-erected on 10 September 1585. 800 men and 75 horses were required to raise the 350 tonnes of granite to its full height of 25.5 m - 84 ft. After giving his blessing the Pope enjoined absolute silence on pain of death and to make sure his order was clearly understood he set up a gallows in the square. The work began but the ropes chafed on the granite and threatened to give way under the friction. Then one of the workers cried out *Acqua alle funi* (water for the ropes) and the Pope congratulated him for disobeying the order. A relic of the True Cross is preserved at the top of the obelisk.

The two fountains are attributed to Carlo Maderno *(right)* and Bernini *(left).* Between them and the obelisk are two discs set into the paving to mark the focal points of the two ellipses enclosing the square; from these points the colonnades appear to consist of only one row of columns. This perspective is achieved by increasing the diameter of the columns from the inner to the outer row and placing them an equal distance from one another.

East Front. — A majestic flight of steps, designed by Bernini, leads up to the east front from the gently sloping square. On either side stand statues of St Peter and St Paul (19C). The east front, which was begun by **Carlo Maderno** in 1607 and completed in 1614, was the object of spirited comment: 45 m - 147 ft high and 115 m - 377 ft wide, it masks the dome. It is from the balcony beneath the pediment that the Pope gives his blessing *urbi et orbi* (to the city and to the world).

The entablature carried Paul V's dedication. The horizontal pediment above it is crowned by statues of Christ, John the Baptist and eleven Apostles (excluding Peter). The clocks at either end are the work of Giuseppe Valadier (19C).

Porch. — It was designed by **Carlo Maderno.** On the left behind a grill stands an equestrian statue of Charlemagne (**1**) (18C). The Door of Death (**2**) with sober sculptures on its bronze panels is by **Giacomo Manzù** (1964); low down on the right in the lefthand section is a low relief figure of John XXIII. The bronze door (**3**) was sculpted in 1445 by Antonio Averulino, known as **Il Filarete**. The true artistic spirit of the Renaissance is seen in the juxtaposition of religious scenes (in the six panels), episodes from the life of Eugenius IV (in the spaces below the panels) and mythological figures, animals and portraits of contemporary personalities (in the frieze surrounding the panels). In the two central panels strange inscriptions in Arab characters appear round the figures of St Peter and St Paul and in their haloes. To the right is the Holy Door: only the Pope may open and close this door to mark the beginning and end of a Holy Year.

The "Navicella" mosaic (**4**) by Giotto dates from 1300. It originally adorned the *atrium* of Constantine's basilica but has been restored and re-sited many times since.

At the north end of the porch in the vestibule of the Scala Regia *(closed to the public)* stands a statue of Constantine (**5**), the first Christian Emperor, by Bernini (1670).

INTERIOR

Here everything is so well-proportioned that the scale, though large, is not over-whelming. The apparently life-size angels supporting the holy water stoops (6) are in fact enormous. St Peter's Basilica, with its 450 statues, 500 columns and 50 altars, and its reputed capacity to hold 60 000 people, is a record of the history of Christianity and art in Rome.

Nave. — The overall length of the church, including the porch, is about 211 m - 692 ft. Comparisons can be made with the length of other world-famous churches by means of marks set in the floor. When Charlemagne received the Emperor's crown from the Pope on Christmas Day 800 AD he knelt on the porphyry disc (7) now let into the pavement of the nave, although in the original church it was placed before the high altar.

The Pietà Chapel (8). — Here is **Michelangelo's** masterpiece, the **Pietà ★★★** which he sculpted in 1499-1500 at the age of 25. The execution of the profoundly human figures is perfect, revealing an amazing creative power. The group was commissioned by a French cardinal in 1498 and immediately hailed as the work of a genius. Even so Michelangelo already had enemies who started a rumour that the work was not his. He therefore added his signature across the Virgin's sash. It is the only signed work of his to have come down to us.

Crucifix Chapel (or Chapel of Relics) (9). — Bernini designed the elliptical chapel which contains a fine wooden crucifix attributed to Pietro Cavallini (early 14C).

Queen Christina of Sweden's Monument (10). — In 1654 Queen Christina abdicated her throne; she was converted to Roman Catholicism and came to live in

(After photo by Gab. Fot. Naz., Rome)
Michelangelo: Pietà

Rome the following year *(pp 100, 191)*. She is buried in the 'grottoes' *(p 78)*. Her monument was executed by G Theodon from designs by Carlo Fontana (18C).

Countess Mathilda of Tuscany's Monument (11). — She was the first woman to be buried in the basilica. At the time of the Investiture Controversy it was she who received the Emperor Henry IV when he submitted to Gregory VII at Canossa (1077). This incident is represented in the low relief carving on the sarcophagus. The monument was designed by Bernini assisted by several of his pupils (1635).

Chapel of the Blessed Sacrament (12). — The wrought iron screen at the entrance is by Borromini. The high altarpiece representing the Trinity is one of the few paintings of St Peter by Pietro da Cortona (most pictures are mosaics). On the altar, the tabernacle, which is similar to the *tempietto* of San Pietro in Montorio *(p 192)*, and the kneeling angels are by Bernini (1675) (the angel on the right is by a pupil).

Bernini brings unity to the Basilica. — The passage (**A**) marks the line between Maderna's later and Michelangelo's earlier work. Bernini's task was to create a harmonized whole. The first problem was the junction of the nave with the eastern wall of Michelangelo's square plan. As this wall supports the oblique thrust of the weight of the dome, it could not be pierced to create a wide monumental doorway similar to the entrance doors in the nave. Bernini's solution was to erect two columns, like those flanking the doorways in the nave, and to fill the space below the arch and the pediment with a shield supported by two angels. As a result the passage suffers a scarcely perceptible narrowing. The second problem was the pier (**B**) which could not be pierced as it supports the dome. He erected two columns and an arch of identical size to those in the passage. The visitor approaching along the north aisle of the church receives an impression of depth accentuated by the two narrow arches.

Gregory XIII's Monument ★ (13). — The low relief carving on the white marble sarcophagus (1723) illustrates the reform of the calendar which the Pope instituted in 1582. The Gregorian calendar has now been adopted world-wide.

Gregory XIV's Monument (14). — According to legend the monument was despoiled to meet the expense of the Pope's illness which had to be treated with a mixture of gold and precious stones. The plaster sarcophagus was not faced with marble until 1842.

Clement XIII's Monument ★★★ (15). — The fine neo-Classical design by Canova dates from 1792. The lack of emotion for which Canova's art is often criticised here contributes to the purity of line; the balance of the whole is however upset by the statue on the left which represents the triumph of religion.

Pictures in mosaic. — It was in 16C that famous pictures began to be copied in mosaic. In the spirit of the Counter-Reformation the church hoped thus to make its glories more intelligible to the faithful. This practice was further developed when Benedict XIII founded a mosaic school in 1727. These mosaics therefore have immense religious significance. They illustrate the power of Peter; his walking on the water (16) and his raising of Tabitha (17); they celebrate the martyrs, popes, saints and angels challenged by the Reformation.

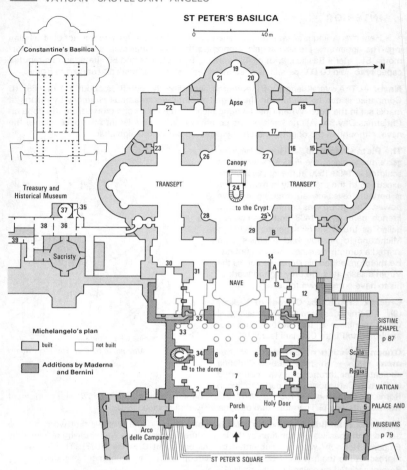

ST PETER'S BASILICA

0   40 m

St Michael's or **St Petronilla's Chapel** (18). — The mosaic illustrates St Petronilla's mar-tyrdom after a painting by Guercino *(p 60)*. St Petronilla, whose relics lie beneath the altar, was venerated in St Peter's from 8C. Pepin the Short built a chapel to her in which Michel-angelo's Pietà was to have stood.

Apse. — The dominant feature is **'St Peter's Chair' ★★★ (19)**, an extraordinary work designed by **Bernini** to contain the remains of an ancient episcopal chair said to have been used by St Peter; these remains, which date from 4C, are encased in a throne, decorated with ivory, which was given to John VIII by Charles the Bold at his coronation in 875. Bernini's throne is made of sculpted bronze apparently supported by the four great doctors of the Church (measuring between 4.50 m and 5.50 m - 15 ft and 18 ft). Above is a gilded stucco ''gloria'', veiled in clouds and a host of cherubs. Silhouetted against a sun-like central opening, which lets in the light, is the dove of the Holy Ghost (its wing span is 1.75 m - just under 6 ft). This work, completed in 1666 when Bernini was in his seventies, is a crowning example of his astounding art, full of movement and light.

Urban VIII's Monument ★★★ (20). — This work by **Bernini**, commissioned in 1628 and finished in 1647, is considered to be the masterpiece of 17C funerary art. His hand raised majestically in blessing, the Pope sits enthroned above the sarcophagus, surrounded by statues of Jus-tice and Charity, while death inscribes his name.

Paul III's Monument ★★★ (21). — **Guglielmo della Porta** (1500?-77), a follower of Michelangelo, conceived a grandiose project: the monument was to be surrounded by eight allegorical statues and placed in the centre of the chancel. Michelangelo objected and asked for the number of statues to be reduced to four. When Bernini altered the apse in 1628 he reduced the number to two (the other two statues are in the Farnese Palace, *p 114*).

St Leo the Great's Altar (22). — The altarpiece is a 'picture in marble' by **Algardi** of the Pope halting Attila at the gates of Rome. This type of sculpture, which resembles a picture owing to the vivid effects it creates, is characteristic of Baroque art.

Alexander VII's Monument ★ (23). — **Bernini** completed this monument in 1678, two years before his death. He was anxious that he himself should sculpt the head of the Pope who was his protector.

The Pope kneels among allegorical statues, the work of pupils who, in their effort to imitate their master, have somewhat exaggerated the effect of movement. Even Bernini's own art gives way to excess here (death is represented by a skeleton draped in mottled marble beckoning the Pope).

Baldaquin ★★★. — **Bernini's** canopy, begun in 1624, was unveiled by Urban VIII in 1633. Despite the weight of the bronze and its great height (29 m - 95 ft - the height of the Farnese Palace), it has captured the light-weight effect of an original baldaquin, usually made of wood and cloth to be carried in processions. As the eye is caught by the wreathed columns, the valance seems to stir. The bees (on the columns and valance) are from the arms of the Barberini family to which Urban VIII belonged.

The work attracted much criticism, first because the bronze had been taken from the Pantheon *(p 105)* and also because it was thought to be too theatrical and in bad taste.

The high altar below the baldaquin, where only the Pope may celebrate mass, stands over the confessio (24), designed by Maderna, which contains St Peter's tomb.

Piers of the Crossing. — Begun by Bramante and completed by Michelangelo, they stand at the crossing of the transepts. Their austerity did not please Baroque taste and in 1629 Bernini faced them in marble and created recesses at the base in which he placed four statues about 5 m - 16 ft high. Above them he designed balcony chapels for the exhibition of relics and re-used the wreathed columns from the baldaquin of the 4C church which had inspired his own canopy.

Each statue represents the relics deposited in the basilica: a fragment of the spear (St Longinus — 25 — by Bernini commemorates the soldier who pierced Jesus' side with his spear, which has become a symbol of pity); the napkin bearing the Holy Image (St Veronica — 26 — wiped Jesus' face on the road to Calvary); a fragment of the True Cross (St Helena — 27 — brought the remains of the Cross to Rome); St Andrew's head (St Andrew — 28). The last three statues are by Bernini's collaborators: Francesco Mochi, Andrea Bolgi and François Duquesnoy.

Dome ★★★. — Bramante's design was for a dome resembling the one on the Pantheon but **Michelangelo** made it larger and raised it higher. He himself carried out the work up to the lantern; it was finished in 1593 by **Giacomo della Porta** and **Domenico Fontana**. It is the largest dome in Rome; the whole building seems to have been designed to support it, a symbol of God's perfection.

The pendentives carry four mosaic medallions, 8 m - 26 ft across, representing the Evangelists. Above in Latin are Christ's words to Peter: "Thou art Peter and upon this rock I will build my church; and I will give unto thee the keys of the kingdom of heaven". The interior of the dome is decorated with figures of the popes and the Doctors of the Church; seated are Christ, Mary, Joseph, John the Baptist and the Apostles; above them are angels. The figure on the ceiling of the lantern is God the Father.

Statue of St Peter ★★ (29). — This 13C bronze by Arnolfo di Cambio is greatly venerated. Countless pilgrims have kissed its foot. It is said to have been made out of the bronze statue of Jupiter on the Capitol.

Pius VII's Tomb (30). — Pius VII died in 1823 after bearing the brunt of the Napoleonic storm. His tomb was designed by Thorwaldsen, a Dane *(p 173)*.

Leo XI's Monument (31). — **Algardi** was responsible for the white marble monument (1642-44). The low relief sculpture on the sarcophagus illustrates Henri IV's conversion to Roman Catholicism; the King is being received by the future Pope who was then Clement VIII's legate.

Innocent VIII's Monument ★★★ (32). — This is a Renaissance work by Antonio del Pollaiuolo (1432?-98), one of the few monuments to be preserved from the earlier church. The tomb is designed in typical 15C style against a wall.

When the monument was re-erected in 1621 the two figures were reversed; originally the recumbent figure was above the Pope, signifying the supreme power of death. An error has crept into the epitaph which says that the Pope 'lived' *(vixit)* rather than reigned for 8 years, 10 months and 25 days.

John XXIII's Monument (33). — The low relief sculpture on the right of the Chapel of the Presentation is by a contemporary artist, Emilio Greco.

Stuart Monument (34). — **Canova** designed this work (1817-19) to the glory of the last members of the Scottish Royal family: James Edward, Charles Edward and Henry Benedict, who are buried in the crypt *(pp 112, 157)*. The monument was commissioned by the Prince Regent and paid for by George III. The angels ★ in low relief were much admired by Stendhal who also remarked that "George IV, in keeping with his reputation as the most accomplished gentleman in the three kingdoms, wished to honour the ashes of the unhappy princes whom he would have sent to the scaffold had they fallen into his hands alive".

Treasury and Historical Museum ★★. — *Open 9 am to 12 noon and 3 to 6 pm (5 pm from 1 October to 31 March). 2 000 L.*

The Treasury has been pillaged on many occasions — by the Saracens in 846, during the sack of Rome in 1527, by Bonaparte under the Treaty of Tolentino in 1797 — but it has always been built up again and today contains gifts from many countries.

The first **room** (35) contains two momentoes of the 4C basilica: the 'Holy Column' which is identical to those re-used by Bernini in the balcony chapels in the piers supporting the dome; the gilded metal cockerel (9C) which Leo IV had placed on top of the basilica. The adjoining **room** (36) houses a fine dalmatic said to have belonged to Charlemagne (it is in fact a Byzantine style liturgical vestment dating from 10C at the earliest); also a copy of the wood and ivory chair contained in Bernini's throne *(p 76)*.

77

In the beautiful **Benefactors' Chapel (37)** is a tabernacle attributed to Donatello, a Renaissance master artist from Florence; the plaster model of Michelangelo's Pietà proved valuable when the original was damaged in 1972. In the next **room (38)** stands the **tomb of Sixtus IV ★★★** by Antonio del Pollaiuolo (1493), a masterpiece of bronze sculpture (accurate portraiture and delicate craftsmanship). Several rooms, glittering with gold and silver ware and liturgical objects, including a terracotta version of Bernini's angel before it was cast in bronze for the Chapel of the Blessed Sacrament *(p 75),* lead into the **gallery (39)** displaying the tiara of silver and gold and precious stones with which St Peter's statue is crowned on ceremonial occasions. **Junius Bassus' sarcophagus ★★★** (4C) was found beneath the basilica and is a remarkable example of Christian funerary sculpture, richly decorated with biblical scenes; on the sides are children gathering the harvest, a symbol of the souls saved by the Eucharist.

Ascent to the top of the Dome. — *Open 8 am to 6 pm (5 pm in winter). 1 500 L by lift; 1 000 L on foot.*

From a broad terrace at the foot of the dome there is a view of the roof of the transept and nave of the basilica and of the fortress-like building of the Sistine Chapel. It is 92 m - 302 ft from the roof terrace to the top of the cross which is 132.5 m - 434 ft above ground level. There is also an extensive view of the city from the east balustrade, which is surmounted by huge statues of Christ and John the Baptist and the Apostles (excluding Peter). From the rear of the terrace a stairway climbs up to a gallery in the drum from which the decorations of the interior of the dome *(p 77)* and the dimensions of the basilica can be appreciated. Two people, diametrically opposite one another and facing the wall, can hold a conversation in a low voice.

The stairway continues up to an external gallery surrounding the lantern at 120 m - 394 ft above St Peter's Square; the **view ★★★** is magnificent: the geometric precision of the square, a model of architectural urban planning; the Vatican City including an interesting aspect of the papal palaces *(p 79);* the whole city of Rome from the Janiculum to Monte Mario.

Vatican 'Grottoes'. — *Access in the northeast pier supporting the dome; open 8 am to 6 pm (5 pm 1 October to 31 March). Only part of the grottoes is open to the public.*

The grottoes embrace the area beneath the basilica containing the papal tombs and parts of the earlier basilica. They consist of a semi-circular section which follows the line of Constantine's apse, with the Ad Caput Chapel *(see below)* on the eastern side, and three aisles projecting eastwards.

In the centre of the apsidal passage are Pius XII's tomb *(west)* and the Ad Caput Chapel *(east).*

The low relief sculptures by Antonio del Pollaiuolo (15C) on the inner wall of the passage illustrate the lives of St Peter and St Paul.

Among the tombs in the aisles are those of Pope John XXIII, Christina of Sweden, Benedict XV and Hadrian IV, born Nicholas Breakspear, the only English Pope.

Vatican Necropolis. — *Guided tour: p 69.* The entrance to the excavations carried out in 1939 on the orders of Pius XII are on the south side of the basilica. Through one of the supporting walls of Constantine's basilica is the **necropolis** he had levelled in order to build his church. Two rows of tombs, dating from 1C to 4C AD are separated by a path sloping down to the Tiber and approximately parallel to the present basilica. One of the tombs, situated at the eastern end of the path, bears the inscription at the entrance indicating the occupant's wish to be buried "in Vaticano ad circum". This discovery confirmed the proximity of Nero's Circus where Peter may have met his death. The earlier tombs were re-used by the Christians, among them the tomb of a child of the Julian family, which contains the earliest known Christian mosaics from before the 4C. A vine pattern surrounds the figure of Christ haloed by sunbeams and driving a chariot.

St Peter's Tomb. — Near to the apse of the present church at right angles to the sloping path is another path bordered on its eastern side by a 2C wall; behind it was discovered a shrine composed of three niches and two small columns which in the 2C may have marked the humble tomb of St Peter. This is why Constantine decided to build his church on this spot although it was uneven and marshy and still in use as a graveyard at the time.

The position of St Peter's tomb has aroused lively controversy among historians, archaeologists and theologians. Until the Vatican excavations were made, his tomb was thought to be in St Sebastian's Catacombs *(p 146).* According to M Carcopino, the saint's relics have had a hazardous existence. Fearing desecration during the Valerian persecution, the Christians may have moved them in 258 to St Sebastian's Catacombs which did not then belong to the church and were therefore unlikely to attract attention from the authorities. Not until 336, when Christians were again entitled to practise their religion, would the relics have been returned to their original resting place in the Vatican.

Clementine Chapel. — This is the **Ad Caput Chapel** (at the head of St Peter). It stands behind the shrine very close to the Apostle's tomb. Some bones, found in one of the walls which in 3C bordered the shrine to the north, are displayed by the guide; they may be the bones of St Peter.

Churches are usually closed from 12 noon to 4 pm.
Visitors are requested not to walk about during services.

■ VATICAN MUSEUMS ★★★ *(Plan pp 80-81)*

They are housed in part of the palaces which the popes began to build in 13C.

The Palaces. — It was probably during the reign of Pope Symmachus (498-514) that some buildings were erected to the north of St Peter's Basilica. Nicholas III (1277-80) intended to replace them with a fortress and towers but his project was only partially realised. Upon their return from Avignon in 1377 the popes gave up living in the Lateran Palace, which had been destroyed by fire, and settled in the Vatican.

Nicholas V (1447-55) decided to enlarge the accommodation. Around the Parrot Court (Cortile del Pappagallo) he constructed a palace incorporating the 13C buildings. He kept the fortress-like exterior but the interior was sumptuously decorated. The chapel by Fra Angelico can still be seen. Almost all the popes have altered or enlarged Nicolas V's palace.

Sixtus IV (1471-84) established a library on the ground floor of the north wing (now a conference room used by the Pope) and built the Sistine Chapel to the west. About 300 m - 984 ft north of Nicholas V's palace, **Innocent VIII** (1484-92) built a summer residence, the Belvedere Palace. From 1493 to 1494 **Alexander VI** added the Borgia Tower to Nicholas V's palace and created his own apartments above Sixtus IV's library.

Pope **Julius II** (1503-13) commissioned Bramante to link Nicholas V's and Innocent VIII's palaces by two long narrow galleries, thus creating the Belvedere Court (Cortile del Belvedere), a huge rectangular courtyard, which provided a setting for grandiose spectacles and was later divided into the present Library and Pine Cone Courts (Cortile della Biblioteca e Cortile della Pigna). He lived above Alexander VI's apartments in the rooms which Nicholas V had had painted by Piero della Francesca, Benedotto Bonfigli and Andrea del Castagno and had them redecorated by Raphael *(p 84)*. The façade of the palace was too austere for his taste so he had another built consisting of three loggias, one above another. The second floor loggia was decorated by Raphael *(p 86)*.

Paul III (1534-49) strengthened the foundations and restored the southwest wing of the early palace.

Pius IV (1559-65) commissioned Pirro Ligorio to alter the Belvedere Court. To the north (on the Belvedere Palace side) the architect constructed a large semi-circular niche before which was erected the Pigna, a huge pine cone, which had adorned the fountain in the *atrium* of Constantine's basilica *(p 73)* . The design is based on Classical architecture, particularly Domitian's Stadium on the Palatine Hill *(p 49)*. To the south, backing on to Nicholas V's palace, he created a semi-circular façade one storey high with a central niche. Later the Belvedere Court was divided by two transverse galleries: between 1587 and 1588 during the reign of Sixtus V, Domenico Fontana built the Papal Library (Sistine Rooms); later, between 1806 and 1823 Pius VII built the New Wing (Braccio Nuovo).

The Belvedere Court was thus divided into three separate courts: the Belvedere Court (Cortile del Belvedere), the Library Court (della Biblioteca), the Pine Cone Court (della Pigna).

During the Baroque period the only addition to the Vatican Palace was the Scala Regia *(not open)*, a monumental stairway constructed by Bernini between 1633 and 1666. From the Great Bronze Door (Portone di bronzo) which is the main entrance to the palace *(plan p 70)* a long corridor along the north side of St Peter's Square leads to the foot of the Scala Regia (Royal Stairway).

The Papal Court. — By providing his nephews with ecclesiastical titles and benefices *(p 18)* and surrounding himself with rich cardinals, artists and men of letters, Sixtus IV (1471-84) created a virtual court like that of a secular prince.

The present Papal Residence. — The 16C buildings surrounding Sixtus V's Court (Cortile di Sisto V) *(plan p 70)* contain the present papal apartments. Heads of State, diplomats and other important people enter the Vatican City by the Bell Arch (Arco delle Campane) **(R)**. Papal receptions are held in the Pope's private library, a large room between Sixtus V's Court (Cortile di Sisto V) and Majordomo Court (Cortile del Maggiordomo).

In the summer the Pope moves to Castel Gandolfo *(p 212)*, a property 120 km - 75 miles southeast of Rome.

The Museums. — Their origins go back to 1503 when Julius II displayed a few Classical works of art in the Belvedere Court. His successors continued to collect Greek and Roman, palaeo-Christian and Christian antiquities. After acquiring a number of antiques with the lottery revenues, Clement XIV created a new museum, which was enlarged by Pius VI and is called the Pio-Clementino after the two popes. The rooms joining the Belvedere Palace to the West Gallery, now occupied by the Apostolic Library, were constructed by the architect Simonetti as an extension.

Following the Treaty of Tolentino in 1797 many works of art were sent to Paris. Those that were left were arranged by Canova, who had been appointed Inspector General of Fine Arts and Antiquities belonging to the State and the Church by Pope Pius VII, in a museum called the Chiaramonti Museum (after the Pope's family name). When the lost works were returned in 1816 Pius VII built the New Wing (Braccio Nuovo) to house them.

In 1838 Gregory XVI opened an Etruscan Museum to house the results of private excavations; an Egyptian musuem followed in 1839.

The Art Gallery (Pinacoteca) was opened in 1932 by Pius XI.

1970 saw the inauguration of a very modern building to house the Antique and Christian Art Collections formerly in the Lateran Palace.

The Missionary collections were transferred from the Lateran in 1973, the same year as the creation of the History Museum and the Museum of Modern Religious Art.

For the interest and diversity of their treasures the Vatican museums rank among the best in the world.

TOUR

Open from 9 am to 2 pm (5 pm in the week preceding and following Easter Sunday, in July, August and September; during these three months closes at 2 pm on Saturday); ticket office shuts 1 hour before closing time.

Closed Sunday, 6 January, 11 February, 19 March, Easter Monday, 1 May, Ascension Day, Corpus Christi, 29 June, 15 and 16 August, 1 November, 8, 25 and 26 December.

In addition the museums are open from 9 am to 2 pm on the first Sunday in the month unless it coincides with one of the holidays listed above. 5 000 L.

Temporary closures are announced at the entrance.

Entrance: Viale Vaticano.

Allow 3 hours for visiting the sections which are highly recommended, 1 day for the whole museum.

The present entrance hall was opened in 1932. A spiral ramp with a sculpted bronze balustrade leads up to the ticket offices from which the museums are reached either through the Cortile delle Corazze (Cuirasses) or through the Atrio dei Quattro Cancelli (Atrium of the Four Gates) and Simonetti's 18C staircase (Ⓐ *on the plan*).

Visitors must follow the official one-way tour, which has options at various points and is liable to variation; see plan below.

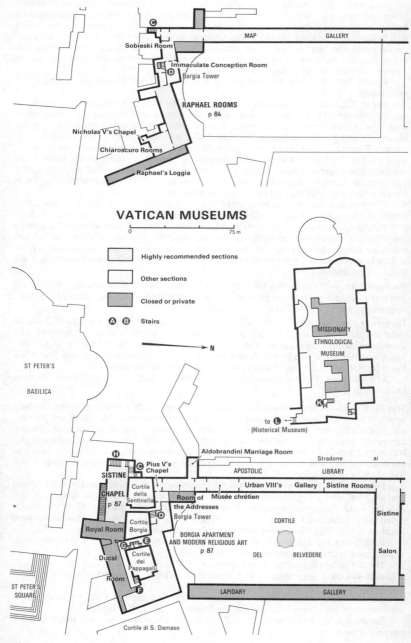

Pio-Clementino Museum ★★★ (Greek and Roman antiquities)

The official tour may pass through the Egyptian and Chiaramonti Museums *(p 83)* before reaching the Pio-Clementino Museum in the Torso Vestibule *(p 83; plan p 82)*. This museum is housed in the Belvedere Palace and the rooms added by Simonetti in 18C.

Greek Cross Room. — Two large porphyry **sarcophagi** ★ predominate: the one (1) belonging to St Helena, the Emperor Constantine's mother, dates from early 4C and is heavily sculptured with conquering Roman cavalry and barbarian prisoners, an inappropriate theme for such a holy woman, which suggests that the sarcophagus was originally intended for her husband, Constantinus Chlorus, or her son Constantine, who may have had it made before moving his court to Constantinople; the other (2) is the sarcophagus of Constance, Constantine's daughter, and dates from 350-60 AD.

Round Room ★. — This fine room by Simonetti (1780) was inspired by the Pantheon. The monolithic porphyry **basin** (3) may have come from Nero's Golden House. The **statue of Hercules** (4) in gilded bronze dates from the late 2C. **Antinoüs** (5), a young favourite of the Emperor Hadrian, drowned himself in the Nile in 130. After his death, the Emperor raised him to the ranks of the gods. He bears the attributes of Dionysius and the Egyptian god Osiris (on his head is the Uraeus, a serpent which formed part of the headdress of the Pharaohs). The **bust of Jupiter ★** (6) is a Roman copy of a Greek original dating from 4 BC.

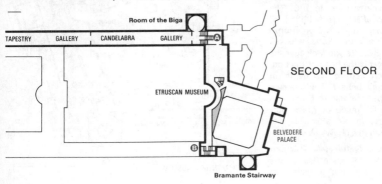

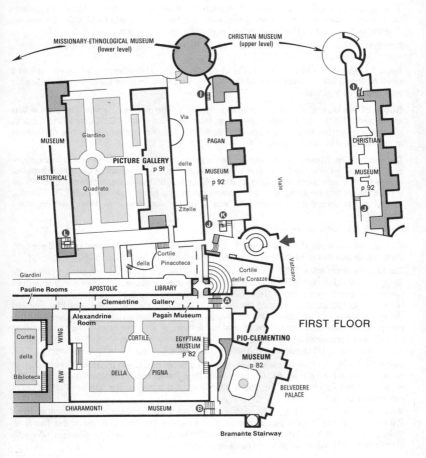

Room of the Muses. — It owes its name to the statues of the Muses which, together with statues of Greek philosophers, are arranged around the room.

The Belvedere Torso ★★★ (7). — Like the statue of the Pugilist (in the National Roman Museum, *p 120*), this is the masterly work of the Athenian Apollonius, Nestor's son, who lived in Rome in 1C BC. The expressive torso, which was part of a statue of Hercules seated, was much admired by Michelangelo.

Room of the Animals. — Various animal sculptures, heavily restored in 19C. The **statue of Meleager ★ (8)** is a 2C Roman copy of a bronze sculpture by Skopas a Greek (4C BC). Beside Meleager the hunter is the head of the boar which caused his death at Diana's behest. The fine **mosaic** pavements are Roman. A **crab (9)** made of green porphyry, a rare stone, is displayed in a show case.

Statue Gallery. — This part of the Belvedere Palace was converted into a gallery in 18C.

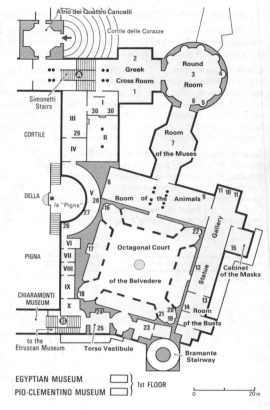

Sleeping Ariadne ★ (10). — Roman copy of a Greek original illustrating the characteristic taste for unusual poses and elaborate draperies of the Hellenistic period (2C BC). On waking Ariadne will be married to Dionysius and carried away to Olympus.

Candelabra (11). — These fine examples of 2C Roman decorative art come from Hadrian's Villa at Tivoli *(p 202).*

Apollo Sauroktonos ★ (12). — This statue of Apollo about to kill a lizard is a Roman copy of a work by Praxiteles, a Greek artist of the 4C BC. An expert in feminine models he made his young god very graceful.

Room of the Busts. — The gallery is sub-divided by fine marble columns. The **busts of Cato and Portia ★ (13)**, a husband and wife group, intended for a tomb (1C BC) are in the typically austere style of the Republican era. The numerous imperial portraits include a particularly expressive bust of Julius Caesar **(14)**.

Cabinet of the Masks. — It owes its name to the mosaic of masks removed from Hadrian's Villa and let into the floor. The **Venus of Cnidos ★★ (15)** is a Roman copy of Praxiteles' statue for the sanctuary at Cnidos in Asia Minor (4C BC) which was famous both for its artistic merits and for being the first representation of a goddess in the nude. The Greeks, versed in the legend of Actaeon who was killed for watching a goddess bathing, were shocked.

Return to the Room of the Animals.

Octagonal Court of the Belvedere ★. — The original internal courtyard of the Belvedere Palace acquired its octagonal outline when Simonetti added a portico in 18C.

The Laocoön Group ★★★ (16). — One morning in January 1506 the architect Giuliano de Sangallo rushed up to Michelangelo inviting him to come and see an extraordinary sculpture which was being unearthed in Nero' Golden House. This was the work of a group of artists from Rhodes (1C BC) representing the death of Laocoön, priest of Apollo, who had incurred the god's anger and, together with his two sons, was crushed to death by serpents. In this composition Hellenistic art attains an intense realism; in an attempt to show the extremes of suffering it achieved an exaggerated style which earned the description "Greek Baroque". The plaster copy **(17)** dates from the time before Laocoön's right arm was discovered.

Apollo ★★★ (18). — The statue was placed in the Belvedere Court by Julius II in 1503. It is probably copied from a 4C BC Greek original by a Roman sculptor who has captured the serenity of the Greek gods. The figure may have held a bow in the left hand and a laurel wreath in the right.

Works by Canova (1757-1822). — Pope Pius VII bought these three neo-Classical statues from Canova to make up for the loss of certain works removed under the terms of the Treaty of Tolentino: **Perseus ★★ (19)**, who conquered Medusa, and the boxers Kreugas **(20)** and Damozenos **(21)**, who met in fierce combat at Nemea.

Hermes★★★ (22). — This 2C AD Roman work, inspired by Praxiteles' Greek style, represents Zeus' son, the messenger of the gods.

The Athlete★★★ (23). — The athlete, scraping his skin with a strigil after taking exercise, is by a 1C AD Roman artist who copied the Greek original by Lysippus (4C BC). No other copies are known. In the weary body the artist reveals the living human being rather than an idealistic image as in the Classical period.

The Bramante Stairway. — The noble spiral stairway, which was used by men on horseback, was designed by Bramante early in 16C during the alterations ordered by Julius II *(p 79)*.

The Torso Vestibule. — The belvedere Torso was displayed here until 1973.

Sarcophagus of Scipio Barbatus (24). — The sobriety of early Roman art shows in the sarcophagus, carved in peperine (3C BC). Its shape is inspired by the Greek models which the Romans discovered after the capture of Rhegium in 270 BC.

"Ara Casali" (25). — Given to Pius VI by the Casali family, this altar is decorated with the legend of Mars and Venus on the front and of Romulus and Remus on the back; it is probably 3C AD.

Chiaramonti Museum and Lapidary Gallery

The **Chiaramonti Museum** was set up by Pius VII, whose family name was Chiaramonti, and has generally kept the appearance given to it by Canova in 1807. It contains Roman copies of Greek works, portraits, funerary monuments; obviously a miller is commemorated by the low reliefs of a millstone, donkey, baskets etc. *(on the right, Row X)*.

The **Lapidary Gallery** houses over 5 000 pagan and Christian inscriptions *(open to specialists on request)*.

Egyptian Museum

Founded by Pope Gregory XVI, it was laid out in 1839 by Father Ungarelli, one of the first Italian Egyptologists to take an interest in Champollion's work. Most of the items come from the Egyptian temple of Isis in the Campus Martius.

In the **hemicycle (V)** are three huge granite statues (26) of members of the dynasty founded by Ptolemy I (366-283 BC).

The fine Pharaoh's head (27) of 11th Dynasty, dating from about 2000 BC and bearing traces of colour, exemplifies the art of the Middle Empire.

The colossal statue (28) is Rameses II's mother who lived about 1300 BC (New Empire art).

In **Room III** is a copy of the Rosetta Stone (29) discovered in 1799 by French troops at Rosetta near the Nile delta and now in the British Museum; it dates from 196 BC and bears three inscriptions, one in hieroglyphics, one in demotic writing and the third in Greek which enabled the French Egyptologist Champollion to decipher the hieroglyphics in 1822. Other exhibits are Roman works inspired by Egyptian art.

In **Room II** is a reproduction of a tomb from the Valley of the Kings: fine sarcophagi in white sandstone, basalt and painted wood and mummies from various periods.

Room I contains two lions (30) bearing the name of a 4C BC pharaoh.

Climb the Simonetti stairs (Ⓐ) or stairway (Ⓑ) to the second floor.

Etruscan Museum ★ *(plan pp 80-81)*

Founded in 1837 by Gregory XVI, the museum houses objects excavated in southern Etruria. The items found in the **Regolini-Galassi tomb** (named after the Archbishop and the General who discovered it in 1836) south of Cerveteri and displayed in **Room II** are particularly fine. A man and a woman of high rank were buried there; a third may have been cremated. In the showcases along the wall on the right of the entrances are displayed the items found in the tomb; belonging to the woman were the bronze throne and jewellery; the incomparable golden **clasp**★★, decorated with lions and ducks in the round and dating from 7C BC, shows the perfection attained by the Etruscans in such work; the incised pectoral medallion lay on the woman's breast surrounded by golden leaves (fragments) sewn on to her dress. The man lay on the bronze couch; the two horse chariot *(biga)* would also have been his.

The little vase in *bucchero (p 21)* is inscribed with an alphabet and a syllabary *(penultimate showcase facing the windows near the door to Room III)*. The **Bronze Room (III)** houses the **Mars**★★ found at Todi, a rare example of a large bronze statue from 5C BC. The style of the work is akin to the rigour of Classical Greek works. The oval cist *(last case to the right of the Mars)*, a toilette receptacle, is attractively decorated with the Battle of the Amazons; fantastic figures adorn the handle.

The subsequent rooms *(often closed)* contain urns, ceramics, bronzes, gilt or *bucchero* items, jewellery and terracotta; Roman and original Greek works are displayed in the rooms next to the Stairway of the Assyrian Reliefs (Ⓒ *on plan*); the hemicycle and the adjoining rooms contain many Greek, Etruscan and Italiot vases from 6 to 3C BC.

Room of the Biga *(plan pp 80-81)*

The **two horse chariot**★★ *(biga)* after which the hall is named is 1C Roman. It was reconstituted in 18C when the body of the chariot was recovered from St Mark's Basilica where it had served as a papal throne.

Candelabra Gallery (plan pp 80-81)

The loggia was transformed into a gallery in 1785 by Pius VI. It is subdivided by arches and pillars flanked by 2C marble candelabra and houses antiquities.

Tapestry Gallery (plan pp 80-81)

The tapestries were hung by Gregory XVI in 1838. Facing the windows: the series was woven by Pieter van Aelst's workshops in Brussels from cartoons by Raphael's pupils. On the window side: the life of Cardinal Maffeo Barberini, later Pope Urban VIII (17C Roman).

Map Gallery ★ (plan pp 80-81)

The ceiling is richly decorated with stuccowork and paintings by a group of 16C Mannerists. The extraordinary maps on the walls were painted by Fr Ignazio Danti between 1580 and 1583, who explained that he had divided Italy in two down the line of the Apennines: the one side bathed by the Ligurian and Tyrrhenian seas, the other bordered by the Alps and the Adriatic. The 40 maps are supplemented by town plans, a map of the region round Avignon (once a papal possession) and two maps of Corfu and Malta. The 16C cartography is fantastically embellished with inscriptions, ships and turbulent seas.

Sobieski and Immaculate Conception Rooms (plan pp 80-81)

In the former hangs a 19C painting of John III Sobieski, king of Poland, repulsing the Turks at the siege of Vienna (1683). The 19C frescoes in the latter illustrate the dogma of the Immaculate Conception pronounced by Pius IX in 1854; an elaborate showcase displays richly decorated books on the same theme.

Raphael Rooms ★★★ (Stanze di Rafaello)

These rooms had been built during the reign of Nicholas V (1447-55) and decorated with frescoes by Piero della Francesca among others. On becoming pope in 1503, Julius II arranged to have them redecorated for his own use by a group of artists which included Sodoma and Perugino. In 1508 on Bramante's recommendation he sent for a young painter from Urbino. Charmed by Raphael's youthful grace, he entrusted the whole of the decoration to him; the other painters were dismissed and their work effaced. The frescoes in what came to be known as the "Raphael Stanze" are among the masterpieces of the Renaissance. They were damaged by the troops of Charles V during the sack of Rome in 1527 but have been restored.

Room of the Borgo Fire (1514-17). — This was the last room to be painted by Raphael. The immediate success of his work and the large number of commissions that followed led him to speed up his work. From 1515 he worked with a group of assistants. In this room he only designed the frescoes which were completed by his assistants. The ceiling frescoes are by Perugino.

To glorify the reign of Leo X, Julian II's successor, who had confirmed Raphael in his appointment, the artist painted the life of the Pope and of his predecessors Leo III and Leo IV. In the fresco of the **Coronation of Charlemagne** (1) the emperor is portrayed as François I and Leo II as Leo X (who signed the Concordat of Bologna with François I in 1516).

The Borgo Fire (2). — According to the mediaeval legend a fire which broke out in 847 in the area near St Peter's (the Borgo) was quenched by Pope Leo IV with the sign of the cross. Inspired, like all Renaissance artists by antiquity, Raphael painted the colonnade of the Temple of Mars Ultor on the left; the old man supported by a youth recalls Virgil (Aeneas fleeing from Troy, carrying his father Anchises, his son Ascanius at his side, while his wife Creusa follows behind).

On the right an elegant young woman is carrying a water jar. In the background stands the mediaeval façade of St Peter's decorated with mosaics.

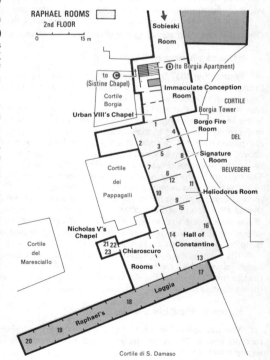

RAPHAEL ROOMS ☐
2nd FLOOR
0   15 m

Sobieski Room

to Ⓒ (Sistine Chapel)
Ⓓ (to Borgia Apartment)

Cortile Borgia
Immaculate Conception Room

Urban VIII's Chapel

CORTILE
Borgia Tower

Borgo Fire Room
DEL

Signature Room
BELVEDERE

Cortile dei Pappagalli

Heliodorus Room

Nicholas V's Chapel

Hall of Constantine

Cortile del Maresciallo

Chiaroscuro Rooms

Loggia

Raphael's

Cortile di S. Damaso

Battle of Ostia (3). — Here Leo X is again represented in the guise of Leo IV who defeated the Saracens at the battle of Ostia in 849.

Oath of Leo III (4). — According to the mediaeval account, when Leo III sought to clear himself of a libel in St Peter's itself, a voice rang out declaring "It is for God not men to judge bishops" (Latin inscription to the right of the window).

Signature Room (Stanza della Segnatura) (1508-11). — It it not clear whether this room was used as a library, a study or for signing papal bulls. Raphael painted it himself after being appointed by Julius II. The decorative theme, probably proposed by a court scholar versed in neo-Platonic philosophy, illustrates the three great principles of the human spirit: Truth, Goodness and Beauty.

The ceiling (medallions) and wall paintings illustrate closely linked subjects: allegories of Philosophy and Theology appear above the School of Athens and the Glorification of Religion (Dispute over the Blessed Sacrament) respectively, representing two aspects of Truth: the rational and the supernatural. Above the fresco illustrating canon law and civil law and the cardinal virtues, representing Goodness, is the allegory of Justice, while Poetry, representing Beauty, crowns Parnassus. Smaller paintings in the pendentives underline the allegorical figures: Adam and Eve — the prime mover of the world (a woman imparts movement to the universe), the Judgment of Solomon, Apollo and Marsyas.

Some of the work on the ceiling is attributed to Sodoma.

Dispute over the Blessed Sacrament (5). — This name is wrongly attributed to the fresco illustrating the Glorification of Religion: at the top surrounding the Trinity, appears the Church victorious with Mary, John the Baptist, the Apostles, Prophets and Patriarchs, martyrs and angels.

On earth, grouped round the altar, stand the Doctors of the Church, the Popes and the faithful including Dante (right, crowned with laurel). The lines converge on the Host, the incarnation of Christ, linking the Church on Earth and the Church in Heaven.

The School of Athens (6). — Beneath the vaults of a Classical building designed by Bramante stands a crowd of philosophers. In the centre are the Greeks, Plato and Aristotle, representing the two main streams of Classical thought: idealism and materialism. Plato's raised finger indicates the realm of ideas, Aristotle's open hand indicates that without the material world ideas would have not existence. Raphael has given Plato the face of Leonardo da Vinci.

On the left, Socrates, in a tunic, is speaking to his pupil Alcibiades. The cynic Diogenes is lounging contemptuously on the steps before a disapproving follower. Epicurus, in a laurel wreath, is giving a dissertation on pleasure, while Archimedes, who resembles Bramante, is tracing geometric figures on a slate. In the righthand corner Raphael has included himself in a black beret standing next to another painter, Sodoma, in a tunic and white beret.

Michelangelo is there also, a solitary figure in the foreground, his head resting on his left hand. At this time he was painting the Sistine Chapel. Raphael added him after the fresco was finished in noble homage to his rival.

The Cardinal Virtues (7). — Above the window are Strength (oak branch, emblem of the della Rovere family to which Julius II belonged), Prudence and Temperance. On the right Raimond de Pennafort hands Gregory IX (1234) the body of rules which make up canon law (Decretals); on the left Justinian approves the "Pandects", a collection of Roman jurisprudence, comprising civil law. Gregory IX is a portrait of Julius I. Beside him stand Cardinal Giovanni de Medici (future Leo X) and Alessandro Farnese (future Paul III).

The "Parnassus" (8). — Around Apollo and the nine Muses are grouped the great poets, starting with Homer and Virgil.

Heliodorus Room (1512-1514). — Not all the paintings are by Raphael.

Expulsion of Heliodorus from the Temple (9). — The biblical subject, taken from the Book of Maccabees (Heliodorus, intent on stealing the temple treasure, is expelled by the angels), was probably chosen by Julius II himself, whose own policy was to expel usurpers from papal property. He appears on the left in the papal chair. It is an excellent portrait revealing the authority of the Pope who fought alongside his own soldiers and one day broke his cane across Michelangelo's back. This fresco is exceptional for Raphael in the vigour and movement of the figures (Heliodorus, the three angels and a person flattening himself against a pillar).

Miracle of the Bolsena Mass (10). — The miracle, which started the feast of Corpus Christi, took place in 1263 when a priest, who doubted the doctrine of the real presence, saw blood on the host at the moment of consecration while celebrating mass in Bolsena. Julius II is kneeling before the priest. The Pope, his suite and the Swiss guards are among Raphael's masterpieces.

The composition is masterly. The problem of the round lunette with its off-centre window is accommodated by the asymetric positioning of the stairs on either side of the altar and by the lively treatment of the crowd on the left where the painting is most restricted.

St Peter delivered from prison (11). — According to the Acts of the Apostles, while in prison in Rome, Peter dreamt that an angel set him free and on waking found that he was free. An essential element in the composition is the use of various light sources: the moon, the guard's torch, the angel.

This painting is a masterpiece in the painting of light anticipating the work of Caravaggio and Rembrandt by more than a century.

St Leo the Great repulsing Attila (12). — On learning of the Huns' approach, Leo I went to meet them and, aided by the appearance of St Peter and St Paul armed with swords, he repulsed Attila.

Raphael has moved the event to the gates of Rome which is indicated by the Coliseum, a basilica and an aqueduct. The calm comportment of the Pope and his suite contrasts with the disorder of the barbarian hordes. The painting was not finished when Julius II died in 1513. Raphael therefore substituted a portrait of Leo X although he already appeared in the picture as Cardinal Giovanni de Medici (left) wearing the cappa magna (a long hooded cloak).

A large part of the painting (right) was done by Raphael's pupils.

Hall of Constantine (1517-1525). — In 1520 Raphael died. The painting of this room, which had been begun during Leo X's reign, was finished in Clement VII's by a group of Raphael's followers led by Giulio Romano and Francesco Penni. This was the beginning of Mannerism; overwhelmed by the legacy of Raphael and Michelangelo, artists tried to imitate them by mixing their styles.

The apparition of the Cross (13) and the Battle of the Milvian Bridge (14). — These two works are by Giulio Romano. Constantine's victory over Maxentius at the Milvian Bridge in 312 suffers from exaggeration.

The Baptism of Constantine (15). — Francesco Penni was the artist. Pope Sylvester who baptised Constantine is shown with the features of Clement VII.

Constantine's Donation (16). — Giulio Romano and Francesco Penni collaborated on this scene which is set inside the old St Peter's and shows the Emperor Constantine (306-37) giving Rome to the Pope and thus founding the temporal power of the Papacy. In his Divine Comedy Dante spoke out vehemently against the gift: "Ah, Constantine, what evil was spawned not by your conversion but by that gift which the first rich pope accepted from you."

The vault. — The old beamed ceiling was replaced at the end of 16C.

Raphael's Loggia ★★ (plan p 84). Open to specialists only

At the beginning of 16C, before the construction of St Damasus' Court (Cortile di San Damaso) and the buildings on its north, south and east sides, the façade of the 13C palace looked out over Rome. Julius II (1503-13) decided to give it a new look. He engaged Bramante to design three superimposed loggias. Work began in 1508 and when Bramante died in 1514 Julius II's successor, Leo X, appointed Raphael to take over.

The loggia takes the form of a vaulted corridor, richly decorated (probably between 1517 and 1519). The walls and arches are adorned with stuccoes and 'grotesques' inspired by Classical models which Raphael and his friends had found in Nero's Golden House (p 66). Various artists collaborated with Raphael: Francesco Penni and Giulio Romano, Giovanni da Udine and Perin del Vaga. Their work abounds with fantastic invention: garlands of fruit and flowers, animals, reproductions of famous statues, people, scenes from contemporary life.

The loggia is divided into 13 bays; the vault of each being decorated with four paintings, representing scenes from the Old Testament except in the first bay (17) which has scenes from the New Testament. The loggia is sometimes called "Raphael's Bible". These charmingly fresh paintings include: Moses in the Bulrushes (18); Building the Ark (19); Creation of the Animals (20).

Chiaroscuro Rooms and Nicholas V's Chapel ★ (plan p 84)

The rooms owe their name to Raphael's chiaroscuro paintings (1517) which were later restored in the late 16C. They also house a wooden model showing the internal construction of St Peter's dome.

Nicholas V's Chapel ★. — The chapel is one of the oldest parts of the Vatican Palace. In 12C it probably formed part of a tower which was absorbed into the first papal palace in 13C. Nicholas V converted it into a chapel and had it decorated by **Fra Angelico** (1447-51), a Dominican monk and master of Florentine art. He was assisted by Benozzo Gozzoli, also from Florence.

In the angles are the Doctors of the Church; the Evangelists are on the ceiling. The two tier wall paintings illustrate the lives of St Stephen and St Lawrence and were extensively restored in 18 and 19C.

Life of St Stephen. — Upper level. On the right (21) are two legendary episodes in the saint's life: St Stephen being ordained to the priesthood (left) by St Peter (whose figure shows great nobility); St Stephen distributing alms (right). Above the entrance door (22): St Stephen preaching in a square in Florence (left) and St Stephen addressing the Council (right). On the left (23): the Stoning of St Stephen.

Life of St Lawrence. — Lower level. Sixtus II, resembling Nicholas V, ordaining St Lawrence (21) whose face shows that saintly expression which only Fra Angelico could impart. Above the door (22): St Lawrence receiving the treasure of the church from Sixtus II and distributing alms to the poor. The portrayal of a blind man (right) is exceptional in the idealised art of the Renaissance. On the left (23); the Roman Emperor Decius pointing to the instruments of torture; the martyrdom of St Lawrence.

On leaving Nicholas V's chapel, return to the first Raphael Room (Borgo Fire). Pass through Urban VIII's chapel and turn right down the stairs to the Borgia Apartment.

Borgia Apartment ★

These rooms, which formed the suite of Alexander VI, the Borgia pope from Spain, now house examples of modern art. They are decorated with paintings by **Pinturicchio**, full of pleasant fantasy.

The first, known as the **Sybilline Room,** is painted with figures of Sybils and Prophets.

In the **Creed Room** the Prophets and Apostles carry streamers bearing the articles of the Creed.

Next is the **Liberal Arts Room,** probably used by Alexander VI as a study. It is decorated with allegories of the Liberal Arts, i.e. the seven subjects taught in the universities in the Middle Ages. On the ceiling are the arms of the Borgias.

The **Saints' Room** was probably painted by Pinturicchio himself whereas in the other rooms he was assisted by many of his pupils. The legendary lives of the saints are combined with mythology, a common practice in the Renaissance period. Facing the window is St Catherine of Alexandria arguing with the philosophers, one of Pinturicchio's best works, against his usual landscape of delicate trees, rocks and hills. In the centre is the Arch of Constantine. Before the Emperor St Catherine expounds her arguments in defence of the Christian faith. The vault is painted with mythological scenes.

The **Mysteries of the Faith Room** depicts the principal mysteries in the lives of Jesus and his mother. On the wall framing the entrance: the Resurrection; on the left: very fine portrait of Alexander VI, in rapt adoration.

The **Pontiffs' Room** was used for official meetings. The ceiling, which collapsed in 1500 narrowly missing Alexander VI, was reconstructed in the reign of Leo X and is decorated with stucco ornaments and 'grotesques'. At one time the room was hung with portraits of the popes, hence its name. Nowadays only the dedications remain.

Return to the Liberal Arts Room and turn left.

In the next room (XIII) on 18 August 1501 Alexander VI suddenly died. Some said he had been poisoned but modern knowledge would suggest he had malaria.

Collection of Modern Religious Art ★★ *(plan p 88)*

This very rich collection brings together some 500 paintings and sculptures, given by artists and collectors. The greatest artists in the world are represented here. On the upper floor the Chapel of Peace by Giacomo Manzù leads into a room devoted to Rouault, followed by a series of smaller rooms revealing traces of the 13C palace and containing works by Chagall, Gauguin, Utrillo, Odilon Redon, Braque, Klee, Kandinsky, Moore, Morandi, De Pisis etc.

Downstairs in rooms partially beneath the Sistine Chapel gleams stained glass by Fernand Leger, Jacques Villon, George Meistermann. There are several canvases by Bernard Buffet, Jugoslavian naive paintings, sculptures by Marini, Lipchitz and Mirko, Picasso ceramics and Bazaine tapestries.

On 23 June 1973 Paul VI declared "Even in our arid secularised world there is still a prodigious capacity for expressing beyond the truly human what is religious, divine, Christian".

Sistine Chapel ★★★

Restoration in progress; most of the paintings are however visible.

It is named after Pope Sixtus IV for whom it was built between 1475 and 1481. As well as being the papal palace chapel, it seems to have served a defensive role in view of the surviving external crenellations *(p 78).*

The long chamber has a vaulted roof and is lit by 12 windows. **Sixtus IV** sent for painters from Umbria and Florence to decorate the walls. His nephew **Julius II** (1503-13) commissioned Michelangelo to paint the roof. Twenty years later the artist was again engaged by **Clement VII** and **Paul III** to paint the wall behind the altar. The chapel is not only the setting for the most solemn ceremonies of the Holy See, where the cardinals meet in conclave *(p 71)* but also a masterpiece of Renaissance art; its dimensions — 40.23 m - 132 ft long, 13.41 m - 44 ft wide and 20.70 m - 68 ft high — are exactly the same as those given in the Bible for Solomon's Temple and the decorations too are charged with spiritual meaning.

Side walls. — In the decoration of the walls (1481-83) Sixtus IV wanted to perpetuate the decorative tradition of the early Christian basilicas. The lowest section represents the curtains which were hung between the columns of the old basilicas. Between the windows are portraits of the early popes from St Peter to Marcel I (308-09). The figures of Christ and the first three popes were obliterated when the Last Judgment was painted above the altar. The series of paintings half way up the walls depict parallel scenes in the lives of Moses and of Jesus, showing the human condition before and after the coming of the Messiah.

Life of Moses. — *South wall.* The first fresco (Moses in the bulrushes) was covered up by the Last Judgment. Moses in Egypt, the work of Perugino and Pinturicchio, is followed by Moses' Youth by Botticelli: the two female figures representing Jethro's daughters, are worthy of the most lyrical Renaissance painter. The next two panels, the Crossing of the Red Sea and the Giving of the Tables of the Law on Mount Sinai, are by Cosimo Rosselli. In the punishment of Korah, Dathan and Abiram for denying Moses' and Aaron's authority over the Jewish people Botticelli has set the scene against a background of Roman monuments (Constantine's Arch - *p 68* and the Palatine Septizonium - *p 47).* The Testament and Death of Moses is by Luca Signorelli.

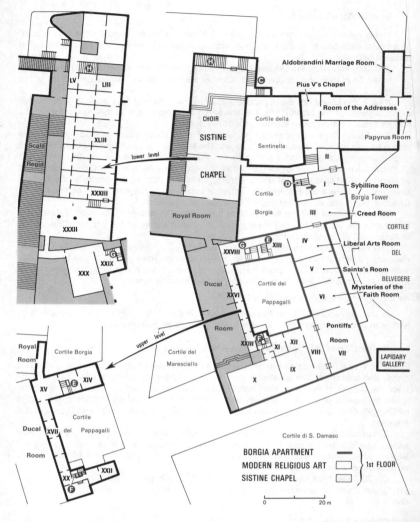

Aldobrandini Marriage Room

Pius V's Chapel

Room of the Addresses

CHOIR

Cortile della

Papyrus Room

SISTINE

Sentinella

II

CHAPEL

Sybilline Room

Cortile

I

Borgia Tower

Borgia

III

Creed Room

Royal Room

CORTILE

Liberal Arts Room

XXVIII   XIII   IV

DEL

V

Saints's Room

BELVEDERE

Cortile dei

Mysteries of the

Ducal

VI

Faith Room

XXVI   Pappagalli

Room

Pontiffs'

XXIII   XI   XII   Room

VIII   VII

LAPIDARY

Cortile del

GALLERY

Maresciallo   IX

Royal
Room   Cortile Borgia   X

Cortile di S. Damaso

XV

BORGIA APARTMENT

Cortile   MODERN RELIGIOUS ART   1st FLOOR

Ducal   XVII   dei   Pappagalli   SISTINE CHAPEL

Room

XX   XXII   0   20 m

Life of Christ. — *North wall.* The first fresco, the Nativity, disappeared beneath the Last Judgment by Michelangelo.

The series now begins with the Baptism of Jesus painted by Perugino and Pinturicchio featuring many of the members of Sixtus IV's court.

The next panel, the Temptation of Christ and the Healing of the Leper, faces the papal throne. Here Botticelli has given greater weight to the Healing scene in deference to Sixtus IV who had written a theological treatise on the subject. He also painted the Temple in Jerusalem to look like the Santo Spirito Hospital which the Pope had reconstructed. Three small scenes at the foot of the painting illustrate the Temptation in the Wilderness: *(left to right)* in a thicket, on a pinnacle of the temple, on a high mountain.

The next painting is an illustration of the calling of St Peter and St Andrew by Domenico Ghirlandaio.

In the Sermon on the Mount and the Healing of the Leper, Cosimo Rosselli assisted by Piero di Cosimo has made one of the first attempts to paint a sunset.

The Delivery of the Keys to St Peter is a masterpiece by Perugino: the Arch of Constantine, so much admired during the Renaissance, appears twice on either side of the Temple in Jerusalem, which is drawn according to the artist's whim.

The final panel is the Last Supper by Cosimo Rosselli in which Judas is set apart from the other Apostles, face to face with Jesus.

The Ceiling. — When Julius II abandoned his project for a funerary sculpture, Michelangelo returned unhappily to Florence. In 1508 he was recalled to Rome by the Pope who asked him to paint the twelve Apostles on the ceiling of the Sistine Chapel. He had barely started, as he later recorded, when he realised the work was going badly; the Pope then gave him a free hand and instead of the blue star-spangled vault (some 520 m² - 660 sq ft) he created a masterpiece. The ceiling is filled with powerful movement; the animated figures compose an epic of the creation of the world and the history of the human race.

Julius II came regularly to ask Michelangelo when he would finish; from the top of the scaffolding came the regular reply "when I can".

On 14 August 1511, bursting with impatience, the Pope insisted on seeing the fresco; he was overwhelmed. About a year later it was finished.

From the Creation to the Flood. — *Starting from the altar.*

1) God divides the light from the darkness.
2) Creation of the sun, the moon and plant life.
3) God divides the waters from the earth and creates living creatures in the seas.
4) Creation of Adam.
5) Creation of Eve.
6) Original sin and expulsion from the Garden of Eden.
7) Noah's sacrifice: contrary to biblical chronology this scene precedes the Flood. Michelangelo may have wanted to give more space to the Flood scene or to stress Noah's loyalty to God thus justifying his being saved in the Ark.
8) The Flood: this was the first scene to be painted. Some of the figures are too small in proportion to their surroundings.
9) Noah's Drunkenness: the whole series could have terminated with the Flood; by including the last scene where Noah is scorned by his son, Michelangelo pessimistically reminds us that life on earth began again under a bad omen.

The "Ignudi" (10). — These are the figures which Michelangelo painted at each corner of the central panels. These remarkable figures, which glorify the human body, are modelled on Classical sculptures and influenced many Renaissance and Mannerist artists.

Prophets and Sibyls. — There is great variety in these twelve portraits: Zacharias (11), the old man with a beard; Joel (12), the critic; the Erythraean Sibyl (13), not knowing where to begin her study; Ezekiel (14),

SISTINE CHAPEL CEILING

in earnest debate; the Persian Sibyl (15), shortsighted and bowed with old age; Jeremiah (16) in his melancholy; Jonah (17), symbol of Christ's resurrection, ejected from the whale in a movement recalled by Baroque artists; the Libyan Sibyl (18), her study completed, descending from her throne with a gracefulness to gratify the Mannerists; Daniel (19), inspired by a new idea; the Cumaean Sibyl (20), a muscle-bound giant apparently puzzled by what she is reading; Isaiah (21), troubled by an angel; the young Delphic Sibyl (22).

Bible Stories. — At the centre of these four scenes are the heroes of the Jewish people — David, Judith, Esther, Moses — in whom Christ reaffirmed the promise of his coming foretold by the Prophets: Judith and Holophernes (23), David and Goliath (24), the Punishment of Haman (25), the Brazen Serpent (26).

Jesus' Forefathers (27). — Their names *(above the windows)* correspond to the scenes painted in the triangular sections. There the Jewish families wait for their deliverance.

The Last Judgment. — Twenty years after painting the ceiling, Michelangelo was sent for by Clement VII in 1534 to complete the decoration of the Chapel. The Pope, who had seen Rome sacked by Charles V's troops in 1527, wanted the Last Judgment to deliver its message boldly from above the altar as a warning to the unfaithful. Paul III took up his predecessor's idea and work began in 1535. The 15C frescoes were obliterated as well as two panels in the series depicting Jesus' ancestors. When the fresco was unveiled on 31 October 1541, people were amazed and dumbfounded. Stamped with the mark of violence and anger, this striking work, with its mass of naked bodies writhing in a baleful light, is an expression of misfortune: Rome had been sacked in 1527; Luther's doctrine was dividing the Western Church. In 16 and 18C the fresco was touched up. The austerity of the Counter-Reformation moved Pius IV to have the naked figures clothed by Daniele da Volterra; in all about thirty figures were clothed.

This fresco introduced a new style in the history of art which led to the Baroque.

The composition follows a strict scheme: the elect are welcomed on high by the angels *(left)* while the damned tumble headlong into hell *(right)*.

At the bottom *(left)* the dead slowly awake; in vain the devils try to restrain them. Up above the elect seem drawn by the movement of Christ's right hand. Beside the terrifying figure of Christ the Judge, the Virgin turns away from the horrific spectacle. Around them are the Saints, bearing the instruments of their martyrdoms: St Andrew with his cross beside the Virgin, beneath them St Lawrence and his gridiron, St Bartholomew with his skin (in its folds appears the distorted face of Michelangelo). In his boat Charon waits for the damned whom he throws into the river of Hell. Minos, the Master of Hell, his body wreathed by a snake *(in the corner)* resembles the Master of Ceremonies at the Papal Court; the latter was shocked that such a work could appear in so venerable a place and complained to the Pope, Paul III, who retorted that he did not have the power to rescue someone from Hell. The fresco as a whole is dominated by angels bearing the Cross, the Crown of Thorns, the Column and the other instruments of the Passion.

Pavement and Choir Screen. — The chapel was paved in 15C in the Cosmati style. The delicate choir screen and the chorister's gallery are by Mino da Fiesole (15C).

Vatican Library ★ (precious objects — *plan pp 80-81*)

Pius V's Chapel. — On display are the Treasures of the Sancta Sanctorum, the private chapel of the popes in the Lateran Palace *(Scala Sancta, p 136)*.

Room of the Addresses. — Secular items from the Roman and palaeo-Christian era are exhibited together with religious items from the Middle Ages to the present day.

Aldobrandini Marriage Room. — On the centre wall is a fresco from the Augustan period depicting a marriage ceremony which is named after its first owner, Cardinal Pietro Aldobrandini.

Christian Museum. — It was founded in 1756 by Benedict XIV for palaeo-Christian antiquities.

Sistine Rooms. — Beyond the Gallery of Urban VIII with its manuscripts are the Sistine Rooms, created by Sixtus V (1585-90) to hold archives and now containing the equipment used in 16C to apply lead seals to papal bulls. Among those upon whom this very lucrative office was conferred were the architect, Bramante, and the painter, Luciani Sebastiano, who was therefore known as Sebastiano del Piombo (Sebastian of the Seal).

Sistine Salon ★. — It was built in 1587 by Sixtus V to house part of the Vatican Library. The decoration by C Nebbia is in the Mannerist style and shows episodes of Sixtus V's papacy, the history of books, the councils of the Church and the inventors of the alphabet *(on the pillars)*; 17C cupboards, painted in 19C.

After the Vatican Library come the two Pauline Rooms, built by Paul V (1605-21), the entrance to the New Wing *(see below)*, the Alexandrine Room by Alexander VIII (1690) and the **Clementine Gallery** by Clement XII.

On display are sketches and studies for works by Bernini. High up on the far side of the last pair of porphyry **columns ★**, separating the last two sections of the gallery, are sculptures of the Tetrarchs (the four emperors instituted by Diocletian in 4C).

The last room contains the **Pagan Museum** which was founded in 1767 by Clement XIII (Etruscan, Roman and mediaeval objects).

New Wing (Braccio Nuovo) (Roman antiquities - *plan pp 80-81*)

The **statue of Demosthenes** *(first recess on the right of the entrance)* is a Roman copy of a Greek bronze (3C BC). The **Nile** *(in the central hemicycle)*, 1C Roman work, probably inspired by a Greek original from the Hellenistic period, represents the river god, surrounded by 16 children corresponding to the 16 cubits by which the river must rise in order to flood the plain and make it fertile. The **gilded bronze peacocks** came from Hadrian's mausoleum (Castel Sant' Angelo). The **statue of Augustus ★★** *(4th recess on the left after the hemicycle)*, known as the Prima Porta head after the place where it was found, is a fine example of official Roman art. The decoration on the Emperor's breast plate is an extraordinarily precise illustration of the King of the Parthians returning the standards lost by Crassus in 53 BC.

The "Doryphoros". — *5th recess on the right after the hemicycle.* The title of this statue is the Greek word for a spear-bearer. It is a Roman copy of a bronze original by Polyclitus (440 BC). The original was probably the model, the "Kanon", which demonstrated Polyclitus' theories about proportion in sculpture.

Return to the Pagan Museum in the Vatican Library; then turn left.

Picture Gallery ★★★ (Pinacoteca)

Italian Primitives (I). — The **Last Judgment** (1) painted on an 11C throne back is an excellent Roman painting similar to Byzantine art.

Giotto and his school (II). — The **Stefaneschi Triptych** (2) is named after the Cardinal who commissioned it and was executed by Giotto, no doubt with the assistance of his pupils, in 1315.

The Florentines: Fra Angelico and his pupil Benozzo Gozzoli, Filippo Lippi (III). — These artists are among the great 15C painters. Fra Angelico's (1400-55) slightly old-fashioned style, which links him to the Middle Ages, nonetheless expresses his deep religious feeling, as a small painting, the **Virgin and Child with saints and angels** (3), demonstrates; the two **scenes from the Life of St Nicholas of Bari** (4) come from an altarpiece predella. The **Coronation of the Virgin** (5) is by Filippo Lippi (1406-69) and **St Thomas receiving the Virgin's girdle** (6) is by Benozzo Gozzoli (1420-97).

Melozzo da Forli (1438-94) (IV). — Among his many works is **Sixtus IV and Platina the Librarian** (7), a fresco, transferred to canvas, which adorned the Pope's library. The Cardinal is a portrait of Sixtus IV's nephew Giuliano della Rovere, later Julius II. The unusual perspective and the vigorous drawing make Melozzo da Forli one of the main exponents of the artistic style of his time. The beautiful **Musical Angels** were, until 18C, part of the decoration of the apse in the Basilica of the Holy Apostles.

Polyptychs (VI). — The Virgin and Child (8) and the Pietà (9) are by **Carlo Crivelli** (1430-93), a Venetian. While the Florentines were experimenting with line, the Venetians were taking an interest in colour. In addition Crivelli had a marked taste for gold decoration (very beautiful painted fabrics).

15C Umbrian School (VII). — The Virgin and Child (10) by **Perugino** and the Coronation of the Virgin (11) by **Pinturicchio** illustrate the clear and poetic style of the Umbrian artists.

Room VIII ★★★; Raphael (1483-1520). — The artistic development of the painter of the *Stanze (p 84)* is illustrated by three works. The **Coronation of the Virgin (12)**, painted in 1503 has a youthful freshness and shows the influence of Perugino. The **Madonna of Foligno (13)** was painted in 1511-12 while Raphael was in Rome at the height of his glory; the fine portrait of Sigismondo dei Conti, on his knees, which dominates the picture, the exquisite pose of the Virgin and the luminosity surrounding her are the work of a master. The **Transfiguration (14)** was intended for Narbonne Cathedral in France but Raphael died in 1520 before finishing the painting. It was completed by Giuliano Romano and Francesco Penni who were probably responsible for the lower part of the picture.

The **tapestries** were woven in Brussels from Raphael's cartoons (now in the Victoria and Albert Museum in London). They represent scenes taken from the Acts of the Apostles. Their lacklustre appearance is due to their having travelled a great deal. Until 1527 they hung in the Sistine Chapel but were dispersed at the sack of Rome. During 16C the popes reunited them; two of them were found in Constantinople.

Room IX. — With his **St Jerome ★★ (15)** Leonardo da Vinci (1452-1519) shows his mastery of anatomy, expression and light. The picture was put together after being discovered in two pieces, one in an antique shop and the other at a shoemaker's.

The **Descent from the Cross (16)** by the Venetian Giovanni Bellini (1429-c1516) combines accurate drawing and deep inspiration with fine tonality.

Room X. — In his **Madonna of San Nicola dei Frari (17)** Titian uses the marvellous colours of the Venetian painters. The **Coronation of the Virgin (18)**, by Giulio Romano *(upper part)* and Francesco Penni *(lower part)*, two artists who often finished off Raphael's work, shows the Mannerist style.

The Mannerists (XI). — The works include The Rest on the Flight into Egypt **(19)** by **Federico Barocci** (1528-1612), as delicate and luminous as a pastel. The fresh and graceful style represented here degenerates into mere affectation with the other Mannerists.

Cortile della Pinacoteca

Caravaggio and his followers (XII). — The **Descent from the Cross ★★ (20)** by **Caravaggio** (1573-1610) clearly expresses his reaction to Mannerist sentimentality. His people, even in the most religious scenes, are drawn from life. The firm line and the way the light falls further emphasise his realism (note how Nicodemus and St John hold the body of the dead Christ). Mary Magdalen, head bowed, is a glorious figure. **Valentin** (1594-1632), a Frenchman, was strongly influenced by Caravaggio: the Martyrdom of St Processus and St Martinian **(21)**. **Guido Reni** (1575-1642) was also inspired by Caravaggio in his Crucifixion of St Peter **(22)**. The Martyrdom of St Erasmus **(23)** was painted by **Nicolas Poussin** for St Peter's Basilica. The picture has been replaced in the basilica by a copy in mosaic.

Rooms XIII-XIV. — They contain 17C works particularly by **Pietro da Cortona**, the great Baroque artist.

Room XV. — The portrait of Clement IX **(24)** is by Carlo Maratta (1625-1713). Sir Thomas Lawrence's portrait of George IV of England was a gift by the king to Pius VII.

Pagan and Christian Museums ★

A fine modern building begun in 1963 houses the Pagan and Christian museums which were opened to the public in 1970. They contain the collections comprising the museum of antique art assembled by Gregory XVI (1831-46) and the museum of Christian art founded in 1854 by Pius IX, formerly kept in the Lateran Palace.

Tour of the Pagan Museum

It is divided into four sections: copies of the imperial period (1C BC to 3C AD); 1 and 2C Roman sculpture; sarcophagi; 2 and 3C Roman sculpture. The modern setting — metal, concrete and wood — shows off the exhibits perfectly and enables them to be viewed from all sides.

Imperial period copies. — The **basalt head (1)** is a fine copy of a Greek original linked to the art of Polyclitus (5C BC). **Sophocles (2)**, the Athenian tragic poet, is represented by a large statue of noble mien with a headband to show he is a priest of Amynos, a healer. The beautiful **mosaic (3)** on the ground is decorated with fantastic designs. There are several **herms (4)**, their head and shoulders springing from a pillar. The **relief of Medea and the daughters of Pelias (5)** is a 1C BC Roman copy of a late 5C BC Greek original; despite being damaged it illustrates the story of the deception of Pelias' daughters by Medea with great elegance. Finally there is a **headless statue (6)**, probably inspired by a 5C original, and also the **"Chiaramonti" Niobid (7)**, a copy of a statue which was part of a group representing the death of Niobe and her daughters.

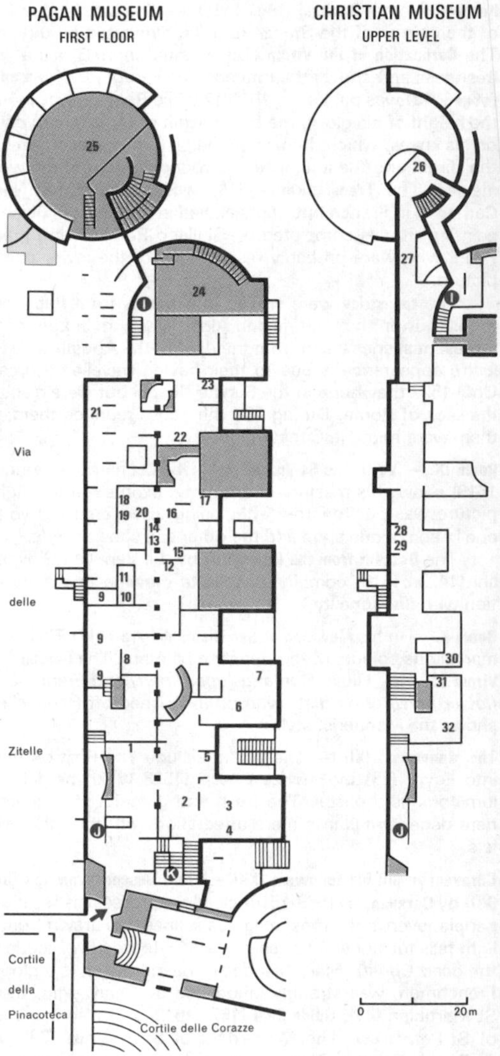

Roman sculpture (1 and early 2C). — The low relief of the **Vicomagistrates' altar (8)** is a particularly fine 1C sculpture which probably decorated the lower part of an altar. It shows a procession of people leading animals to the temple for the sacrifice; following the four Vicomagistrates (street magistrates) are the assistants bearing statues of the Lares (the gods of the household and the crossroads). The narrative style of the sculpture and its naturalism make it a truly Roman work.

There is a fine collection of **urns and funerary altars (9)**, dating from 1C, which come from the Via Appia in particular, and also the **base of a column** from the Basilica Julia in the Roman Forum (**10**), a fine example of Roman decorative art.

Among the major pieces in the section are the **Chancery Reliefs ★**, so called because they were discovered beneath the Chancery Palace in the Campus Martius. Classical in style, they illustrate two events in the life of the Emperor Vespasian and his son Domitian. One sculpture (**11**) shows Vespasian's arrival in Rome after his election to the imperial throne; the Emperor makes a noble figure in his toga on the right. His son Domitian greets him. Between them is the genius of the Roman people, bearing the horn of plenty, with one foot resting on a milestone, showing that the meeting is taking place at the limit of the

PAGAN MUSEUM
FIRST FLOOR

CHRISTIAN MUSEUM
UPPER LEVEL

pomerium (the sacred boundary of Rome). The other sculpture (**12**) shows Domitian's departure on a campaign. When the Senate banned memorials of Domitian, his head was replaced by that of his successor, Nerva.

The **Haterii tomb sculptures** are the remains of a family tomb from the end of 1C. They represent the popular taste in Roman art which developed parallel with the official style (realism and detailed precision to the detriment of the overall affect). The family concerned was probably that of Haterius Tychicus, constructor of public buildings; two low reliefs in particular allude to the building trade: one (**13**) represents the monuments of ancient Rome (the unfinished Coliseum is easily recognisable); the other (**14**) shows a huge funerary monument in the form of a temple; appearing above the building are the scenes which took place inside the tomb; the detailed treatment lacks proportion: to the left of the scenes the sculptor has placed a crane. The portraits are particularly realistic: a woman in a recess with wavy hair (**15**) is executed with great skill; likewise the little pillar wreathed in finely modelled roses (**16**) is exquisite.

There are several fine **decorative sculptures**: two pillars ornamented with foliated scrolls (**17**) and fragments of 2C friezes (**18, 19, 20**).

Sarcophagi. — Many are illustrated with mythical subjects. The fragment of the "philosopher's" sarcophagus (**21**) shows a group of scholars: the faces are so realistic that they seem like portraits; they date from about 270 AD.

Roman sculpture (2 and 3C). — The **porphyry torso** (**22**) probably belonged to an imperial statue (2C). The statue of a **young woman arrayed like Omphale** (**23**) (Queen of Lydia who assumed Hercules' attributes) is typical of 3C style which aimed at immortalising the subject in the disguise.

Mosaics from the Baths of Caracalla ★. — *Both of them (**24** and **25**) are visible from the stairs and the Museum of Christian Art.* They date from 3C and show the figures of athletes, gladiators and their trainers; their brutality is evidence of the Roman taste for violent spectacles.

Tour of the Christian Museum

Statue of the Good Shepherd (26). — Heavily restored, it probably dates from 3C. The Christian artist has taken the pagan image of a shepherd offering his finest animal to the gods or of Hermes leading the dead into the next world but here the figure is suffused with the meaning of the new religion and illustrates the parable of the lost sheep saved from the wolf by the good shepherd: "When he hath found it, he layeth it on his shoulders, rejoicing."

Sarcophagi. — The Christian sarcophagi are similar to the pagan ones in their decoration: figures in relief in a continuous band; the sides divided into panels separated by arcades; strigils and central medallion.

The first Christian artists decorated the sarcophagi with garlands, baskets and children, using the pagan motifs to which they added the symbolic themes of sheep — Christ's flock, vine branches — symbol of union with God through the Eucharist, etc. From the middle of 3C scenes and figures were added to the symbols, as for example on the **side of a sarcophagus found in St Lawrence Without the Walls (27)** which shows Christ and the Apostles as well as sheep representing the Christian flock.

In 4C new subjects appear: on a **covered sarcophagus found in St Callixtus' Catacombs (28)** and also on a **sarcophagus with two bands of decoration (29)** are two scenes often shown together: Peter's arrest and Moses striking water from the rock *(on the righthand side of the former and in the lower section of the latter).*

On a 4C **sarcophagus found in St Lawrence Without the Walls (30)** are various scenes including: Adam and Eve receiving a grain of wheat and a sheep from God *(upper section left of the central medallion),* symbols of the labour to which they were condemned after their fall from grace.

On another 4C **sarcophagus from St Paul Without the Walls (31)** the cross is placed in the centre as a sign of triumph while the Christian monogramme is surrounded with a crown of laurel.

Note also the **moulding of the sarcophagus of Junius Bassus (32)** *(p 78).*

Missionary-Ethnological Museum
(Open: Wednesday and Saturday — Plan pp 80-81)

It was founded in 1927 by Pius XI and first housed in the Lateran Palace but moved into ultra modern premises in the Vatican during Paul VI's reign.

It comprises a large collection of articles illustrating the great world religions (Buddhism, Hinduism, Islam) and Christian artefacts designed in the ethnic style of the local artists from every continent except Europe.

Historical Museum *(Open: Wednesdays and Saturdays — Plan pp 80-81)*

The underground building, opened in 1973 during the reign of Paul VI, houses a varied collection of papal memorabilia: sedan chairs, coaches for long journeys and ceremonial occasions, weapons, standards and uniforms belonging to the former armed forces which were disbanded in 1970.

■ VATICAN CITY AND GARDENS ★★★ *(Tour p 69 — Plan p 70)*

The Bell Arch (Arco delle Campane) (**R**) leads into the Piazza dei Protomartiri Romani, which is situated more or less in the centre of the Circus of Caligula and Nero where many early Christians were martyred; a black stone with a white border set in the ground marks the site of the obelisk *(p 74).* On the left is the German and Dutch burial ground (**S**) which, according to a pious legend, consists of earth brought from Jerusalem. Next comes a visit to the **Mosaic School** (Scuola del Mosaico) and then the various buildings from which the Vatican State is administered. There are fine views of the Leonine City *(p 69).* The tour finishes with a view of the dome of St Peter's, designed by Michelangelo, rising majestically above the magnificent **gardens** ★★★; the fountains and statues are gifts from various countries. Pius IV's 'Casina' is a charming 16C building decorated with paintings and stucco work.

■ CASTEL SANT' ANGELO ★★★

Hadrian's Mausoleum. — This fortress-like building was intended as a sepulchre for Hadrian and his family. Begun by the Emperor in 135 AD it was finished four years later by his adopted son and successor to the imperial throne, Antoninus Pius.

The base, 84 m - 276 ft square, is surmounted by a drum 20 m - 66 ft high, on which was heaped a *tumulus* (small mound of earth). It was crowned by a statue of the Emperor and a bronze *quadriga* (four horse chariot). The mausoleum contained the cinerary urns of all the emperors from Hadrian to Septimius Severus (211 AD).

When Aurelian surrounded the town with a wall in 270 he incorporated the mausoleum within the precinct and turned it into a fortress.

Castel Sant' Angelo. — In 590 Pope Gregory the Great led a procession against the plague which was decimating the city. Suddenly there appeared on top of the mausoleum an angel sheathing his sword. The gesture was interpreted as a sign that the plague would abate and in gratitude the Pope had a chapel built on the mausoleum.

During the mediaeval struggle between the papacy and the noble Roman families, the building became a fortified stronghold. Nicholas V (1447-55) built a brick storey on top of the original construction and added turrets at the corners.

The octagonal bastions were the work of Alexander VI (1492-1503). In 1527 Clement VII took refuge there from the troops of Charles V and made several rooms habitable. These were later improved by Paul III who already knew the castle as he had been imprisoned there by Innocent VIII when he was only Cardinal Alexander Farnese. In his autobiography Benvenuto Cellini, the sculptor and metalworker, admits that he too had been in the castle gaol, as had Cagliostro, so it is said. After the unification of Italy the Castel Sant' Angelo became a barracks and military prison but today, surrounded by a public garden, it knows only the assaults of tourists.

A high defensive wall, the **Passetto**, built by Leo IV (847-55) links the castle to the Vatican Palace. Alexander VI created a passage along the top of the wall so that the pope could reach the fortress from the palace in case of siege.

TOUR *(Opening times: p 69)*

From the outside the Castel Sant' Angelo looks like a solid squat mass, the original part distinguished by the huge blocks of travertine and peperine of which it is built. The statue of the angel dominates the whole.

Access is gained by the old entrance to the mausoleum, although the threshold is now some 3 m - 9 ft higher.

Spiral ramp. — When the castle was a mausoleum the ramp led up 125 m - 137 yd to the chamber where the urns were placed. The walls were covered in marble, the floor was paved with mosaic (several traces remain) and the vault was decorated with stucco work. The holes in the vault were air vents except for the first one *(on the left in the entrance hall)* which was made in 18C to take a lift.

At the top of the ramp is a transverse stairway. Originally it ended in the cinerary chamber but Alexander VI extended it into a passage leading from one side of the castle to the other following the north-south diameter of the drum. In 19C a permanent bridge was built above the central chamber. The stairway emerges in the main courtyard.

Main courtyard. — It is also known as the Angel Court owing to the 16C statue which was transferred there from the top of the castle in 18C.

There are piles of cannon balls which from 15 to 17C supplied the catapults, bombards and cannons.

On the right (west side) is a suite of rooms: **guard room** restored to its 16C state; **display of arms** (Greek, Roman, Etruscan and mediaeval helmets).

The north end is filled by the chapel, designed by Michelangelo for Leo X; it probably stands on the site of Gregory the Great's Chapel *(p 93).* Slight alterations were carried out in 1910.

Enter the suite of rooms on the east side of the courtyard.

Clement VIII and Clement VII's Rooms. — Clement VIII's rooms are the rooms in Pope Leo X's apartment which were later rearranged by Paul III and Clement VIII whose names appear over the doors.

Apollo Room. — Over the doors and chimney is the name of Pope Paul III, 1547. The room takes its name from the painted scenes framed by grotesques, which are probably by Perin del Vaga (16C) assisted by other followers of Raphael. One of the openings in the floor was made in 18C to take a lift *(see above).* Beneath another opening is a shaft, 9 m - 30 ft deep, leading into a small chamber with no exit. The building has several such traps which have given rise to hair-raising legends.

Clement VII's Rooms. — Wooden ceilings and 15 and 16C paintings.

Hall of Justice. — Early in 16C a court used to hold its sessions here. Display of weapons and armaments.

Leave by the passage leading into the semi-circular court on the east side of the castle.

Alexander VI's Court. — The handsome well dates from the reign of this pope (1492-1503). The alternative name — Theatre Court — recalls the theatrical performances given here by Leo X and Pius IV, both men of letters.

Clement VII's bathroom. — *Access by stairway in southwest corner of court.* The beautiful décor by Giulio Romano, a pupil of Raphael, is evidence of the civilised lifestyle of the Pope in 16C.

Prisons. — *Access by steps leading down from Alexander VI's Court.* Beatrice Cenci *(p 116),* Giordano Bruno the heretic monk *(p 113)* and Benvenuto Cellini are supposed to have been imprisoned here.

Oil and grain store. — The jars could hold 22 000 litres of oil and the capacity of the five large silos was about 3 700 cwt of grain. It was Alexander VI who made these provisions in case of siege.

Return to Alexander VI's Court and take the steps up from the centre of the semi-circle which lead to the Loggias of Pius IV, Paul III and Julius II (walking anti-clockwise).

Pius IV's Loggia. — The rooms opening off the loggia *(right and left of staircase)* served as quarters for the castle staff and then as prisons. Here for many years the midday gun was fired.

Proceed anti-clockwise.

Paul III's Loggia. — The pope commissioned Antonio da Sangallo (the Younger) to design the loggia *(which faces north)* in 1543 and had it decorated with stucco work and grotesques. There is a view of the bastions and the defensive wall.

Julius II's Loggia. — It faces south with a fine view of the St Angelo Bridge (Ponte S Angelo) and of the city of Rome. It was probably built by Bramante for Julius II.

From here steps lead up to the papal apartments.

Papal Apartments ★. — After the unhappy experience of the siege of 1527 when Clement VII was forced to take refuge in Castel Sant' Angelo, Paul III had a suite of rooms constructed on top of the castle which was well protected by the succession of ramps and steps.

Council Room (Sala Paolina). — Here visitors waited to see the Pope. The frescoes are by a group of artists instructed by Perin del Vaga; the marble floor was restored in 18C by Innocent XIII.

Persian Room. — The name is derived from the subject of the frieze which was painted by Perin del Vaga. Fine coffered wooden ceiling (16C).

Cupid and Psyche Room. — *Temporarily closed.* The frieze below the ceiling illustrates the story of the young woman who was loved by Venus' son.

Return to the Council Room.

Two sets of steps linked by a passage lead up to the Library and two series of rooms *(one above the other)* named after their decorations: Hadrian's Mausoleum room, the Festoon Room, which opens into a smaller room where Cagliostro was imprisoned, the Stork Room and the Dauphin and Salamander Room.

Return to the Library.

Treasure and Secret Archives Room. — At the centre of the fortress is a circular chamber, lined with walnut presses containing the papal records which were transferred here from the Vatican in 1870. The cupboards (probably 14C) originally held the precious objects, the relics and the silver belonging to Julius II, Leo X and Sixtus V.

Roman Staircase. — The steps were part of Hadrian's mausoleum.

Terrace. — *Closed for restoration.* The bronze statue of the angel (repaired in 18C) presides over a **panorama ★★★** of Rome, one of the most famous that there is. From left to right: the Prati district and the green patch of the Villa Borghese; close to the castle, the great white mass of the Law Courts, then the Quirinal Palace, the Militia Tower and the shallow dome of the Pantheon; further right, the monument to Victor Emmanuel II and the domes and turrets of the city: the Gesù Church, St Ivo's corkscrew tower, the belfry of Santa Maria dell' Anima with its ceramic tiles, Sant' Andrea delle Valle, San Carlo ai Catinari, the Synagogue. On the extreme right is the Janiculum Hill, San Giovanni dei Fiorentini, the Via della Conciliazione, St Peter's and the Vatican Palace linked to Castel Sant' Angelo by the "Passetto", Monte Mario.

It is also possible to take the parapet walk linking the four bastions: St John's, St Matthew's, St Mark's (which gives access to the "Passetto", *p 94*) and St Luke's.

St Angelo Bridge ★ (Ponte S. Angelo)

This is one of the most elegant bridges in Rome. It goes back to the time of Hadrian who built a fine bridge (136 AD) linking the Campus Martius with his mausoleum; its three central arches have survived. The other arches date from 17C and were altered when the Tiber embankments were built in 1892-94. The statues of St Peter and St Paul *(left (south) bank)* were erected by Clement VII in 1530; the ten Baroque angels are the work of Bernini commissioned by Clement IX (1667-69).

Walk upstream on the left (south) bank and then cross the Umberto Bridge.

■ LAW COURTS

They were built from 1889 to 1911 by Guglielmo Calderini and are one of the most conspicuous modern buildings in Rome. With its bronze quadriga by Ximenes (1855-1926) and its colossal statuary, it can claim both Classical and Baroque inspiration.

Distance: 3 km - 3 miles. Time: about 3 1/2 hours. Start: Piazza del Populo.

In the days of the 'Grand Tour' before the railway came to Rome, English travellers usually approached from the north down the Via Flaminia and entered the city through the Porta del Populo. They took lodgings in the neighbouring streets between the Piazza del Populo and the Piazza di Spagna (Spanish Square) so that the district came to be known as the English Ghetto. Henry Matthews set down his first impressions in his diary in 1820: "We were soon in the Piazza di Spagna, the focus of fashion and the general resort of the English. Some travellers have compared it to Grosvenor Square but the Piazza di Spagna is little more than an irregular open space, a little less nasty than the other piazzas in Rome because the habits of the people are in some measure restrained by the presence of the English… The English swarm everywhere. We found all the inns full. It seemed like a country town in England at an assizes".

This district also recalls the numerous French interventions in Italian affairs in 18 and 19C. In 1798 General Berthier marched on Rome and deposed Pope Pius VI, establishing a Republic; in 1800 Pope Pius VII was elected by the Venice conclave and regained possession of the Papal States; after the Concordat of 1801 had re-established religious peace in France, Pius VII crowned Napoleon emperor in Notre-Dame Cathedral in Paris on 2 December 1804; but the emperor decided on a continental blockade: all the European sovereigns obeyed except Pius VII; on 2 February 1809 General Miollis breached the walls of Rome at the Porta del Populo with a force of 8 000 men; finally on 17 May 1809 Napoleon recorded that 'the Papal States are reunited to the French Empire'. This action led to a complete breach and excommunication followed by five years of French government while the Romans hurled continuous insults at the accomplices of the man whom they called the Antichrist.

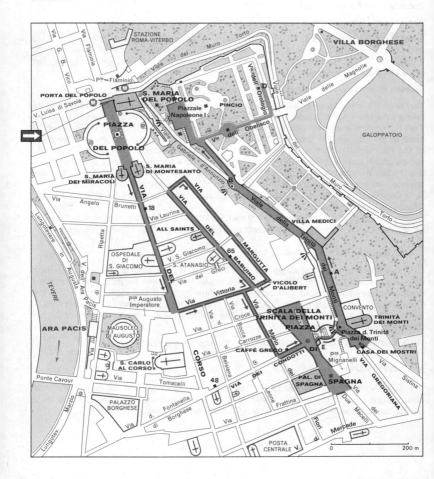

Piazza del Popolo ★★. — The square was laid out by **Giuseppe Valadier** (1762-1839), the favourite architect and town planner of Pius VI and Pius VII. In an effort to open up Rome, he made the Piazza del Popolo one of the largest squares in the city. He retained the Popolo Gate, the central obelisk and the twin churches flanking the Via del Corso, and opened out the space into two semicircles adorned with fountains and allegorical neo-Classical statues. The east side of the square was linked to the Pincio gardens above by a series of monumental arcaded terraces screened by trees and shrubs.

On 18 December 1813 a guillotine was set up in the square by the French government to deter the gangs of thugs who roamed the streets.

Popolo Gate ★ . — This gateway in the 3C Aurelianic wall stands more or less on the site of the ancient *Porta Flaminia.* The exterior façade was built between 1562 and 1565 by Pius IV who wanted to impress visitors arriving from the north with an entrance worthy of the splendour of his capital. The Medici arms are the dominant feature. When Queen Christina of Sweden, newly converted to Roman Catholicism, arrived in 1655 the internal façade was decorated by Bernini with two scrolls supporting a garland beneath the star of the Chigi coat of arms which belonged to the then pope, Alexander VII.

Obelisk. — It was brought from Heliopolis in Lower Egypt in the reign of Augustus and set up in the Circus Maximus *(p 193).* It was Sixtus V and his architect, Domenico Fontana, who raised it in the centre of the Piazza del Popolo in 1589. The basins and marble lions at the base were added by Valadier at Leo XII's request in 1823.

'Twin' churches. — From the obelisk there is a fine view of **Santa Maria di Montesanto** and **Santa Maria dei Miracoli** flanking the beginning of the Corso. They are a good example of town planning by **Carlo Rainaldi,** providing a background to the obelisk and a theatrical entrance to the Via del Corso. Their similarity is more apparent than real since the site of Santa Maria di Montesanto is narrower than the other. The church on the left is built on an elliptical plan beneath a twelve-sided dome whereas the righthand church is circular in plan with an octagonal dome. The illusion that they are the same is given by the sides of the drums facing the square having the same dimensions.

Santa Maria di Montesanto was the first to be built: by Carlo Rainaldi from 1662 to 1667 and then by Bernini from 1671 to 1675. Carlo Rainaldo was also responsible for the construction of Santa Maria dei Miracoli until 1677 but it was completed by C Fontana in 1679. Both domes were recovered in slate in 1825 under Leo XII.

Santa Maria del Popolo ★★ . — Despite its simple exterior, the church contains **art treasures ★** worthy of a museum.

The building which was commissioned by Sixtus IV in 1472 and finished in 1477 is one of the first examples of the Renaissance style in Rome; its façade rises, almost devoid of ornament, to a triangular pediment; the plainess is relieved by typical Renaissance features: shallow pilasters and simple scrolls linking the lower and upper stages of the façade (the elaborate curves are Baroque additions).

The **interior** abounds in Renaissance features: a Latin cross plan in preference to a basilical one. The nave, which has groined vaulting, is flanked by two aisles lined by side chapels. The usual columns and walls of a basilical church have been replaced by massive square pillars composed of engaged columns.

During the Baroque period stucco statues were added above the arches of the nave by Bernini.

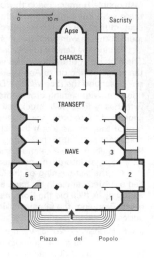

Della Rovere Chapel (1). — The chapel rail contains the arms of the della Rovere family to which Pope Sixtus IV belonged. Above the altar is a **fresco ★** of the Adoration of the Child by **Pinturicchio** (1454-1513) who came from Umbria. The Virgin's face is a marvellous example of his gentle touch. He liked to illustrate a landscape by painting individual details and including picturesque elements: note the ox's expression and the goat grazing and the lamb suckling on the cliff top.

On the left is the tomb of two members of the della Rovere family; the decorative motifs were carved by Andrea Bregno late in 15C; the oval medallion of the Virgin, its simple lines expressing a harmony of strength and gentleness, is by Mino da Fiesole, who worked at the Papal court from 1473 to 1480.

Cybo Chapel (2). — The Baroque chapel was designed by Carlo Fontana (1682-87) on a Greek cross plan beneath a dome.

Basso della Rovere Chapel (3). — The tomb of Giovanni Basso della Rovere (15C) on the righthand wall is by a pupil of Andrea Bregno and the frescoes above the altar and on the lefthand wall are by the Pinturicchio school.

Transept. — The chapels opening off the east side of the transept and the apses at either end are characteristic of the Renaissance. The Baroque style is represented by the cherubs supporting the picture frames above the transept altars.

The dome above the crossing was probably the first to be produced by the Renaissance in Rome.

The chancel arch is decorated with gilded stucco low reliefs, one *(right)* showing Pope Pascal II (1099-1118) chopping down a walnut tree. According to legend the church was built on the site of the tomb of the terrible Nero which was marked by a walnut tree. The population which went in fear and trembling of Nero's ghost appealed to Pascall II who felled the tree, threw Nero's remains into the Tiber and erected a chapel which under Sixtus IV became Santa Maria del Popolo.

Apse and Chancel. — *Go round behind the high altar.* The apse was extended by Bramante for Julius II (1503-13). The ceiling fresco is by Pinturicchio. The stained glass in predominantly neutral tones picked out with flashes of brilliant colour is the only old glass in Rome; it is the work of a Frenchman, Guillaume de Marcillat (16C).

The two **tombs** ★, carved in about 1505 by **Andrea Sansovino,** are elegant works of art in which the influence of Classical architecture (commemorative arches) mingles with the decorative style of 15C Florence.

Caravaggio's Paintings ★★★. — *In the Cerasi Chapel* (4). Two pictures, painted in 1601, illustrate two scenes from Holy Scripture.

In the Conversion of St Paul *(right),* as in all Caravaggio's works, light is the dominant feature. The effect of the divine light illuminating St Paul on the road to Damascus should have been sublime but it falls first of all on the horse, which is out of proportion, before touching the foreshortened figure of the saint.

The Crucifixion of St Peter *(left)* illustrates Caravaggio's taste for creating a diagonal focus. The treatment of the subject avoids all reference to the sublime: three brawny men whose faces are hidden are raising a cross bearing a man of rugged but noble mien.

Chigi Chapel ★ (5). — The design was entrusted to Raphael in 1513 by his champion, Agostino Chigi, banker, patron and consort of princes and popes. The dome mosaic, from a drawing by Raphael, dates from the Renaissance as do the figures of Jonah (after Raphael) and the prophet Elijah in their niches and the altarpiece, a Nativity in muted tones by Sebastiano del Piombo.

In the Baroque period Bernini was commissioned by Fabio Chigi, the future Alexander VII; he faced the base of the pyramid shaped tomb of Agostino and Sigismondo Chigi with green marble, carved the figures of Daniel and the lion and Habakkuk and the angel, which seem to burst from their niches, and inserted in the floor a winged skeleton with the Chigi coat of arms.

Bishop Foscari's Tomb (6). — In the last chapel is a recumbent figure in bronze of Girolamo Foscari sculpted by Vecchietta in 15C.

Via del Corso ★★. — Following the route of the ancient Via Flaminia the modern street runs in a straight line for 1 500 m - 1 640 yds from Piazza del Popolo to Piazza Venezia. Its mediaeval name was Via Lata but now it is called after the famous horse races organised by Pope Paul II in 15C. It is lined by handsome Renaissance palaces. Nowadays the 'Corso' is the main street of central Rome; its fashionable shops and cafés attract the crowds.

At the heart of the festivities. — Throughout the years, the Corso has been the place where fashionable Romans made their appearance. In 18C it was good form for a lady to be seen there with her *sigisbeo,* a faithful admirer. The *sigisbeo* became so firmly fixed in local custom that the church tolerated the practice and clauses permitting a wife to have one or more admirers were included in marriage contracts.

During the **Carnival** in February processions and mascarades proceeded along the Corso. The high point of the festivities was reached when the horse racing began. Each evening in the week leading up to Ash Wednesday the grooms led the horses round the course. Dickens described the race vividly "Down the whole length of the Corso they fly like the wind: riderless, with shining ornaments upon their backs and twisted in their plaited manes; and with heavy little balls stuck full of spikes dangling at their sides to goad them on. The jingling of these trappings and the rattling of their hoofs upon the hard stones, the dash and fury of their speed along the echoing street; nay, the very cannon that are fired — these noises are nothing to the roaring of the multitude: their shouts: the clapping of their hands. But it is soon over — almost instantaneously. More cannon shake the town. The horses have plunged into the carpets hung across the street to stop them".

On the last evening of the Carnival the *Moccoli* (wax tapers) appeared; everyone carried a lighted candle in his hand and tried to put out his neighbour's flame.

Only in 1809 did the Romans boycott the Carnival in protest against the French government. Pasquino, the famous talking statue *(p 160)* observed mockingly 'The bear may dance under the rod but not men'.

Goethe Museum. — *No 18, Via del Corso. Temporarily closed.*

This museum commemorates the German poet's residence here. On 9 February 1788 he wrote "The idiots made another great din on Monday and Tuesday, particularly Tuesday evening when the craze for *Moccoli* was at its height".

Turn left into the Via Vittoria.

On either side are workshops involved in the restoration of works of art.

Via del Babuino. — The street was opened by Clement VII for Jubilee Year in 1525. Its present name was given to it by popular usage when the statue of a Silenus was discovered in such a hideous state that the Romans compared it to a baboon. The statue is now to be found next to the fountain on the corner by St Athanasius' Church (S. Atanasio).

Today the street is known for its antique shops often situated in 17 and 18C buildings.

All Saints Anglican Church (Ognisanti). — *Open mornings only.* The church, which is now a protected building, was designed by **G E Street** in the early 1880s shortly before his death. It is built in the English Gothic style of specially made bricks, with a distinctive white travertine spire erected in 1937. The spacious interior is enriched by a variety of coloured marbles from different parts of Italy: white and green Carrara, red Perugia, black Verona, yellow Sienna and white Como. The pulpit designed in 1891 by A E Street, the architect's son, is reminiscent of the early Christian basilicas. Above the high altar hang seven lamps bought in Venice by a former Hon Asst Chaplain out of money given him by the congregation 'to be spent on himself'. The stained glass, depicting various saints and commemorating people connected with the church, is English, as is also the organ, a large and complex instrument, originally made in Huddersfield and presented in 1894, which has been used by famous guest organists for recitals and master classes.

The first Anglican services, for which papal permission was sought and granted, were held in Rome in 1816. After several years in hired rooms the congregation found a more permanent base in 1824 in the granary chapel outside the Porta del Popolo, until the building was demolished in a road widening scheme in 1882.

Via Margutta. — This street in the artistic heart of Rome is named after à famous little 15C theatre where they performed parodies of chivalrous epic poems such as Luigi Pulci's comedy *Morgante* with its two heroes, Morgante and Margutta.

The houses in the Via Margutta, often decorated with balconies and courtyard gardens, are occupied on the ground floor by art galleries. In June and October this peaceful backwater comes to life for the Via Margutta Exhibition — *Fiera di Via Margutta* — when artists exhibit their work in the street.

Via Margutta leads into **Vicolo d'Alibert** which in 18C contained the Dames Theatre; here for the first time women sang on stage in the Papal States. Formerly the female roles in opera had been sung by *castrati*.

Cross over the Via del Babuino and turn left into Via Mario dei Fiori.

Via dei Condotti. — The street is named after the conduits *(condotti)* which brought water to Agrippa's baths in 19 BC.

It was in this street in 1760 that a Greek opened the famous **caffè Greco**, a meeting place for artists and men of letters: Goethe, Berlioz, Wagner, Leopardi, d'Annunzio. Here Elizabeth Barrett Browning, who lived in Via Bocca di Leone, was introduced to Hans Andersen, who lived above. Tennyson, Thackeray and Keat's friend, Joseph Severn lodged in the house opposite.

The room at the back of the café, called the omnibus owing to its narrow width, is still hung with portraits of famous people. One can imagine its elegance and the unpopularity of Pope Leo XII when on 24 March 1824 he forbade his subjects to enter the café. The door was to remain locked and the owner was restricted to serving his customers through an opening in the window. The penalty was three months in the galleys.

Spanish Square ★★ — Spanish Steps (Piazza di Spagna — Scalla della Trinità dei Monti). — The square is world famous. The celebrated steps are no longer occupied by flower sellers but by peripatetic salesmen who spread out their wares: jewellery and arts and crafts.

Shaped like two triangles joined at their points, **Spanish Square ★★** got its name in 17C when the Spanish Ambassador to the Holy See took up residence in the **Palazzo di Spagna**. Thereupon the area bounded by Via dei Condotti, Via del Corso and Via della Mercede became Spanish territory and any foreigner crossing the boundaries at night often disappeared, having been impressed into the Spanish army. The French however, who owned the land round the convent of the Trinità dei Monti, claimed the right to pass through the square. They named part of it 'French Square' and set out to rival the Spanish by giving ever more sumptuous entertainments. In 1681 the Spanish celebrated the birthday of their queen, Marie-Louise by transforming the square with a variety of paste-board decorations. In 1685 it was the turn of the French; to celebrate the Revocation of the Edict of Nantes they covered the whole hillside with candelabras and decorated the church to look like a wayside altar from which they set off fire works which lit up the whole town.

Boat Fountain (Fontana della Barcaccia). — *At the foot of the steps.* It was designed by Bernini's father, Pietro (1627-29) for Pope Urban VIII. The boat, which is decorated at either end with the suns and bees of the Barberini coat of arms, seems to be letting in water. The sculptor is supposed to have conceived the idea from seeing a boat stranded in Spanish Square by the flood waters of the Tiber.

Keats' House (Casina di Keats) (E). — *26 Piazza di Spagna. Open Monday to Friday from 9 am to 1 pm and 3.30 to 6.30 pm (9 am to 1 pm and 2.30 to 5 pm in winter). 2 000 L.*

The house on the right at the foot of the Spanish steps where Keats died of tuberculosis in February 1821 was purchased in 1903 by the Keats-Shelley Memorial Association. The rooms which Keats occupied on the first floor now contain a collection of manuscripts, letters, momentoes and documents on the lives not only of Keats but also of Shelley, Byron and Leigh Hunt, together with a library of 10 000 volumes. In the entrance hall on the ground floor hang portraits of Keats and his contemporaries by English artists of the period.

Spanish Steps ★★ (Scala della Trinità dei Monti). — Built between 1723 to 1726 by de Sanctis in accordance with designs by Specchi (a pupil of C Fontana), the steps show the Baroque taste for perspective and *trompe-l'œil*.

Construction was preceded by fierce diplomatic struggles between the Holy See and France which are recalled in the eagles from the Conti coat of arms for Innocent XIII and the Lily of France. The idea of a flight of steps linking Spanish Square with the Church of the Trinità dei Monti had first been proposed in 17C. The French Ambassador even contributed 10 000 écus towards the cost, while Cardinal Mazarin proposed to make the steps a symbol of the greatness of the French monarchy in Rome. A grandiose design was prepared dominated by an equestrian statue of Louis XIV. The idea of a king's statue in the papal city! Alexander VII objected. Neither the Cardinal's death in 1661 nor the Pope's death in 1669 ended the quarrel. It was not finally settled until Innocent XIII (1721-24) agreed to the French architect and the French abandoned the statue of Louis XIV. De Sanctis designed three successive flights of steps, some broader, some narrower, some divided, exaggerating the effect of height and creating a graceful and majestic décor.

From the upper terrace there is an excellent view of the city.

In the square in front of the Church of the Trinità dei Monti stands an imitation Egyptian obelisk transported from Sallust's gardens near the Salaria Gate by Pius VI.

Church of the Trinità dei Monti★. — The church — Holy Trinity on the Hill — was founded in 1495 by Charles VIII at the request of St Francis of Paola for the Minims who lived in the neighbouring convent. The building rose slowly during 16C. It was severely damaged by French revolutionaries and completely rebuilt in 1816 by the architect Mazois assisted by several students from the Villa Medici. It is now French property and the convent is occupied by the Ladies of the Sacred Heart.

Façade. — An elegant stair, built in 1587 by Domenico Fontana leads up to the façade which is surmounted by two belfries, erected in 1588 by the Duc de Joyeuse and modelled on those designed by Giacomo della Porta for St Athanasius' in Via del Babuino. In 1613 a clock was added to tell the time in the "French manner".

Interior. — *Open Sundays and holidays 8 am to 1 pm and 4 to 6 pm.* The single nave flanked by intercommunicating chapels is reminiscent of the Gothic churches in the south of France. It is quite possible that it was designed by an architect from the southwest of that country (the windows which formerly decorated the chancel were sent for by Cardinal Briçonnet from Narbonne). The decorative latticework in the transept vaults, the oldest part of the church, is typical of late Gothic art. The side chapels are decorated with Mannerist paintings. The third on the right contains a fresco of the Assumption by Daniele da Volterra. The figure in red on the right of the picture is a portrait of Michelangelo; his assistants were responsible for the paintings on the side walls: the Massacre of the Innocents *(left)* and the Presentation in the Temple *(right)*.

Deposition from the Cross★. — *Second chapel on the left.* This fresco (1541), which has been much restored, is a masterpiece by **Daniele da Volterra** who was a great admirer of Michelangelo. See how skilfully he has arranged his composition around the pale body of Jesus.

Monsters' House (Casa dei Mostri). — *At the beginning of Via Gregoriana.* The door and windows are framed by curious carved monsters with gaping mouths.

In 17C and 18C Via Gregoriana and its neighbour Via Sistina usually provided lodgings for the wealthier visitors to Rome.

Take Viale della Trinità dei Monti.

On the right is a **bust of Chateaubriand (A)**, better known as a writer, who was the French Ambassador in Rome from 1828 to 1829.

Villa Medici. — *Guided tour Wednesday 9 am to 1 pm and Sunday 10 am to 1 pm in English, French or Italian according to the majority language of the party.*

The villa itself was built about 1570 for Cardinal Ricci di Montepulciano and passed to Cardinal Ferdinando de' Medici in 1576. In 1C BC the site was covered by the gardens of Lucullus. There is a fine view of Rome from the terrace opposite the entrance. The fountain which was installed in 1587 by Cardinal Ferdinando de' Medici, is the one which Corot painted. Legend has it that the ball in the centre of the basin is a canon ball fired at the Villa from Castel Sant'Angelo by Queen Christina of Sweden who adored practical jokes. She wanted to wake up the master of the house to invite him to join a hunting party.

French Academy. — It was founded by Colbert under Louis XIV in 1666 and occupied various buildings in Rome before moving to the Villa Medici in 1803. Its previous home, the Palazzo Salviati had been closed, sacked and burned during the Revolution. Originally the pupils were chosen by competition, the Prix de Rome; the first batch comprised six painters, four sculptors and two architects. After 1803 the field was widened to include engravers and musicians. The struggle for Italian unity and the second world war forced the Academy to move to Florence, then Nice and finally Fontainebleau before returning to the Villa Medici in 1946. Since then new areas of study have been admitted: literature, cinema, history and restoration of art. There are now about 25 students, chosen by the Ministry of Culture on the recommendation of specialists, and they study for one or two years.

Continue along Viale della Trinità dei Monti.

Where the road widens out on the left to afford a fine view of the city stands a **monument to the brothers Enrico and Giovanni Cairoli (B)**, Italian patriots who fought with Garibaldi's troops against the Pope's forces. They died in 1867 during the struggles for Italian unity.

The Pincio. — The Pinci family, who had a garden here in 4C, have left their name to this little hill which is still covered by a garden, one of the pleasantest in Rome. The Pincio was laid out in its present style during the Napoleonic occupation (1809-14) according to the designs of **Giuseppe Valadier**. The avenues are shaded by magnificent umbrella pines, palm trees and evergreen oaks. The statues of Italian patriots were added by Giuseppe Mazzini (1805-72).

From the terrace of Piazzale Napoleone I there is a magnificent **view★★★** particularly at dusk when the golden glow so typical of Rome is at its mellow best. Below the terrace is the Piazza del Popolo with the domes of the twin churches marking the beginning of the Corso. Opposite are the buildings of the Vatican grouped round the dome of St Peter's next to the green slopes of the Janiculum; just in front stand Castel Sant' Angelo and the white bulk of the Law Courts. The line of the Corso is marked by the domes of San Carlo, San Giovanni dei Fiorentini, Sant' Andrea delle Valle, the Pantheon (shallow) and the Gesù Church ending with the monument to Victor Emmanuel II.

Half way along Viale dell' Obelisco which leads to the gardens of the Villa Borghese *(pp 169, 174)* stands an obelisk which was set up here in 1822 by Pius VII after being found near the Porta Maggiore in 16C; it was originally erected by the Emperor Hadrian in memory of his young friend Antinoüs.

The water clock **(D)** in Viale dell' Orologio was built in 1867 by a Dominican monk, Giovan Battista Embriago and presented to the Universal Exhibition in Paris (1889).

PANTHEON

Distance: 2.5 km — 1 1/2 mile. Time: about 4 hours. Start: Piazza Venezia

This walk covers the ancient Mars' Field (Campus Martius) at the heart of Baroque Rome. The dark narrow streets provide a kaleidoscope of human activity: the hurrying tourist, the long established trader who observes the passing crowds from the back of his little shop, men and women of the church, busy or meditative or strolling along Via dei Cestari past the shops which specialise in religious habits.

Every visitor to Rome gravitates towards the Pantheon: seeking peace and quiet after the noise and bustle of the Corso or looking for one of the many small restaurants *(trattoria)* in the area.

HISTORICAL NOTES

For many years the **Campus Martius** was merely a marshy plain used for drilling the soldiery or conducting a census of the citizenry. In 2C BC however, under the influence of the urban manners they had observed in their new provinces in Greece, Macedonia and Pergamum, the Romans began to divide up the area into lots. In the eastern half, between the Pantheon and the present Corso, Caesar erected the *Saepta*, an enclosure for the assemblies which elected the tribunes of the people *(comitia tributa)* bordered on the south side by the *diribitorium* where the votes were counted and on the east and west by two porticos: the Meleager and the Argonauts. In about 43 BC two Egyptian temples dedicated to Isis and Serapis were built beside the *Saepta (plan pp 14-15)*.

Each imperial dynasty felt honour bound to leave its mark on the Campus Martius. Augustus' son-in-law, Agrippa, built the Pantheon and, between 25 and 19 BC, the first public baths in Rome. Domitian was responsible for a temple to Minerva and a portico to the deified Flavians. Under the Antonines a temple to the deified Hadrian was built. Alexander Severus, the last of the Severans, rebuilt Nero's baths.

In 4C the Christians held sway. The Bishop of Rome, henceforward in control of the Caesars' capital, constructed Christian buildings often on the ruins of pagan monuments.

During the mediaeval struggle between the princes and the popes Rome was peppered with towers and became *Roma Turrita* (turreted Rome) *(p 12)*. Near the Pantheon stood the Crescenzi fortress which gave its name to the adjoining street: Salita dei Crescenzi. A tower was built nearby by the Sinibaldi. Then came the Renaissance and the Papacy was triumphant. The higher clerics and the wealthy citizens bought up whole blocks of hovels and replaced them with unostentatious but luxurious palaces.

Time seems to have stood still here since the Baroque age cast its veil of illusion over the buildings.

TOUR

For a description of Via del Corso see p 98.

Palazzo Bonaparte. — This 17C palazzo of modest appearance became the property of Napoleon's mother and she took up residence in 1815 when the Empire fell. Without rancour Pius VII granted asylum to all the exiled members of the imperial family. Lucian, Jerome and Louis, the ex-king of the Netherlands, formed the old lady's circle in the palace. From the enclosed balcony on the first floor she liked to see what was going on in the street below. On 8 February 1836 attended by her son Jerome and Cardinal Fesch she died. She was buried quietly in the nearby church, Santa Maria in Via Lata, while the Carnival was in full swing.

Palazzo Salviati. — It was built by the Duke of Nevers, Cardinal Mazarin's nephew, in 17C to house the French Academy *(p 100)*.

Palazzo Doria Pamphili ★. — *Contains a picture gallery: p 102.* This palazzo, one of the largest in Rome, was begun in 15C and gradually enlarged by the succession of noble families which owned it. First acquired by the della Rovere family, it then passed to Pope Julius II's nephew, the Duke of Urbino. Clement VIII, a member of the Aldobrandini family, then bought it for his nephew. Finally Donna Olimpia, Clement VIII's niece and heir, married Camillo Pamphili whose family was later allied with that of the Dorias.

The façade facing the Corso is an imposing 18C construction in the Baroque style whereas the front looking into Via del Plebiscito dates from 1643. The palazzo extends the whole length of Via della Gatta behind a 19C façade and round two sides of Piazza del Collegio Romano.

Since 1966 part of the Palazzo has housed the Anglican Centre in Rome, a tangible outcome of the formal visit paid by Archbishop Michael Ramsey to Pope Paul VI in that year, where students of any age, particularly Roman Catholics, who wish to learn about the Anglican Communion can consult the library of Anglican authorities, books of reference and of history.

Santa Maria in Via Lata. — The façade ★ of the church is its most interesting feature. It was built between 1658 and 1662 by **Pietro da Cortona** at the point in the evolution of the Baroque style when the detached column began to play an essential role. The two storeys of columns comprising the façade seem to support the whole building and create beautiful effects of light and shade.

Palazzo del Banco di Roma. — Originally built between 1714 and 1722, the palace served as the French Ambassador's residence in 18 and 19C before being converted in 20C; it is now occupied by the Banco di Roma.

San Marcello. — The Church of St Marcellus was founded in 4C on the site of a *titulus,* a private house used as a place of Christian worship.

The church was burned down in 1519 and completely rebuilt in 16C and 17C. In 1683 Carlo Fontana designed the slightly concave Baroque façade. The palms linking the two storeys are typical of the Baroque style which delighted in the unusual. The empty frame above the entrance has never received its intended sculpture.

The single nave flanked by side chapels, typical of the Renaissance, was designed by Jacopo Sansovino in 16C. The late 16C coffered ceiling is richly decorated in gold, blue and red.

Works of art from the Renaissance to the Baroque period are to be found here. To the left of the entrance is the tomb of Cardinal Giovanni Michiel, who was poisoned on Alexander VI's orders in 1503. Below it is the tomb of his nephew, Bishop Antonio Orso who died in 1511. The work was begun in 1520 by Andrea Sansovino and finished in 1527 by his pupil Jacopo Sansovino. The books at the base recall the Bishop's bequest of several works to the convent of St Marcellus.

In the fourth chapel on the right is a fine 15C wooden crucifix. The realistic figure of Christ in agony gave rise to a lugubrious legend: the sculptor was so obsessed with the desire to depict the suffering as realistically as possible that he killed a poor fellow who happened to be passing that way and studied the death throes to inspire his own carving. When the church burned down in 1519 the crucifix was recovered intact in the ruins. The frescoes in the vault are by Perin del Vaga, one of Raphael's pupils. In the base of the altar is a 3C Roman stele which was decorated with incrustations of marble in 12C to serve as a reliquary.

The fourth chapel on the left contains busts of the noble family of the Frangipani; the three on the right were carved by Algardi in 1625.

Turn back into Via Lata between the Banco di Roma and the church of Sta Maria in Via Lata.

Facchino Fountain (A). — Tucked against the wall *(right)* is an amusing little fountain composed of a water-carrier *(facchino)* holding a barrel with water issuing from the bung hole into a basin. According to legend the sculptor took as his model a Renaissance water carrier with a reputation for drunkenness, who is thus obliged to make do with water for the rest of time.

Turn left out of Via Lata into the square.

Doria Pamphili Gallery★. — *Entrance in the southwest corner of Piazza del Collegio Romano. On the first floor. Open 10 am to 1 pm. 2 000 L; 2 000 L extra for the private apartments. Closed Monday, Wednesday, Thursday, 1 January, 1 May, Christmas.*

The Palazzo Doria Pamphili *(p 101)* houses a fine collection of paintings and sculpture. Some of the more outstanding are mentioned below. *The numbers used in the text correspond with those in the gallery.*

First gallery *(bear right):* Portrait of a young man *(15)* by Jacopo Tintoretto (1518-94). The portrait of two people *(23)* is attributed to Raphael. Salome with the head of John the Baptist is an early work by Titian.

Three paintings by **Caravaggio** (1573-1610) are among some of his most famous; he returned to realism thus saving the art from becoming enmeshed in Mannerism. The Magdalen *(40)* is simply painted as a despairing young woman without any reference to the New Testament story. The bottle of perfume and the jewellery at her side are shown in remarkably clear detail. In the **Flight into Egypt★★★** *(42)* the Virgin asleep with her child is shown in a similar attitude to Mary Magdalene. The scene on the left of the composition is unusually romantic for Caravaggio. John the Baptist as a child *(44)* recalls the painting which hangs in the Conservators' Palace *(p 60)*. Caravaggio had probably seen the nude figures painted by Michelangelo in the Sistine Chapel or by Carracci in the Farnese Palace.

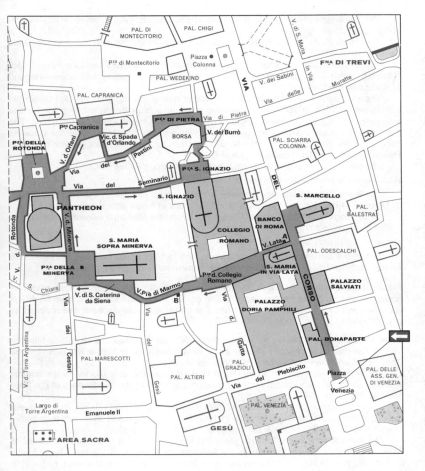

At the far end of this gallery is a **bust of Olimpia Maidalchini Pamphili ★★** by **Algardi.** She is said to have pestered and hounded her brother-in-law, Giovanni Battista Pamphili, until he attained the papal throne as Innocent X. Algardi who was an accomplished portraitist knew precisely how to express the energy and ambition of Donna Olimpia, as she was called by the Romans; she is shown in the distinctive headdress which she alone wore.

Several steps lead down into the Aldobrandini salon which is hung with some fine 16C Brussels tapestries illustrating the battle of Lepanto (7 October 1571).

Second gallery: Saint Sebastian *(135)* is by Ludovico Carracci (1555-1619) who together with his cousins, Agostino and Annibale, had Caravaggio as a pupil. The bronze and porphyry bust of Innocent X is by Algardi.

The suite of four rooms, branching off right at the junction of the second and third galleries and ending in an octagonal room, contains *(3rd room)* a charming portrait of Agatha van Schoonhoven *(279)* painted in 1523 by Jan van Scorel, a painter from Utrecht, who was in Rome when his compatriot Adrian VI became Pope, and *(4th room)* Portrait of a Franciscan *(291)* by Rubens, Earthly Paradise *(295)* by 'Velvet' Brueghel and the unusual Naval Battle in the Bay of Naples *(317)* by Brueghel the Elder.

Third gallery: decorated in 18C style with mirrors and gilding, it ends in an alcove containing the **Portrait of Innocent X ★★★**, a masterpiece by **Velazquez**, painted in 1650 during his second visit to Rome; the painter has succeeded in painting an official portrait quite lacking in nobility. Here also is a bust of Innocent X by Bernini, a very expressive interpretation of the Pope's authority.

Fourth gallery: it is dominated by two **works ★★** by **Annibale Carracci.** They are semi-circular in shape and were part of a series painted from 1603 to 1604 for the palace chapel. In Flight into Egypt *(359)* the gentle but realistic landscape takes up almost all the picture presaging a taste which was to develop throughout 17C. At the end of the gallery is an early version of Bernini's bust of Innocent X.

Private Apartments ★. — *Guided tour; last tour at 11 am.* These are the rooms inhabited from 16C to 18C by the families who owned the palace. In the Wintergarden are a small sleigh used in 18C and a fine sedan chair, painted and gilded (18C). The Andrea Doria room bears the name of the most famous member of the Genoese Doria family; a mercenary *(condottiere)*, he commanded the French fleet for Francis I before being employed by Charles V. The 16C Brussels tapestries depicting the Battle of Lepanto are part of the same series as those in the Aldobrandini salon.

The smoking room, which is decorated in 19C English style, contains a 15C Tuscan polyptych.

The frieze in the dining room depicts the various properties belonging to the Doria Pamphili family (19C).

In the Green Drawing Room: a graceful Annunciation by the Florentine Filippo Lippi (1406-69), Botticelli's master; a large 15C Tournai tapestry illustrating the mediaeval legend of Alexander the Great.

The tour continues with a suite of reception rooms starting with the Ball Room, its walls lined with silk in 20C, which contains a beautiful table decorated with hard stone marquetry and supported on a 17C gilded wooden base in the shape of four dolphins. The walls of the Yellow Drawing Room are hung with tapestry panels made at the Gobelins factory in Paris for Louis XV. In the Small Red Drawing Room hangs a portrait of James Edward Stuart, the Old Pretender, by A S Belle.

The tour ends in the Chapel which is decorated in *trompe-l'œil* (18C).

Walk along the south side of Piazza del Collegio Romano.

The **Roman College** (Collegio Romano), formely the Jesuit College, was founded in 1583 by Gregory XIII who strove to re-establish the primacy of Rome after the Council of Trent.

At the corner of Via della Gatta there is a charming Madonna beneath a canopy so typical of Rome *(p 161).*

Continue westwards along Via Piè di Marmo.

The street is named after the enormous stone **foot** (B) which probably belonged to a Roman statue although no one knows how it came to be in its present position.

Piazza della Minerva. — It was Bernini's idea to embellish this charming square with an obelisk supported on an elephant's back. The obelisk is Egyptian and dates from 6C BC; it was once part of the nearby Temple of Isis. The fantastic marble elephant was sculpted by one of Bernini's pupils, Ercole Ferrata (1667).

Santa Maria sopra Minerva ★. — Founded in 8C near the ruins of a temple to Minerva built by Domitian, the church has undergone many alterations. In 1280 it was rebuilt in the Gothic style and then modified towards the middle of 15C.

The façade was constructed in 17C; it is rectangular and very plain with the original 15C doorways. Six plaques *(right)* mark the heights reached by the flood waters of the Tiber between 1598 and 1870.

The construction of the side chapels began in 15C, the chancel was rebuilt in 17C and the pillars were covered in grey marble in 19C. The broad nave and aisle with their heavy intersecting rib vaulting can give the impression of a Gothic church.

The **works of art ★** in the Minerva place it in the first rank of the 'museum churches' of Rome. Just inside the central door is the Renaissance tomb (1) of Diotisalvi Neroni who died in 1482 after being exiled from Florence for plotting against Piero de Medici; by the side door is the tomb (2) of Virginia Pucci-Ridolfi adorned with a beautiful female bust; the two holy water stoops (3) date from 1588.

South aisle. — In the fifth chapel (4) the painting by Antoniazzo Romano on the subject of the Annunciation recalls the beneficence of Cardinal Juan de Torquemada who provided poor girls with dowries. This work against a gold background is typical of the style of this late 15C painter which is marked with a certain religious conventionality.

The sixth chapel (5) was designed late in 16C by Giacomo della Porta and Carlo Maderno. In the spirit of the Counter-Reformation the extravagance of the marble is tempered with a certain severity. The tombs of Clement VIII's parents are by Giacomo delle Porta and Nicolas Cordier (a French sculptor who spent almost all his life in Rome).

The next chapel (6) contains one of Andrea Bregno's most famous works *(right):* the restrained and delicate decoration on the tomb of Cardinal Coca who died in 1477.

In the last chapel before the transept (7) is a beautiful 15C wooden crucifix.

South transept. — The Carafa chapel (8), which has a finely carved marble altar rail, was built and decorated between 1489 and 1493 with frescoes ★ by **Filippino Lippi:** above the altar in a typical late Renaissance frame is an Annunciation in which Thomas Aquinas presents Cardinal Oliviero Carafa to the Virgin. The expressive faces, the slender figures and the deeply pleated garments are characteristic of Filippino Lippi's art. The rest of the wall is taken up with an Assumption in fine colours. The righthand wall shows scenes from the life of Thomas Aquinas.

On the left of the Carafa chapel is an example of the Italian Gothic style *(pp 55 and 64):* the tomb of Guillaume Durand (9), Bishop of Mende in France who died in 1296.

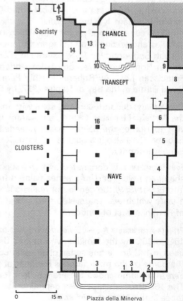

Piazza della Minerva

Chancel. — The heavy and inexpressive statue of Christ (10) was commissioned by a Roman nobleman from Michelangelo. The artist has returned to Florence in 1520; he started the statue but then sent it to Rome where it was finished by his pupils. The gilded bronze drapery was added later.

The funeral monuments of the Medici popes, Clement VII (11) and Leo V (12), modelled on commemorative arches, are the work of Antonio da Sangallo (1483-1546); contemporary taste preferred architectural to decorative features in funerary art.

North transept. — The first chapel (13) contains many fine **tombs ★ :** in the Gothic style *(right)*; dating from 15C *(on either side of the rear door)*; in the Baroque style *(above the door and on the right)*; the tomb with the dead man resting on his elbow *(left)* is by Giacomo della Porta (late 16C).

Let into the floor is the tomb of Fra Angelico, Giovanni da Fiesole, the Dominican painter who died in 1455.

In the next chapel (14) is a 15C tomb composed of an antique sarcophagus (Hercules and the lion).

St Catherine of Siena's Chapel (15). — It was built in 17C using the walls of the room in which the saint died in the neighbouring Dominican convent.

North aisle. — Monument to Venerable Sister Maria Raggi (16): flowing garments, an ecstatic expression and lively cherubs exemplify the art of Bernini (1643). The Renaissance tomb of Francesco Tornabuoni (17), who died in 1480, is one of Mino da Fiesole's most successful works owing to its fine decorative carving.

Bear right into Via della Minerva which leads to the Pantheon.

Pantheon Square (Piazza della Rotonda). — This is a typical Roman scene: the grandiose portico of the Pantheon, flanked by the elegant orange and ochre façades of the houses overlooking the square, the friendly simplicity of the cafés and the continual coming and going of the tourists.

The fountain at the centre was set up in 1578 by **Giacomo della Porta;** in 1711 Clement XI added the obelisk. Like the one in Piazza della Minerva, it comes from the Temple of Isis; the base is decorated with dolphins and the papal coat of arms.

■ PANTHEON ★★★

Open 9 am to 1 pm and 2 to 6 pm (4 pm in winter). Closed Sunday morning, Monday and 15 August, Christmas and 26 December.

Originally it was a temple, built by Agrippa, the great town planner, in 27 BC; it was dedicated to all the gods and faced south. In 80 AD it was damaged by fire and restored by Domitian. Then Hadrian (117-38) rebuilt it and gave it its present orientation to the north. It was closed in 4C by the first Christian emperors together with all other places of pagan worship, sacked by the barbarians in 410 but saved from destruction by Pope Boniface IV who received it as a gift in 608 from Phocas, the Emperor in Byzantium *(p 43)*. It was then converted into a church dedicated to St Mary *ad martyres.*

Until 756, when the Papal States came into being, Rome was subject to Byzantium. The only Eastern Emperor to visit the Christian capital was Constantinus II in 356 when the Pantheon was despoiled of its bronze tiles for the embellishment of Constantinople. It was restored early in the Renaissance and then Urbain VIII removed the nails and bronze plates which covered the beams of the porch roof and had them made into the magnificent baldaquin now in St Peter's. Pasquino *(p 160)* responded with a neat pun on the Pope's family name: *Quod non fecerunt Barbari, fecerunt Barberini* (what the barbarians did not do, the Barberini have done). During Alexander VII's reign (1655-67) the porch was 'improved' by the addition of two belfries. Bernini was the architect responsible; immediately Pasquino talked about "Bernini's ass' ears". They were removed in 1883.

Exterior. — The Pantheon is a compact building comprising the main circular chamber and a pillared porch *(pronaos)* beneath a pediment. The porch cornice bears two inscriptions: one concerns the original building by Agrippa and below, scarcely visible, the other mentions restorations carried out by Septimius Severus and Caracalla.

From the side street, Via della Rotonda, the powerful relieving arches are visible set into the massive walls which are 6.20 m - over 20 ft thick. At the rear of the building are an apse, some hollow niches and sculpted fragments; they belonged to the Neptune basilica which stood between the Pantheon and Agrippa's baths *(map pp 14-15)*.

Interior ★★★ . — The entrance is under the porch which is supported on 16 monolithic granite columns, all original except for the three on the left which were replaced owing to weakness under Urban VIII and Alexander VII; the papal emblems (the Barberini bees and the Chigi stars) can be seen on the capitals.

The bronze doors which date from the Empire were restored under Pius IV (16C). The harmony and grandeur of the interior have an immediate impact. The proportions are striking; the diameter of the building is equal to its overall height: 43.30 m - 142 ft. The dome is an incredibly bold feature; its weight is distributed via relieving arches incorporated in the walls on to the eight piers of masonry which alternate with the deep recesses. At the centre of the coffered ceiling is an enormous round opening through which the interior is lit.

A series of superb monolithic columns marks the alternating rounded or rectangular recesses. The piers between the recesses are decorated with shrines with alternating triangular or rounded pediments to which later Renaissance architects turned for inspiration in designing palazzo windows.

The upper stage between the cornice and the base of the dome was redesigned in 18C with the present series of panels and blind windows. A section above the third chapel on the west side has been returned to the original décor.

The recesses have been converted into chapels: in the first to the west of the entrance is an attractive Annunciation attributed to Melozzo da Forli. The next chapel contains the tomb of Victor Emmanuel II (1820-78), the first king of unified Italy.

Between the fifth and sixth chapels is the tomb of Raphaël, who died aged 37 in 1520, composed of a fine antique sarcophagus. On the upper edge is an inscription by Cardinal Pietro Bembo, poet and humanist (1470-1547) which Alexander Pope translated without acknowledgement for another epitaph:

> *"Living, great nature feared he might outvie*
> *Her works; and dying fears herself to die."*

Turn right down Via del Seminario to Piazza S. Ignazio.

Piazza S. Ignazio ★. — The square is best observed from the steps of the church. It was designed in imitation of a theatre set, in ochre and stone, and has an unusual charm with curved façades on the street corners where people make their entrances and exits like actors on a stage.

St Ignatius' (Sant' Ignazio). — The church, which is dedicated to the founder of the Jesuits, is typical of the Counter-Reformation *(p 25)* and was begun in 1626 to the plans of a Jesuit, Orazio Grassi. It stands within the precincts of the Roman College and served for many years as the college chapel.

Another Jesuit, Andrea Pozzo, designed the high façade; the two superimposed orders linked by scrolls produce a solemn and austere effect.

Central ceiling fresco ★★. — For the best effect stand on the disc in the centre of the nave. The fresco is the work of **Andrea Pozzo** (1684). A Jesuit, he chose a subject dear to the Counter-Reformation which exalted the saints in the face of Protestantism. Here St Ignatius is bathed by a divine light which is reflected on the four corners of the world shown allegorically. Pozzo used his knowledge of perspective to create the *trompe-l'œil* effect. Against an architectural background he has ranged an animated crowd of figures.

Apsidal fresco. — Also the work of Andrea Pozzo, it glorifies the miracles worked by St Ignatius' intercession.

Transept. — Above the crossing rises a 'cupola' in *trompe-l'œil* painted by Andrea Pozzo. Between 1696 and 1702 he wrote a treatise entitled *Perspectiva pictorum et achitectorum* which had considerable influence on painters and architects in 18C.

The chapel at the end of the right transept is dedicated to St Luigi Gonzaga. Above the lapis lazuli urn containing the saint's relics and between the beautiful green marble columns wreathed in fronds of bronze is an admirable 'marble picture' carved by **Pierre Legros**, a French student at the French Academy (1629-1714), who collaborated with Andrea Pozzo in most of his works. The Director of the Academy however did not appreciate one of his students working to the glory of the Roman Jesuits rather than the king of France, so Pierre Legros had to leave the Academy.

Opposite in the left transept is a corresponding chapel in honour of St John Berchmans. The high relief sculpture of the Annunciation is the work of Filippo Valle. Both chapels boast bold interpretations by Andrea Pozzo of the pediments so dear to Borromini.

Take Via dei Burrò.

It owes its name to the administrative offices established in the area by Napoleon Bonaparte.

Piazza di Pietra. — The south side of this colourful square is occupied by a building which now houses the Stock Exchange but in 18C was the Customs House where any visitor to Rome was obliged to present himself.

Incorporated in the present building are eleven beautiful marble columns in the Corinthian order which belonged to a **temple** which stood here in antiquity. It was erected in honour of the deified **Hadrian** by his adopted son Antoninus Pius and consecrated in 145 AD. The grandeur of the ancient columns contrasts strangely with the intimate character of the square.

Take Via dei Pastini turning right into Vicolo della Spada d'Orlando.

On the base of one of the columns in this street is a scoremark left by Roland's sword during a street brawl.

Return to Piazza della Rotonda by Via degli Orfani.

On the left on the corner of Salita dei Crescenzi and Via di S. Eustachio two ancient columns belonging to the baths of Alexander Severus have been re-erected.

San Luigi dei Francesi ★★. — *Closed Thursday afternoons.* The first stone of this building was laid in 1518 by Cardinal Giulio de' Medici, the future Pope Clement VII. After very slow progress between 1524 and 1580 the church was completed in 1589 partly with the aid of subsidies from France given by Henri II, Henri III and Catherine de Medici and was consecrated as the national church of the French in Rome.

The façade, which bears the salamander of Francis I of France, was probably designed by Giacomo della Porta. Its elegant lines accord well with the Piazza di San Luigi dei Francesi. The prominent columns hint at the flamboyance of the Baroque style.

The interior, consisting of a nave, side aisles and lateral chapels, was embellished in the Baroque period and in 18C with marbles, paintings, gilding and stucco work.

The vault was decorated in 1754 with the Glory of St Louis by Natoire; beneath it many Frenchmen have been laid to rest: Cardinal de Bernis (1) who lived in style in the Palazzo del Banco di Roma *(p 101)*; Pauline de Beaumont (2), Chateaubriand's romantic friend: the Pope turned a blind eye to their illegal liaison and Chateaubriand, then the French Ambassador, commissioned her memorial; Claude Gellée, also known as Lorraine, who captured the Roman light so marvellously in his paintings, has a memorial here (3) although he was buried in the Trinità dei Monti.

Domenichino's frescoes ★. — *In St Cecilia's chapel* (4). They illustrate the legend of St Cecilia and were painted in 1614. Domenichino, who arrived in Rome in 1602, rejected the exuberance of the Baroque style in his desire to express balance and clarity.

The five scenes chosen by the artist for illustration are: on the right St Cecilia distributing her riches; on the left St Cecilia's death; on the vault St Cecilia and her husband Valerian are crowned by an angel; St Cecilia refuses to sacrifice to the pagan gods; St Cecilia in glory.

Piazza di San Luigi dei Francesi

Caravaggio's paintings ★★★. — *In St Matthew's chapel* (5). There are three paintings depicting St Matthew's life. The vault is by Cavaliere d'Arpino whose Mannerist style so exasperated Caravaggio.

Above the altar: St Matthew and the Angel; the artist's delight in contradiction is expressed here in the rather acrobatic posture of the old man writing his Gospel at the angel's dictation.

— *On the left:* the Calling of St Matthew; in a dark room five men seated at a table are distracted from their occupation by the entrance of Christ accompanied by St Peter; His pointing finger singles out Matthew seated beside an old man in spectacles who is counting out the money; the shaft of light striking the wall and illuminating the faces is typical of Caravaggio's art; the young man with a feather in his cap watching with a slightly scornful air is a familiar figure in Caravaggio's paintings.

— *On the right:* the Martyrdom of St Matthew; the naked figure *(centre)* and the gesture of the young boy *(right)* are in the academic style although the forms are defined by the play of light and shade in Caravaggio's usual manner.

Turn right into Via del Salvatore, then left into Corso del Rinascimento.

This broad street was opened up in 1938 during the renovation of the historic centre of the City.

(After photo by Gab. Fot. Naz., Rome)
Caravaggio:
Calling of St Matthew (detail)

Palazzo Madama. — *Since 1870 when Rome became the capital of Italy the Senate has occupied the building. Not open to the public.*

It was built by the Medici in 16C. In the days of Cardinal Giovanni de' Medici, the future Leo X, a succession of banquets and literary gatherings was held here. Later Pope Clement VII made it the residence of his great niece, Catherine de Medici. When she became the queen of France she renounced her Medici possessions and the palace passed to Alessandro de' Medici, whose wife, Madam Margaret of Austria (1522-86) gave the palace its name.

The Baroque façade in the Corso del Rinascimento was built *c*1642.

At the southern end of the street rises the façade of Sant' Andrea delle Valle.

Palazzo della Sapienza. — Until 1935 it was occupied by Rome University. Now it houses among other things the archives of the Papal States from 9 to 19C. The simple façade, begun in 1575 to a design by Giacomo della Porta and coloured burnt umber, gives no hint of the elegance of the inner courtyard nor of the audacity of **St Ivo's Church ★** by Borromini. The courtyard is surrounded by a two-storey portico terminating in the concave façade of the church at the far end. Just as Bernini aimed at extensiveness so Borromini tried to confine his ideas within a restricted space, using such exaggeratedly curved lines that his architecture was termed perverse and contrary. An amazing variety of curves is used in this building: in the many-faceted drum, in the convex line of the dome and the concave buttresses, in the spiral surmounting the lantern.

The interior, very high and light, is a constant interplay of concave and convex surfaces, a foretaste of the Rococo style *(to visit, apply to the porter during office hours)*.

It is worth taking a stroll in the narrow streets behind St Ivo's: from Piazza Sant' Eustachio, where the best coffee in Rome is served and which provides a very fine view of the spiral atop St Ivo's, to Via del Teatro Valle, where basket makers still work at their craft, and to the **Valle Theatre** with its old fashioned décor. In 1817 Stendhal was a frequent patron and complained vigorously about the lack of comfort and the disorderly behaviour of the public, despite the law which prescribed of 100 strokes of the cane for taking another's seat.

Distance: 8 km - 5 miles. Time: about 5 hours. Start: Corso Vittorio Emanuele II.

The walk follows the narrow streets of the district lying between the Tiber, the Corso Vittorio Emanuele II and the Capitol. In antiquity the district was just to the south of the Campus Martius and was chosen by Pompey for the construction of several important buildings in 55 BC: a huge theatre, the first in Rome to be built of stone, a temple to Venus and a Curia to house occasional meetings of the Senate. It was in Pompey's Curia that a decisive event in Roman history occurred: on the Ides of March 44 BC Julius Caesar was assassinated at the foot of Pompey's statue. Almost nothing remains of this building.

Archaeologists working on a nearby site in 1926 uncovered a religious enclave dating from the Republican era (Area Sacra del Largo Argentina: *p 110*).

The first Christian sanctuary in the district was San Lorenzo in Damaso, founded in 380 in the reign of Pope Damasus.

In the Middle Ages churches and castles grew in number. The churches were quite simple buildings serving the needs of the tradesmen, who in their various guilds gave a certain character to the district:

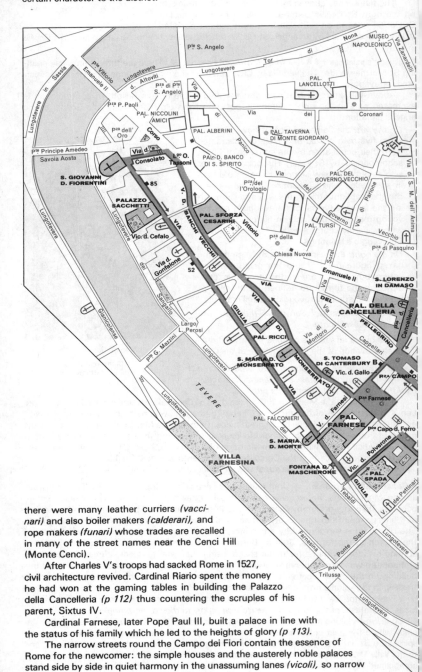

there were many leather curriers *(vaccinari)* and also boiler makers *(calderari),* and rope makers *(funari)* whose trades are recalled in many of the street names near the Cenci Hill (Monte Cenci).

After Charles V's troops had sacked Rome in 1527, civil architecture revived. Cardinal Riario spent the money he had won at the gaming tables in building the Palazzo della Cancelleria *(p 112)* thus countering the scruples of his parent, Sixtus IV.

Cardinal Farnese, later Pope Paul III, built a palace in line with the status of his family which he led to the heights of glory *(p 113).*

The narrow streets round the Campo dei Fiori contain the essence of Rome for the newcomer: the simple houses and the austerely noble palaces stand side by side in quiet harmony in the unassuming lanes *(vicoli),* so narrow in places that the two sides are linked by an arch.

■ GESÙ CHURCH ★★★

The salient features of the Piazza del Gesù are the church and the wind. According to a Roman legend it has been so since the Devil asked the wind to wait for him while he went into the church. But he never came out and the wind has been waiting ever since.

This building is the main Jesuit church in Rome. The Society of Jesus was founded in 1540 by Ignatius Loyola, a Spaniard. After the Council of Trent the Society became the prime mover in the Counter-Reformation which sought to rebut the ideas put forward by Martin Luther and Calvin. In 1568 the decision was taken to build a church in the centre of Rome. Cardinal Alexander Farnese undertook the provide the funds and insisted on his choice of architect: Vignola. The Vicar General of the Society engaged his own Jesuit architect, Father Giovanni Tristano, to see that the demands of the Jesuit rule were met.

For the **façade** Giacomo della Porta's design was chosen (1575). Very solemn and severe, it became a model for a transitional style, half-way between Renaissance and Baroque art, long known as the 'Jesuit style'. Art historians no longer use the expression since the Jesuits neither invented nor promoted a new style of architecture; at the most Rome gave practical advice on the construction of the Society's churches abroad.

The façade consists of two superimposed orders linked by powerful scrolls and has a double pediment, one curved and one triangular. These are the features which later became characteristic of Baroque architecture: several engaged columns are used instead of the flat pilasters of the Renaissance; projecting features and effects of light and shade are more pronounced. The height and width of the façade to some extent mask the dome which is seen to best advantage from above.

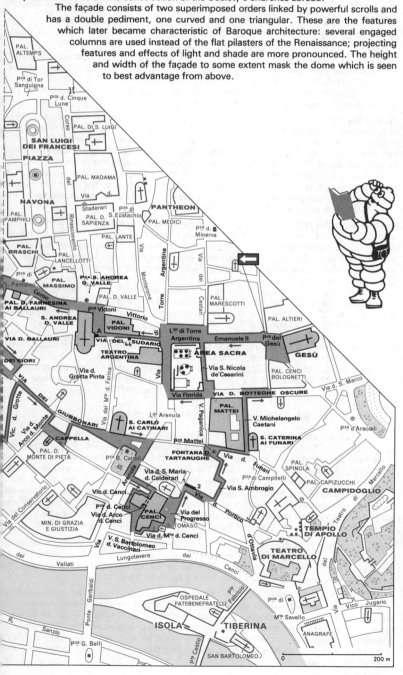

Interior

Compared with the purity of Gothic or the austerity of Romanesque, the richness of the décor is astonishing. A distinction must be made between the architecture of the building, a fairly plain product of the Counter-Reformation, and the decoration; which was added a century later in the Baroque period when the Papacy was triumphant.

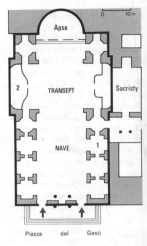

The majestic Latin cross **plan** was ideal for the Society's main purpose: preaching which enabled the congregation to understand the ceremonies which they attended. In the single broad nave, unobstructed and well lit, the worshippers could concentrate on the celebrant and read the prayers with him. Special attention was paid to the acoustics to give resonance to the canticles, which were essential to the worship of God.

The **decoration** inspired by the Counter-Reformation was intended to reinforce the conclusions of the Council of Trent: for example, the third chapel on the right (1) which is decorated with angels and the Virgin interceding for the souls in Purgatory illustrates ideas which were contested by the reformers. The 17C Baroque decoration expresses the victory of the Roman church: against the Turks at Lepanto in 1571; against Protestantism renounced by Henri IV, king of France, in 1593.

The abundance of polychrome marble, paintings, sculptures, bronzes, stuccowork and gilding which covers every inch of space is overwhelming.

Baciccia frescoes ★★. — In 1672, thanks to Bernini, Giovanni Battista Gaulli, called 'Il Baciccia', was commissioned to do the paintings in the Gesù Church. The Triumph of the Name of Jesus on the ceiling of the nave was certainly his masterpiece and entitled him to be considered as the main exponent of Baroque decoration. The work, which was completed in 1679, combines the technique of composition with the exuberance of *trompe-l'œil;* the eye moves without check from the painted surface to the sculptures by Antonio Raggi. The damned, who spill over the edge in a tumult of plunging bodies, do not break the unity of the composition imparted by the rays of divine light. He also painted the Adoration of the Lamb in the apse and the Assumption on the dome.

Chapel of St Ignatius Loyola ★★★ (2). — This chapel, where the remains of St Ignatius rest in a beautiful urn, was built by **Andrea Pozzo**, a Jesuit, between 1696 and 1700. Behind a bronze rail embellished with cherubs bearing torches, stands the altar bearing a statue of the saint in marble and silver. The original statue, which was the work of Pierre Legros, a Frenchman, was of solid silver but was melted down by Pius VI to pay the taxes imposed by Napoleon under the treaty of Tolentino (1797).

Andrea Pozzo used precious stones and metals with which he achieved impressive colour combinations: four columns faced with lapis lazuli rest on green marble bases adorned with low reliefs in bronze gilt. Above, among the figures of the Trinity, is a child supporting a terrestrial globe in lapis lazuli.

The altar is flanked by two groups of allegorical statues illustrating the activities of the Society of Jesus: Faith triumphing over idolatry *(left)* by Giovanni Theodon; Religion crushing heresy *(right)* by Pierre Legros, in the style of Andrea Pozzo *(p 106).*

In the building to the right of the church are the rooms where St Ignatius lived and died *(open 8 am to 12.30 pm and 4 to 7 pm).* The ceiling and walls of the flanking passage are decorated all over in *trompe-l'œil* paintings by Andrea Pozzo (17C).

■ AREA SACRA DEL LARGO ARGENTINA ★★

This is the name given to a group of ruins excavated between 1926 and 1929 in the Largo Argentina. The remains, which date from the days of the ancient Roman Republic, are among the oldest found in Rome. This marshy ground on the banks of the Tiber near the Campus Martius was often flooded. The necessary work of draining and embanking meant raising the ground level and modifying the buildings on the site. Traces of five building levels from 5C BC to the beginning of the Empire have been revealed by the archaeologists. In antiquity this large precinct was at the heart of a busy district: to the southeast stood the theatre built by Balbus in Augustus' reign, to the west Pompey's theatre and Curia, to the north the rear façade of Agrippa's baths and the Saepta *(plan pp 14-15).*

Tour. — *It is best to look at the ruins initially from the east side, Via S. Nicola de' Cesarini.* The Area Sacra consists primarily of four temples, including a round one, all facing east on to a square paved in travertine in the imperial period. As it is not known to which gods the temples were dedicated, they are known as temples A, B, C and D.

Temple C. — This is the oldest temple. Excavation of the podium has revealed the presence of blocks of tufa similar to those used in the construction of the Servian Wall (Mura Serviane); the original building therefore dates back to 6 to 5C BC. The plan is that of the early Roman temples which followed the Etruscan model: a triple *cella* (containing three shrines), a fairly high podium without columns at the rear. In the imperial period the *cella* was rebuilt at a higher level, the columns and the podium were faced with stucco and the floor was covered with mosaics.

The tower and portico in the southeast corner of the site, which were preserved during the excavations in 1932, were originally part of a group of mediaeval houses, built in 12C near the church of San Salvatore which stood in front of temple C.

Temple A. — The first building on this site dates from 4 to 3C BC. The present remains of a temple surrounded by columns date from 2 to 1C BC.

By 12C the ground was level with the top of the podium; temple A was converted into a church dedicated to St Nicholas, with a nave and south aisle both ending in an apse.

AREA SACRA DEL LARGO ARGENTINA

0   30 m

—— Extant parts
—— Non-extant parts
—— Remains of St Nicholas' Church

Temple B. — This circular building dates from 2C BC and may have been dedicated to Juno (a statue which is probably a representation of this goddess was found in the temple). The podium of tufa was covered by one of peperine which was in turn covered in stucco. The *cella* was enlarged and the surrounding columns were linked by tufa walls. The floor was raised and recovered in mosaics.

Temple D. — The greater part of this temple lies beneath the road (Via Florida).

The north and east sides of the precinct were bounded by a portico (1). The high wall (2) on the west side behind Temple A belonged to a public lavatory. The drainage trough is still visible. Further south several large blocks (3) have been identified as the remains of the podium of Pompey's Curia.

Argentina Theatre. — The first performance of the Barber of Seville took place here in 1816 and was one of the most resounding failures in the annals of opera. It is said that Pauline Borghese *(p 122)* was behind it: she had wanted to help the tenor who was a friend of hers to avenge himself on Rossini who had refused to alter the score.

■ VIA DEL SUDARIO

Palazzo Vidoni. — The decision to build a palace here was taken by the Caffarelli, a rich Roman family, in 1500 and Raphael was asked to design it. One of his pupils, Lorenzo Lotto, supervised its construction. The robust elegance of the palace was altered in 18 and 19C when the façade was enlarged and re-sited to face the Corso Vittorio Emanuele II and the top storey was added.

Tradition would have it that Charles V lodged here in 1536. In 1853 the Bishop of Perugia, the future Leo XIII lived on the ground floor. Later the building became the offices of the Fascist party.

Johannes Burckard's House: at no 44. — There used to be a tower on the site where Burckard, the papal master of ceremonies, built his house in 1503. He called it Torre Argentina after the Latin name (Argentoratum) of Strasbourg, his home town.

The house, which has been restored, is in the Gothic and Renaissance style. It is now the home of the Society of Dramatic Authors and contains a library and a collection of masks, theatrical costumes, play bills etc. connected with the theatre *(open 9 am to 1.30 pm. Closed Sundays and holidays and in August)*.

Via del Sudario ends in Piazza Vidoni.

Statue of Abate Luigi (A). — This statue of a Roman in a toga is one of the famous 'talking' statues which exchanged comments with Pasquino *(p 160)*, Madam Lucrezia *(p 125)* and Marforio *(p 60)*.

■ CHURCH OF SANT'ANDREA DELLA VALLE★

The fountain in **Piazza Sant'Andrea della Valle** is thought to be by Carlo Maderno. It is decorated with the eagle and dragon of the Borghese and was probably put up for Pope Paul V.

Construction of the church began in 1591 and continued slowly until 1665. The **façade★★**, which was built between 1655 and 1665 by Carlo Rainaldi, who took over from Carlo Maderno, is one of the most elegant of the Baroque period, with a fine effect of movement created by the numerous projections and columns.

The usual scrolls, uniting the lower and upper stages, are here replaced by an angel with one wing spread (only the lefthand statue has been executed).

Interior. — The Latin-cross plan with one nave flanked by inter-communicating side chapels, as in the Gesù Church *(p 109)*, is typical of the Counter-Reformation. The severity typical of the art of this period is to be found in the extremely sober architecture in the second chapel on the right and on the altar in the right transept (the nave vaulting and the left transept were decorated early in 20C).

Dome ★★. — This is the work of Carlo Maderno; it is one of the lovliest domes in the city and second only to St Peter's in size. It was painted between 1621 and 1625 by **Lanfranco** who was the first artist to adapt successfully to the technique of painting a curved surface. The Glory of Paradise, with its rich colouring, is an imitation of the fresco painted by Correggio on the dome of Parma cathedral. The Evangelists on the pendentives were painted by Domenichino. The vigour of these figures is reminiscent of Michelangelo's art.

Apse ★. — The upper section, which is subdivided by ribs of white and gold stucco and painted by Domenichino (1624-28), is in late Renaissance taste: St Andrew is led to his death *(right)*; the Calling of Sts Andrew and Peter *(centre)*; the Flagellation of St Andrew *(left)*; St Andrew being received into heaven *(above)*; Peter and Andrew are shown the Saviour by John the Baptist *(arcade centre)*.

The large painted panels (1650-51) round the main altar depicting the death of St Andrew are by Mattia Preti inspired by Caravaggio and Lanfranco.

Piccolomini popes' tombs. — *Above the last bay in the nave before the transept.* The monuments to Pius II *(left)* and Pius III *(right)* are typical of late 15C funeral art.

Almost opposite the church stands the Palazzo Massimo *(p 159)* and overlooking the Piazza di S. Pantaleo is the Palazzo Braschi *(p 159)*.

■ PALAZZO DELLA FARNESINA AI BALLAURI

This little Renaissance building was begun in 1523 for Thomas le Roy, a French diplomat accredited to the Holy See. Raised to the peerage by François I of France he added the lily of France to the Ermine of Brittany, his country of origin. The lily was mistaken for the iris of the Farnese and the building was called the "Piccola Farnesina". As it overlooks the **Via dei Ballauri** (luggage makers: *baule* means trunk) it acquired the name of Farnesina ai Ballauri. The façade giving on to the Corso Vittorio Emanuele II was erected from 1898 to 1904.

The interior, which was radically restored in 19C, houses the collection of antique sculpture left by Baron Giovanni Barraco.

Barracco Museum. — *Open 9 am to 1.30 pm (1 pm Sunday and holidays; also 5 to 8 pm Tuesday and Thursday. Closed Monday and 1 January, Easter, 15 August, 25 December. 500 L.*

The collection ranges over Egyptian, Assyrian, Greek and Roman sculpture from their origins to the end of antiquity.

It is worth admiring the elegant internal courtyard before taking the stairs to the first floor. **Room I:** series of Assyrian low relief sculptures showing five women in a palm grove (late 8C BC). **Room II:** Egyptian sculptures from 3rd millennium (a Pharaoh's head which could be Rameses II; two low relief sculptures from the tombs of wealthy people dating from the Old Empire; stucco head of a mummy from Faynum, Egyptian art from the Roman period). **Room III:** Greek originals or copies from the archaic and pre-Classical periods (6 and 5C BC), including the head of an ephebe, an original work, and a head of Marsyas, a rare copy of a work by Myron who brought together the goddess Athena and the satyr Marsyas in the same composition.

Take the stairs to the second floor.

Room IV: Greek sculpture from the Classical period (5C BC) including a head of Apollo, a fine copy of a work by Phidias, and, on a cushion, a head of Diadumenos (victorious athlete), a copy of a work by Polyclitus.

Room V: Greek art from 4C BC.

On leaving the Museum turn left out of the Corso Vittorio Emanuele II into Piazza della Cancelleria.

■ PALAZZO DELLA CANCELLERIA ★★

The Chancery Palace was built between 1483 and 1513 for Cardinal Raffaele Riario, great nephew of Sixtus IV who loaded him with honours and riches. The architect could have been Andrea Bregno, nicknamed Antonio da Montecavallo, or perhaps his brother, assisted by Bramante.

During 18C it was the official residence of Cardinal Henry, Duke of York and brother of Bonnie Prince Charlie, the Young Pretender, whose wife, Princess Louise Stolberg, was granted a suite of rooms in the palace between deserting her husband and rejoining her lover, Alfieri, after his banishment from Rome on account of their illicit liaison. Here also the Cardinal later received his brother's illegitimate daughter, Charlotte, Duchess of Albany, after her father's death.

The inscription above the balcony states that the building housed the Corte Imperiale, the law courts during the Napoleonic occupation (1809-14). Between 1937 and 1945 it was strengthened and restored and is now occupied by the papal chancery which drafts canon law. It therefore enjoys the privilege of extra-territoriality granted to Vatican property by the Lateran Treaty *(p 71)*.

A fifteen hundred year old Cupid. — Cardinal Riario moved into the palace in 1496. His well known taste for antiquities gave Michelangelo the idea of sculpting a magnificent Cupid, skilfully applying an artificial patina of age and selling it to the Cardinal for 200 ducats as a genuine antique. The collector got wind of the deceit and decided to recover his money and return the statue to the artist but Michelangelo never saw his Cupid again; it was transferred to France and disappeared no one knows where.

Façade and courtyard. — These two features make the building the most elegant product of the Renaissance in Rome. The broad smooth surfaces, the straight lines and the shallow pilasters of the travertine façade give it a majestic quality. A light and delicate touch is added by the roses of Riario which decorate the second floor windows.

The central doorway was added in 1589 by Cardinal Alessandro Peretti, great nephew of Sixtus V.

The granite columns which support the two storeys of the arcading surrounding the courtyard — a harmonious composition — come from the early building of the Church of San Lorenzo in Damaso.

It was the Chapter of this church which received the rents from the ground floor shops behind the arcades in Via del Pellegrino; the upper floors are decorated with fine balconies overlooking this street.

The coats of arms on the corners of the palace are those of Sixtus IV and Julius II (the oak of the della Rovere family) whose reigns marked the beginning and the end of the construction.

San Lorenzo in Damaso. — The church, which was founded by Pope Damasus I in 4C, was rebuilt as part of the palace. It became a stable during the first French occupation in 1798, was restored several times during 19C and then became an annex to the Imperial Court during the second French occupation (1809-14). Following incendiary damage in 1939 the ceiling has been entirely renewed.

The church consists of a nave and side aisles preceded by a vestibule. The first chapel on the right contains a 14C wooden crucifix; the last chapel on the left in the nave contains a 12C painting of the Virgin inspired by Byzantine icons.

■ PIAZZA CAMPO DEI FIORI★

The origin of the name (which means Field of Flowers Square) probably goes back to the Middle Ages when the area was one vast meadow dominated by the fortress of the powerful Orsini family who were lords of the manor. By 16C the area had become the centre of Rome, a meeting place for people of all ranks, crowded with inns. The **"Hostaria della Vacca"** (B) belonged to Vanozza Catanei (1442-1518), famous for her liaison with Rodrigo Borgia, who became Pope Alexander VI. She bore him several children including Cesare and Lucretia. The façade of her hostellery still bears an escutcheon showing the Borgia arms alongside those of Vanozza and those of one of her husbands *(p 126)*.

The Campo was the site of all sorts of festivals as well as a place of execution. At the centre stands a statue of Giordano Bruno, a monk who was burned for heresy on 17 February 1600 during the Counter-Reformation. The statue has replaced the 'Terrina' fountain which is now in Piazza della Chiesa Nuova *(p 161)*.

Every morning the Campo dei Fiori is filled with the bustle of an extensive food market.

Take one of the three narrow streets which lead into Piazza Farnese.

■ FARNESE PALACE★★★

At either end of the Piazza Farnese are two huge granite tanks found in the Baths of Caracalla and converted into fountains in 1626. On the far side stands the most beautiful of Roman palaces, now the French Embassy, which bears the name of the family which built it. The fame of the Farnese began when Cardinal Alessandro was elected pope in 1534 taking the name of **Paul III**. As the first pope of the Counter-Reformation he set up the Council of Trent, yet conducted his reign like a Renaissance monarch: he had four children whose mother has not been identified, made three of them legitimate and loaded them with riches. He was a patron of the arts, continuing the work on St Peter's and the Sistine Chapel and building the Farnese Palace. He and his descendants amassed a magnificent collection of works of art. One of his grand children, Ranuccio (1530-65), commissioned Salviati to celebrate the glory of the Farnese in a series of frescoes. Another, Odoardo (1573-1626), invited the Carracci to paint the gallery on the first floor. The last of the Farnese was Elizabeth (1692-1766) who married Philip V of Spain. Their son, Don Carlos of Bourbon, who became king of Naples in 1735, inherited the Farnese family riches; almost all the works of art from the Farnese Palace are now in the Naples Museum or in the royal palace at Capodimonte.

TOUR

Not open to the public at present.

Façade. — The absence of pilasters and the clear horizontal lines contribute to a masterpiece of balance and proportion. Construction began in 1515 on Cardinal Alessandro Farnese's orders, to the designs of his favourite architect, Antonio da Sangallo, the Younger. When Sangallo died in 1546, Michelangelo took over. He retained the first floor windows, framed by columns with alternate pediments, curved or triangular like the recesses in the Pantheon. He added the impressive upper cornice and over the central balcony he carved the irises of the Farnese coat of arms (not to be confused with the French lily).

Courtyard and garden. — The entrance hall is divided into three by powerful granite columns with stucco decoration. The courtyard is a model of Renaissance elegance. It was designed by three men — Sangallo, Vignola and Michelangelo (second floor) — and is composed of the three Classical orders — Doric (ground floor), Ionic and then Corinthian. Until the end of 18C gigantic statues stood under the arches of the ground floor. In 19C the north and south galleries on the first floor were glassed in.

The garden and **rear façade** look on to Via Giulia. The façade is by Vignola who succeeded Michelangelo as architect. In 1573 he was succeeded by Giacomo della Porta who built the loggia. Last to be built in 1603 was the bridge over Via Giulia, linking the palace to the convent of Santa Maria della Morte and to several rooms where the Farnese kept their collection of antiquities.

(After photo by Gab. Fot. Naz., Rome)

Farnese Palace: courtyard

The finest rooms in the palace are on the first floor but are not open to the public.

Guard Room. — Allegorical statues of Abundance and Charity which were designed as part of Paul III's tomb in St Peter's. Reproduction of the Farnese Hercules, itself a Roman copy of the original by Lysippus.

Great Gallery. — The **frescoes★★★** (1595-1603) are by Annibale Carracci with the assistance of his brother Agostino and his pupils Domenichino and Lanfranco. With their illusion of celestial infinity and the fact that they can be viewed from any angle they herald the arrival of Baroque art. The subjects are taken from Greek mythology: Triumph of Bacchus and Ariadne; Pan offering wool from his sheep to Diana; Hermes offering the apple of Discord to Paris.

Take Via di Monserrato.

Under the kindly eye of its many beautiful madonnas (on the corner of Via dei Farnesi) the **Via di Monserrato** is lined by craft and antique shops, by palaces where the many Spanish prelates, who came to Rome in the suite of the Borgia popes (Calixtus III and Alexander VI), used to live. Many of the courtyards are worth a glance: the beauties of the Renaissance have not all disappeared.

St Thomas of Canterbury (San Tommaso di Canterbury). — *Open October to mid-June (during term time); ring at the Porter's Lodge, 45 Via di Monserrato.*

The present church was begun in 1869 by Camporese the Younger and finished on his death by Poletti and Vespignani; it contains a fine recumbent white marble effigy of Card. Christopher Bainbridge, Archbishop of York and Henry VIII's first Ambassador to the Holy See (d. 1514). The original church was founded in 775 by Offa, King of the East Saxons; it was destroyed by fire in 817, rebuilt in 1159 and dedicated to St Thomas à Becket, who had stayed in the adjoining hospice which is now the Venerable English College. The hospice was started in 1362 by John and Alice Shepherd as a hostel for English pilgrims and is said to have survived owing to "national pride, national piety and a national distaste for being fleeced by foreigners". It was converted into a college in 1579 by Gregory XIII. Those who have stayed there include Thomas Cromwell, Milton, John Evelyn and Card. Manning.

The church of **Santa Maria di Monserrato** is the Spanish national church.

The **Palazzo Ricci,** tucked in at the back of its little square, has great charm; the façade bears traces of decorations by P da Caravaggio and M da Firenze *(p 162).*

The **Via del Pellegrino** was created by Sixtus IV in 1483; where it merges with Via di Monserrato the corner house, which otherwise follows the line of the streets, has been cut back to open up the crossroads; this was an innovation in town planning for those days.

Continue along **Via dei Banchi Vecchi** (the bankers' street in 15C), where Alexander VI built his palace **(Palazzo Sforza Cesarini)** while he was still a cardinal.

■ VIA GIULIA ★

The street gained its notoriety in 16C. It was named after Pope Julius II, its creator, and is one of the few straight streets in Rome. It had a good reputation during the Renaissance but lost favour in 17C when Innocent X had the state prisons transferred there. Owing to recent restoration work and the arrival of antique shops and modern art galleries, it has regained some of its former standing.

S. Giovanni dei Fiorentini. — It was Pope Leo X, a Medici from Florence, who decided to build a 'national' church for his fellow countrymen in Rome. The most famous Renaissance artists were invited to compete for the commission: Peruzzi, Michelangelo, Raphael. The artist chosen was Jacopo Sansovino. Work began early in 16C; it was continued by Antonio da Sangallo and Giacomo della Porta and completed in 1614 by Carlo Maderno. The façade which dates from 18C is in the style of the late Counter-Reformation. The decoration of the chancel is Baroque: in the centre is the Baptism of Jesus, a marble group by Antonio Raggi, one of Bernini's pupils. The tombs on either side were designed by Borromini.

Continue along Via Giulia. No 85 is one of the houses where Raphael is said to have lived.

Palazzo Sachetti. — *No 66, Via Giulia.* It may have been designed by Sangallo the Younger, architect of the Farnese Palace or by Annibale Lippi, the architect of the Villa Medici; both buildings were commissioned in 16C by Cardinal Ricci di Montepulciano.

Between the next two side turnings on the right, Vicolo del Cefalo and Via del Gonfalone, are huge blocks of masonry which were the foundations for Julius II's law courts designed by Bramante but never built. The Romans have christened them 'the Via Giulia sofas'.

No 52 is the prison which Innocent X had built in 1655. The inscription on the face of the building speaks of a model institution designed for a more humane type of detention.

Santa Maria della Morte. — The 18C façade of this church, by F Fuga, is reminiscent of the Baroque.

The Via Giulia here passes beneath the beautiful arch designed to link the Farnese Palace with the Farnesina over the river *(pp 114, 191)*.

Gargoyle Fountain (Fontana del Mascherone). — It was built in 1626. The marble mask and the huge granite basin probably come from an ancient building.

Turn left into Vicolo del Polverone to reach Piazza Capo di Ferro.

■ PALAZZO SPADA ★

It was built in about 1540 for Cardinal Gerolamo Capo di Ferro probably by an architect in Sangallo's circle. In 1632 it was acquired by Cardinal Bernardino Spada and in 1927 it became the property of the Italian Government for the Council of State.

Although it was built only a few years after the Farnese Palace, the Spada Palace is quite different in conception. The noble austerity of Renaissance architecture has been replaced by fantastic decorations in the Mannerist style. The façade is nearly smothered in statues, stucco garlands, medallions and scrolls bearing Latin inscriptions about the famous Classical figures which appear in the niches on the first floor. On the second floor, which is dominated by the Spada coat of arms, the decoration becomes overwhelming.

The delicate execution of the three friezes in the courtyard is quite admirable. On the wall facing the entrance is the French coat of arms flanked by the arms of Julius III, a souvenir of Cardinal Capo di Ferro who was papal legate to France and a friend of Julius III.

Spada Gallery ★. — *Open 8.30 am to 2 pm (9 am to 1 pm Sundays and holidays). Closed Monday, 1 January, 25 April, 1 May, 15 August, Christmas. 1 000 L. The numbers in the text are the same as those in the gallery.*

The gallery presents the works of art collected by Cardinal Spada in their original setting and is typical of the private collection of a wealthy Roman in 17C. The Cardinal was the patron of Guercino and Guido Reni, whose noble manner pleased him, while at the same time he was interested in *bambocciate*, realistic paintings which appeared in Rome in about 1630 in the circle of the painter Pieter van Laer, a Dutchman nicknamed *Il Bamboccio*.

Room I. — Two canvasses by Guido Reni (1575-1642) are outstanding: a portrait of Cardinal Bernardino Spada *(25)* which exemplifies the artist's style; Judith *(35)*, which was painted in 1625. Another portrait of Cardinal Spada *(38)* by Guercino (1591-1666).

Room II. — The two console tables date from 17C. The carved walnut tabernacle is from the late 16C. Among the paintings: the Portrait of a Musician *(56)* is an early work by Titian (c1515). Three fine portraits by Bartolomeo Passarotti (1529-92) — the Astrologer *(60)*, the Botanist *(63)*, the Surgeon *(57)* — show naturalism tempered by delicate posing. The Portrait of Pope Paul III *(74)* is a copy of a 16C portrait painted by Titian (Naples Museum).

Room III. — The console tables in gilded wood are late 17C Roman workmanship.

In the Allegory of the Massacre of the Innocents *(97)* Pietro Testa (c1607-50) painted his masterpiece. The violent contrast between light and dark accentuates the dramatic aspect of this work. The Triumph of the Name of Jesus *(108)* by Baciccia is a sketch for the fresco which decorates the nave of the Gesù Church *(p 109)*. The Death of Dido *(109)* by Guercino, assisted by his pupils, shows the artist's lyrical manner (the winged cupid). The Landscape with Windmills *(138)* is a masterly work by 'Velvet' Bruegel painted in 1607.

Room IV. — These works are by artists who were influenced by Caravaggio. The small octagonal painting of the Halt at the Inn *(142)* is a *bambocciata*. Michelangelo Cerquozzi (1602-60) was one of the chief exponents of this fashion: the Revolt of Masaniello *(149)* is a later work; the subject taken from Neapolitan history allows the painter to give full reign to his narrative passion. Among the French artists who followed Caravaggio is Valentin (1594-1632): Holy Family with St John *(169)*.

Borromini Perspective. — *On the ground floor behind the library and visible from the courtyard.* This is an optical illusion created by Borromini: the diminishing girth of the pillars and the particular angle of the arches make the gallery appear longer than it really is (9 m - 30 ft).

Bear left into Vicolo delle Grotte and then right into Via dei Giubbonari.

From Via dei Giubbonari to Via delle Botteghe Oscure

The Via dei Giubbonari runs very close to the site of Pompey's theatre of which nothing remains except the semi-circular line followed by the houses in the Via di Grotta Pinta. By tradition it is the street where doublet makers (*giubbone* = doublet), silk merchants and garment repairers were to be found. It has remained very commercial.

Chapel of the Monte di Pietà ★. — *Apply preferably 24 hours in advance for permission to view. Closed Saturday afternoon, Sunday, Monday and holidays.*

This small oval chapel within the Monte di Pietà palace is a gem of Baroque art. The chief architects were Giovanni Antonio de Rossi (who worked with Bernini) and Carlo Bizzaccheri (a pupil of Carlo Fontana) who took over on his death in 1695 and was responsible for the entrance hall and the dome.

The theme of the décor is the aim of the institution: to put down usury. The chapel was consecrated in 1641. The work of decoration went on until 1725. Starting from the entrance and moving anti-clockwise: the allegorical statue of Faith is by Francesco Moderati; the low relief of Tobias lending money to Gabelus is an exuberant work by Pierre Legros, a student at the French Academy in Rome; the allegory of Charity is by Bernardino Cametti whose figures seem about to leap from their recess; the low relief of Mercy by Domenico Guido, who collaborated with Bernini, was finished in 1676; the statue of Charity by Giuseppe Mazzuoli is followed by a low relief of Joseph giving corn to the Egyptians by Jean-Baptiste Théodon, also a student at the French Academy; the last statue is an elegant expression of Hope by Agostino Cornacchini.

San Carlo ai Catinari. — The grandiose but rather heavy façade of this church was erected between 1635 and 1638. It is in the style of the Counter-Reformation.

The **interior** ★, which is shaped like a Greek cross, is dominated by a handsome coffered dome. The artists who painted Sant'Andrea della Valle *(p 111)* are to be found here too: Domenichino painted the Cardinal Virtues on the pendentives of the dome; in the apse Lanfranco accomplished his last work (1647), the Apotheosis of St Charles Borromeo; above the high altar is St Charles Borromeo leading a procession in Milan to ward off the plague by Pietro da Cortona (1650); the 17C St Cecilia's Chapel *(right of the chancel)* is verging on the rococo with its strained effects at perspective and its broken lines and animated stucco figures.

Cross over Via Arenula and turn left into Via di Santa Maria dei Calderari.

The arch and two columns on the left are the remains of a 1C building.

Palazzo Cenci. — The narrow streets which surround the palace repeat like variations on a theme the name of the great family which hit the scandal headlines in 16C: Via dell'Arco de Cenci, Vicolo dei Cenci, Piazza de' Cenci, Via Beatrice Cenci, Via del Monte dei Cenci.

The palace itself stands on a slight rise (Monte Cenci) formed by the rubble from ancient buildings (perhaps the Circus Flaminius).

An 'angelic parricide'. — The scandal broke on 9 September 1598. In those days a bold man could get away with almost anything. The head of the rich Cenci family was Francesco Cenci, whose father had been Pius V's treasurer. A cruel and perverted man, Francesco was eventually murdered at the instigation of his daughter Beatrice with the support of her brother Giacomo and Francesco's wife Lucrezia. Pope Clement VIII sentenced them to death despite public opinion which supported the plea of self defence. The scandal, in which incest, opium and crime were all involved, set Rome in a ferment. The guilty parties were beheaded on 11 September 1599 in the Piazza di Ponte Sant'Angelo. Each year on 11 September a mass is celebrated in St Thomas' Church in the Piazzetta di Monte Cenci for the soul of Beatrice Cenci.

Take Via del Progresso turning right into Via del Portico d'Ottavia.

Lorenzo Manili's house (nos 1, 1b and 2) was built in 1468 with shops on the ground floor. It is decorated with low reliefs and has the proprietor's name written up in Latin and Greek. Above the name is an inscription praising the owner for contributing to making the city beautiful.

Turn left into Via Sant'Ambrogio which leads to Piazza Mattei.

Turtle Fountain ★ **(Fontana delle Tartarughe).** — This is a late Renaissance work (1581-84) full of grace and charm by Taddeo Landini probably from a design by Giacomo della Porta. Local legend tells how Duke Mattei, the owner of the neighbouring palace and an inveterate gambler, lost his fortune in one night. His prospective father-in-law obliged him to look for another fiancée. To prove that a Mattei, even when ruined, could achieve wonders, he had the fountain built in one night.

Palazzo Mattei. — Five palaces were built by the Mattei in 16 and 17C; they occupy the confined space bordered by Piazza Mattei, Via dei Funari, Via Caetani, via delle Botteghe Oscure and via Paganica. Carlo Maderno (1598-1611) was the architect of the palace with two entrances (31 Via dei Funari or 32 Via Caetani). The decoration of the courtyards (statues, busts and low reliefs) shows the taste for antiquities which was then the fashion.

Santa Caterina ai Funari. — This church has a very graceful façade, which was built from 1500 to 1564; the shallow pilasters are typical of the Renaissance but the many garlands indicate an attempt at the decorative effects typical of the Counter-Reformation. Unusual bell tower.

Take Via Caetani which leads into Via delle Botteghe Oscure.

This street was famous in the Middle Ages for its dimly lit shops which had probably been set up in the ruins of Balbus' theatre. The street was widened in 1935 as part of a government plan for renovation.

Distance: 2 km — 1 1/4 miles. Time: about 4 hours. Start: Stazione Termini
The first part of the route is to be followed on foot from Stazione Termini to Piazza Galeno; St Lawrence Without the Walls is reached by tram from Piazza Galeno.

To the east of the historic centre of the City lies a modern district which developed after 1870 as Rome assumed its new role as the capital of Italy. Several ministries established their offices around Piazza dell'Indipendenza and the civil servants took up residence in the neighbouring streets. The Castro Pretorio, the barracks of the Emperors' personal bodyguard (the Pretorian Guard founded by Augustus), is now used by the soldiers of the modern Italian state. In 1935 the University, which had grown too large for the Palazzo Sapienza *(p 107)*, moved to a new site next to the municipal hospital (Policlinico Umberto I) founded in 1890.

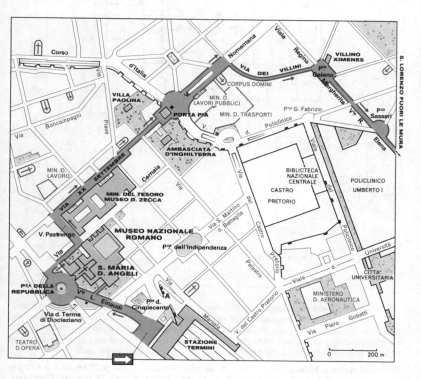

Central Station (Stazione Termini). — The railway arrived in Rome during the reign of Pope Pius IX (1846-78). Three lines were opened: from Frascati to the Porta Maggiore Station in 1856; from Civitavecchia to Ostiense Station in 1859, from Ceprano to Statione Termini in 1862.

Just before the Second World War the government began a new building to replace the old central station. The two wings were completed before work was interrupted by the war. Work was resumed in 1942 and completed for Holy Year in 1950. The undulating roof over the central concourse is one of the successes of modern architecture. Today Statione Termini is the main railway station in Rome, where all the international trains begin and end their journeys.

On the north side of the station square, Piazza dei Cinquecento, are traces of the **city walls (A)** which were put up round Rome after the Gauls invaded in 4C BC.

Cross Piazza dei Cinquecento.

Between Viale Luigi Einaudi and Via delle Terme di Diocleziano is a monument to the memory of 500 Italians who died at Dogali in Eritrea in 1887; this was an incident in the wars of Italy's colonial expansion. The obelisk surmounting the monument comes from the Temple of Isis in the Campus Martius.

■ BATHS OF DIOCLETIAN *(plan p 118)*

In 4C there were some 900 bath houses in Rome but the largest and most beautiful were the baths of the Emperor Diocletian which covered over 13 ha - 32 acres. Building took ten years from 295 to 305 under the direction of Maximian acting for Diocletian who lived in Nicomedia in Asia Minor until he moved to Split after his abdication in 305; he never visited Rome.

As well as the suite of rooms, each at a different temperature, in the bath house itself, which could accommodate up to 3 000 people simultaneously, there were libraries, concert halls, gardens with fountains playing, galeries for the exhibition of sculpture and paintings and exercise rooms.

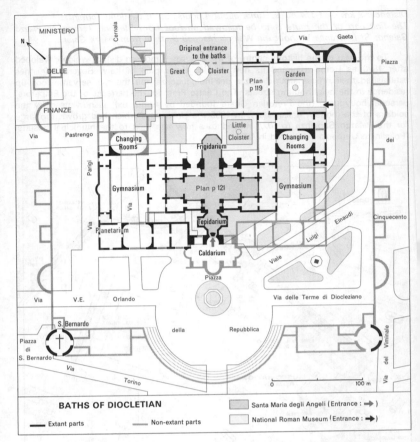

BATHS OF DIOCLETIAN

— Extant parts   — Non-extant parts

Santa Maria degli Angeli (Entrance : ➡)

National Roman Museum (Entrance : ➡)

The baths were abandoned in 538 when the aqueducts were destroyed by the Ostrogoths under Witigis. Michelangelo was commissioned by Pius IV (1559-65) to convert the ruins into a church and Sixtus V (1585-90) removed a great deal of material from the site for his many building projects. Today the grandiose construction is reduced to a few scattered remains and some boldly vaulted halls housing the National Roman Museum.

National Roman Museum ★★★ (also Museo delle Terme). — *Open 9.30 am to 2 pm (1 pm Sundays and holidays). Closed Monday, 1 January, Easter, 1 May, 15 August, Christmas. 1 500 L. The greater part of the Museum is closed for restoration; only the room containing the Ludovisi Throne, the Great Cloister and the first floor are open.*

The museum is housed in the Charterhouse which, like the Church of Santa Maria degli Angeli *(p 121)*, dates from 16C and some rooms belonging to the Baths of Diocletian; it was inaugurated in 1889. It has continually made new acquisitions, in particular the Ludovisi collection in 1901, and is one of the great museums of Greek and Roman antiquities. Owing to the acquisition of the paintings from the Villa Farnesina and the frescoes from Livia's Villa at Prima Porta it now closely rivals the Museum of Naples for Classical painting.

Garden. — In Diocletian's day there was already a garden here. Set among the cypresses and pink and white oleanders is a collection of archaeological fragments. The huge tank in the centre once adorned the villa of a rich Roman citizen (there is a similar tank in the courtyard of St Cecilia's Church in Trastevere: *p 187*).

On the northeast side of the garden is what must have been a luxurious room, panelled with marble and paved with mosaic; the curved inner wall decorated with columns faced a screen wall pierced with niches in which stood statues.

The entrance to the sculpture galleries (plan p 119) is a glass panelled door in the west corner of the garden.

On the right of the path leading to the entrance is a sarcophagus lid; the clothing covering the dead couple is very well sculpted. In front of the sarcophagus is the headless statue of a young boy; hanging round his neck is a *bulla*, a medallion filled with amulets that he would have worn until the age of 17.

Room 1. — The face on the statue of a young girl dressed to represent Diana (1) is certainly a 1C portrait while the body resembles the Amazon of Ephesus for which Phidias, Polyclitus and Kresilas competed (5C BC).

Room 2. — The famous **Ludovisi Throne ★★★** (2) is displayed here. This curious monument, which suggests a throne for a cult statue, was found in 1887 in the Villa Ludovisi. It is a Greek original from the early Classical period (5C BC). The high quality of the decorative low relief sculptures make it a masterpiece of antique art.

The main face shows the bust of a young woman being assited to rise by two other young women who are holding a veil in front of her body. Archaeologists have interpreted this scene as the birth of Aphrodite, goddess of Love who sprang from the foam, accompanied by Seasons whose feet brush the stones of the sea-shore. The very light garments are used with great skill: the one masking the lower half of the goddess' body echoes the curves of the tunic about her neck. The artist has endowed Aphrodite's face with a beautiful expression of joy. The sides of the 'throne' are decorated with scenes connected with the cult of Aphrodite: a naked woman playing the flute and another fully clothed burning incence are often interpreted as symbols of the sensuality of a courtesan and the modesty of a wife.

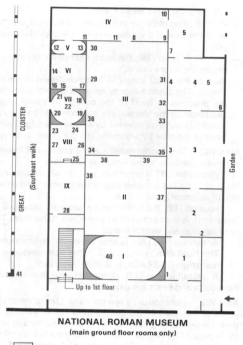

NATIONAL ROMAN MUSEUM
(main ground floor rooms only)

Highly recommended rooms

0   10 m

Room 3. — The statue of Diony-sius (3), a very young figure clothed in the goat skin given him by his father, Zeus, comes from Hadrian's Villa near Tivoli. The figure is also known as Bacchus, god of wine, and holds a goblet in the right hand. It is probably a copy made during Hadri-an's reign (117-38) of a 4C BC bronze original.

Room 4. — The low relief sculpture of a Maenad holding an ox by the horns (4) is a copy, dating from Hadrian's time, of a Greek work in the Hellenistic style; the grace of the gown and the abandoned attitude of the Maenad, a votary of Dionysius, are typical of this style.

The sleeping Hermaphrodite (5) is a replica of a work from the Hellenistic period which delighted in the representation of creatures with particular physical or moral features.

The **Head of a dying Persian** ★ (6) is the work of the Pergamum School in Asia Minor, one of the most productive centres of Hellenistic art. The artist has carried realism to the point where the expression of death shows in the eyes of the dying man. This work belongs to a series of sculptures which the kings of Pergamum commissioned to celebrate their victory over the barbarians, particularly the Galatians in 3C BC.

Room 5. — The statue of a Child on horseback (7), in marble and alabaster, was an ornament on a late Empire tomb. It was found broken into hundreds of pieces. The body of the child and of the horse are hollow so as to contain the urn holding the ashes of the corpse.

A suite of rooms follows, identified by Roman numerals and containing the most outstand-ing exhibits.

Room IV. — Devoted in particular to Hellenistic art (post 4C BC) and including:
— The supple beauty of the Palatine Grace (8) (so called because it was discovered in 1862 at the foot of the Palatine): the statue's relationship with the work of Callimachus is evident in the very thin garment which is closely moulded to the body as if it were wet.
— The Tivoli Dancer (9), found in Hadrian's Villa. This Roman work is inspired by Greek Hellenistic art. The young woman's pose is one of great elegance.
— The group representing an Amazon on horseback charging against a fallen Gaul (10): the Amazon's head, which had been sculpted separately, has disappeared but the Gaul is recognizable from his traditional hair style *(pp 60-61)*. The sculpture was found in Nero's country house at Anzio and is attributed to the Pergamum School.
— Two statues of the Muse seated (11) found on the Palatine Hill (3C BC).

Room V. — It contains two beautiful **altars** ★. One (12) in marble (1C AD) is decorated with ox heads and sprays of delicately carved leaves framed by remarkably detailed friezes.

The other (13) shows the frenzied dancing of two Maenads and several *camilli,* young men preparing a sacrifice and a wedding ceremony. The cinerary urn has been placed at the bottom of the altar; the upper part is decorated with beautiful decorative motifs: garlands suspended from ox heads, various objects (a mirror, a pitcher...), birds, small trees, etc. The sculpture is executed with skill and distinction.

Room VI. — This room could well be named after the **statue of Augustus** ★★★ (14) which is so famous. The Emperor is shown at about the age of fifty wearing the High Priest's toga. The face is treated with a simple realism, perhaps with a little flattery: age does not seem to have wrought any change since the Emperor was portrayed at the time of the Battle of Actium when he was 32 years old. This earlier statue, which is in the Capitoline Museum *(p 61),* and the later one displayed here convey the solemn majesty and authority of Augustus; no psychologist's report could give a better portrait of the Emperor.

Among the other **works** ★ are:
— Portrait of an old woman (**15**), with a tight chignon and receding chin and deep wrinkles on either side of the nose; a Roman work which clearly expresses the woman's personality.
— Portrait of Nero (**16**); the facial expression is remarkable for its hint of restlessness; the execution is very skilful.
— Bust of the Chief Vestal (**17**); it was found in the House of the Vestals in the Roman Forum. The austere dignity emanating from the portrait is appropriate to the function of the priestess as head of the college of Vestal virgins. The bust shows the robe and headdress of the Vestals: the hair was held back by a band with the ends resting on the shoulders and was covered by a white veil edged with purple which was attached to the front of the robe by a brooch. The grey cloth tunic was covered by a purple mantle.

Room VII. — This room contains a fine **collection of Roman portraits** ★. Among them are some admirable portraits of the Antonine Emperors.

Vespasian (**18**) is an official portrait which does not reveal the plebeian origins of the Head of State but it shows clearly the strength and determination of the soldier with even a hint of sceptical good nature.

Hadrian (**19**), the first Emperor habitually to wear a beard (hitherto it had been a sign of mourning), is the portrait of an active and stable man. This work is of high quality as regards both material and workmanship.

Antoninus Pius (**20**), despite his youth, appears very serious.

The head of a young girl (**21**), her hair dressed in the style which was fashionable in Tiberius' reign (14-37 AD), is skillfully executed.

A beautiful altar (**22**), decorated with scenes depicting the origins of Rome, comes from Ostia and bears the date 124 AD.

Room VIII. — Here too are a few portraits: Lucius Verus (**23**), associated with Marcus Aurelius in the government of the Empire from 161 to 169; the Emperor Gallienus (**24**) who reigned during a period of great anarchy and whose portrait reveals great weariness; a man of the same period (**25**) who seems to exhibit the same emotions.

The sarcophagus (**26**), which was found near Acilia on the outskirts of Rome and is somewhat damaged, dates from 3C and betrays the exaggerated techniques used by the sculptors of that period to render the effects of light and shade: the deeply cut folds of the garments and the unsubtle treatment of the hair and beard. By comparison the young man's head is sculpted in a more delicate style. The beautiful oval sarcophagus (**27**) is decorated with lively rural scenes and has the name Julius Achilleus on the lid.

Room IX contains an impressive torso of Hercules (**28**) from the Baths of Caracalla (2C) and a fine collection of mosaics arranged on the floor and walls.

Room III. — This room contains several **masterpieces** ★★★ of antique sculpture:
— **Pugilist resting** (**29**); this masterly work in bronze is an original from the Hellenistic period. The realism which characterises Greek works from 3C BC is evident here; this fighter is no longer the ideally handsome hero, represented by the Classical artists, but a man overwhelmed with fatigue. The statue was found in 1884 at the same time as the young man leaning on a spear (**30**). They are both very rare and well preserved examples of antique bronze statues.
— **Ephebe from Subiaco** (**31**); a beautiful imitation of a late 4C BC Greek original, found in Nero's house in Subiaco (east of Rome), which represents a young man, naked and kneeling on one knee.
— **Venus of Cyrene** (**32**): this statue is made of a beautiful Parian marble which has the consistency of ivory. It was discovered during the excavation of the baths at Cyrene in Libya. Venus is engaged in twisting up her hair while still rising from the sea. The statue is a copy of a Greek original typical of the female divinities sculpted by Praxiteles. To support the statue the sculptor has devised a garment draped over a dolphin which has a fish in its gullet.
— **Daughter of Niobe** (**33**); this original Greek work (5C BC) was found in the gardens of Sallust where it had probably adorned the pediment of a temple. The statue represents an episode in Greek mythology: Niobe, who had fourteen children, was scornful of Leto, who had only Artemis and Apollo, but they avenged their mother by killing all Niobe's children. The statue represents one of Niobe's daughters trying to withdraw the arrow that kills her. The statue is one of the first representations of the naked female figure in Greece.
— **Discobolos**; this is the title given to the statue of an athlete throwing the discus. Room III contains two 2C Roman copies of the original Greek bronze by Myron (5C BC). The Discobolos of the 'Casa Lancellotti' (**34**), which is named after its former owner, is considered to be an excellent copy. The artist has chosen to represent the moment where the athlete has already grasped the discus in his right hand and is flexing the muscles of his whole body prior to the throw. The impassive face, devoid of any reflection of the physical effort, is typical of Greek works in the Classical period. The hair and the veins in the arms are sculpted in great detail.
The other replica is the Discobolos of 'Castel Porziano' (**35**) and is named after the estate where it was found in 1906; it is less complete and also less well executed.
— **Maiden of Anzio** (**36**); original Greek work, probably from the early Hellenistic period, representing a young girl engaged in carrying the implements required for a sacrifice; the nobility and detail of the face are admirable.
Set into the floor of this room are some beautiful Roman mosaics.

Room II. — At the centre a beautiful mosaic; **the works** ★★ in this rooms are mostly drawn from the 'severe' or 'pre-Classical' art which is typical of the period between archaic art and Classical art (end 6 to early 5C BC).

— **Apollo of the Tiber** (37); the statue was found in the river in 1891. It is a copy of a Greek original dating from early 5C BC which still shows signs of archaism.

— **Three statues** *(incomplete)* of robed female figures which show artistic development from 5C BC slowing shedding its rigidity. The two older figures (38) are modestly dressed while the one dating from the end of the century (39) is of a young girl in a floating dress.

Room I. — Numerous Roman vases and cinerary urns decorated with garlands and fruit. The great basin (40) belonged to a fountain. It dates from the early Empire and rests on three feet in the form of animals' paws and on a wreathed column.

On leaving turn right into the Great Cloister of the Charterhouse.

Great Cloister. — It is sometimes attributed to Michelangelo although he died in 1564 aged 89 and the cloister was completed in 1565 if one believes the date inscribed on the corner pillar near the entrance (41). At the centre is a pleasant garden containing sculpted fragments and many inscriptions. In the northeast walk particularly sarcophagi are on display. At the north end of the walk is a very fine mosaic in vivid colours representing the banks of the Nile. It was found in a vineyard on the Aventine and is typical of the exotic and pittoresque art which was in fashion in 1 and 2C. The huge pieces of sculpture, the animal heads, which rear up above the bushes, probably come from Trajan's Forum.

First Floor. — At the top of the stairs are several mosaic panels, depicting fish and animals, which are remarkable for their rich colours and lively design. Next one sees the **stuccoes and paintings** ★★★ found in a building of the Augustan era near the Villa Farnesina. The stuccoes, which decorated the ceilings of the rooms, are marvellously delicate; the paintings are typical of the 'second' and 'third' styles *(p 22)*. The collection of 1C **frescoes** ★★★ which comes from the villa at Prima Porta (north of Rome), which belonged to Livia, Augustus' wife, is admirable. Around the four walls of the room runs a band of decoration representing an enclosed orchard, with fruit trees, flowers and birds. The muted colours and the artist's use of chiaroscuro to obtain the effect of perspective and relief have created a masterpiece of Classical painting.

Piazza della Repubblica. — Despite the choking traffic the circus is one of the better post 1870 pieces of town planning.

It is sometimes called Piazza dell'Esedra on account of the semi-circle formed by the two buildings which flank the southwest side. They were designed in 1896 by Gaetano Koch to trace the line of the exedra in the southwest wall of the baths of Diocletian. The porticos are reminiscent of the architecture of Turin; the unified kingdom of Italy, with Rome as its capital, had as its king Victor Emmanuel II, head of the House of Savoy, who lived in Turin. The Naiad Fountain at the centre of the circus dates from 1885.

Santa Maria degli Angeli ★★. — This prestigious church which is dedicated to St Mary of the Angels is often used for official religious services.

According to tradition the baths of Diocletian were built by 40 000 Christians condemned to forced labour; in 1561 Pius IV decided to convert the ruined baths into a church and a charterhouse.

Michelangelo, by then 86 years old, was put in charge. His design, which closely followed the architecture of the original baths, was continually altered after he and the Pope had died within a year of one another (1564 and 1565 respectively) so that by 1749 the church was a jumble of disassociated features and Vanvitelli was commissioned to reintroduce a degree of uniformity.

The outer façade which he designed was demolished in early 20C revealing the unusual unadorned curved wall of the caldarium of the original baths.

The interior, which is designed to the Greek cross plan, was considerably altered by Vanvitelli.

Vestibule. — This was the *tepidarium* of the baths. On either side of the entrance are two stoops; the one on the right is 18C Baroque, the other is a modern copy. On the left is the tomb (1) of the Neapolitan poet and painter Salvatore Rosa who died in 1673; on the right the tomb (2) of Carlo Maratta (1625-1713) who designed it himself.

Between the vestibule and the transept the statue of St Bruno (3 - *right*), founder of the Carthusian order, is by the French sculpture Houdon (1741-1827) who spent eight years in Rome (1764-78), staying originally at the French Academy. The niche opposite once contained a plaster statue by the same artist of John the Baptist. Unfortunately it was broken by the Sacristan, re-made to a smaller size and placed in the Borghese Gallery.

SANTA MARIA DEGLI ANGELI

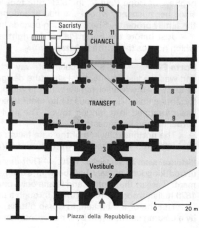

Piazza della Repubblica

Transept★. — This part of the church gives the best idea of the solemn magnitude of the ancient building.

It occupies the central hall of the baths with its eight monolithic granite columns. To create a uniform effect, Vanvitelli copied the columns in painted masonry, adding four more in the two recesses leading to the vestibule and the chancel. In addition to the present entrance, Michelangelo had intended two more, one at each end of the transept but eventually two chapels were created instead and painted in *trompe-l'œil* with architectural effects.

The transept is a virtual picture gallery, particularly of 18C works. The majority of them come from St Peter's where they were replaced by mosaics. Here in St Mary's Vanvitelli arranged them to cover the wall spaces between the pillars. 'St Basil celebrating mass before the Emperor Valens' (4) is by the French painter Subleyras (1669-1749). The Emperor, overwhelmed by the dignity of the ceremony, has fainted; his military costume and the background are treated in the Classical manner. 'The Fall of Simon Magus' (5) by Pompeo Batoni (1708-86) is typical of this artist's work with its fine colours and contrasting light and shade. 'St.Bruno's vision of the Virgin' (6) is a luminous painting by Giovanni Odazzi (1663-1731), a pupil of Baciccia and exponent of the Baroque Mannerist style.

The south transept contains the tombs of three First World War heroes: Marshal Armando Diaz (7) who won the battle of Vittorio Veneto in 1918; Admiral Paolo Thaon di Revel (8), commander in chief of the allied forces in the Adriatic 1917-18; Vittorio Emanuele Orlando (9), Minister of State.

Running across the floor from the south transept to the chancel is a meridian (10). Between 1702 and 1846 the clocks of Rome were regulated by it. Nowadays midday is announced by the firing of a canon on the Janiculum *(p 192)*.

Chancel. — Like the transept it is generously decorated with paintings including 'The Martyrdom of St Sebastian' (11) by Domenichino (1581-1641), 'The baptism of Jesus' (12) by Carlo Maratta; note the affectation of the figures of Christ and John the Baptist.

Behind the high altar is a much venerated picture (13) showing the Virgin surrounded by adoring angels. It was commissioned in 1543 from a Venetian artist by Antonio del Duca, a Sicilian priest, who had a vision in which he saw a cloud of angels rising from the Baths of Diocletian. From then on he never stopped demanding the construction of a church on the site of the baths; eventually Pius IV acceded to his request.

■ TOWARDS THE PORTA PIA

On leaving the church, walk along the northeast side of Piazza della Repubblica; turn right into Via Cernaia and then left into Via Pastrengo.

Via XX Settembre. — The street is named after the date — 20th September 1870 — when Italian troups entered the papal capital *(see below)*. It replaced the old Strada Pia and was the first street to be developed in the post 1870 town planning. It was designed to link the Ministries and to reflect the grandeur of the city's new status. It was therefore lined with pompous buildings in imitation of the Renaissance and Baroque styles.

Currency Museum (Museo della Zecca). — *Housed on the ground floor in the northeast wing of the Treasury. Open 9 to 11 am; proof of identification necessary to obtain permit issued by Information Office (Ufficio informazioni) on the left of the entrance. Closed Saturday, Sunday and holidays.*

The Treasury building dates from 1877. The numismatic museum displays the currencies of every country in the world including coins issued by the Popes from 15C. There is also a fine collection of wax impressions (about 400) by Benedetto Pistrucci (1784-1855) who was chief engraver to the Bank of England for 40 years: heads of George IV, Victoria, Duke of Wellington, Napoleon during the 100 days, Paulina Borghese.

Continue northeast along Via XX Settembre.

Pauline Bonaparte's Villa (Villa Paolina). — *Seat of the French Ambassador to the Holy See.* The villa is named after Napoleon's sister who married Prince Camillo Borghese, great nephew of Pope Paul V, in 1803. She took up residence here after the fall of the Empire since her husband, whom she had abandoned a few years earlier, had banished her from the family property. She spent long periods in the house until her death in 1825.

Just before the Porta Pia on the right is a very modern building by Sir Basil Spence which houses the **British Embassy.**

Porta Pia★. — This spectacular gateway was built between 1561 and 1564 by Pope Pius IV and was the last architectural structure designed by Michelangelo. In the centre is the coat of arms of the Medici family with the famous balls *(palle)* which represent the bezant, a Byzantine coin. The curious white motif which occurs several times is said to be a barber's basin wrapped in a fringed towel. The sculptor wished to remind Pius IV that he had a barber among his ancestors.

The northeast façade of the gate facing down Via Nomentana is by Benedetto Vespignani (1808-82) who together with Giuseppe Valadier was extremely active in 19C.

Historical note: 20 September 1870. — That day was the culmination of the Risorgimento. The united kingdom of Italy had been in existence since 1861; Cavour had declared in parliament: 'I assert that Rome, and Rome only, ought to be the capital of Italy'. On 20 September 1870 Italian troops entered Rome through a breach in the Aurelianic wall.

The site of the breach, in Corso d'Italia, on the left on leaving the Porta Pia, is marked by a column surmounted by a representation of Victory.

Walk down Via Nomentana.

This very broad street is bordered by luxury dwellings in a modern residential district.

Go past the Church of the Corpus Domini and turn right into Via dei Villini.

The name **Via dei Villini** evokes early 20C town planning. In 1909 a new development plan defined two types of dwellings: the *palazzo,* a 4 or 5 storey block of flats for letting, and the *vilino,* a smart little house with its own garden.

Beneath this district run St Nicomedes' Catacombs.

The road comes out into Piazza Galeno opposite the **Villino Ximenes,** an unusual little house, built for himself by Ettore Ximenes (1855-1926), sculptor, painter and illustrator, who had designed many official buildings in Rome and abroad.

In Piazza Galeno take a tram going southeast down Viale Regina Elena to Piazzale San Lorenzo.

■ BASILICA OF ST LAWRENCE WITHOUT THE WALLS★
(San Lorenzo Fuori Le Mura)

The church is also known as San Lorenzo al Verano since it is built on land that belonged to a certain Lucius Verus in antiquity. To the north runs Via Tiburtina, lined, like other roads on the outskirts of Rome, with pagan tombs and then with underground Christian cemeteries, the catacombs. One of them contains the grave of St Lawrence who was martyred in 258 under the Emperor Valerian.

As pilgrims to the tomb of St Lawrence became more and more numerous the Emperor Constantine had a sanctuary built (330). By 6C it was in such a poor state of repair that Pope **Pelagius II** (579-90) had it rebuilt.

It was probably enlarged in 8C but underwent major alterations in 13C under Pope **Honorius III** (1216-27): the apse of Pelagius' church was demolished, the church was extended westwards and its orientation reversed. The original nave was raised and became the chancel of the new church.

Later Baroque additions were removed by Pius IX in 1855; he also revealed the original nave while retaining Honorius' chancel.

On 19th July 1943 a bomb fell on the church; the roof, the upper part of the walls and the porch were destroyed.

Repair work was put in hand immediately with the aim of restoring the church to its 13C appearance.

Façade. — The very elegant porch, which dates from the time of Honorius (13C), was reconstructed after the 1943 bomb damage using some of the original material. Above the architrave which is supported on simple columns is a beautiful mosaic frieze in vivid colours. Above this is a cornice delicately carved with flowers, fruit and acanthus leaves punctuated with lion head gargoyles. This fine example of mediaeval decorative sculpture is attributed to the Vassalletti, a family who worked in marble with the Cosmati from early in 12C to late in 13C.

The Romanesque bell tower *(right)* was erected in 12C, probably at the same time as the cloisters *(p 124);* it was restored in 14C, possibly because of damage caused by an earthquake or a fire.

In the porch is a fairly rare sarcophagus (1) with a small pitched roof which dates from 11C. It must have marked the site of a tomb on the floor of a church.

Next to it is a 4C sarcophagus (2) with a likeness of the occupant in a medallion. The concise decoration depicts scenes from the Old and New Testaments.

The **'harvest' sarcophagus** (3 - *left)* is quite remarkable. It is shaped like a funeral bier and decorated with vine leaves, bunches of grapes garnered by Cupids, birds and animals, very varied and lively. It was carved in 5 or 6C; the clear cut relief and the large smooth surfaces are characteristic of the Middle Ages.

Two modern works honour Pope Pius XII (4) and Alcide de Gasperi (5), President of the Council from 1945 to 1953, in recognition of their assistance in the work of restoration following the bomb damage.

The two lions (6) on either side of the main door are Roman.

Interior. — It is immediately obvious that the church is composed of two buildings — the churches of Honorius III (13C) and Pelagius II (6C) — which are joined by the present chancel arch and aligned on different axes.

Honorius III's church. — The funerary monument (7 - *right of entrance)* of Guglielmo Fieschi (died in 1256), nephew of Pope Innocent IV, was reconstructed in 1943. Beneath a small temple resembling a 13C baldaquin is a 3C sarcophagus decorated with a marriage scene.

Honorius' church comprises a nave and two aisles separated by beautiful antique granite columns of varying diametres. The Ionic capitals, like those in the porch, date from the Middle Ages and are attributed to the Vassalletti. They show with what happy results the mediaeval marble workers adapted their technique to ancient columns.

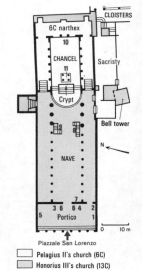

Pelagius II's church (6C)

Honorius III's church (13C)

The lighting of the nave has hardly changed since 13C. After 1943 the ceiling was rebuilt exactly as it had been in 19C when Vespignani, who was working for Pius IX, had inserted a wooden coffered ceiling beneath the open roof frame.

The floor, which was damaged by the bomb, is bright with the colours of the 13C Cosmati work.

The two **ambones** ★ are not identical. They are Cosmati work: a combination of white marble, porphyry and serpentine marble, with multicoloured insets gleaming with touches of gold. The one on the right (8) was used for reading the Gospel and was more sumptuously decorated (early 13C) than the one on the left (9) which was used for reading the Epistle and has the simple elegance of late 13C Cosmati work.

Pelagius II's church. — The central section containing the high altar has been raised and is approached by two sets of steps. Its original orientation with the apse projecting west of the present chancel arch was reversed so that it could serve as the chancel of Honorius' church, as it does today. Pelagius' church comprised a nave and two aisles. From the raised nave only the tops of the ancient fluted columns are visible, supporting a magnificent sculpted architrave composed of disparate fragments which once belonged to a frieze or a door lintel. Over the aisles are galleries *(matrones)* for the women; the arcades rest on fine slim columns, their capitals decorated with leaves (6C).

The chancel arch which opened into the apse of Pelagius' church is decorated with a late 6C mosaic. At the centre is Christ, his hand raised in blessing. On his right are Sts Peter and Lawrence and Pope Pelagius II offering his church to the Saviour. On his left are Sts Paul, Stephen and Hippolytus.

The **papal throne** (10) at the east end of the chancel is by the Cosmati (1254). The whiteness of the marble contrasts with the vivid colours and the gold inlays to create a fine decorative effect. The elegance of the throne is enhanced by the fine craftsmanship of the screen which closes off the choir.

The **baldaquin** (11) over the high altar is supported by four porphyry columns. The last two sections of the columns were repaired in 1862. This is Cosmati work (1148) and is signed by the four sons of Paolo, the oldest of the group. It is one of the earliest examples of this sort of miniature temple with columns supporting an architrave.

Beneath the high altar in the **crypt** are the remains of Sts Lawrence, Stephen and Justin.

It was during some work commissioned by Pope Pius IX in 19C that the lower part of the 6C church and the narthex were discovered. There are two sets of steps leading down, one on each side of the chancel *(if the gates are closed, enquire in the Sacristy)*.

The narthex is decorated with modern mosaics by craftsmen of the Venice school and contains the **tomb of Pius IX** (1846-78).

Cloisters. — *Entrance through the Sacristy in the south aisle or from the outside on the right of the bell tower.*

The 12C cloister with its archaic charm formed part of the fortified convent which was like a citadel in the Middle Ages. St Lawrence' Basilica, being outside the walls of Rome, was easy prey for thieves and looters. The cloister walk contains many inscriptions from the neighbouring catacombs *(not open)*.

IMPERIAL FORA

Distance: 3 km — 2 miles. Time: about 4 hours. Start: Piazza Venezia

This walk from the Capitoline to the Esquiline evokes several crucial moments in Roman history: the apogee of the Empire with its legacy of the imperial fora, a magnificent series of buildings erected by the Emperors during a century and a half; the Risorgimento, which resulted in the unification of Italy in 1870 with Rome as its capital, is traced in a museum housed in the monument to Victor Emmanuel II.

■ PIAZZA VENEZIA ★

This is the usual meeting place recommended to tourists by their guides who feel sure that even someone just arrived in Rome would be able to find the Piazza Venezia and the monument to Victor Emmanuel II.

The main streets of the city meet in the Piazza Venezia and the worst traffic jams occur here too. The modern pedestrian trying to reach the other side of the square may be consoled to learn from Juvenal that conditions were worse in 1C: "Hurry as we may, we are blocked by a surging crowd in front, and by a dense mass of people pressing in on us from behind: one man digs an elbow into me, another a hard sedan-pole; one bangs a beam, another a wine cask against my head. My legs are bespattered with mud; soon huge feet trample on me from every side and a soldier plants his hobnails firmly on my toe. If that load of marble overturns on to the crowd, what is left of their bodies? Who can identify the limbs, who the bones? The poor men's crushed corpses wholly disappear, just like their souls."

The major political parties have their offices near the Piazza Venezia and the square is often the scene of rallies and marches; it is also the rendezvous of the taxi drivers when they go on strike and jam the square with a sea of yellow cabs.

■ PALAZZO VENEZIA ★

With this building which extends from the Piazza Venezia to Via del Plebiscito and Via degli Astalli, the Renaissance made a timid debut into civil architecture.

Historical note. — When Pietro Barbo was made a cardinal by his uncle Eugenius IV, he took a small house near the Capitol. He prided himself on doing everything with great show and in 1455 he began to build a palace worthy of his rank. When he became Pope in 1464 as **Paul II** he continued his project on a larger scale. Like the majority of the Renaissance popes Paul II was both a military chief concerned with defence and a lover of the arts; but he was not very fond of the humanists. His quarrels with Platina, legal draughtsman at the Vatican Chancery, are recorded in the papal annals: Platina, who was dismissed for sedition, threatened to incite the princes to call a council against the Pope and he formed his friends into an academy which held well publicised meetings in the catacombs. Paul II imprisoned his opponent and talked of chopping off his head; Platina finally got off with milder corporal punishment and the dissolution of his academy.

In 1471 the Pope died before his house was finished. His nephew completed it. It was later altered several times: under Sixtus IV (1471-84) a smaller palace *(palazzetto)* was added opening on to a garden surrounded by a portico. Several popes lived in this agreeable residence from Alexander VI to Clement VIII early in 17C. On his way to the conquest of the kingdom of Naples, Charles VIII of France stayed in the house in 1494 and 1495.

Under Paul III (1534-49) a covered passage was built linking the papal palace with the Aracoeli Convent on the Capitol where the popes liked to spend the summer. It was Pius IV who gave the palace its present name in 1564 when he allowed the ambassadors of the Republic of Venice to lodge in part of the building. Following the treaty of Campoformio between Austria and Napoleon in 1797, the Republic of Venice ceased to exist and almost all its property (including the Palazzo Venezia) reverted to Austria.

By order of Napoleon in 1806 it became the seat of the French administration and was again at the forefront of Roman history in 1910 when the Italian government decided to lay out a huge square in front of the monument to King Victor Emmanuel II; Paul III's covered passage was demolished; the *palazzetto* which stood at the foot of the tower in the southeast angle was pulled down and immediately put up again where it stands today on the corner of the Piazza di San Marco and the Via degli Astalli. At the same time the **Palazzo delle Assicurazioni Generali di Venezia** was built on the other side of the square in imitation of the Palazzo Venezia.

Mussolini set up his office on the first floor of the palace. Now the Palazzo Venezia is one of the prestigious buildings in the capital housing a museum and the library of the Institute of Art and Archaeology. It was restored several times in 18 and 19C and again from 1924 to 1936.

Exterior. — The crenellations on the façade overlooking the Piazza Venezia and the huge tower in the southeast corner show how the severe style of the fortified houses of the Middle Ages persisted. The mullion windows, the doors on to the square and in Via del Plebiscito and above all the attractive façade of St Mark's Basilica are pleasing manifestations of the Renaissance.

Statue of Madam Lucrezia (A). — It stands in the Piazza di San Marco in the angle where the Palazzo Venezia and the *palazzetto* join and may have belonged to the Temple of Isis which stood on the Campus Martius.

It was one of the four talking statues of Rome, the others being Pasquino *(p 159)*, Marforio *(p 60)* and the Abate Luigi *(p 111)*, which was Madam Lucrezia's favourite.

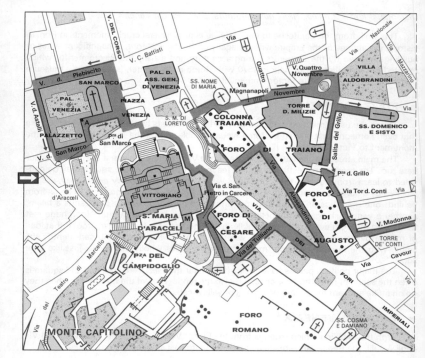

Interior. — *There are three entrances to the palace: from Piazza di San Marco by the Madam Lucrezia statue, from Piazza Venezia, from Via del Plebiscito.*

The unsophisticated outward appearance of Roman Renaissance palaces gives no hint of the elegant décor often to be found within.

Courtyard. — At the centre is a flourishing garden, partially flanked on two sides by an elegant but incomplete portico by Giuliano da Maiano (1432-90). The east side is formed by St Mark's Basilica, which stands within the palace beneath its mediaeval belfry. The attractive fountain dates from 18C: Venice, the lion of St Mark at its feet, is throwing a ring into the sea, a symbol of the marriage between the Serenissima and the sea.

Palazzo Venezia Museum. — *On the first floor. Open 9 am to 1.30 pm (12.30 pm Sundays and holidays). Closed Monday, 1 January, Easter Tuesday, 1 May, 1st Sunday in June, 15 August, Christmas; 2 000 L. As the Museum is being re-organised, it may not be possible to visit the rooms in the order described below.*

Paul II's suite of rooms with their fine Renaissance door casings (overlooking Via del Plebiscito and Piazza Venezia) displays 15C and 17C tapestries and 15C and 18C arms. In the Royal Room ambassadors waited to be received by the Pope. The Battle Room (from the battles of the First World War) is the former Consistory Room where the Pope brought the Cardinals together in assembly. The Map Room owes its name to the map of the world which was displayed there in 15C. The architectural features painted on the walls are by Mantegna, extensively restored in 20C. From the balcony Mussolini used to address the crowds gathered in Piazza Venezia.

Next to the Map Room there is a fine collection of painted wooden statues (13 to 15C). The statue of a pope seated (corner room overlooking Piazza Venezia and Piazza di San Marco) is attributed to Arnolfo di Cambio (13C). The other rooms display ceramics, 17C tapestries and silverware.

St Mark's Basilica. — Founded by Pope Mark in 336 and dedicated to St Mark the Evangelist this basilica was rebuilt by Gregory IV in 9C. Excavations beneath it have uncovered traces of an earlier 4C building and of the 9C crypt where Gregory IV caused the relics of Abdon and Sennen, Persian martyrs, to be deposited.

In 12C a belfry was added and then in 1455 the church was rebuilt and incorporated in the Palazzo Venezia by Cardinal Pietro Barbo. In 17 and 18C further restoration and alterations took place.

The **façade** ★ overlooking Piazza di San Marco is attributed to Giuliano da Maiano or Leon-Battista Alberti: the double row of arches, in which the upper ones are carried on slimmer supports, lends elegance to this charming Renaissance composition.

In the porch, among the various fragments, are the mediaeval stone surround of a well and the tomb stone *(right)* of Vanozza Catanei, mother of Pope Alexander VI's children, Caesar and Lucrezia Borgia *(p 113)*.

The sumptuous **interior** ★ is a typical Roman example of the overlapping of styles down the centuries. The mediaeval basilical plan of a nave and two aisles remains. In 15C the elegant coffered ceiling was added with the arms of Paul II and high windows were inserted in the nave above the alternate panels of stucco and 18C paintings which illustrate the legend of Abdon and Sennen.

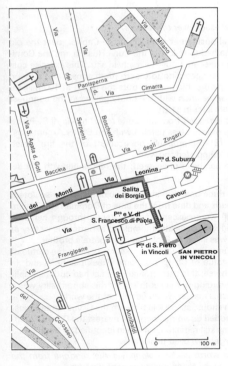

The mosaic in the apse was commissioned in 9C by Gregory IV. To the right of Christ among a group of saints is the Pope offering his church; on his head is a square nimbus showing that he was still alive.

Below are twelve sheep, representing the Apostles, advancing towards the Lamb, symbol of Christ, over a flowered meadow.

The chancel arch shows a bust of the Saviour, the Evangelists and St Peter and St Paul.

In the sacristy is a charming 15C tabernacle carved by Mino da Fiesole in collaboration with Giovanni Dalmata; it stood originally on the high altar but was moved in 18C.

Walk to the foot of the monument to Victor Emmanuel II (Vittoriano: p 53).

To the left of the monument is a typical Roman scene composed of Trajan's Column rising above a group of umbrella pines flanked by the domes of the Churches of Santa Maria di Loreto in the foreground and Il Santissimo Nome di Maria (The Most Holy Name of Mary) in the background.

Walk round the monument on the left into Via di San Pietro in Carcere.

■ RISORGIMENTO MUSEUM ★ (M)

Closed for restoration.

This museum, which is housed in the base of the monument to Victor Emmanuel II, traces the history of the *Risorgimento,* the revival of Italy which resulted in 1870 in a united kingdom. This period, which is of major importance in the history of Italy and of contemporary Europe, is one of the subjects most frequently studied by historians (every university in Italy has a chair of Risorgimento history) and is very popular with the general public owing to a few heroic figures such as Garibaldi.

The significant events in this period are retraced from the spread of new ideas in the Age of Enlightenment (18C), the beginnings of unification in the Napoleonic period, the Restoration of the old regime after the Congress of Vienna (1814-1815), the uprisings in 1820-21 and the activities of the secret societies (the Carbonari and Young Italy founded by Giuseppe Mazzini).

Then Cavour, founder of the newspaper 'Il Risorgimento', and Charles Albert, king of Piedmont-Sardinia entered the action and the revolution of 1848 followed. In February 1849 a Republic was declared in Rome and Pius IX was deprived of his temporal power. It was the French General Oudinot who defeated Garibaldi and re-instated the Pope in authority in Rome. Progress towards unity continued under the aegis of Piedmont with Victor Emmanuel II, Cavour, the assistance of the troops of Napoleon III (paid for by the session of Nice and Savoy to France) and the return of the South achieved by Garibaldi's 'red shirts' (the expedition of the Thousand, 1860). In 1861 Victor Emmanuel II was proclaimed king of Italy and Florence became the capital from 1865 to 1870 when Rome took over.

■ IMPERIAL FORA ★★★

These are the fora built by the Emperors when the old forum, the Roman forum, had become too small to hold the assemblies of the people, the judicial hearings, the conduct of public affairs and of commercial matters. Caesar was the first to build a new forum to the north of the old one; he was followed by Augustus, Vespasian, Nerva and Trajan. The imperial fora extended approximately from the Piazza Venezia to the Basilica of Maxentius and formed a monumental expression of imperial prestige with their porticoes, their temples, their libraries, their basilicas. The old forum was not in any way abandoned. Octavius erected a temple to the divinity of Caesar; as the Emperor Augustus he was himself honoured with a commemorative arch in 19 BC while he had begun construction of his own forum some ten years earlier; the temple to Vespasian stood at the foot of the Capitol.

The fora were excavated in 19C and the mediaeval buildings which had been put up on the site were removed from 1924 to 1932 when the Via dei Fori Imperiali was being constructed.

Via dei Fori Imperiali (Imperial Fora Way). — The road was opened in 1932 as Via dell'Impero and drives straight through the middle of the imperial fora in a straight line from Piazza Venezia. 30 m - 98 ft wide and 850 m - 930 yds long, it opens up a clear view of the Coliseum, a solid reminder of Roman grandeur *(p 67).*

Caesar's Forum ★★

It is usually closed but it can be clearly seen over the railings.

For his forum Caesar chose a central position at the foot of the Capitol, near the old Roman forum. In order to clear the site he had to re-locate the Curia Hostilia and the Comitium *(p 37)* and purchase and demolish the elegant houses already in situ. This exercise cost him the exorbitant sum of 60 million sesterci according to Cicero (then consul and a friend of Caesar's) although Suetonius, the Emperors' biographer, puts the figure at 100 million. Negotiations began in 54 BC when Caesar was rich with the booty gained in the conquest of Gaul (58-51 BC); work began three years later in 51 BC.

Caesar's forum was rectangular and extended from the Curia *(east)* to Via di S. Pietro in Carcere *(west)*, the long sides running more or less parallel with the Clivus Argentarius. Domitian engaged in restoration work (81-96) probably on account of the fire which destroyed part of the Capitol in 80. Trajan completed the work.

About two thirds of Caesar's forum has been uncovered; the rest is beneath Via dei Fori Imperiali.

The ruins. — First to catch the eye are three beautiful standing columns, richly sculpted, which belonged to the **Temple of Venus Genitrix** and date from the time of Domitian and Trajan. Caesar claimed that his family (the Julii) were descended from Venus through her son, Aeneas, and Aeneas' son, Iulus. He decided to dedicate a temple to her after his victory at Pharsalus in 48 BC against Pompey who was killed by Ptolemy, Cleopatra's brother.

This temple, to the north of the Forum, was a veritable museum: besides the statue of Venus in the *cella,* there was a golden statue of Cleopatra, some Greek paintings and, in front of the temple, a statue of Caesar's horse: this extraordinary animal had curiously split hooves, which resembled human feet; according to the sooth-sayers this abnormality was a sign of divine intervention and meant that his master would be ruler of the world.

The edge of the forum was lined with shops, still visible beneath the Clivus Argentarius. During Trajan's reign (2C) a portico was added down the long side nearest the Clivus Argentarius; its two long rows of granite columns still remain. It has been identified as the Basilica Argentaria where the money changers *(argentari)* plied their trade.

After crossing Via dei Fori Imperiali, it is worth walking along Via Alessandrina from the junction of Via Cavour and Via dei Fori Imperiali for an overall view of the fora.

This road junction stands more or less on the point where the Fora of Nerva *(west)* and Vespasian *(east)* met. There are very few remains.

Vespasian's Forum

It was built by Vespasian from 71 to 75 and formed a square adjoining the old Forum and extending approximatively from the Basilica of Maxentius in the south to the Conti Tower (Torre dei Conti) in the north. In the south corner there was a library which is now occupied by the Church of Sts Cosmas and Damian.

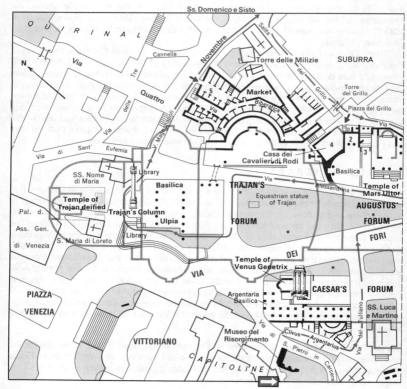

It was also called the Peace Forum. To commemorate his consquest of the Jews in 71 Vespasian erected a Temple of Peace which contained the treasures looted from the Jewish Temple in Jerusalem: the golden 7 branched candlestick, the tablets of the Law of Moses and the silver trumpets *(p 46)*.

Nerva's Forum

Although begun by Domitian, it was completed and inaugurated by Nerva in 98. It was long and narrow in shape and traversed by the Argiletum, a street linking the old Roman forum with the Suburra district; for this reason it was also known as the Forum Transitorium. Here stood the Temple of Minerva; its fine ruins were still visible early in 17C until Pope Paul V had them demolished; the columns and cornices were used in the construction of the Pauline fountain on the Janiculum *(p 192)*.

Against the east wall stand two beautiful **columns ★** (1) and some fragments of a frieze which adorned the wall enclosing the Forum.

Augustus' Forum ★★

The entrance is in Piazza del Grillo but it is better to view it first from Via Alessandrina.

Octavian, who took the name Augustus when he became Emperor, wanted to avenge the murder of his adopted father Caesar. When he finally defeated the murderers, Cassius and Brutus, at Philippi (a town in northern Greece) in 42 BC, he vowed to dedicate a temple to Mars Ultor (the Avenger) to be sited in a new forum, which would be added to the two which already existed (the Roman forum and Caesar's Forum) and would be particularly devoted to the administration of justice. Building began in 31 BC after a considerable amount of demolition work. The site extended from the old Forum to the edge of the unsavoury Suburra district; a high wall, forming the back of the new forum was built to isolate it from the hovels and frequent fires of Suburra; its irregular line reveals the difficulties the builders had to overcome. The two sides facing southeast and northwest bowed out in two semi-circles which are still visible. In the recesses in the walls stood bronze statues of the most famous Romans 'who had brought Rome from insignificance to greatness' (Suetonius): Aeneas, the kings of Alba, the founding fathers of the Julian family, Romulus, Marius, Sulla and other great generals of the Republican era.

Against the centre of the back wall stood the **Temple of Mars Ultor** which was approached by a majestic flight of steps. A few columns to the front and side still stand.

This temple played an important role in public life; it served as a reliquary for Caesar's sword. It was here that members of the imperial family came for the ceremony of the *toga virilis* which they received on passing from adolescence to manhood (at about 17). It was here too that magistrates appointed to the provinces were invested with their authority *(imperium)* and here that they deposited the trophies of their victories on their return.

The basilicas. — These were formed by two porticoes, one on each side of the temple, in front of the semi-circular recesses. Marble statues stood between the columns.

IMPERIAL FORA

0   100 m

Extant parts
Non-extant parts
Sightseeing route

Two columns have been re-erected in front of a room (2), which housed a colossal statue of Mars or Augustus.

Two flights of steps flanking the temple linked Augustus' forum with Suburra. At the top of the steps near the three re-erected columns is a fine arch, known as Arco dei Pantani. There is a better view of it from Via Tor de' Conti.

Augustus' successors made further embellishments: Tiberius (14-37) erected two commemorative arches (3), one on each side of the temple, in honour of Drusus and Germanicus, who pacified Germany and Pannonia (western Hungary). The Emperor Claudius (41-54) continued to dispense justice there as, according to Suetonius... 'one day when he was hearing a case in Augustus' forum he was attracted by the cooking smells coming from the Temple of Mars next door: leaving his court, he went to join the Salian priests at their table'.

Trajan's Forum ★★★ (Foro di Traiano)

High above the northeast corner of the forum is a charming roof-top loggia, part of a 15C building (4) belonging to the Knights of Rhodes *(p. 131)*.

Trajan's forum consisted of a covered market with a concave façade and the forum itself which comprised a public place, the Basilica Ulpia, Trajan's column, two libraries and the Temple of Trajan.

The forum was inaugurated by Trajan, the best of the Antonine emperors, in 113. Its construction had involved work on a huge scale including the cutting back and levelling of a spur of the Quirinal which extended towards the Capitol. Just as Caesar had financed the construction of his forum with booty taken from the Gauls, so Trajan used the spoils of war won from the Dacians, a redoubtable people who lived in what is now Romania. Even after Trajan's death the prestige of his forum did not fade; it was the setting for official demonstrations: here Hadrian publicly burned the records of debts owed by certain of his citizens; here Marcus Aurelius (161-80) held an auction of his personal treasures to finance his wars against the Marcomanni, a German tribe, who were threatening the Empire.

Trajan's forum which extended from Caesar's forum to beyond the two domed churches of St Mary of Loretto and the Holy Name of Mary, was the largest of the imperial fora and certainly the most beautiful, if one is to believe the historian Ammianus Marcellinus (*c*330-400); he gives an account of a visit made by Constantinus II (356), Emperor in the East, to the superceded imperial capital; already on seeing the old Forum, 'the sanctuary of the old power' he had been speechless. 'But on arriving in Trajan's forum... he was stupified'. Even today, few Roman ruins so nobly evoke the ancient civilisation.

Forum. — It extended from Caesar's forum to the edge of the market. The entrance was set in a slightly curved wall facing southeast. The northeast and southwest walls were relieved by two apses, one of which is still visible, running parallel with the concave façade of the market and marked by two columns (one of which is standing). To the left of this column are a few traces of a small mediaeval church.

The wall on the far left of the apse is the outer wall of the forum and is composed of huge blocks of peperine and travertine.

At the centre of the forum stood an equestrian statue in gilded bronze of the Emperor Trajan which Constantinus II dreamed of imitating. Ammianus Marcellinus recounts that a prince in the imperial suite made a subtle suggestion: 'Begin, Sir, by building a stable in this style... so that the horse you envisage will be as well housed as this one'. Down the sides of the forum were porticoes ornamented with statues of illustrious men as in Augustus' forum.

Basilica Ulpia and Libraries. — The basilica was named after Trajan's family. The ends open into two semicircles, one of which is beneath the building at the corner of Via Magnanapoli. The basilica was opulent with five aisles, a marble floor and two storeys of marble and granite columns (some standing, some marked by their bases).

Beyond the basilica were two public libraries: one contained Greek works, the other Latin works together with Trajan's personal records. Between the two libraries was a court-yard at the centre of which stood Trajan's Column, a masterpiece of Classical art which is beyond compare.

Trajan's Column ★★★ (Colonna Traiana). — Originally there were roof top terraces on the libraries which made it easier than it is today to view this extraordinary work. It was invented by Apollodorus of Damascus; no earlier model has been found. It stands about 38 m - 125 ft high and consists of 17 marble drums sculpted in a spiral of panels showing episodes in Trajan's wars against the Dacians. If the spiral of panels were laid out in a straight line it would be 200 m - 656 ft long.

No other imperial victories have ever been celebrated with so much talent and genius. Both wars (101-02 and 105-06) are illustrated; their respective incidents are separated by the winged figure of victory inscribing the imperial victories on a shield *(visible from the terrace in front of the churches)*.

There are over 100 scenes. The artistic ability of the sculptor and the technical skill required to achieve a perfect fit between two parts of a panel at the junction of two drums are matched by such precision of detail that the column serves as a faithful historical record of the Dacian campaigns and of Roman military technique.

The diameter of the shaft is not uniform from top to bottom; two thirds of the way up it increases slightly to prevent the illusion of concavity which would otherwise result from the effect of the height. The size of the panels and of the figures increases towards the top of the column which was originally brilliantly coloured.

A bronze statue of Trajan was placed on top of the column probably after his death. In 1587 Pope Sixtus V had it replaced with the statue of St Peter that one sees today. Although a pagan monument Trajan's Column was never maltreated by the Christians who believed that Trajan's soul had been saved by the prayers of St Gregory. A golden urn containing the Emperor's ashes was placed in a funerary chamber within the column; the urn was stolen in the Middle Ages. Trajan's successor, Hadrian, erected a temple to the deified Emperor after his death but nothing remains to be seen.

The base of the column, which is sculpted with war trophies, bears a Latin inscription (on the side facing the Basilica Ulpia) which has given rise to lively polemics; does the height of the column indicate the height of the Quirinal hill before it was levelled to make room for Trajan's forum?

Inside the column is a spiral staircase *(not open)* leading to the top which is lit by windows in the decorative panels; part of the designer's skill lies in the fact that these windows are scarcely visible from the outside.

Market ★★★ . — *Entrance Via Quattro Novembre. Open 9 am to 1 pm and 3 pm to 6 pm. 1 October to 31 May, 10 am to 4 pm. Sundays 9 am to 1 pm. Closed Monday, 1 January, Easter, 1 May, 15 August, Christmas. 500 L.*

There were about 150 shops arranged in terraces against the Quirinal hill above the forum. The market was not simply a retail market like the Forum Boarium and the Forum Holitorium *(p 148)* but a centre for the acquisition, division and redistribution of supplies, administered by the imperial authorities, under the Prefect of Rome and the Prefect of the Annona *(p 151)*.

First comes a magnificent vaulted room (5) where the civil servants may have worked. The buttresses which support the pillars on which the vaulting rests are of interest; no equivalent structure has been found among the monuments of ancient Rome.

Via Biberatica ★ . — This street serves the upper part of the semicircle which forms the façade of the market and the shops which lined it dealt in exotic commodities. It is still covered with its original paving and runs in a curve from the Torre del Grillo to the present Via Quattro Novembre.

From Via Biberatica the visitor walks down through the market. The shops on the first floor, which are long and vaulted, were probably used for the sale of wine and oil; they open on to a vaulted arcade.

Façade. — The semicircular façade and the arrangement of the shops in tiers demonstrate the genius of Appollodorus of Damascus who gave a monumental appearance to this utilitarian complex.

The shallow shops on the ground floor opened directly on to the curving street which still has its original paving; they may have sold fruit and flowers; one has been reconstructed.

The elegance of the first floor arcades is enhanced by the curved and triangular pediments.

Militia Tower ★ (Torre delle Milizie). — *Closed for restoration.*

This is one of the best preserved buildings of mediaeval Rome. It was the keep of a castle built by Pope Gregory IX (1227-41) at a time when the Pope often had to use force to establish the faith in the Empire. The tower leans slightly owing to an earthquake in 14C; it has lost its top storey and crenellations. It has been known as 'Nero's Tower': according to the legend it was from the top of this tower that the mad Emperor, dressed in theatrical costume, watched the fire that he himself had caused, 'charmed by the beauty of the flames', in Suetonius' account, and reciting one of his poems.

From Via Quattro Novembre there is a view of the beautiful trees in the terraced public gardens of the **Villa Aldobrandini** and of the baroque façade of the **Church of Sts Dominic and Sixtus** (completed in 1655).

Turn into Salita del Grillo. No 1, Piazza del Grillo is the entrance to Augustus' Forum (p 129).

House of the Knights of Rhodes (Casa di Cavalieri di Rodi). — *Not open to the public at present.*

Marco Bembo, Bishop of Vicenza and Cardinal of St Mark's Basilica, was appointed Grand Master of the Order of the Knight Hospitallers of St John by his uncle Pope Paul II (1464-71). He reconstructed this building in 15C in part of a mediaeval convent construted round the remains of the Temple of Mars Ultor. Some of the windows show that Venetian craftsmen were employed. The beautiful 15C loggia (4) overlooking Trajan's Forum is supported on Roman columns, their capitals carved with leaves and rosettes; the walls are decorated with frescoes.

Continue down Via Tor de' Conti.

The street skirts the huge wall constructed of blocks of tufa and travertine which separated Augustus' forum from the Suburra district. Notice the fine arch (Arco dei Pantani) which marked the entrance to Augustus' forum.

■ TOWARDS SAN PIETRO IN VINCOLI

Turn left into Via Madonna dei Monti and continue into Via Leonina.

The district of **Suburra,** the most disreputable in ancient Rome, the haunt of robbers and murderers, has given its name to a tiny square. The narrow streets still seem to be haunted by the spectre of the scandalous Empress Messalina who frequented the local brothels in secret.

Turn right up the steps in Salita dei Borgia, cross Via Cavour and continue up the steps of Via di San Francesco di Paola.

The steps are overlooked by what was once a palace belonging to the Borgia family (attractive 16C loggia).

The sad end of an Etruscan king. — The modern flight of steps leading up to Piazza San Francesco di Paola covers a site linked with the legendary history of early Rome when the city was administered by Etruscan kings. King Servius Tullius' daughter, Tullia, was married to Tarquin. Devoured by ambition she incited her husband to unseat her father, who, wounded in a struggle fomented by his son-in-law in the old Curia, died in the street linking Suburra to the Esquiline which followed the line of the present steps. Seven centuries later Livy tells in his Roman History how Tullia, led astray by her husband's fury, "drove her chariot over her father's body", the street was then called Vicus Sceleratus (Crime Street).

Go up through the covered passage into Piazza di San Pietro in Vincoli.

■ ST PETER IN CHAINS ★ (San Pietro in Vincoli)

The church was consecrated in 5C by Sixtus III (432-40) although it was probably built on a much older construction. During the Renaissance the Cardinals of the della Rovere family were the incumbents: Francesco, who became Pope Sixtus IV (1471-84), and then Giuliano, who became Julius II (1503-13) had it restored.

The church attracts many visitors: tourists who come to admire Michelangelo's Moses and pilgrims who come to see the chains that bound St Peter.

In 1475 Cardinal Giuliano della Rovere added the porch which would be quite elegant if an upper story had not been added in 16C.

The broad interior is divided into a nave and two aisles by two rows of Doric marble columns, beautiful in their solemn austerity. The mediaeval décor was altered in 17 and 18C: the nave was vaulted and painted with frescoes.

On the left of the main door is the tomb of Antonio and Piero del Pollaiuolo, famous Renaissance sculptors from Florence.

Julius II's Mausoleum. — This monument occasioned the meeting of two of the most powerful personalities of the Renaissance: Julius II and Michelangelo. The pope, with his unquenchable appetite for grandeur, conceived the idea of a tomb of such splendour that it would reflect the glory of his pontificat for ever. In 1505 he summoned Michelangelo from Florence to assist in the project. The tomb was to be placed in the centre of St

Peter's Basilica, three storeys high, with 40 huge statues, bronze low reliefs, surmounted by the sarcophagus. Michelangelo left for Carrara where he spent 8 months choosing the blocks of marble from which this superhuman work was to be created. While in Carrara he dreamed of sculpting a single gigantic figure out of the mountain of marble. Then he returned to Rome and to the indifference of the Pope who now swore only by Bramante. Michelangelo returned to Florence hurt. After Julius II's death in 1513 the project for his tomb declined steadily; Michelangelo sculpted only the Slaves (in Florence and Paris) and the Moses; he began the statues of the daughters of Laban, Leah and Rachael, but left the mausoleum itself to his pupils.

Moses ★★★. — Pope Paul III grew tired of seeing Michelangelo working on the tomb of Julius II and, being anxious for him to start as soon as possible on the Last Judgment in the Sistine Chapel, he went one day to see the sculptor at work. There in front of the Moses one of his Cardinals remarked with great diplomacy that the statue was so beautiful that it alone would suffice to honour the Pope's grave.

(After photo by Gab. Fot. Naz., Rome)
Michelangelo: Moses

The authoritative attitude of the huge seated figure is enhanced by the steady gaze of the eyes.

St Peter's Chains. — The chains are displayed in the confessio beneath the chancel. Originally there were two chains: one which had bound the Apostle in Jerusalem, the other in Rome. The legend of the miraculous joining of the two chains arose in 13C.

Crypt. — The relics of the 7 Maccabees, whose martyrdom is recounted in the Old Testament, are preserved in a beautiful 4C sarcophagus which can be seen through a circular grill in the confessio beneath the monstrance containing St Peter's chains.

When planning your sightseeing

Read the Introduction (pp 10 to 29):

This will give you a broad outline of the city's history and appearance, of the art and way of life in what was the cradle of Christian and western culture.

Work out a programme:

Using the itineraries suggested for 3 or 8 days (pp 31 and 32);

Choosing from among the 29 walks described (pp 37 to 212) with the help of the Plan showing the walks and principal sights (pp 4 to 9).

The visitor with time to spare will find enough to occupy a stay of about one month.

Refer to the Practical Information (pp 30 to 35) when planning the material details of your journey.

Consult the index (p 213) for references to famous people, technical terms explained in the text and sights and monuments described in the walks under their English and Italian names.

ST JOHN LATERAN

Distance: 2.5 km - 1 1/2 miles. Time: about 3 1/2 hours.
Start: Piazza di Porta San Giovanni

Rome is a holy city with three hundred churches. It is this aspect of the capital that predominates in the walk described below; seven churches are visited, from an impressive basilica to a humble oratory, leaving the visitor with an unforgettable memory of incomparable works of art or other treasures.

■ LATERAN DISTRICT

The name is taken from the Laterani family who owned a rich property which was confiscated by Nero and restored by Septimius Severus. Excavations in Via dell' Amba Aradam (beneath the INPS building) have revealed traces of a house identified as belonging to the Laterani. It was combined with a neighbouring property in 4C and may have been the residence of Fausta, Maxentius' sister and Constantine's wife, who in 313 lent her house to Pope Melchiades so that he could hold a council of bishops. This was one of the first official manifestations of Christianity.

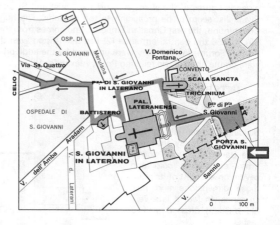

Beneath the St John Lateran Hospital are traces of a building which has been identified as the house of the Annii, Marcus Aurelius' family; the remains of the base of a statue were found in a peristyle; it may have carried the statue of the Emperor which now stands in Capitol Square *(p 56)*.

The walk begins at **St John's Gate** (Porta San Giovanni) which was made in 16C in the Aurelianic Wall (Mura Aureliane) which was built round Rome in 3C and is very well preserved at this point.

Outside the gate in Via Sannio a busy clothing market takes place each morning.

The **monument to St Francis of Assisi** (**A**) is a reminder that the saint and his companions came to the Lateran one day in 1210 to have their rule approved by Innocent III.

From Piazza di Porta San Giovanni bear left towards the basilica.

There is a marked contrast between the noisy square which is a busy road junction and the calm solemnity diffused by the east front of the basilica.

■ BASILICA OF ST JOHN LATERAN ★★★ (San Giovanni in Laterano)

This basilica was the first church to be dedicated to the Holy Redeemer; it symbolised the triumph of Christianity over paganism and thus deserved its title of 'Mother and Head of all the churches in the City and the world'. It is the cathedral of Rome. The dedication to St John came later.

Constantine's Basilica. — On 28 October 312, after defeating Maxentius in battle, Constantine made a triumphal entry into Rome and immediately forbade the persecution of the Christians. In 314 Pope Sylvester I took up residence in the Lateran (a group of buildings comprising a palace, a basilica and a baptistry); the palace became the official papal residence from 5C until the papacy departed to Avignon in France.

Before starting St Peter's in the Vatican, Constantine built the Lateran basilica on the site of Maxentius' bodyguards' barracks. He thus asserted his victory by destroying one of the signs of his enemy's greatness and by stressing his intention of giving the Christians his approval.

After being laid waste by the barbarians in 5C, damaged by an earth tremor in 896 and destroyed by fire in 1308, the basilica was rebuilt in the Baroque era and in 18C. In all over 20 popes contributed to its rebuilding, restoration and embellishment, from Leo the Great (440-61) to Leo XIII (1878-1903).

A strange trial. — It took place in 896 in the Lateran. The accused was the corpse of Pope Formosus, dressed in his papal vestments; his enemies had not forgiven him for having bestowed the Emperor's crown on the 'barbarian' Arnoul, last of the Carolingians. He was set up opposite his judge, Pope Stephen VI, declared unworthy and a perjuror, and finally thrown into the Tiber.

Stephen VI was punished in his turn and was strangled in prison.

The Great Lateran Councils. — Some of the most decisive councils in the history of the Church took place in the Lateran. In **1123** the Diet of Worms was confirmed putting an end to the Investiture Controversy. The council of **1139** condemned **Arnold of Brescia**, a canon, who challenged episcopal authority and preached in favour of a return to the poverty of the early church; he founded a free commune in Rome and drove out Eugenius III.

In **1179** Alexander III called for a crusade against the Albigensian heresy. Following the Council in **1215**, which was attended by 400 bishops and 800 abbots and at which every court in Europe was represented, it was laid down that the faithful must go to confession once a year and take communion at Easter. Innocent III decided to put an end to the Albigensian (Cathar) heresy and launched a crusade in the Languedoc. In **1512** Julius II opened the fifth Lateran Council by asserting the supremacy of the Church of Rome.

EXTERIOR

The well-balanced 18C **façade** is the major work of Alessandro Galilei (1691-1736), one of the architects who used the Baroque style in Rome. He had a masterly touch in contrasting the clear lines of the columns with the dark cavities behind them. On the roof, the gigantic figures of the saints surrounding Christ and St John the Baptist and St John the Evangelist seem to be preaching to the heavens. The huge statue (1) in the porch is of Constantine, the first Christian Emperor, and comes from the imperial baths on the Quirinal. Since 1656 the central entrance (2) has been fitted with the doors from the Curia in the Roman Forum; in 1660 they were enlarged by the addition of a border decorated with the stars on the arms of the reigning Pope, Alexander VII.

INTERIOR

It is hard to envisage the basilical plan of Constantine's building. The central nave and four aisles of today are those of a Baroque church, sometimes considered cold and severe on account of its grandiose dimensions and pale stuccoes. In fact it is a very old building dressed in 17C taste.

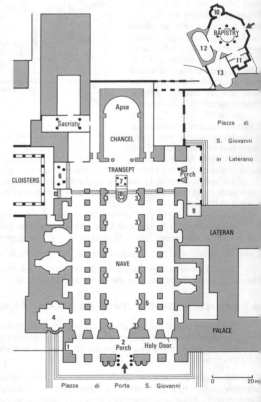

Nave and Aisles. — This part of the church was designed by the great Baroque architect Borromini. Just as Urban VIII had commissioned Bernini to complete St Peter's, so his successor Innocent X in his desire to mark his reign in a prestigious manner invited Borromini in about 1650 to refurbish St John Lateran. Whereas Bernini knew exactly how to adapt Baroque art to earlier styles of construction, Borromini was unable to submit completely to the restrictions imposed by an already existing building. To express his extravagant imagination, which delighted in curves and counter curves and broken lines, he needed to work on a small scale where every detail would be important. The ceiling seems to crush the pillars in the nave which replace the ancient columns; the prominent niches faced with dark marble spoil the effect of the low relief sculptures and the oval medallions above them.

Ceiling ★★. — It was begun by Pius IV in 1562; his arms are in the centre. It was completed in 1567 by Pius V, whose arms are near the chancel. In 18C it was restored by Pius VI who added his arms near the main door. The original design was by a group of Michelangelo's pupils.

Statues of the Apostles ★ (3). — They are in the late Baroque style by some of Bernini's followers. Borromini created twelve huge recesses in the pillars of the nave to receive them. The columns of green flecked marble, which Borromini shortened and re-employed, originally separated the nave and aisles in the ancient basilica. Above each recess he placed the dove from the arms of Innocent X. The low relief sculptures (above), executed under the direction of Algardi, depict stories from the Old and New Testaments. The Prophets in the oval medallions (top) were painted in 18C. This decoration replaced the 15C frescoes painted by Pisanello and Gentile da Fabriano for Martin V and Eugenius IV.

Corsini Chapel ★ (4). — Alessandro Galilei, who designed the east front, was also responsible for this chapel which is built on the Greek cross plan beneath a dome. The red porphyry coffer (left) beneath Clement XII's tomb came from the Pantheon. The allegorical statues are fine 18C work. The fragment of heavily restored **fresco** (5), attributed to Giotto, shows Boniface VIII announcing the Jubilee Year in 1300.

Transept. — The nave is as bare of ornament as the transept is adorned with frescoes, marble and gilding. It was renovated in about 1595 by Clement VIII with Giacomo della Porta as architect. It is a good example of Mannerist decoration: the great wall frescoes resemble a theatrical décor and were painted principally by Cesare Nebbia, Pomarancio and Cavaliere d'Arpino who, in the Ascension *(end of left transept)* imitated the Transfiguration by Raphaël (Vatican Gallery).

The elaborate marble decoration includes high relief angels, placed in small niches, which do not show the liberty of movement which characterises Baroque art. The ostentatious **ceiling** ★★ bearing the arms of Clement VIII is rich in colour and gilding and was designed by Taddeo Landini (late 16C).

The pediment in the **Chapel of the Holy Sacrament** (6) is supported by four beautiful antique **columns** ★ in gilded bronze, the only ones of this kind in Rome. Legend has it that in 1C BC they belonged to the Temple of Jupiter on the Capitol.

The 14C **baldaquin** (7) was repainted at the Renaissance. At the top are kept some relics of the heads of Sts Peter and Paul placed in silver reliquaries, partly paid for by Charles V of France (repaired in 18C). In 19C Pius IX had the high altar faced in marble. During this work it became apparent that the wooden altar contained some much older planks one of which very probably belonged to the altar at which Pope Sylvester I officiated (314-35).

The confessio (8), created in 9C, contains the tomb of Martin V, the first pope to reign after the Great Schism. His tomb is the work of Donatello's brother.

Apse. — The apse of Constantine's basilica was rebuilt in 5C and again in 13C but was not substantially altered until 19C when Leo XIII moved it back in order to extend the chancel. The ogival windows and particularly the **mosaic** in the top of the apse were retained. This mosaic had already been restored in 13C by **Jacopo Torriti** who took several features from the original model: the representation of the cross, celestial Jerusalem with the palm and the phoenix, symbols of the resurrection *(beneath the cross)* and the Jordan full of fishes, birds and boats, which forms the base of his composition. To these he added the Virgin and Nicolas IV kneeling, Sts Peter and Paul *(left),* Andrew and the two Johns *(right).* He also included two smaller figures: St Francis of Assisi *(left)* — Torriti was a Franciscan monk — and St Anthony of Padua *(right).*

The mosaic is dominated by the figure of Christ; the first representation of Christ in the apse dates from 4C. Not long before paganism was still the state religion so that when Pope Sylvester consecrated the basilica, the appearance of such an image was considered miraculous by the faithful. In his desire to perpetuate the 'miracle' Jacopo Torriti managed to transfer the ancient figure to his own composition. During the 19C alterations this original figure was broken and replaced by a copy.

Cloisters ★. — This charming 13C construction is one of the most remarkable by the Vassalletti (father and son). Their art, like that of the Cosmati, consisted of cutting and assembling fragments of antique marble. The twisted columns with varied capitals, the mosaic frieze and the delicate carving of the cornice make this a poetic place where one would like to linger. A fine 9C well has been placed in the middle of the garden.

Leave the basilica by the right transept.

In the **porch** is a bronze statue of Henri IV of France (9) by Nicolas Cordier (1567-1612) in recognition of the king's gift to the Lateran Chapter of the abbey of Clairac in Agenais. In memory of France's beneficence to the Lateran the President of the French Republic belongs as of right to the Lateran Chapter (a mass is said for France on 13 December).

The **façade of the north transept** is so majestic it could be the main front; it was built by Domenico Fontana in 1586.

BAPTISTRY ★

Like the basilica it was built by Constantine. In 4C every Christian was baptised there; nowadays it is used for the ceremonies of Holy Saturday. It was rebuilt in 5C by Sixtus III who set up the eight porphyry columns in the centre and had verses appropriate to baptism inscribed on the octagonal entablature. The upper colonnade and the lantern are 16C additions. Various popes built the adjoining chapels and Urban VIII gave it its present appearance when he added the wall frescoes in 17C.

Chapels. — *Ask the keeper to open the doors.*
The **Chapels of St John the Baptist** (10) and **St John the Evangelist** (11) were built by Pope Hilary (461-68). While legate to Pope Leo the Great, Hilary was sent to the Council of Ephesus to argue against a heresy. During the hearing there was a disturbance and Hilary took refuge on the tomb of St John the Evangelist where he made a vow to build a chapel to the two Sts John.

The Chapel of St John the Baptist has kept its original door which is made of an alloy of silver, bronze and gold and is very heavy; it makes a very special sound when it swings on its hinges.

The Chapel of St John the Evangelist was given a new bronze door in 12C. The ceiling is covered with a beautiful 5C mosaic (delicate colours on a gold ground).

Chapel of Sts Rufina and Secunda (12). — In 12C the original narthex which was the entrance to the Baptistry was converted into a chapel; it is rectangular in shape with an apse at either end, one of which is decorated with a fine 5C mosaic.

Chapel of St Venantius (13). — Built in 7C by John IV, it is decorated with mosaics in the Byzantine style (slim slightly stiff figures) and has a fine cedar ceiling.

LATERAN PALACE (Palazzo Lateranense)

When Gregory XI returned to Rome in 1377 after the popes' period in Avignon he found that the palace had been gutted by fire and he was obliged to instal his household in the Vatican.

The present building was constructed in 1586 by Domenico Fontana during the reign of Sixtus V. The Lateran Treaty *(p 71)* was signed here in 1929. The palace is now the head-quarters of the diocese of Rome (Vicariate) with the Pope at its head in his capacity as Bishop of Rome.

In the square — **Piazza di San Giovanni in Laterano** — stands a fine Egyptian obelisk made of granite, the tallest in Rome. It dates from 15C BC and was brought to Rome in 4C by Constantinus II to adorn the Circus Maximus at the foot of the Palatine where it was found in 1587. It was repaired and re-erected in its present position by Domenico Fontana at Sixtus V's behest.

Traces of the mediaeval palace. — In the Middle Ages the papal palace extended from its present site as far as the Via Domenico Fontana. Two features from this building, the *triclinium* of Leo III and the Scala sancta, have been reconstructed on the east side of the square.

Triclinium of Leo III. — This Pope (795-816) built two rooms in the palace. All that remains of the *triclinium* (dining room) is an apse decorated with a mosaic, repaired in 18C. It cele-brates the alliance of Leo III with Charlemagne: the Emperor re-instated the Pope on his throne and the Pope crowned the Emperor in St Peter's in the Vatican.

Scala sancta. — Sixtus V (1585-90) demolished what remained of the mediaeval palace with two exceptions: the stairs, which according to tradition came from Pontius Pilate's palace and had been used by Christ, and the private chapel of the popes, which was resited not far from its original position in a building specially designed by Domenico Fontana to incorpo-rate the famous steps, which are climbed by the faithful on their knees. There are other stairs on either side for those who prefer to go up on foot.

At the top is the popes' chapel, known as the Holy of Holies *(Sancta Sanctorum),* by analogy with the temple in Jerusalem, because of the precious relics it contained. It is always closed and can be seen only through heavy grills decorated with fine Cosmati work. Above the altar is the famous icon of Christ called the Acheiropoeton, which means it was not made by human hand: St Luke began it and it was completed by an angel; it arrived in Rome miraculously from Constantinople in 8C. The ancient bronze door with its impressive locks which gives access to the popes' chapel can be seen from St Lawrence's chapel *(right).*

These treasures are in the custody of the Passionist Fathers who live in the adjoining convent.

Leave Piazza di S. Giovanni on the west side by Via Ss. Quattro Coronati.

■ COELIAN HILL (Celio)

The Coelian is the greenest and pleasantest of the seven hills of Rome. It was incorpo-rated into the city in 7C BC: when the city of Alba broke the peace treaty which had united it with Rome since the combat between the Horatii and Curiatii, the king Tullus Hostilius captured the rebellious city and transferred its population to the Coelian hill. It was continu-ously inhabited until 11C when the Investiture Controversy brought war to Rome. In 1084 the army of Robert Guiscard 'liberated' the papal capital from the German troops at a terri-ble cost in devastation. Since then there has been little building on the Coelian hill.

CHURCH OF THE FOUR CROWNED SAINTS (Santi Quattro Coronati)

In the Middle Ages this church was part of a fortress which protected the papal Lateran Palace against attack, always possible, from the strongholds of the noble families on the Palatine and in the Coliseum.

The early Christian church (4C) was developed by Leo IV (847-55) into a building which lasted until 1084 when it was left in ruins by Robert Guiscard's troops. Pascal II (1099-1118) built a much smaller church, shorter and without side aisles. From 12C to 15C it belonged to Benedictine monks but in 16C the whole building passed to a community of Augustinian nuns.

Neither archaeologists nor historians have been able to identify the four saints to whom the church is dedicated. The story of four martyred soldiers is mixed up with the story of five sculptors martyred in Pannonia (western Hungary). According to a list of martyrs drawn up by Leo IV their remains were all placed in the crypt of this church.

Tour. — The door beneath the tower, which served as a belfry in 9C, leads into an outer courtyard. The wall opposite the entrance was the eastern façade of the early church. In the inner courtyard on the right are the columns which separated the nave and north aisle now incorporated into a wall.

The **interior** of the church is as Pascal II built it. The space taken up by the nave and aisles corresponds to the width of the nave only in the early church. This makes the apse seem abnormally large. In the walls of the side aisles, as in the inner courtyard, the columns which separated the nave and aisles in the early church are incorporated in Pascal II's build-ing. The wooden ceiling and the women's galleries *(matronea)* date from 16C. In 17C the apse was decorated with paintings and stuccoes depicting the history of the two groups of saints venerated in the church with a glory of saints in the cap.

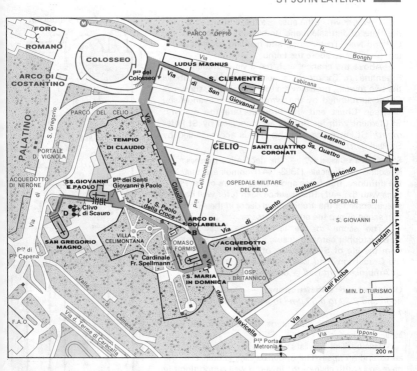

Against the pillar on the left of the chancel arch is a 15C tabernacle, its fine carving picked out in gold. The surrounding paintings were added in 17C.

The crypt goes back to the time of Leo IV. The sarcophagi of four martyrs were found in it together with the silver reliquary containing St Sebastian's head.

Cloisters ★. — *Ring the bell beside the door in the south aisle.* This delightful construction was added in 13C by the Benedictines. The Augustinian nuns replaced the simple roof with vaulting. The ornamental basin placed at the centre of the garden dates from the time of Pascal II. The charming simplicity of the small columns is offset by the capitals which are decorated with water lily leaves. In the eastern walk is St Barbara's Chapel, with three small apses, added by Leo IV (9C).

St Sylvester's Chapel ★. — *Entrance beneath the portico in the inner courtyard. Key available in the convent entrance on the north side of the inner court.* It was built in 13C and is decorated with a curious collection of frescoes, very naive in execution. Beneath the figure of Christ who is flanked by Mary, John the Baptist and the Apostles, is an illustration of the legend of Pope Sylvester (314-35): the leprosy of the Emperor Constantine (lying down and covered in sores), his being cured by the Pope, his baptism, the offering of his power to the Pope and the Pope's entry into Rome preceded by the Emperor.

Continue downhill bearing right and then left into Via di San Giovanni in Laterano.

ST CLEMENT'S BASILICA ★★ (San Clemente) *(plan p 138)*

The church was founded in 4C in a private house belonging to a Christian *(a titulus)* and was immediately dedicated to St Clement, the fourth Pope. It is therefore one of the oldest Roman basilicas. It was ruined in 1084 but rebuilt on the same site by Pascal II in 1108.

Present basilica. — The main entrance through an atrium shows the simple austerity of mediaeval buildings *(usual entrance in south aisle)*. The interior has preserved its 12C basilical plan with a nave and two aisles divided by ancient columns taken from a variety of sources. The unity of style has however been broken by the addition of Baroque stucco decorations and 18C alterations (ceiling and wall frescoes). The marble furnishings are particularly remarkable: in the *schola cantorum* (1) where the choristers sang, the sober *ambones* where the Epistle and Gospel were read and the pascal candlestick are very fine 12C work; the screen separating the *schola cantorum* from the chancel belonged to the early church and dates from 6C. The Cosmati floor (12C) is one of the best preserved in Rome.

Apse Mosaic ★★★. — This composition with its dazzling colours dates from 12C. The richness of the symbolism is enhanced by the diversity and beauty of the style. At the top of the apse against a background of ornamental foliage interspersed with small decorative objects in the manner of the mosaicists of the early centuries is an illustration of the Crucifixion: on the cross itself are 12 doves symbolising the Apostles, flanked by the Virgin and St John. Above is Paradise shown in irridescent colours *(fan-shaped)* with the hand of God the Father holding out the crown to his Son. Below the cross are stags coming to quench their thirst (symbolising candidates for baptism) while humanity gets on with its work.

Lower down in the apse is a frieze of sheep leaving the cities of Jerusalem and Bethlehem, symbols for the Old and New Testaments, and heading towards a distant prospect to adore the Lamb.

Above the chancel arch the style is influenced by Byzantine art. The prophets, Jeremiah and Isaiah (above the two towns), proclaim the triumph of God, shown as Christ surrounded by the symbols of the Evangelists. Between Christ and the Prophets are the martyrs: St Clement with his boat is accompanied by St Peter *(right)*; St Lawrence with his grill is accompanied by St Paul *(left)*.

St Catherine's Chapel (2). — The decorative **frescoes** ★ by Masolino da Panicale (1383-1447) combine a taste for the attitudes, thin faces and subtle colours of the Primitives with the early Renaissance search for well defined space: consider the architectural décor in the Annunciation scene above the entrance arcade.

The scene to the left of the arcade shows St Christopher carrying Jesus; in the chapel are scenes from the life of St Catherine of Alexandria *(left wall)*, the Crucifixion *(end wall)* and scenes from the life of St Ambrose *(right wall — damaged)*.

Underground constructions. — *Open 9 am to 12 noon and 3.30 to 6.30 pm (10 am to 12 noon Sundays. 1 000 L.*

From the north aisle steps lead down to the **lower basilica** (4C).

This basilica consists of a narthex, a nave and two aisles and an apse. The upper basilica is built over the nave and south aisle of the lower; a wall supporting the upper construction (3) divides the lower church into four.

Frescoes. — Some of them (4) date from 11 and 12C; others are older (9C). Those in the nave (5) which are notable for their good state of preservation and their lively scenes illustrate the legend of Sisinius, Prefect of Rome: he went to arrest his wife who was attending a

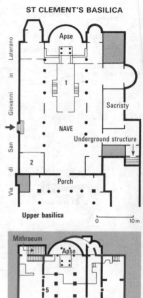

ST CLEMENT'S BASILICA

Upper basilica

0   10 m

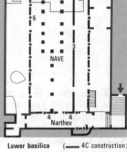

Lower basilica   (▬▬▬ 4C construction)

clandestine mass celebrated by Pope Clement but was struck blind in the presence of the holy man; above this scene his servants, also blinded, are carrying off a column thinking it to be his wife.

Mithraeum. — Beneath the 4C basilica are the remains of two houses built in Republican times. The house beneath the apse was converted in 3C into a *mithraeum,* a small temple for the cult of the god Mithras. Ancient steps lead down to the mithraeum, which is well preserved with two parallel stone benches, where the initiates sat. A statue of the god was placed at the far end; in the centre is the altar showing the god cutting the throat of the bull while the dog, the serpent and the scorpion, symbols of evil, try to prevent the sacrifice which releases life-giving forces.

Continue down Via di San Giovanni in Laterano.

The ruins on the right at the end of the street may have belonged to the **Ludus Magnus,** a gymnasium built by Domitian for training gladiators.

Turn left past the Coliseum (p 67) and bear left into Via Claudia.

On the right are the retaining walls of the huge platform which supported the **Temple of Claudius,** altered by Nero and incorporated into his Golden House.

The entrance to a narrow lane between high walls (Via S. Paolo della Croce - *right*) is marked by **Dolabella's Arch** (1C) carrying the remains of **Nero's aqueduct** which supplied water from the Porta Maggiore to the Palatine; there are further traces of the aqueduct in Via della Navicella (a pillar) and at the west end of Via di Santo Stefano Rotondo.

Next to Dolabella's arch is an attractive **doorway (B)**: it was decorated by Roman marble workers in 13C with a mosaic showing Christ flanked by two figures, one in black and one in white, representing the Trinitarians who devoted themselves to ransoming captives. There used to be a Trinitarian hospice next to the Church of S. Tomaso in Formis.

SANTA MARIA IN DOMNICA

The **Navicella Fountain,** in front of the church porch, was created in 1931 out of a 16C sculpture in imitation of an ancient boat.

This church, a favourite with the Romans for weddings, has retained the charm of a country church. It was founded in 9C and was greatly altered at the Renaissance. The elegant porch was added for Pope Leo X (1513-21) by Andrea Sansovino; the Pope's name is echoed by the lions on the key stones.

The interior has retained certain 9C features: the basilical plan with a nave and two aisles, the columns with antique capitals and the beautiful apsidal **mosaic** ★ , an example of the artistic renewal which took place in the reign of Pascal I (817-24).

The artist has abandoned the Byzantine rigidity for a more lifelike representation: a current of air seems to stir the raiment of the angels, attractively grouped round the Virgin; similarly the apostles above the arch are shown as men rather than in the symbolic form of lambs joyfully approaching Christ and his two angels. The green meadows of the background are dotted with brightly coloured flowers. Enthroned at the centre of the cap is the Virgin: Pope Pascal kneels at her feet, identified by the square nimbus of the living.

Walk through the Villa Celimontana park to Piazza dei Santi Giovanni e Paolo.

BASILICA OF STS JOHN AND PAUL

The quiet square is dominated by the porch and the bold campanile both dating from 12C. The campanile rests on the foundations of the Temple of Claudius *(p 138),* which are visible beneath the porch of the convent of the Passionist Fathers. Its history is similar to that of other buildings on the Coelian Hill: in 4C a certain Pammachius established a church in a private house; it was sacked by Robert Guiscard's Normans in 1084 but rebuilt in 12C.

The five arches above the porch and the gallery, which comprise the upper stage of the façade, belong to the original building.

Two handsome mediaeval marble lions guard the entrance. The interior dates almost entirely from 18C. The main interest lies underground in the rooms of the **ancient house** ★ which have been excavated revealing traces of beautiful paintings: *Access by steps at the west end of the north aisle, 8 am to 12 noon and 3.30 to 5.30 pm; closed holiday mornings.* At the foot of the stairs is a *nymphaeum* decorated with a marine fresco (1) dating from 2C; its fine state of preservation is due to a coat of whitewash which was probably applied to cover up the pagan décor when the house became a Christian place of worship. There follows a suite of parallel rooms beneath the nave and the south aisle; one (2) contains traces of sophisticated paintings of adolescents and spirits among garlands of flowers, vine tendrils and birds. The introduction of Christianity is evoked in a vaulted room where one wall (3) bears a representation of a woman at prayer, her arms extended as if on the cross, surrounded by a décor of scrolls and animals.

Two stairways lead to a small chapel, a confessio, built by Pammachius' family and painted with 4C frescoes depicting the martyrdom of two oriental saints whose relics, which were placed in the confessio, had led to the construction of the basilica.

ANCIENT HOUSE BENEATH THE BASILICA OF SS JOHN AND PAUL

Take Clivo di Scauro on the left of the church.

Look back up at the apse of the basilica, the only one of this kind in Rome. With its small columns it is reminiscent of the Romanesque churches in Lombardy.

ST GREGORY THE GREAT (San Gregorio Magno)

Its imposing 17C façade rises at the top of a steep flight of steps framed by cypresses and umbrella pines. It was begun in 1633 by G B Soria for Cardinal Scipione Borghese (the eagle and dragon of his arms appear above the lower arches). Legend tells how in 6C Gregory converted his house into a church and convent. It was from here that he sent a group of monks to evangelise England; among them were St Augustine, the first Archbishop of Canterbury, and St Lawrence, St Melitas, St Justus and St Honorius who all succeeded him to the see of Canterbury. In 12C the church was rebuilt and dedicated to the saintly Pope. The present building was restored in 17C and 18C.

In the chapel at the head of the south aisle stands Gregory's altar (15C), decorated with low reliefs depicting his legend. To the right of this chapel is a little cell containing an ancient throne which passes for the one used by the saint. At the head of the north aisle is a chapel decorated with 17C paintings; it contains a curious Virgin painted on the wall (13C) and, opposite, a 15C tabernacle.

A door in the north side of the Atrium opens into an enclosure to the left of the church.

Here stand three charming **chapels** (D) *(open Sunday 10 am to 12 noon)* linked by a portico of antique columns. Two of them were built in 17C; the other is older but was restored at that time.

In St Sylvia's Chapel *(right),* dedicated to St Gregory's mother, the apse is painted with a concert of angels by Guido Reni (1608).

The walls of St Andrew's Chapel *(centre)* are decorated with the Flagellation of St Andrew painted by Domenichino in 1608 and with the saint going to his martyrdom by Guido Reni.

St Barbara's Chapel *(left)* was restored in 17C. According to legend the table in the centre is the one on which St Gregory used to offer a meal to the poor; one day an angel came to sit among them. A fresco records this event.

ST PAUL WITHOUT THE WALLS

This walk describes two sites which lie outside the Aurelianic Wall and are linked with the story of St Paul: the Basilica of St Paul Without the Walls contains his tomb and Three Fountains Abbey a few miles further south was the site of his martyrdom.

Access: *by underground or bus — see transport map (p 30); by car — map in the Michelin Red Guide Italia (hotels and restaurants).*

Tour: *allow about 1 hour for St Paul Without the Walls and 3/4 hour for Three Fountains Abbey.*

Saint Paul. — Paul was a Jew called Saul, who was born early in the 1C AD at Tarsus in Cilicia in Asia Minor (southeast Turkey, not far from Adana). At first he persecuted Christ's disciples; then on his way from Jerusalem to Damascus one day, he was blinded by a light, fell from his horse and heard Jesus's voice saying: "Saul, Saul, why persecutest thou me?" This event precipitated his conversion: he changed his name from Saul to Paul and became the chief agent in preaching Christianity to the Gentiles.

His very active life as an apostle contrasted with his mean physique. According to an apocryphal account dating from mid-2C, he was a pale little man, bald but bearded, with a hooked nose and knock knees; he made long missionary journeys throughout Syria, Cyprus, Asia Minor, Macedonia and Greece.

Accused by the Jewish community of Caesarea in Palestine he demanded to be brought before the Emperor Nero (Paul was a Roman citizen). This is why he set out for Rome in about 60 AD. He landed in Pozzuoli and from there travelled to Rome where he was welcomed by the Christians. Two years later he appeared before the imperial court and was acquitted.

The date of Paul's martyrdom is not known for certain. He may like Peter have been a victim of the persecution of the Christians organised by Nero after the terrible fire in 64 AD which destroyed the greater part of Rome. When the rumour began to spread that Nero himself had started the fire to clear the land for his Golden House, he quickly found someone to take the blame. Innumerable Christians died a variety of deaths. Tacitus writes: "Mockery was added to their suffering; covered with the skins of beasts, they were torn by dogs and perished; or were nailed to crosses; or were doomed to the flames to serve as human torches as daylight waned. Nero threw open his garden for the spectacle...".

As a Roman citizen, St Paul was sentenced to be beheaded.

■ BASILICA OF ST PAUL WITHOUT THE WALLS ★★★
(San Paolo Fuori le Mura)

Together with St Peter's in the Vatican, St John Lateran and St Mary Major, St Paul Without the Walls is one of the major basilicas in Rome. Its historical significance attracts visitors from all over the world. Pilgrims to the tomb of the Apostle to the Gentiles are united by a common spirit of veneration.

St Paul's body was buried beside the Via Ostiense which was lined with tombs as were all the major roads leading out of Rome. A small shrine *(memoria)* was erected over his grave. In 4C the Emperor Constantine undertook to build a basilica over the tomb, as he had done for St Peter's tomb. This first basilica was consecrated by Pope Sylvester I in 324. It was smaller than St Peter's Basilica and faced the Via Ostiense. The apostle's tomb was enclosed by the apse on the spot where the high altar now stands. By 386 it had become such a popular place of pilgrimage that three emperors — Valentinian II, Theodosius I and his son Arcadius — decided to enlarge the building. It could not be extended across the Via Ostiense (because of the rising ground) and since the Apostle's tomb could not be moved the orientation was reversed, with the apse on the Via Ostiense and the façade facing the Tiber so that the tomb occupied a central position at the head of the nave.

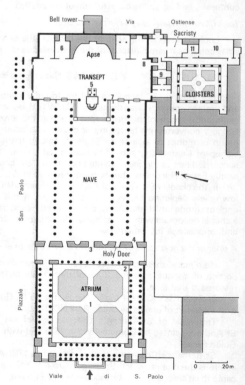

The new basilica was magnificent; it was larger than the contemporary basilica of St Peter in the Vatican. The huge project was not completed until 395 in the reign of the Emperor Honorius. For the next fourteen centuries the basilica was maintained with great care and attention.

When the building was sacked by the Lombards in 8C and by the Saracens in 9C, the damage was immediately repaired. John VIII (872-82) had a defensive wall built enclosing both the basilica and the community which had grown up around it; this came to be known as 'Johannipolis' after the Pope.

The greatest artists were employed to embellish the basilica: from Pietro Cavallini and Arnolfo di Cambio to Carlo Maderno.

When therefore on the night of 15 to 16 July 1823 fire broke out in the roof and almost totally destroyed the basilica it was a great catastrophe.

Reconstruction began immediately and it was decided not to preserve the undamaged parts which had survived. Thus the nave and aisles were rebuilt in their entirety although the south side of the basilica had not been touched by the flames; the apse and transepts were extensively restored.

Although St Paul's basilica is now adorned with gleaming marble and vivid colours, it still follows the original plan and manifests the grandeur of the early Christian basilicas in Rome.

TOUR

Enter by the main doors facing the Tiber (Viale di S. Paolo) to appreciate the size of the building.

The west front is preceded by a huge courtyard *(atrium)* surrounded by covered arcades which was built early in 20C.

The statues of St Paul (1) and St Luke (2) date from 19C.

The mosaic on the pediment is a replacement of the one created by Pietro Cavallini in 14C.

The centre doorway (3) is flanked by statues of St Peter and St Paul; the doors themselves are decorated in bronze and silver with scenes from the lives of the two saints. They replace the 11C bronze door which has been preserved inside the basilica.

Interior ★★★. — No visitor can fail to be impressed by the multitude of columns — eighty granite monoliths — which divide the nave and four aisles. No church interior can be more truly likened to a forest.

The gold and white coffered **ceiling** bears the arms of Pope Pius IX (1846-78) who consecrated the new basilica.

At the west end of the south aisle is the 11C bronze door (4) which was made in Constantinople for Gregory VII (1073-85).

During the reconstruction every alternate window in the **nave** was suppressed; the daylight is filtered by a screen of alabaster.

The 5C portraits of the popes have been replaced by mosaic medallions showing the long line of succession from St Peter to John Paul II.

In the long **side walls** windows and recesses alternate. The recesses contain statues of the Apostles sculpted by various 19 and 20C artists.

Two gigantic granite columns support the **chancel arch** above which are two inscriptions recalling the construction of the basilica by Theodosius and Honorius and its embellishment by Galla Placidia, Theodosius' daughter, who was responsible for the 5C mosaic, which was reconstructed after being badly damaged in the fire. It shows Christ flanked by two angels and the twenty four elders of the Apocalypse; above are the symbols of the Evangelists; below are St Peter and St Paul. On the reverse side of the arch fragments of the original mosaic have been re-employed.

The **baldaquin ★★** (5) is a Gothic work by Arnolfo di Cambio (1285). It is supported on four fine porphyry columns with gilt capitals.

Detail and proportion are delicately blended: the many decorative figures are executed with great skill, from the pairs of angels supporting the pierced roses on each of the four pediments to the animals on the vault.

The side facing the nave shows Abbot Bartolomeo, who commissioned the baldaquin, offering it to St Paul.

Beneath the baldaquin is the high altar; the table is 1.37 m - 4 1/2 ft above a 4C marble plaque engraved with the name of Paul, Apostle and Martyr. The plaque marks the position of Paul's grave and has never been moved.

The mosaic in the **apse** dates from 13C and is the work of Venetian artists commissioned by Pope Honorius III; it is in the characteristic style of the Venetians who even at that time still followed Byzantine models: the little figure at Christ's feet represents Pope Honorius in all humility. The whole work was restored in 19C.

(After photo by Gab. Fot. Naz., Rome)

St Paul Without the Walls:
baldaquin by Arnolfo di Cambio

The ceiling of the broad **transept** is richly decorated with the arms of St Paul (an arm and a sword) and the arms of successive popes from 1800 to 1846 (Pius VII who died a few days after the fire in 1823, Leo XII, Pius VIII, Gregory XVI). The altars which face one another from the far ends of the transept are symmetrical and decorated with lapis lazuli and malachite.

To the left of the apse is the **Chapel of the Holy Sacrament** ★ (6) which contains a 14C wooden crucifix attributed to Pietro Cavallini, a statue of St Bridget kneeling by Stefano Maderno (c1576-1636) and a wooden statue of St Paul dating from 14C or 15C.

The paschal **candlestick** ★★ (7) by Nicolà di Angelo and Pietro Vassalletto (12C) is a remarkable piece of Romanesque art. The base is decorated with monsters while on the shaft are decorative motifs, scenes from the life of Jesus (note the expressions of the squat figures), tendrils and more monsters supporting the candle socket.

The **stoop** (8) is a charming piece of sculpture by Pietro Galli (1804-77) showing a child threatening a terrified demon with holy water.

The **baptistry** (9), rebuilt in 1930, is an elegant chamber in the shape of a Greek cross, incorporating four ancient columns.

Cloisters ★. — These probably formed part of the work done by Vassalletto (13C) who, like the Cosmati, was skilled in marble incrustation work. The north gallery (backing on to the church) is particularly fine.

The great variety among the columns, their marble incrustation picked out in gold and the exquisite workmanship of the mosaic frieze above the arcades make the cloisters a charming composition.

The galleries contain numerous archaeological specimens, some of which come from the old basilica.

In the **picture gallery** (10), among the 13 to 19C pictures, are a series of engravings showing the basilica, particularly in its ruined state after the fire in 1823; the "St Paul Bible", a 9C illustrated manuscript; a reproduction of the slab over St Paul's tomb; several papal portraits from the series painted in the nave in 5C for Leo the Great.

Very precious treasures are housed in the **Relics Chapel** (11) including a beautiful crucifix reliquary in silver gilt dating from 15C.

■ **THREE FOUNTAINS ABBEY** ★ (Abbazia delle Tre Fontane)

Take Via Laurentina and turn left (eastwards) up a drive which leads to Three Fountains Abbey.

The place known in antiquity as *Ad Aquas Salvias* is where St Paul was beheaded. Legend has added an epilogue: the Apostle's head bounced three times and from the ground spouted three fountains.

Pilgrims have been coming here since the Middle Ages. Many oratories were built; one of them, still decorated with traces of 9C painting, is now the entrance gateway. Surrounded by green hillsides and the scent of eucalyptus trees is a group of buildings: a Trappist monastery, a convent of the Little Sisters of Jesus and three churches.

Santa Maria "Scala coeli". — Cistercian monks settled here in 1140. The history of the church is connected with one of St Bernard's ecstatic visions: while celebrating mass in the crypt he had a vision of the souls in Purgatory ascending into heaven, released by his intercession.

The present church, which was restored in 1925, was built in 1583 by Giacomo della Porta to an octagonal plan beneath a shallow dome. In the lefthand chapel there is an attractive 16C mosaic above a painting of St Bernard's vision.

Behind the altar in the crypt is a room supposed to be where St Paul waited before his execution.

Sts Vincent and Anastasius. — This is the abbey church of the Trappists who have occupied the neighbouring monastery since 1868. The origins of the church go back to 7C when Pope Honorius I (625-38) built a convent to house some oriental monks (as at St Sabas: *p 195*).

The church, which was rebuilt in brick in 13C, is austere in appearance with its unusually high elevation and its solid pillars which still bear traces of paintings of the Apostles executed by some of Raphaël's pupils.

St Paul at the Three Fountains. — Giacomo della Porta designed this church in 16C to replace two chapels built on the spot where, according to legend, the fountains had spouted from the earth. Excavations beneath the church in 19C uncovered traces of a small building which in 7C marked the site of Paul's martyrdom; some tombs were also discovered belonging to a Christian cemetery dating back to 4C and beyond.

The statues of St Peter and St Paul on the façade are by Nicolas Cordier. The ancient mosaics set into the floor come from Ostia. The sites of the three fountains are marked by three shrines set at different levels.

Each year the Michelin Red Guide Italia (hotels and restaurants) presents a multitude of up-to-date facts in a compact form.

Whether on a business trip, a weekend away from it all or on holiday take the guide with you.

The part of the Old Appian Way (Via Appia Antica) which holds most interest for the tourist is the stretch which passes the catacombs and the nearby ancient monuments (Romulus' tomb, Maxentius' Circus and the tomb of Cecilia Metella).

Access: *by bus (starting from the Coliseum for the Catacombs of St Callistus and St Sebastian and from Piazza di Porta S Giovanni for the Domitilla Catacombs), consult a transport plan (p 30); by car, consult the plan in the Michelin Red Guide Italia (hotels and restaurants).*

Tour: *follow the itinerary shown on the plan below. Allow about 4 1/2 hours (i.e. 1 hour for St Callistus, 1 hour for Domitilla and 1 hour for St Sebastian).*

Between the tomb of Cecilia Metella and the Casale Rotondo the Old Appian Way is accessible only by car: p 147.

The Appian Way is named after Appius Claudius Caecus, under whose magistracy the road was opened in 312 BC. Before the Aurelianic Wall was built in 3C the Appian Way left Rome by the Capena Gate *(p 179)* and followed more or less the same line as the Via delle Terme di Caracalla and the Via di Porta San Sebastiano. It passed through Capua and Benevento on its way to Brindisi.

In the early stages it was lined by tombs owing to a law, which was already in force in 5C BC, forbidding burials within the city. In the Middle Ages the Appian Way became unsafe; the Caetani converted the tomb of Cecilia Metella into a fortress and plundered the passing travellers. This led to the opening of the New Appian Way. Late in 17C the Old and New Appian Ways were linked by the Via Appia Pignatelli.

Nowadays, with its Catacombs and the Quo Vadis Church, the Old Appian Way is an important part of Christian Rome.

The **"Domine, quo vadis?" Church** recalls a famous legend. While fleeing from persecution in Rome Peter is supposed to have met Christ on the road and asked him "Domine, quo vadis? (Lord, whither goest thou?)". "To Rome, to be crucified a second time", replied Christ and disappeared leaving his footprints in the road. Ashamed of his weakness Peter returned to Rome and met his death.

■ THE CATACOMBS ★★★

In mediaeval Rome the Latin expression *ad catacumbas* referred to St Sebastian's cemetery which lay in a hollow beside the Appian Way. When other similar cemeteries were discovered in 16C they were referred to by the same name. 'Catacomb' now means an underground Christian cemetery composed of several storeys of galleries which generally extended downwards. When there was no more room in an upper gallery, excavation began on a lower one, so that the galleries nearest to the surface are usually the oldest.

Catacombs have been found elsewhere on the outskirts of Rome and also around Naples, in Sicily, North Africa and Asia Minor.

Christians in the Catacombs. — Until the middle of 2C there were no formal Christian cemeteries. Very often a private burial ground belonging to a family some of whom were pro-Christian would be made available to Christians of their acquaintance for burying the dead. The situation changed early in 3C when Pope Zephyrinus put Callistus in charge of the cemetery on the Appian Way. This was the first step in the organisation of Christian burials and cemeteries for Christians only began to be established on land belonging to the church.

For a long time the catacombs were simply graveyards where Christians came to pray at the tomb of a loved one. Visits became more frequent in 3C when the persecutions (by Septimius Severus in 202, Decius in 250, Valerian in 257 and Diocletian in 295) created many martyrs; the popes strongly urged the faithful to pray at the martyrs' tombs. The catacombs however were never a place of refuge where Christians lived in hiding; they were known to the imperial authorities who closed them at the height of a persecution. It was only rarely, when they had broken the closure rule, that Christians were killed in the catacombs.

After a period of great popularity in 4C when Christianity experienced a great expansion, the catacombs were abandoned (except for St Sebastian's which was always a place of pilgrimage). In 5 and 6C the Roman countryside was ravaged by Barbarians; gradually the martyrs' relics were transferred to the town where churches were built to house them. It was not until 16C, when an underground cemetery was discovered in the Via Salaria by Antonio Bosio, an Italian archaeologist, that interest in the catacombs started up again. Their systematic investigation is primarily due to another archaeologist Giovanni Battista de Rossi (1822-94).

TOUR OF THE CATACOMBS

The most typical of the many catacombs beside the Appian Way are those of St Callistus, Domitilla and St Sebastian.

Visitors to the catacombs are shown round in guided parties. Owing to the poor lighting in the galleries and the pressure of numbers, which means that the parties move quickly, it is adviseable to keep close to the guide.

Special terms used in the catacombs. — A **hypogeum** is an underground tomb belonging to a noble Roman family.

From the *hypogeum* a network of galleries developed; each gallery was about a metre - 3 ft wide and 2 or 3 metres - 7 ft or 10 ft high. Opening off the galleries were small rooms, **cubicula**, where the sarcophagi were laid; sometimes there was a **lucernarium**, an opening in the roof through which air and light could enter.

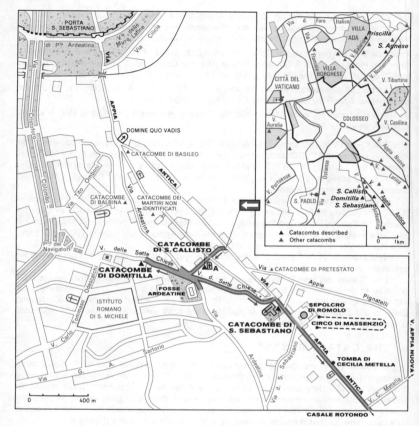

When lack of space became acute, recesses, **loculi,** were hollowed out one above another in the gallery walls; the corpse was wrapped in a shroud and laid in the recess which was sealed off with a marble slab or a row of terracotta tiles inscribed with the name of the dead person and a sign to show his religion. Sometimes when a tomb was set into a wall, it was sealed with a horizontal slab of marble and the vault, **arcosolium,** was often decorated with paintings.

As the cult of the martyrs developed so did the custom, borrowed from the pagans, of holding a funeral feast, called **refrigerium** by the Christians. The faithful would gather round a martyr's tomb to ask him to intercede on their behalf and to share a meal.

Near to the catacombs there is often a **columbarium;** this is a communal burial chamber, containing niches where the urns holding the ashes were placed, and was usually reserved for pagans of modest means.

Decorative motifs used in the Catacombs. — Originally the Christians decorated their tombs with motifs found on pagan tombs (garlands of flowers, birds and cherubs). Then various other motifs begin to appear, illustrating the metaphors of the Holy Scriptures, depicting scenes from the Bible and symbolising manifestations of the spiritual life. The meaning of the paintings and symbols found in the catacombs is still the subject of much controversy.

The **dove** holding a twig in its beak is a symbol of reconciliation between God and man. The **anchor** signifies hope; sometimes the horizontal bar is stressed to form a cross. The **fish** is a symbol for Christ: the Greek word for 'fish' is composed of the initial letter of each word in the Greek phrase meaning "Jesus Christ, God's son, Saviour".

The **dolphin** which comes to the rescue of shipwrecked sailors indicates Jesus the Saviour.

The **fisherman** means a preacher because of Jesus' words to his disciples "I will make you to become fishers of men".

Jonah and the whale foretells the Resurrection.

The **Good Shepherd** or Jesus searching for the lost sheep was one of the most popular ways of representing Christ among the early Christians.

Other favourite scenes were the miracle of the feeding of the five thousand, the healing of the man sick of the palsy and the Baptism of Jesus or the institution of baptism.

Join us in our never ending task of keeping up to date.
Send us your comments and suggestions please.

Michelin Tyre Public Limited Company
Tourism Department.
81 Fulham Road, LONDON SW3 6RD.

ST CALLISTUS' CATACOMBS ★★★

Guided tour 8.30 am to 12 noon and 2.30 to 6 pm (5 pm October to April). Closed Wednesday, 1 January, Easter and Christmas. 2 000 L.

The catacombs extend over an area bounded by the Appian Way, the Via Ardeatina and the Via delle Sette Chiese. The cemetery where almost all the 3C popes were buried is also famous for its exceptional collection of paintings. In G B Rossi's opinion, the Christian cemetery could have grown out of the family tomb of the Caecilii who were patricians. By 3C the property belonged to the Church and was developed as a huge burial ground for Christians.

It was probably **Callistus** who was chiefly responsible for the Church becoming the legal owner of the cemeteries. This change in circumstances occurred at the very end of 2C during the reign of the Emperor Commodus (180-92) which was a peaceful period for the Christians: it was said that Commodus' concubine, Marcia, was a Christian.

Callistus, who may have been a native of Trastevere, was a slave whose Christian master entrusted him with his money matters. Financial failure caused Callistus to flee. He was caught, denounced as a Christian by some Jews and sentenced to hard labour in the Sardinian quarries. He was released under an amnesty but excluded from Rome by the Pope, Victor I, who regarded him as an adventurer.

Returned to favour under Zephyrinus, Victor's successor, he was made a deacon and appointed as administrator of the cemetery which bears his name. In 217 he succeded Zephyrinus as pope; five years later he died. He was not however buried in his cemetery on the Appian Way but in Calepodius' cemetery on the Aurelian Way near the Janiculum where his tomb was found in 1962.

Near the entrance to the underground is a **chapel with three apses (A)**, probably built in 4C, which may have contained the remains of Pope Zephyrinus.

Papal Crypt. — Callistus decided that his cemetery should be the popes' official burial place and the remains of the 3C popes were placed in the *loculi* hollowed out of the walls of this chamber. Among them was Sixtus II who was put to death on 6 August 258 together with four of his deacons; they had been surprised while holding a meeting in the cemetery, an act which contravened an edict issued by the Emperor Valerian forbidding Christian assemblies and closing the catacombs.

The marble plaques sealing the *loculi* bear the names and titles of the dead popes. The Greek letters M T P, which are the main consonants (MTR) in the Greek word 'martyr' meaning witness, have been added to the names of Pontianus and Fabian; the former was deported to Sardinia where he died in 235, the latter was a victim of the Emperor Decius who organised one of the worst persecutions ever suffered by the Christians.

The wreathed columns and the *lucernarium* date from 4C.

Also 4C is the inscription to the glory of all the saints who lie buried in this place, which was put up by Pope Damasus to commemorate the martyrs with a few verses in their honour.

St Cecilia's Crypt. — This chamber was already being venerated by pilgrims as St Cecilia's tomb in 7C. Her sarcophagus was found by Paschal I in 9C in the *loculus* which now contains a copy of the statue of the saint sculpted by Maderno *(p 187)*.

Sacraments' Crypt. — This group of chambers contains an extraordinary collection of paintings dating from the late 2C or early 3C. The majority of the subjects generally found elsewhere in the catacombs appear here. There are no purely decorative motifs, except in a simple band framing the scenes.

Callistus' cemetery also contains the crypt in which Pope **Eusebius** (309-10) is buried (he was deported to Sicily where he died but his body was recovered by his successor); the crypt where Pope **Caius** (283-96) is buried; the crypt where, in the opinion of G B de Rossi, Pope **Miltiades** (311-14) was buried.

Lucina's precinct, which is named after a noble Roman lady, and the Papal Crypt are the oldest part of the cemetery; Lucina is thought to have recovered the remains of Pope Cornelius (251-53) and to have buried them in a chamber decorated with paintings showing Cornelius with his friend Cyprian, Bishop of Carthage. In another chamber in Lucina's precinct, also decorated with paintings, are two very faint illustrations of the mystery of the Eucharist: two fish together with two baskets of bread and glasses of wine. These paintings, which are on the left wall of the chamber, date from 2C.

DOMITILLA'S CATACOMBS ★★★

Entrance at no 282, Via delle Sette Chiese. Same opening time as St Callistus' but closed on Tuesday.

This extensive network of galleries began in the private cemetery of Domitilla, whose uncle, the Emperor Domitian (81-96), belonged to the rich Flavian family. In 95 Domitilla's husband, Flavius Clemens, was denounced as a Christian and executed on Domitian's orders. Domitilla was exiled to the Isle of Pandataria (now called Ventotene).

Domitilla's catacombs became famous in 4C when a basilica was built over the graves of St Nereus and St Achilleus. According to legend they were two of Domitilla's servants who like their mistress were converted to Christianity. In fact they were two soldiers martyred under Diocletian (284-305). Not far from their tomb lay St Petronilla whose sarcophagus was transferred to the Vatican *(p 76)* in 8C.

Domitilla's cemetery was discovered in 16C by Antonio Bosio; in 19C it was excavated by G B de Rossi and then by the Papal Commission on Sacred Archaeology.

Basilica of St Nereus and St Achilleus. — The basilica, which consisted of a nave and two side aisles preceded by a narthex, was built between 390 and 395 to the detriment of the upper galleries which belonged to one of the oldest parts of the cemetery. The sarcophagi of the two saints must have been placed in the apse near Petronilla's. Pieces of the original structure, in particular of the *schola cantorum* which separated the chancel from the rest of the church, have been put back in place. In front of the chancel on the right one of the small columns which supported the canopy now bears a sculpture of Achilleus the martyr.

In this basilica in the late 6C Gregory the Great preached one of his homilies deploring the misery that Rome was suffering under the barbarian menace. By the end of 8C the basilica was deserted; in future the saints were venerated within the city walls in the new church built by Leo III *(p 181)*.

Veneranda's Cubiculum. — This chamber behind the apse proves popular enthusiasm for the cemetery in 4C. The faithful were very keen to be buried near to the tomb of a saint, just as Veneranda managed to be buried next to St Petronilla. A painting on the *arcosolium* shows them both entering Paradise.

"Flavian Vestibule". — This is the name given to the *hypogeum (p 143)* on the right of the basilica. It is one of the oldest parts of the cemetery and dates from 2C. It is like a long wide gallery decorated with vine tendrils, birds and cupids; opening out of it are *cubicula* to contain the sarcophagi; when there was no more room, *loculi* were created. Late in 3C a room for the funeral meal was created on the right of the entrance. Linked to it is a *cubiculum* named after Love and Psyche on account of its decorations which date from 3C but have been partially damaged by the creation of *loculi*.

Flavian-Aurelian Hypogeum. — To the left of the basilica is another *hypogeum* containing the names of the freedmen employed by the Flavians and the Aurelians. It is contemporary with the Flavian Vestibule. There are examples of the simple symbols such as the anchor or a monogram used by the early Christians.

Domitilla's Catacombs contain a multitude of galleries and *cubicula* such as the *cubiculum* of Diogenes, a grave digger, or the *cubiculum* of Ampliatus etc.

Turn right out of Via delle Sette Chiese into Via Ardeatina.

Ardeatine Graves (Fosse Ardeatine). — *Open 9 am to 12 noon and 4 to 7 pm, mid May to September, 8.30 am to 12 noon and 2.30 to 5 pm, October to mid May.*

This is a moving memorial of a particularly painful episode during the second World War. Here on 24 March 1944 the Nazis killed 335 Italians as a reprisal for an attack by the Resistance in Rome in Via Rasella in which 32 German soldiers were killed. The tombs of the victims are sheltered by a santuary and a museum gives information on the period.

Return to Via delle Sette Chiese.

ST SEBASTIAN'S CATACOMBS ★★★

Same opening times as St Callistus' but closed on Thursday.

Beside the area covered by the catacombs, the Appian Way entered a valley. On its slopes houses and dovecotes were built. In the valley bottom three mausoleums were built which probably marked the beginning of the cemetery.

When the Church became the owner of the site in 3C the mausoleums were covered by a platform arranged as a covered courtyard called *triclia*.

In 4C a basilica with a nave and two aisles was built above the earlier structures and surrounded by mausoleums (those round the apse and on the south side have been preserved). It was here, near where the Apostles Peter and Paul were venerated, that St Sebastian was buried; he was a soldier martyred during the persecution in Diocletian's reign (284-305). His cult became so popular that in 5C a crypt was excavated around his tomb. The basilica was altered in 13C and then rebuilt in 17C for Cardinal Scipio Borghese; the new church was built above the nave of the previous building.

The tour of St Sebastian's Catacombs includes a *colombarium;* there are other graves of the same type parallel with the one that is visited.

The three mausoleums. — These three structures with their brick façades, pediments and travertine door frames probably date back to the early 1C. At first they were used by pagans and then by Christians. The lefthand and central mausoleums have some beautiful stucco decorations. From these and the inscriptions found within it seems that the structures belonged to religious sects which developed alongside Christianity; the central mausoleum contains the Greek symbol for the Son of God, Saviour *(p 144)* left by the Christians. The righthand mausoleum is decorated with paintings and bears the name of its owner, Clodius Hermes.

The 'triclia'. — This section of the catacombs has proved the most controversial among archaeologists. The many graffiti on the walls invoking the Apostles Peter and Paul suggest that from 258 onwards Christians used to meet here to celebrate their memory. But did they meet here because the relics of the two saints had been lodged here temporarily while the basilicas of St Peter in the Vatican and St Paul Without the Walls were being built? *(p 78)*

The participants sat on the stone benches for the meal *(refrigerium)*.

St Sebastian's Crypt and Catacombs. — The network of galleries which began to develop in 4C round the martyr's tomb was badly damaged in the Middle Ages by a ceaseless procession of pilgrims who came to invoke St Sebastian's name against the plague.

St Quirinus' Mausoleum and "Domus Petri". — *Open to specialists only.* These two chambers are supposed to have housed the relics of Peter and Paul. One contains the graffito *Domus Petri* (Peter's house) which may indicate that Peter's remains rested there.

The other, built in 5C, was the mausoleum of St Quirinus who was martyred in Pannonia (western Hungary).

Present Basilica. — The atmosphere in the single nave with its white walls and beautiful 17C painted wooden ceiling is fairly solemn and chill. In the relics chapel *(right)* is exhibited the stone in which Christ is said to have left his foot prints *(p 143)*. It may in fact be an old votive offering.

St Sebastian's Chapel *(left)*, which was built in 17C over his tomb, contains a statue of the saint by one of Bernini's pupils (17C).

In the Sacristy *(right of St Sebastian's Chapel)* there is a beautiful 14C wooden crucifix.

■ ROMULUS' TOMB AND MAXENTIUS' CIRCUS

When his young son Romulus died in 309 the Emperor Maxentius had a handsome tomb built for him beside the Appian Way. The tomb itself was cylindrical with an internal chamber. What is left of it is partly covered by undergrowth and partly hidden by a house built on to the front.

On its southern side in a natural depression Maxentius built a large hippodrome for chariot races. The oblong shape of the circus is well preserved as are the remains of the two towers which stood at the western end flanking the stalls and the magistrates' box where the starting signal was given.

■ CECILIA METELLA'S TOMB *

Open 10 am to 7 pm (4 pm October to March). Closed Monday, 1 January, Easter, 1 May, 15 August, Christmas.

This handsome tomb dates from the late Republic. The crenellations were added in 14C when the Caetani family turned it into a keep and incorporated it into the adjacent 11C fortress which extended across the road. Its bulky silhouette is one of the best known in the Roman countryside.

The cylindrical mausoleum standing on a square base was the tomb of the wife of Crassus, son of the Crassus who was a member of the first triumvirate with Caesar and Pompey in 60 BC. The decorative frieze of ox heads has caused the locality to be known as 'Capo di Bove'.

Fragments of tombs from the Appian Way can be seen within the ruins of the mediaeval fortress *(right of the entrance)*.

On the left of the entrance is the way in to the conical funeral chamber of the original tomb.

From Cecilia Metella's tomb to Casale Rotondo

5 km - 3 miles. 800 m - 875 yds after Cecilia Metella's tomb the Old Appian Way becomes a one way road. Return to Rome by the Ring Road (Grande Raccordo Anulare) and one of the radial roads leading to the city centre (map pp 4-5-6).

Although it is sometimes frequented by the unsavoury element in the population, this stretch of the Old Appian Way provides a pleasant view of the Roman countryside where the reddish tones of the tombs and the ruined aqueducts blend with the dark green of the cypresses and umbrella pines.

The tombs on the Appian Way were some of the most elaborate in Rome; shaped like pyramids or tumuli and topped by a mound covered in undergrowth; sometimes only an inscription or a few carvings remain.

The tomb on the right just after the junction with Via Erode Attico was long thought to be the **tomb of one of the Curiatii**, who took part in the famous combat with the Horatii *(pp 179 and 212)*.

The **Quintilian Villa** (villa dei Quintili) was a huge property going back to the time of Hadrian (117-38); part of it was turned into a fortress in 15C.

The **Casale Rotondo** was a cylindrical mausoleum dating from the Republican era; it is now topped by a farmhouse.

From this point there is a fine view *(left)* of aqueduct ruins.

(After photo by Carlo Guidotti, Rome)

Old Appian Way

Distance: 2 km — 1 1/4 miles. Time: about 3 hours. Start: Via del Portico d'Ottavia

To visualise the unity of this part of the town, hemmed in by the Capitoline, the Palatine and the Tiber, one must go back 2 500 years to the time of the Etruscan kings and the Republic. As early as 6C BC crowds thronged the vegetable market (Forum Holitorium) at the foot of the Capitoline and the cattle market (Forum Boarium) at the foot of the Palatine. This area was also a religious centre, containing several temples, some of which were thought to have been founded by King Servius Tullius (578-34 BC).

At the end of the Republican period Caesar began the construction of the magnificent Theatre of Marcellus. Nearby was the Circus Flaminius, a vast oblong arena, built in 221 BC, where chariot races, hunting events and processions took place.

When Rome declined these buildings fell into ruins. In the Middle Ages the area was heavily populated, particularly by artisans. Small businesses abounded, owned particularly by Jews who congregated there from 13C. The removal of the Ghetto in 1888, the clearances undertaken in 1926 to reveal the ancient monuments and the opening of new roads, have all destroyed a proportion of the narrow lanes and old houses.

Forum Holitorium and Forum Boarium. — From the earliest days not far from the Roman Forum, the administrative and political centre, there were other fora devoted to trade.

One of them, the vegetable market **(Forum Holitorium)** extended from the Porticus of Octavia along the riverbank to Vicus Jugarius. Another, the cattle market **(Forum Boarium)** extended further south to the foot of the Aventine and reached as far east as the Arch of Janus (Arco di Giano) and the Arch of the Money-changers (**B**). These two markets were next to the Port of Rome; the boats sailed up the Tiber which was then navigable and moored by the left bank level with the Pons Aemilius (Ponte Rotto).

From the beginning this district had contained altars for the worship of the gods. Hercules, who was thought to have driven Geryon's cattle through the Forum Boarium, was honoured near to Santa Maria in Cosmedin, in recognition of his victory over Cacus, the blind cattle thief *(p 50)*. Parallel to the Temple of Apollo, traces have been found of another temple attributed to the Roman goddess of war, Bellona. Three temples stood side by side on the site the Church of San Nicola in Carcere. Not far from the Church of St Omobono, beside the Vicus Jugarius a group of sanctuaries has been uncovered; further south stands the Temple of Fortune which Servius Tullius, the slave who became king, dedicated to the god who changes men's destinies. Naturally Portumnus, the protector of harbours, had a place of worship near the port; this has sometimes been identified as the very old sanctuary known as the Temple of Fortuna Virilis *(p 152)*.

Upstream from the Forum Boarium and its quays, must have been the military port, known as 'Navalia inferiora' (later on another port 'Navalia superiora' was built on the Campus Martius). In 338 BC when Rome embarked on the conquest of the Mediterranean, her citizens came to the port to admire the ships captured at Antium; the prows were displayed on the Rostra in the Forum *(p 42)*. It was here too that Cato of Utica disembarked in 58 BC laden with treasures from King Ptolemy Auletes after an expedition to Cyprus.

Ghetto. — The Jews who formerly lived in Trastevere moved to the left bank of the Tiber in 13C. Pope Paul IV (1555-59) had the area enclosed within a wall thus creating the Roman ghetto. The wall ran from Ponte Fabricio along Via del Portico d'Ottavia returning to the riverbank along Via del Progresso. The gates were opened at dawn and closed in the evening on the 4 000 inhabitants (in 1656). The ghetto ended in 1848; the walls were taken down and the houses demolished in 1888. The Synagogue was built in 1904 among other new constructions.

TOUR

Portico of Octavia (**A**). — This was one of the richest monuments in Rome. It was vast, extending back as far as the present Piazza di Campitelli and the Church of Santa Caterina dei Funari *(p 116)*.

All that now remains is part of the entrance porch *(propylaea)* which faces the Tiber. The remaining Corinthian columns supporting sections of the entablature belonged to a portico built by Septimius Severus (193-211).

The original portico had been built in 2C BC by Cecilius Metellus, who defeated the Macedonians, as an enclosure for two temples dedicated to Juno and Jupiter respectively. Augustus rebuilt the portico, which he dedicated to his sister Octavia, and included two public libraries, one Latin and one Greek, as well as an assembly hall where the Senate sometimes met.

Sant'Angelo in Pescheria and the fish market. — Nowadays the *propylaea* of Octavia's Portico serves only as a monumental entrance to the little Church of Sant'Angelo in Pescheria (founded in 8C).

The name, like those of the neighbouring streets, recalls the fish market which occupied the antique ruins in 12C. The activity surrounding the stalls set out on the huge paving stones in front of the church and in Via di Sant'Angelo in Pescheria made this one of the most picturesque corners of Rome.

On the right of the portico is a stone bearing a Latin inscription which says that fish above a certain length went to the Conservators of Rome *(p 56)*. This privilege was abolished in 1798.

Take Via di Sant'Angelo di Peschieria bearing right into Via della Tribuna di Campitelli; turn right into Piazza di Campitelli.

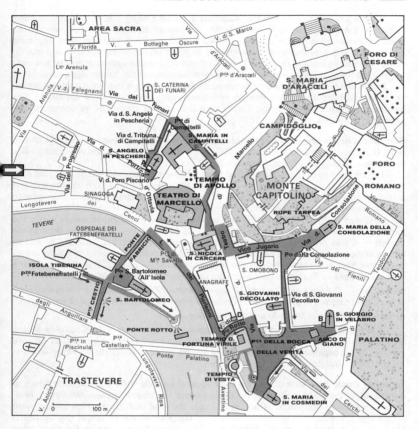

Church of Santa Maria in Campitelli. — *Open 10 am to 12 noon.* When Rome was struck by the plague in 1656 the Romans prayed ceaselessly in front of an image of the virgin in the Church of Santa Maria in Portico; now demolished, this church stood on the site of the present Anagrafe on the riverbank. When the epidemic ceased it was decided to build a new sanctuary to house the holy image. The first stone of Santa Maria in Campitelli was laid in September 1661. The building was entrusted to Carlo Rainaldi (1611-91) who drew up his own design and executed it himself.

The exterior, like the interior, is a forest of columns. Those on the façade are clearly detached and form a pleasant harmony. Variety and movement are provided by the broken and curved pediments, the jutting cornices and multiple recessing.

The **interior ★** space is defined by the advanced columns. The variation on the Greek cross plan which is extended and constricted towards the apse, the grandiose elevation of the vault and the dome and the alternating projections and recesses create a bold effect of perspective.

The church contains a few fine 17C paintings including a canvas of St Anne, St Joachim and Mary *(second chapel on the right)* by Luca Giordano (1632-1705), an exponent of the Baroque style. The picture frame is supported by two kneeling angels. Another Baroque painting *(left of the choir)* is by Giovanni Battista Gaulli, called Baciccia (1639-1709), who painted the vault of the Gesù Church *(p 109).* Below the painting is the tomb of Cardinal Massimi, designed by Verroi and sculpted by Qualieri (1975). Above the high altar is a Baroque glory surrounding the 11C enamel of the Virgin which came from the Church of Santa Maria in Portico.

From Piazza di Campitelli, turn right into Via del Teatro di Marcello.

Temple of Apollo ★★. — The Greek god Apollo was venerated by the Romans chiefly for his power to ward off disease (Apollo medicus). The first temple dedicated to him was raised on this site in 5C BC. In 34 BC Caius Sosius, governor of Cilicia and Syria, rebuilt the sanctuary in marble and it became known as the Temple of Apollo Sosianus. The three elegant fluted **columns ★★** with Corinthian capitals belonged to the porch *(pronaos)* of the temple and were re-erected in 1940.

Theatre of Marcellus ★★. — The building was begun by Caesar and completed between 13 and 11 BC by Augustus who dedicated it to Marcellus, his sister Octavia's son.

The two tiers of arches which remain were probably topped by a third row of Corinthian pilasters. They form the semi-circular part of the building which contained the tiers of seats; the stage, of which nothing is left, backed on to the riverbank. It was the second largest theatre in Rome after Pompey's Theatre in the Campus Martius; it could hold about 13 500 spectators. Its severe and sobre style, with the three architectural orders — Doric, Ionic and Corinthian — one above the other, served as a model for the Coliseum which was built of the same stone, travertine from the Tivoli quarry.

On the day of the inauguration Augustus suffered a slight mishap which Suetonius recorded: 'the official chair *(sella curulis)* gave way beneath him and he fell backwards'. The theatre was damaged both in the fire in 64 AD and during the struggle between Vespasian and Vitellius and was finally abandoned early in 4C. It was soon being used as a quarry; some of the stone went to repair the Ponte Cestio in 4C. Houses were built against the walls and in 1150 it was transformed into a fortress and thus saved from further depredations.

In 16C the noble family of Savelli turned it into a palace. It is the remains of this house, which was built by Baldassarre Peruzzi, which are visible today above the old arches. The palace later passed to the Orsini. The ancient theatre was cleared of its accretions and excavated from 1926 to 1929.

San Nicola in Carcere and the temples of the Forum Holitorium. — The little church of St Nicholas by the Gaol was built in 11C on the ruins of three temples which stood side by side overlooking the Forum Holitorium.

The church has been restored several times: the façade was designed by Giacomo della Porta in 1599. The nave is built on the site of the *cella* and *pronaos* of the middle temple and is flanked by aisles so that the side walls of the church incorporate columns belonging to the side walls of the two outer temples. The lefthand temple was the oldest; it was built in the Doric style in 2C BC and probably dedicated to Janus. The righthand temple was in the Ionic style — two columns from its righthand side stand on their own to the right of the church — it was probably dedicated to Hope and has been dated to 1C BC. The middle temple is the most recent and was probably dedicated to Juno. The tower, originally defensive, dates from 12C when the district belonged to the Perleoni family. The words *in carcere* in the title refer to a Byzantine gaol which occupied the lefthand temple in 7 and 8C.

Excavations. — *Guided tour 10 am to 12 noon Thursday.* The tour includes the foundations of the pagan temples in the crypt and portions of a frieze seen from the roof of the church.

Cross Via del Teatro di Marcello and turn into Vico Jugario.

In antiquity Vicus Jugarius (now Vico Jugario) ran at the foot of the Capitoline linking the Forum Holitorium to the Roman Forum and was lined with the workshops of yoke makers. At the beginning of the street on the left are traces of the porticoes which stood at the foot of the Capitoline in the Republican era.

Tarpeian Rock (Rupe tarpea). — Vico Jugario runs into Via della Consolazione which is dominated by the southern face of the Capitol which has been identified, after much hesitation, as the Tarpeian Rock. In antiquity it was the rock bluff from which traitors were hurled into the void. It is named after Tarpeia, daughter of the keeper of the Capitoline citadel, who opened the gates of the city to the enemy Sabines during Romulus' reign *(p 55).*

Santa Maria della Consolazione. — The broad white façade at the top of the steps is an invitation to pause. A 14C chronicler recounts how a prisoner condemned to death asked for an image of the Virgin to be placed near the Capitol, the place of execution. Because she brought comfort to poor wretches about to die she was called the Virgin of Consolation.

The first church was built in 1470. In 16C a hospital was added; it was constructed between 1583 and 1600 according to plans by Martino Longhi the Elder. He also began the façade of the church which was eventually completed in 19C in a style inspired by the Counter-Reformation.

From Piazza della Consolazione turn south down Via di S. Giovanni Decollato.

Oratory of St John the Beheaded ★ (San Giovanni Decollato). — *To visit ring at no 22.* The brotherhood of St John the Beheaded was founded in the late 15C to assist those condemned to death. Those who died in a state of grace were buried beneath the cloisters.

The members of the brotherhood hold their meetings in the Oratory which is decorated with paintings by the Mannerists who drew their inspiration from Michelangelo and Raphael without sinking to slavish imitation. Starting on the right of the altar: the Angel Gabriel appearing to Zacharias (Jacopino del Conte): on the left of the painting there is a portrait of Michelangelo who was a member of the brotherhood; the Visitation (Salviati); Birth of John the Baptist (Salviati); Preaching of John the Baptist (Jacopino del Conte); Baptism of Christ (J del Conte); Arrest of John the Baptist (Battista Franco); Dance of Salome (Pirro Ligorio); Beheading of John the Baptist; on either side of the altar St Andrew and St Bartholomew (Salviati); above the altar, Deposition (J del Conte).

The church *(right of the entrance)* is decorated with paintings and stuccos (late 16C).

Via di S. Giovanni Decollato leads to the Velabrum.

The **Velabrum,** the valley between the Palatine and the Capitoline hills, was for a long time a stagnant marsh before it was drained by the Cloaca Maxima *(p 37).*

Arch of Janus (Arco di Giano). — This massive 4C construction with four faces, each one being pierced by an arch, was a *janus,* i.e. a public gateway spanning a busy crossroads. It marked the northern edge of the Forum Boarium. The name reflects the power of the god Janus to protect road junctions.

Arch of the Money-changers (B). — This construction is more like a monumental gate against the west wall of San Giorgio in Velabro. It was built in 204 by the guild of Money-changers in honour of the Emperor Septimius Severus and his wife, Julia Domna, who both appear on the arch *(inside right panel)* making an offering before a tripod. The sharp relief and the abundance of decoration are characteristic of 3C art.

San Giorgio in Velabro. — Founded originally as a deaconry *(see below)* in the 7C, the church was rebuilt and enlarged by Pope Gregory IV (827-44). Since its restoration in 1926 San Giorgio in Velabro has recaptured the charm of the Roman churches of the Middle Ages. The facade, the porch and the bell tower date from 12C. The interior is essentially simple. In the Middle Ages Rome was poor: architects used existing foundations resulting in asymetrical designs; columns and capitals were also re-employed in an arbitrary fashion. The apsidal fresco of Christ flanked by the Virgin and Sts George, Peter and Sebastian is attributed to Pietro Cavallini (1295).

Piazza della Bocca della Verità

Piazza della Bocca della Verità ★. — This open space more or less covers the site of the Forum Boarium. The combination of ancient, mediaeval and Baroque buildings, framed by umbrella pines and pink and white oleanders, makes a typical Roman scene.

Opposite the mediaeval façade of Santa Maria in Cosmedin stands an 18C fountain supported by two tritons.

Santa Maria in Cosmedin ★. — The soaring **bell tower ★** with its bold arcading was built in the early 12C and is one of the most elegant in Rome.

In 6C the district between the Aventine and Tiber was inhabited by Greeks, who like other foreign colonies in Rome, formed themselves into a fighting force *(schola)* to protect Rome from the threat of the Lombards. In order to feed these soldiers the Church was obliged to form **deaconries** *(diaconiae),* composed of religious and lay people who inherited the duties performed by similar bodies under the Roman Empire. Their duty had been to fix the price of wheat and to distribute it, sometimes free of charge. The imperial organisation had been administered by the *praefectus annonae* from the *Statio annonae.* It was on the site of this building that the Church set up one of its deaconries, with an oratory in one of the store rooms. It was enlarged in 8C by Pope Hadrian I and became the Greek church under the name of Santa Maria in Schola Greca, which later became Santa Maria in Cosmedin in memory of the name of a district of Constantinople. Early in 12C the church was restored; the porch and campanile were added by Popes Gelasius II and Callistus II. The church was restored to its mediaeval appearance in 19C.

Tour. — In the porch is the **Bocca della Verità** (Mouth of Truth) (1). According to popular legend the mouth would snap shut on the hand of anyone with a guilty conscience. The name was also attributed to the fact that the mouth had never spoken. The face is that of a marine divinity, perhaps the Ocean, with two bull's horns symbolising the surging power of the sea. The plaque is in fact a drain cover, possibly from the nearby Temple of Hercules.

In the north aisle, on either side of the entrance door and in the Sacristy, now incorporated into the construction of the church, are the huge Corinthian columns which belonged to the *Statio Annonae* which extended from left to right across the back half of the church.

The three parallel apses, inspired by the plan of oriental churches, date from the period of Pope Hadrian I (8C) and the columns dividing the nave and aisles come from ancient monuments.

The beautiful floor and the marble furnishings (ambones, paschal candlesticks, canopy above the high altar and the episcopal throne) are all Cosmati work. The *Schola cantorum* (2) for the choristers and the presbytery (3) for the priests are 19C reconstructions. The presbytery has been screened off by a *pergula,* a colonnade hung with curtains which are drawn at certain moments in the eastern liturgy.

Piazza della Bocca della Verità
● Columns of the "Statio Annonae"

The crypt (8C) with its nave and aisles separated by small columns is an original design for this period when it was usual to follow the semi-circular plan designed by Gregory the Great (590-604) for the confessio in St Peter's in the Vatican.

The beautiful 8C mosaic (4) in the Sacristy comes from St Peter's Basilica.

Temple of Vesta ★. — It has been given this name because of its circular shape; there was in fact only one temple dedicated to Vesta, the one in the Roman Forum *(p 44).* It is not known to which god this temple was dedicated.

With its well proportioned fluted columns and its Corinthian capitals it is an elegant building which dates from the reign of Augustus. A church was established in the *cella* in the Middle Ages; in 16C it was dedicated to St Mary of the Sun after an image of the Virgin which had been found in the Tiber was placed there: when the coffer containing the image was opened a ray of light shone out.

Temple of Fortuna Virilis ★. — The attribution of this temple to Manly Fortune is without foundation. Some archaeologists think it is a sanctuary dedicated to Portumnus, the god of rivers and harbours. It dates from the late 2C BC and is one of the best preserved temples in Rome. It has an air of austere solemnity typical of the rigour of the republican era. At this period the Romans were still greatly influenced by the Etruscans and built rectangular temples, set on a high podium. The temple was used as a church probably from 9C and dedicated to St Mary the Egyptian in 15C.

The Crescenzi House (D). — This curious building, one of the rare remains of 'Roma Turrita' *(p 12),* was built in 12C as a fortress to defend the Aemilian Bridge (Ponte Rotto) on which the Crescenzi family had the right to collect tolls. The random use of antique elements (in the cornices and in the arch over the main door) shows how insensitively the Roman monuments were despoiled in the Middle Ages.

Follow the bank of the river upstream, Lungotevere dei Pierleoni.

Fabrician Bridge. — It is sometimes also known as the Bridge of Four Heads on account of the Hermes with four heads set at the far end. It is the only Roman bridge to survive intact from the Classical period. Above the arches is an inscription stating that the bridge was built in 62 BC by the Consul Fabricius. It links the left bank with Tiber Island.

Tiber Island ★ (Isola Tiberina). — This peaceful spot was the subject of many legends connected with the origins of Rome. The island is said to have been created by silt piling up on the crop of Tarquins thrown into the Tiber when the last King of this line, Tarquin the Proud, was driven out of Rome in 6C BC. It it also said that the island's shape is that of the boat which brought Aesculapius, the god of medecine, from Epidauros in Greece. To stress the ressemblance the southern point of the island has been paved with slabs of travertine round an obelisk, set up like a mast. Aesculapius arrived in Rome in 293 BC in the form of a serpent. The boat had scarcely come along side when the serpent disembarked and hid on the island; the Romans interpreted this as the serpent's desire to have a temple built on that spot. The sanctuary was built on the site now occupied by St Bartholomew's Church. The hospital of the Brothers of St John of God (*Fatebenefratelli* — literally do-good-brothers) continues the island's medical tradition.

Pointing towards the southern tip of the island on the far side of an open square is St Bartholomew's Church with its Baroque façade and Romanesque bell tower. According to tradition it was in the hospital attached to this church that Rahere, courtier to Henry I of England, recovered from an attack of malaria, usually fatal in those days. He had vowed, if he was spared, to found a priory and a hospital and on his return Henry granted land in Smithfield in London where the church and the hospital still stand.

From the square take the steps down to the river on the right.

Ponte Rotto. — In origin the Broken Bridge goes back to the Aemilian Bridge (Pons Aemilius) which was built here towards the middle of 2C BC. It had already collapsed twice when Pope Gregory XIII rebuilt it in about 1575. It collapsed again in 1598. Only one arch remains to challenge the Tiber; poets have been attracted by the strange spectacle of a single span stranded in midstream cut off from the roar of the traffic.

Horatius Cocles and the Sublician Bridge. — Downstream from the Ponte Rotto and its modern neighbour, the Palatine Bridge, is the Sublician Bridge (Pons Sublicius), the first to span the Tiber, which was built to foster relations between the Latins on the Palatine and the Etruscans on the right bank. Each year on 14th May human figures made of willow were offered to the river to appease it. The bridge was made of wood and the law forbad any iron to be used in its repair: it had to be easy to dismantle in the event of relations between the two peoples deteriorating. This of happened when the last Etruscan king, Tarquin the Proud, was driven out of Rome in 6C BC. Livy gives a good description; the Etruscans marched on Rome under the banner of Lars Porsenna; Horatius Cocles was guarding the bridge. While his men were dismantling the bridge, he held back the enemy single-handed: 'withering the Etruscan leaders with his look, he challenged them one by one or taunted them'. Finally the bridge was breached. Horatius jumped into the Tiber and rejoined his men. He was treated as a hero: he was granted land, his statue was put up in the Comitium and 'every citizen set aside part of his own income to be given to Horatius'.

The incident is also well known to many through Lord Macaulay's stirring ballad *Horatius* from his *Lays of Ancient Rome.*

Cestian Bridge. — It links Tiber Island to the Trastevere district *(p 186).* Its origins go back to 1C BC; it was partially rebuilt in 19C. To the left there is a view of the bell tower of Santa Maria in Cosmedin and to the right of the Janiculum Hill with its lighthouse.

> *Traces of the origins of Rome are rare.*
> *The oldest include:*
> — *the items displayed in the Antiquarium in the Roman Forum (11 - 7C BC) (p 46);*
> — *the necropolis in the Roman Forum (8 - 7C BC) (p 45);*
> — *the traces of huts on the Palatine (8 - 7C BC) (p 51);*
> — *the Black Stone (Lapis Niger) in the Roman Forum (6C BC) (p 42).*

Distance: 2 km — 1 mile. Time: about 4 hours. Start: Piazza Barberini.

The **Quirinal** (61 m - 200 ft) was the highest of the seven hills of Rome. The traditional home of the Sabines, the hill took its name from one of their gods, Quirinus who, with Mars and Jupiter, formed the basis of Roman religion.

Until the end of 19C the Quirinal stood on the fringes of the city: the Flavian mausoleum was built there by Domitian (81-96); Caracalla built a temple to Serapis of which the ruins survived until the Middle Ages; Constantine built a bath house which disappeared in 17C.

Nowadays the name Quirinal is synonymous with Italian politics since the Quirinal Palace is the official residence of the President of the Republic.

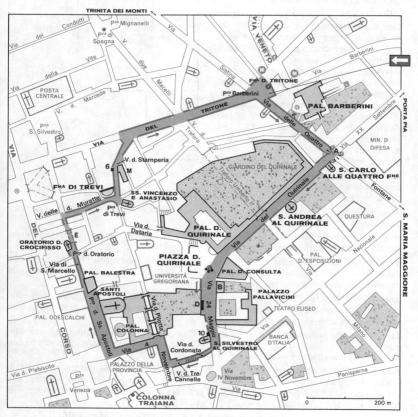

Towards Quirinal Square

Triton Fountain ★. — Bernini's fountain (*c*1642) is a happy example of Roman Baroque. The composition — four dolphins supporting an open scallop shell in which sits a triton blowing into a conch — demonstrates the powerful and lively qualities of his art. The Barberini bees on the coat of arms are an echo of the Barberini Palace that was built by Urban VIII on the north slope of the Quirinal.

■ BARBERINI PALACE ★★ *(Entrance in Via delle Quattro Fontane)*

In 1623 Cardinal Maffeo Barberini became Pope Urban VIII and decided to build a Baroque palace to house his family. Work began in 1627 under Carlo Maderno; the palace was completed from 1629 to 1633 by Borromini and Bernini.

The main façade, which is framed by two wings, in the style of a Roman country villa, is the work of Bernini. By super-imposing three stages of attached columns and shallow pilasters to frame two floors of huge windows (slightly splayed on the upper storey) over an open porch at ground level, he created a sense of the dignity and solemnity appropriate to the Barberini family.

Borromini has left his mark in the two small curiously pedimented upper windows in the intermediate sections linking the wings to the central block of the palace.

The windows in the rear façade were decorated by Borromini who also designed the oval spiral staircase at the righthand (south) end of the front porch.

Picture Gallery ★★. — *Open 9 am to 2 pm Tuesday to Saturday; in summer only 9 am to 1 pm Sundays. Closed Monday, 1 January, 1 May, 15 August.*

A monumental staircase *(lefthand (north) end of entrance porch)* designed by Bernini leads up to the gallery which is housed in some of the finest rooms in the palace (17C painted ceilings). The rooms on the first floor are devoted to 13C to 16C works.

First floor

The first floor of the gallery is being restored; some of the pictures mentioned below may have been moved, others may have been withdrawn for restoration.

Room I. — Virgin and Child by Simone Martini (**1**), typical of the elegant and meticulous drawing of the great 14C Siennese painter. Curious painting (**2**) by Bonaventura Berlinghieri, a native of Lombardy who died in 1243 and painted several crucifixes with a calligrapher's touch.

Room II. — **Triptych by Fra Angelico ★★★** (**3**) showing the Last Judgment, the Ascension and Pentecost; this painter, who experienced the silence of the cloister, expressed his deep faith by painting serene and saintly faces (central panel of the Last Judgment) and a Christ which inspires adoration (Ascension, righthand panel).

Annunciation (**4**) and Virgin and Child (**5**) by Filippo Lippi, painted in 1437. The architectural elements which Lippi introduced into his paintings (windows, columns) were a novelty in early Italian art.

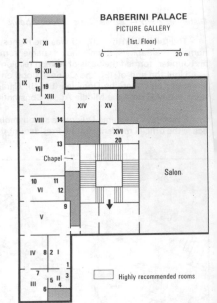

BARBERINI PALACE
PICTURE GALLERY
(1st. Floor)
0   20 m

☐ Highly recommended rooms

Room III. — Virgin and Child with Saints (**6**) and St Sebastian (**7**) by Antoniazzo Romano, chief exponent of the firm style practised in Latium at the end of 15C.

Room IV. — Sacra Conversazione (**8**) by the Venetian Lorenzo Lotto (c1480-1556) using unusual colours.

Room V. — Portrait of Pope Urban VIII (**9**) painted by his protégé, Bernini (1625). Only a few paintings from this artist's immense pictorial work now remain.

Room VI. — Rape of the Sabines (**10**), Mystic marriage of St Catherine (**11**) and the Three Fates (**12**) by Sodoma (1477-1549); this painter was a great admirer of Raphael's elegant contours and was his friend and collaborator in Rome.

Room VII. — Portrait of Stefano Colonna (**13**) by Bronzino (1546), a sophisticated painter and portrait painter who sought to present his subjects in an appropriate noble pose rather than with their characteristic expression.

Room VIII. — **The Fornarina ★★★** (**14**) by Raphael is a painting of his beautiful mistress. The attribution of this work to Raphael has been disputed and it has also been attributed to one of his pupils and later to Sebastiano del Piombo.

Room IX. — Two paintings by El Greco — the Baptism of Jesus (**15**) and the Nativity (**16**) (c1590) with their drawn and contorted figures — flank a work by Tintoretto — Christ and the Woman taken in Adultery (**17**) (1546), an example of the dramatic tendency which was to develop until it influenced El Greco.

Room XII. — Very expressive **portrait of Erasmus ★★★** (**18**) by Quentin Metsys (1517).

Room XIII. — **Portrait of Henry VIII ★★★** (**19**) by Hans Holbein the Younger (1540); he became the official painter of the English court and produced portraits of the important members of the court with impartiality and psychological insight.

Rooms XIV and XV. — Works by Hubert Robert, Greuze, Fragonard, Lancret and Le Nain.

Room XVI. — Together with Judith and Holophernes (**20**) by Caravaggio are hung works in Caravaggio's style by Carlo Saraceni, Valentin and Simon Vouet.

Central Salon ★★★. — The ceiling is the main work of Pietro da Cortona who showed the measure of his talent here. It was painted between 1633 and 1639 to celebrate the glory of the Barberini family whose coat of arms (in a crown of laurel) is carried by allegorical figures representing the Virtues. On the left, Divine Providence holding a sceptre, reigns from the clouds. The painter has used sections of grisaille to separate the scenes with admirable skill.

The walls of the Salon are hung with cartoons by Baroque painters (Andrea Sacchi, Lanfranco, Bernini) for the mosaics for one of the small cupolas in St Peter's in the Vatican and for tapestries produced by the Barberini factory (17C).

Second floor

The rooms on the second floor are devoted to 17C and 18C works mostly by artists who worked in Rome.

The first rooms contain mainly religious paintings, several of which are small scale sketches of larger works commissioned for churches or palaces in Rome and elsewhere; in particular two studies in perspective by **Andrea Pozzo** *(pp 106 and 110).*

Several foreign artists who worked in Rome are represented here.

The portrait of Henry Peirse is signed and dated 1775 by **Pompeo Batoni** (1708-87) who painted many portraits of the British gentry on the Grand Tour *(p 29);* the classical background is typical of this kind of portraiture. By contrast the portrait of Pope Clement XIII illustrates the official style.

The melodramatic quality of **Alessandro Magnasco** (1667-1749), known as **Il Lissandrino**, is exemplified by "Demons tempting monks" and "Hermits in Prayer".

The corner room *(no pictures)* contains a finely modelled white marble fireplace; the walls are decorated with monochrome frescoes in the neo-Classical style, representing alcoves containing statues of famous heroes and ladies from antiquity.

The last four rooms are devoted to *vedute* (views), a genre probably invented by **Gaspar van Wittel** (*c*1655-1736), a Dutchman known as **Vanvitelli**, as a result of his work as a draughtsman on a scheme for regulating the Tiber; he broke with the tradition of romantic ruins set in landscapes. The small corner room contains two series of paintings by him: topographical views of Rome *(p 58)* and several imaginary views *(vedute ideate)*.

Panini (1692-1765/8) was the first painter to specialise in ruins; his work, particularly his *capricci* (fantasies based on original elements), was very popular with visitors on the Grand Tour.

Hubert Robert (1733-1808), a Parisian who spent eleven years in Italy, worked with Panini and Piranesi and also specialised in ruins.

Francesco Guardi (1712-93), who produced views of Venice in great numbers as souvenirs for tourists, and **Luca Carlevaris** (1665-1731), also a painter of views of Venice, were both eclipsed by the more famous **Canaletto** (1697-1768), four of whose views of Venice hang in the room opposite the entrance.

Also in this room are two canvasses by **Bernardo Bellotto** (1720-89), Canaletto's nephew and pupil, who sometimes used his uncle's name; he left Italy for Germany in 1747, finally settling in Warsaw.

In the south wing of the palace on the second floor is a suite of late **18C** rooms overlooking the gardens and the *ponte ruinante,* an imitation ruined bridge, designed by Bernini in keeping with the fashionable taste for ruins. The series of seven rooms is decorated in the high Baroque Italian style with low ceilings that give an echo. The dining room leads into the Marine Room with seascapes painted on the walls. A few steps lead up into the Small Gallery. The walls of the Silk Room are covered with silk panels painted with scenes inspired by the tales of travellers returned from the New World. The Battle Room was probably decorated on the occasion of the marriage of Cornelia Costanza, last of the Barberini name, with Giulio Cesare Colonna di Sciarra, Duke of Bassanello; the walls depict episodes in the Colonna family history.

Continue up Via della Quattro Fontane.

Four Fountains Crossroads (A). — The crossroads was created by Sixtus V (1585-90) whose efforts at town planning introduced more alterations to Rome than the city had known since the end of the Roman Empire. His aim was to link the main basilicas and the main districts by means of broad straight roads. The creation of these four straight streets opened up **views ★** of the obelisks in front of the Trinità dei Monti *(west),* the Porta Pia *(north),* the west end of St Mary Major in Piazza dell'Esquilino *(east)* and in Quirinal Square *(south).* The corners of the crossroads are canted to make room for four fountains decorated with statues (16C).

Turn right (south) into Via del Quirinale.

■ SAN CARLO ALLE QUATTRO FONTANE★★

The Church of St Charles by the Four Fountains, which is also known as San Carlino, is probably the best expression of Borromini's creative genius. Commissioned in 1638, it was his first known work. The façade, which was added some thirty years later, was his last; it was unfinished when he committed suicide in 1667. It reveals the torment of a man whose art was full of contradictory statements: every curve is followed by a counter curve (in particular the façade and the cornices). Against the central concave section of the upper storey is set a convex shrine (below the medallion).

The concave surfaces of the belfry and the lantern on the dome also express Borromini's contrary spirit in architectural terms.

The **interior ★ ★** is based on an ellipse and oriented on the longer axis; the movement is supplied by the alternating concave and convex surfaces of the walls. The confined space — no larger, it is said, than one of the pillars supporting the dome of St Peter's — is perfectly suited to the architect's distinctive style: both affected and austere, bizarre and elegant, quite out of sympathy with the Baroque taste for sheer size. Above the intricate design of the coffering in the dome, the Holy Ghost looks down from the lantern.

Cloisters ★. — Borromini's cloisters — two orders of Doric columns and slightly convex canted corners — are perfectly proportioned.

■ SANT'ANDREA AL QUIRINALE★★

The Church of St Andrew on the Quirinal by Bernini and San Carlo by Borromini are striking illustrations of the contrast between two opposing geniuses.

Over the semicircular porch beneath a crown are the arms of Cardinal Camillo Pamphili, Innocent X's nephew, who commissioned the church in 1658.

The **interior ★ ★**, as in San Carlo, is elliptical but oriented on the shorter axis. The deep rectangular side chapels and the impression of depth created by the false portico in front of the high altar, give a feeling of spaciousness which helps to disguise the true proportions of the church. Bernini's sure taste in the use of coloured marbles, gilding and stucco figures has created a rich and beautiful décor.

The chapels contain three paintings by Baciccia (1) (17C) and the Crucifixion of St Andrew (2) by Jacques Courtois called the Burgundian (17C). The gilt glory over the high altar, which is lit from above, is a reminder that Bernini had a great liking for theatre décor. On the left is a chapel (3) dedicated to the glory of St Stanislas Kostka, a young Pole who came to Rome to enter the Jesuit noviciate. The painting by Carlo Maratta (17C) shows the Virgin appearing to St Stanislas.

St Stanislas' Rooms (4) *(apply to the Sacristan)* contain a recumbent statue of the saint by Pierre Legros (1629-1714) in polychrome marble.

In the **Sacristy** (5) is a vault in *trompe-l'œil*.

Continue down Via del Quirinale.

Along the west side is a wing of the Quirinal Palace built in 17 and 18C.

■ QUIRINAL SQUARE ★★ (Piazza del Quirinale)

Lined by handsome palaces, adorned with an obelisk and ancient statues and refreshed by a fountain, the square typifies Roman elegance.

Its embellishment was begun by Sixtus V (1585-90) who transferred the statues of the Dioscuri from Constantine's Baths nearby; they are fine Roman copies of original Greek works. Some two centuries later, Pius VI moved them slightly apart to make room for one of the obelisks which had stood at the entrance to Augustus' mausoleum *(p 167)*. Finally Pius VII (1800-23) completed the group with a handsome antique basin which had served as a water trough when the Forum was known as Campo Vaccino and used for grazing cows *(p 38)*.

Quirinal Palace ★★ (Palazzo del Quirinale). — This building is the work of some of the finest architects of the Counter-Reformation and the Baroque period. It was begun in 1573 by Gregory XIII who asked Martino Longhi the Elder to design a summer residence for the popes. Sixtus V commissioned Ottaviano Mascherino, Domenico Fontana and Flaminio Ponzio. Under Paul V Carlo Maderno added the monumental door with its two half reclining statues of St Peter and St Paul. Bernini was brought in by Alexander VII. The palace was completed by Ferdinando Fuga for Clement XII.

Napoleonic Storm. — In 1808 Napoleon was declared king of Italy and his brother Joseph king of Naples but Pius VII, as head of the Papal States, refused to apply an economic blockade or to recognise any king other than Ferdinand IV of Naples. On 2 February General Miollis was ordered to enter Rome with 8 000 French soldiers to bring His Holiness to reason. Pius VII shut himself up in the Quirinal Palace. On the evening of 17 May 1809 in Vienna Napoleon wiped the Papal States off the map of Europe. Pius VII issued a Bull of excommunication: "Let sovereigns learn once and for all that they are subject by the law of Christ to our throne and our commands." Several French soldiers were found dead at dawn in the streets of Rome. On 7 July 1809 French troops broke down the door of the palace. The Pope in cape and stole, awaited them. Despite their great respect for the Pope the soldiers took him away to spend the rest of the Napoleonic era at Fontainebleau. Thus Napoleon rendered "unto Caesar the things which are Caesar's and unto God the things that are God's".

Interior. — *To visit, apply in writing a week in advance to the Palace Administration (Via della Dataria). Closed Wednesday, Saturday, Sunday, holidays and in August.* The sentries on duty are members of the Republican Guard who must be at least 6 ft tall. From the palace courtyard the grand staircase leads up to the first floor: the fresco of Christ *(above the arch)* by Melozzo da Forli was originally part of the Ascension painted on the apse of the Church of the Holy Apostles *(pp 90 and 157)*. The tour includes the chapel painted by Guido Reni (Annunciation on the altar piece), the Pauline chapel with its 17C stucco decoration and a suite of opulent rooms (Venetian chandeliers and Chinese vases).

Palazzo della Consulta. — The facade ★ is by Ferdinando Fuga (18C) who often used Baroque motifs. The three doorways, their pediments crowded with statues and sculptures, and the coat of arms of Clement XII, supported by a swarm of cherubs, make a lively contrast with the bare façade of the Quirinal Palace. This is now the seat of the Constitutional Court.

Towards the via del Tritone

Walk down Via 24 Maggio.

Palazzo Pallavicini. — The courtyard with its palm trees, laurels, pines and holm oaks is lined on two sides by the palace which was built in 1603 by Cardinal Scipio Borghese, Paul V's nephew, more or less on the site of Constantine's baths.

On the left, just inside the main gates, stands the palace **Casino ★** (B) *(open 9 am to 12 noon and 2 to 5 pm on the first day of each month).* This charming 17C pavilion opening on to a terraced garden is famous for the **Aurora fresco** painted on the ceiling by Guido Reni, a pupil of the Carraccis. This is a fine example of the academic style. The goddess is shown opening the gates of heaven to the sun's chariot.

On the right of the street (Via 24 Maggio) the impressive doorway approached by a flight of steps is the entrance (D) to the **gardens of the Palazzo Colonna.**

San Sylvestro al Quirinale. — *Entrance to the left of the façade. If this door is closed, ring at no 10.*

The façade of the Church of St Sylvester on the Quirinal is purely decorative; it was constructed in 19C to disguise the difference of level between the church and the street which had been widened and lowered, while the church itself was truncated. The interior décor is surprisingly rich. The coffered ceiling is 16C (restored in 19C). Among the Mannerist decorations are some paintings in the **first chapel on the left** by Polidoro da Caravaggio and Maturino da Firenze *(p 162)*. The floor has been paved with the remains of a ceramic pavement which used to decorate the Raphael Loggia in the Vatican.

In the left arm of the transept is a beautiful octagonal domed **chapel ★**. Domenichino painted the medallions in the pendentives (1628) while the stucco statues of Mary Magdalen *(left of the entrance)* and St John *(left of the chancel)* were sculpted at the same time by Alessandro Algardi.

The **chancel** vault is decorated with a late 16C fresco on a beautiful grey base.

To the left of the chancel is a door opening on to a quiet terrace where Vittoria Colonna, who had composed poems to the glory of her dead husband, spent many hours in the company of scholars and holy men. Sometimes Michelangelo came to join them. He developed a great affection for this noble and cultivated lady and was present at her death.

Turn right into Via della Cordonata and right again into Via 4 Novembre.

Colonna Palace Gallery ★. — *Entrance in Via della Pilotta. Open Saturday 9 am to 1 pm. Closed in August. 2 000 L. The numbers given in the text are the same as those in the gallery.*

The palace dates from 15C but was rebuilt in 1730. It is linked to its gardens, which have an entrance in Via 24 Maggio *(see above)*, by four arches spanning the Via Pilotta. Pope Martin V (1417-31), a member of the Colonna family, took up residence here when he returned to Rome after the Great Western Schism *(p 12)*.

The gallery, which consists of a suite of richly furnished rooms, contains many 16 and 17C paintings.

Column Room. — Narcissus at the fountain *(189)* by Tintoretto (1518-94). Portrait, which may be of Vittoria Colonna *(see above) (37)*, long attributed to G Muziano but more recently to B Cancellieri.

In the middle of the half dozen steps leading down into the Salon is lodged a cannon ball which was fired by the French troops besieging Rome in 1849 so as to re-establish Pius IX on the papal throne.

Salon ★★. — A very handsome perspective, resplendent with gilt, mirrors, crystal chandeliers, yellow marble and paintings. The vault is painted with a 17C fresco depicting the triumph of Marcantonio Colonna who led Pius V's troops at the Battle of Lepanto (1571).

Casket Room. — Two **caskets ★**, small 17C chests: one in ebony decorated with ivory low relief carvings (in the centre, copy of Michelangelo's Last Judgment); the other in sandalwood, inset with precious stones and bronze gilt. A dozen paintings by Gaspard Dughet (1613-75).

Apotheosis of Martin V Room. — The name of the room comes from the subject of the ceiling decoration. Fine portrait of a gentleman *(197)* by Paul Veronese (1528-88). The painting of a 'Peasant eating beans' *(43)*, which is attributed to Annibale Carracci, is a fine example of naturalism.

Throne Room. — This room was intended for the reception of the Pope.

Continue down Via 4 Novembre and then turn right into Piazza Santi Apostoli.

Holy Apostles Basilica ★ (Santi Apostoli). — The church goes back to 6C when a basilica on the site was dedicated by popes Pelagius I and John III to the Apostles Philip and James the Less whose relics they had received. The greatest alterations were carried out by Sixtus IV (1471-84), of which only the lower part of the porch remains. The loggia above the porch was closed with rectangular windows in the Baroque era and topped with a balustrade and statues. The upper section is a 19C neo-Classical composition.

In the porch, guarding the entrance, are three lions from the mediaeval building.

On the nave vault Baciccia painted the Triumph of the Franciscan Order (1706). A few years earlier this artist had painted his masterpiece on the ceiling of the Gesù Church *(p 110)*. The chancel contains the Renaissance tombs of the two Riario cardinals, Pietro and Raffaele, who helped their uncle, Sixtus IV to reconstruct the church: **Cardinal Pietro Riario's tomb ★** *(left)* is the result of three masters of funerary art working in collaboration: Andrea Bregno, Mino da Fiesole and Giovanni Dalmata; Raffaele's tomb *(right)* is inspired by Michelangelo's favourite designs. On the chancel ceiling Giovani Odazzi (18C) has achieved a fine *trompe-l'œil* effect with the Fallen Angels.

The **monument to Clement XIV** at the top of the left aisle is the first work executed in Rome by the neo-Classical sculptor Antonio Canova (1787).

The second pillar on the right bears a red marble plaque inscribed in memory of Maria Clementina Sobieska *(see below)*.

Palazzo Balestra. — At the end of the square stands a Baroque palace (now occupied by the Banco di Roma) where the Stuarts lived in exile. Originally known as Palazzo Muti since it was built in 1644 for the Muti-Papazzuri family, it was given by Clement XI to James Stuart, the Old Pretender, in 1719 when he married Maria Clementina Sobieska of Poland. His two sons, Charles Edward, the Young Pretender, and Henry, Cardinal York, were born in the palace and 'Bonnie Prince Charlie' returned to die there in 1788.

Take Via di San Marcello which leads to Piazza dell'Oratorio.

Oratory of the Crucifix ★ (Oratorio del Crucifisso). — *If closed, apply to the Suore Mission-arie di Gesù, Piazza dell'Oratorio, 68a (left).*

It is such treasures as this little oratory that reveal the intimate charm of Rome which makes the city so attractive. The building's construction was entrusted to Tommaso dei Cavalieri, a young Roman noble, who inspired a warm affection in Michelangelo yet chose as his adviser one of Michelangelo's bitterest enemies, Nanni di Baccio Bigio. The façade was designed by Giacomo della Porta in 1561. It marked the beginning of a brilliant career which led to his being in charge of work on the Capitol and at St Peter's (1573). The façade, which was finished in 1568 and which harmonises so well with the square it overlooks, bears traces of Michelangelo's teaching (the pediments over the recesses flanking the door). The interior is decorated with a series of frescoes by Mannerist artists. On the reverse side of the façade is the history of the Confraternity of the Crucifix of San Marcello. The wall paintings, which are reminiscent of a theatre décor, are by Giovanni de' Vecchi, Pomarancio and Cesare Nebbia and illustrate the story of the Cross.

Take the alley on the right of the Oratory.

The **Galleria Sciarra** (E), with its metal framework, its glass canopy and its painted façade, is a highly original late 19C arcade.

Turn right into Via delle Muratte which leads to Piazza di Trevi.

Trevi Fountain ★★★. — This late Baroque creation is one of the most famous sights of Rome. The key to the work is given in two low relief carvings: in 19 BC Agrippa decided to build a 20 km - 13 miles long canal to bring water to Rome *(left)*; the canal was called Acqua Vergine after a young virgin who revealed the spring to the Roman soldiers *(right)*. Repairs were made under Pope Nicholas V and Urban VIII. It was Clement XIII who commissioned Nicolà Salvi (1762) to adorn the end of the canal with a fountain. Salvi's fountain fills the whole width of the façade which forms a backdrop to it and gives the impression of a triumphal arch. Salubrity and Abundance stand in the wings flanking the central figure, the Ocean, who rides in a chariot drawn by two sea horses and two tritons and provides a photogenic spectacle for the faithful tourists, who continue to play their traditional role by throwing two coins over their shoulders into the fountain — one coin to return to Rome and the other for the fulfilment of a wish.

Echoing the flamboyance of the fountain is the ornate Baroque façade of the **Church of Sts Vincent and Anastasius** built for Cardinal Mazarin in 1650 by Martino Longhi the Younger; it is a study in light and shade created by advanced pediments and a host of detached columns.

Take Via della Stamperia on the right of the Trevi Fountain.

No 6 in this street is the **Calcographia** where over 20 000 old engravings are kept; among them are some by Piranesi (1720-78) who produced remarkable views of Rome. *Open 9 am to 1.30 pm to see the engravings. Closed Monday.*

St Luke's Academy Gallery (M). — *Closed for restoration.*

In **Room I**: portrait of Clement IX by Baciccia (1639-1709); fine fragment of a fresco by Raphael. In **Room II**: Judith and Holophernes by Piazzetta (1682-1754).

In **Room III**: self-portrait by Mme Vigée-Lebrun (1755-1842); self-portrait and Hope by Angelica Kauffmann, a woman artist and friend of Goethe's in Rome. **Room V** is dominated by Sir Anthony Van Dyck's Virgin and Angels.

Via del Tritone. — This street is full of shops and is one of the busiest in Rome; it links the city centre with the northeastern suburbs.

The 29 walks described in this guide cover
historic sites and districts,
the art treasures in the museums.

Make your choice using the maps on pp 4 to 9.

Programmes for a 3-day and an 8-day stay
are laid out on pp 31 and 32

Distance: 2 km — 1 mile. Time: about 4 hours. Start: Corso Vittorio Emanuele II.

In antiquity the district bordered by the Corso Vittorio Emanuele II (opened in late 19C), the Corso del Rinascimento (1936-39) and the Via Zanardelli (c1906), was part of the Campus Martius which had been the admiration of the Greek geographer Strabo when he visited Rome in about 7 BC for being covered with grass throughout the year. Domitian (81-96 AD) built a large stadium and an Odeon where poetry readings and musical concerts were given (approximately on the site of the Palazzo Massimo and the Piazza di San Pantaleo).

Except for the outline of Domitian's stadium which is preserved in the shape of the Piazza Navona, no trace of ancient Rome has survived here.

The network of picturesque lanes and streets between the Piazza Navona and the Tiber recalls the splendour of the papal era in the heart of Renaissance Rome.

Starting with Sixtus IV (1471-84), the Popes turned this once dilapidated area, where the overcrowded houses were undermined by floods, into the commercial and financial centre of the city. It lay on the processional path between the Vatican and St John Lateran. Magnificent palaces began to line the papal route: along the Via Banco di Santo Spirito, the Via dei Banchi Nuovi which formed the Papal Way (via Papalis) and the Via del Governo Vecchio.

Early in 16C it became the residential district for Cardinals, Ambassadors, papal officials, rich bankers and distinguished courtesans. Around them grew up an intellectual circle: booksellers, engravers, illuminators settled round the Piazza Navona and the Piazza di Pasquino and many artisans are to be found in the district to this day.

TOUR

This walk passes many 15 and 16C palaces containing delightful surprises for the curious visitor who is prepared to turn aside into the courtyards; the rustic façades with their plain rectangular windows and regular pediments often conceal some fine Renaissance architecture: a colonnaded loggia, cornices with antique motifs, escutcheons, walls decorated with grisailles, friezes and medallions.

Palazzo Massimo. — The palace comprises three separate buildings belonging to the oldest family in Rome, the Massimi. The one adjoining **St Pantaleon's Church** (façade by Valadier 1806) on the right is called "Pyrrhus' Palace" because of a statue which was kept there. The Palazzo Massimo *alle colonne* opens on to the Corso Vittorio Emanuele II with a handsome pillared portico in the Doric order following the curve of the street front. It was designed by Baldassarre Peruzzi (1532-36). The windows of the upper storey are in the Mannerist style. The oldest building of the three is at the back overlooking a small square (Piazza dei Massimi - *access by the first turning to the left in the Corso Rinascimento);* the column may have belonged to Domitian's Odeon. It is known as the "illustrated palace" because of the grisailles painted on the façade by some of Daniele da Volterra's pupils in about 1523.

From the square there is a glimpse of the fountain in the centre of Piazza Navona.

Palazzo Braschi ★. — It is named after the family of Pope Pius VI who had it built in late 18C for his nephews. It was the last papal family palace to be built in Rome. The neo-Classical style then in vogue was used for the ponderous façades which dominate the surrounding streets: Via della Cuccagna, Via di Pasquino and Via di San Pantaleo.

Rome Museum ★. — *Open 9 am to 1.30 pm (1 pm Sundays and holidays); also 5 to 7.30 pm Tuesdays and Thursdays. Closed Mondays, 1 January, Easter, 21 April, 1 May, 15 August, Christmas. 1 000 L.* Rome since the Middle Ages is the subject of the museum housed in the Palazzo Braschi.

The colossal staircase with its antique granite columns and decorative stucco is by Cosimo Morelli who designed the palace.

In the third room are three anonymous paintings depicting the jousts held in 16 and 17C in the Belvedere courtyard in the Vatican, the Piazza Navona and on the Testaccio. In the fifth room are **frescoes ★** from demolished buildings; the sixth room contains chiaroscuro decorations by Polidoro da Caravaggio and Maturino da Firenze (16C) *(p 162);* the delicate frescoes in the next room showing Apollo and the nine Muses belong to the 16C Umbrian school and come from a papal residence. In the ninth room are various anonymous paintings illustrating the bustle of the old market near the Capitoline in 17C and the pageantry of the Corpus Christi processions in St Peter's Square. The next room is hung with 18C Gobelins tapestries. The subjects, children in a garden, are taken from the paintings of Charles le Brun (1619-90) for the Aurora Pavilion in the Parc de Sceaux near Paris. From the windows there is a fine view of the Piazza Navona.

In the first room on the second floor hang three huge canvases on Greek mythological themes by Gavin Hamilton (1723-98) a Scots painter who settled in Rome in 1755 and spent most of his working life in Italy *(p 29).* Also on the second floor are the famous **water colours ★** in the series "Lost Rome" *(Roma sparita).* The sixth room contains fragments of the mosaics from the old St Peter's Basilica (late 12 - early 13C).

On the ground floor *(entrance in northeast corner of the courtyard)* is the papal train built for Pius IX in 1858 at Clichy in Paris. It consists of an open-sided coach, upholstered in damask, containing two long sofas and a throne, which is linked to a closed coach by an open platform where the Pope could stand in full view of the crowds; the third coach is fitted out as a small chapel.

Take Via di San Pantaleo which leads into Piazza di Pasquino.

Piazza di Pasquino. — The statue of Pasquino, which was probably part of a 3C BC group, was found in the Piazza Navona in 15C. It was in such a pitiable state that no collector wanted it and so it was placed on the corner against the building which occupied that site before the Palazzo Braschi and there it stayed. People called it Pasquino after a local tailor with a very caustic tongue and used it as their mouthpiece. During the night satirical or even libellous comments, criticising morals and politics and expressing popular claims, sometimes in Roman dialect, were secretly hung on Pasquino. The following day the 'Pasquinades' spread through Rome as far as the doors of the papal officials; some were even carried to the ears of foreign sovereigns and started more than one diplomatic incident. The draconian laws sentencing the perpetrators of these libels to death were rarely applied; or if they were the prisoner was immediately pardoned.

Pasquino was the most loquacious of the Roman 'talking statues'.

Via del Governo Vecchio. — This was one of the main streets of the district, continuing the Papal Way *(p 159)* as Via di Parione. It is lined with craft shops, junk shops and antique dealers occupying the ground floor premises of the Renaissance palaces, some of which still bear the coat of arms of the noble family which once lived there.

Palazzo del Governo Vecchio. — The building was completed in 1478. In 1624 it became the residence of the Governor of Rome. When the Government was transferred to the Palazzo Madama under Benedict XIV (1740-58), the building became known as the Old Government Palace. It has an attractive doorway decorated with sculptures and diaperwork.

Turn left into Via della Chiesa Nuova to reach the square of the same name.

New Church ★ (Chiesa Nuova). — The church was founded in 12C as Santa Maria in Vallicella; the name is probably an allusion to the little valley *(vallicella),* the Tarentum, which lay near the Tiber in antiquity.

The history of the church is linked to the memory of **St Philip Neri,** the Florentine founder of the Oratorians who were promoted into a Congregation in 1575 by Gregory XIII, who also offered the Church of Santa Maria in Vallicella to Neri as a base for his order. Reconstruction was set in hand and the new building, which was finished in 1605, was called the New Church. It was restored in 19C.

The façade is decorated with the shallow pilasters and attached columns of the Counter-Reformation.

Philip Neri wanted the interior to be very plain but during the Counter-Reformation it was given a Baroque décor inspired by Pietro da Cortona. On the coffered stucco ceiling he painted one of St Philip's visions (1664-65): during the building of the church he had a vision of the Virgin holding up a piece of the ceiling of the old building which threatened to collapse on to the altar where mass was being celebrated. Pietro da Cortona who had become the acknowledged master among decorative painters enjoyed equal celebrity in Rome with Bernini. He had already (1648-51) painted the dome depicting Christ presenting the instruments of the Passion to God and cancelling human punishment. In the pendentives he placed the prophets Isaiah, Jeremiah, Ezekiel and Daniel (1659-1660). In the interim he had begun to paint an Assumption in the apse.

The three paintings in the chancel are youthful works by Rubens (1608).

The chapel on the left of the chancel contains the remains of St Philip Neri and is splendidly decorated with gold, bronze and marble incrusted with mother-of-pearl.

The chapel in the left transept contains a picture by Barocci, a Mannerist painter, very typical of the style current in the second half of 16C.

On the altar in the sacristy *(entrance in the lefthand aisle)* stands a beautiful marble sculpture of St Philip and an angel by Alessandro Algardi executed in 1640.

The Oratory (Oratorio dei Filippini). — The building adjoining the New Church was built between 1637 and 1662 to house the assemblies of the Congregation of the Oratory where laity and clergy met under the spiritual direction of St Philip Neri.

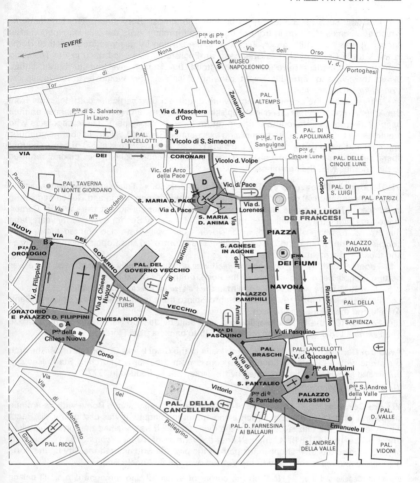

Nowadays the Oratory is also known as the Borromini Hall and is used for conferences and various cultural activities. In addition to the Oratorian priests the vast palace also houses the Vallicelliana Library, the Roman Library, the archives of the city of Rome, which include a collection of Roman newspapers dating back to 18C, and various cultural institutes.

The **façade** ★ overlooking the Piazza della Chiesa Nuova is in fact the side elevation of the Oratory. It was designed by Borromini so as to form a unit with the church. It is monumental and yet subtle too, being a combination of the attention to detail and the delight in contrasting curves which are characteristic of this great Baroque architect. It is composed of two orders; the central section showing the use of contrasting curves: convex on the lower floor and concave on the upper. The windows are richly ornamented with curved and broken lines, those on the ground floor being recessed as well. The roof line is crowned by a slightly concave trilobed pediment.

"Terrina" Fountain (A). — The fountain was transferred here in 1925 after standing in the Campo dei Fiori until 1899. The basin was carved in 1590 but a few years later was covered with a travertine lid bearing the inscription: "love God, do good and let others talk".

Piazza dell' Orologio. — The plain front which the Oratory presents in Via dei Filippini ends unexpectedly on the corner of Via del Governo Vecchio in a graceful clock tower. The wrought iron scroll work on the bell cage is recognisable as Borromini's work (1647-49). Beneath the clock is a mosaic of the Virgin of Vallicella.

On the corner of the building a beautiful **Madonna ★ (B)** surrounded by a 'glory' of cherubs, in typical Baroque taste, keeps watch over the square.

(After photo by Carlo Guidotti, Rome)
Madonna, Piazza dell'Orologio

In Rome such madonnas are to be found in almost every street. The little lanterns which sometimes still burn in front of them were for many years the only illumination after sunset. It was not until January 1854 that street lighting by gas was introduced to Rome in the Via del Corso by James Shepherd, an Englishman, who is buried in the Testaccio Cemetery. Foreigners have never understood the Roman aversion to bright lights. When they walked abroad at night carrying a lantern they would hear the locals cry *Volti la luce* (Dim the light).

In December the street madonnas were the object of a particular cult: peasants from the Abruzzi mountains, dressed in sheep skins, would come and give performances on their bagpipes before their favourite shrine in return for a small payment. These bagpipers who would begin to play at four in the morning exasperated Stendhal. "To gain your neighbours' approval and avoid denunciation by the parish priest, anyone who is afraid of being thought liberal subscribes for two novennas". Their devotions accomplished, the "pipers" returned to their homes with their earnings.

Via dei Banchi Nuovi and Via Banco di Santo Spirito. — These streets gave the district the air of a commercial centre. By 15C bankers from Florence, Siena and Genoa had set up in business. Their fortunes were immense. Under the supervision of the Cardinal Camerlengo the Chigi family administered the finances of the Holy See for over twenty years; later the Strozzi, relatives of the Medici, took over. The Papal State also granted the bankers concessions on mining and customs dues. They controlled the Pope's personal finances and those of the great Roman families.

Together with money changing, which was conducted freely in the streets, there was betting: people bet on the election of the Pope, on the sex of babies...

Until 1541 there was a working mint in the **Palazzo del Banco di Santo Spirito.**

From the end of the Via Banco di Santo Spirito there is a pleasant view of Castel Sant' Angelo and the bridge leading to it.

Early in 16C the **Palazzo Niccolini-Amici** was built by Jacopo Sansovino for the Strozzi. The **Palazzo Alberini** opposite was rented in 1515 to bankers from Florence.

Arco dei Banchi. — The Bankers' Arch leads to the Chigi bank. On the left under the arch is a stone with a Latin inscription which comes from the nearby Church of Sts Celsus and Julian and shows the height reached by the Tiber when it flooded in 1277.

Turn right into Vicolo del Curato.

Via dei Coronari ★. — This is one of the most attractive streets in Rome with its antique shops and its palaces glowing in ochre and stone. In antiquity it was part of the Via Recta which led from the Piazza Colonna to the river. Overall it has retained the form it acquired under Sixtus IV (1471-84). It is named after the vendors of rosaries *(corone)* and other pious objects who set up their shops in the path of the pilgrims who entered the City by the Porta del Popolo and made their way to the Vatican over the St Angelo Bridge.

Via della Maschera d'Oro. — No 9 on the corner of Vicolo di San Simeone is a small palace which shows how civil architecture developed in 16C as a result of Sixtus IV's essays in town planning. The streets of Rome were lined by charming façades engraved and painted with monochrome frescoes. **Polidoro da Caravaggio** and **Maturino da Firenze** were the masters of this technique. The wall was first given a rough rendering blackened with smoke and then covered with a coat of plaster. The artist then engraved mythological scenes or motifs taken from antique art so as to reveal the dark undercoat. These decorations were extremely fragile and have almost all disappeared.

Return to Via dei Coronari and turn right into Vicolo della Volpe.

This street took its name from an inn at the sign of the 'Fox' *(volpe).*

Santa Maria della Pace ★. — *Closed for restoration. The cloisters are open on Sunday morning (entrance no 5 Vicolo del Arco della Pace).*

There was already a small church on this site in 12C. Sixtus IV had it rebuilt in 1480. In the Baroque era it changed in appearance when Alexander VII (1655-67) invited Pietro da Cortona to design a new façade. He created a pleasing combination of contrasting effects: a semi circular porch with six columns beneath a double pediment — a curved one within a triangular one — flanked by two concave wings. To provide a suitable setting for his work the architect designed a charming square lined with elegant colour washed façades.

Cloisters (D). — They were built in 1504 and were one of Bramante's earliest Roman works. The handsome proportions give an air of great simplicity. The columns on the ground floor are complemented by those on the first floor which alternate with smaller columns placed centrally over the lower arches.

Interior. — The 15C plan in very unusual; it comprises a short rectangular nave and an octagonal domed section. The arch of the first chapel on the right in the nave was decorated by Raphael in 1514; he painted the four **Sybils ★** inspired by the angels no doubt after seeing Michelangelo's Sybils in the Sistine chapel. His skill in turning an awkward surface to good account is to be admired. The prophets were painted by one of his pupils. The first chapel on the left is decorated with elegant frescoes by Baldassarre Peruzzi (1481-1536) who also worked on the Farnesina *(p 191)*. The very rich decoration on the arch leading into the second chapel on the right is typical of the Renaissance.

In the octagonal section over the high altar is an image of the Virgin which is supposed to have bled when struck by a stone in 1480; Sixtus IV had the church rebuilt to house the miraculous image. In the chapel on the left of the choir is a 15C wooden crucifix and in the next a fine painting by Sermoneta, one of the first Mannerists to imitate Raphael.

Santa Maria dell' Anima. — *As the main entrance is usually closed, enter by the side door in Via della Pace and start with the interior.*

This is the church of German speaking Roman Catholics. There had been a pilgrim hostel on the site since 1386 when the present building was begun in 1500. It was restored in 19C.

Interior. — Its design — a hall church *(Hallenkirche)* where the aisles are as high as the nave — is surprising in Rome where Gothic architecture is rare. The décor dates from 19C. There are several works by lesser artists imitating the great masters: a painting *(first chapel on the right)* by Carlo Saraceni (1618), a follower of Caravaggio; a Pietà *(fourth chapel)* by Nanni di Baccio Bigio (1532), in clumsy imitation of Michelangelo; a painting of the Holy Family *(above the high altar)* by Giulio Romano, one of Raphael's assistants; the tomb of Ferdinand van der Eynde *(third pillar on the left in the nave)* by Duquesnoy (1594-1643) who worked with Bernini.

The **façade** in the Via dell'Anima was designed by Giuliano da Sangallo and built in 1511. Its flatness, which gives it the appearance of a screen, belongs to the Renaissance period. The pediment above the central door contains a sculpture of the Virgin between two figures each representing a soul (*anima* in Italian) which is a copy of a painting which gave the church its name. The original is kept in the Sacristy *(apply to the Sacristan)*. To the right of the façade there is a view of the bell tower which is capped by a slim cone faced with multicoloured ceramics (1516-18).

Take Via dei Lorenesi to reach Piazza Navona.

Piazza Navona ★★. — Set apart from the noise and smell of the traffic, the Piazza Navona seems to be permanently on holiday: the balloon seller has his pitch beside a caricaturist who sketches his customer with a few deft strokes of charcoal; a dear old body lovingly feeds the pigeons next to a trades unionist exhorting his comrades; tourists and locals come to savour a *tartuffo* on the terrace of the *Tre Scalini*.

The long and narrow shape of the square is due to Domitian: in 86 AD he had a stadium built on this site and immediately instituted a series of games in the Greek style. Unlike the games in the amphitheatre where the gladiators confronted one another with violence, these games were contests of wit and physical fitness; the speaking, poetry and musical competitions were held in the Odeon *(p 159)* while running, wrestling, throwing the discus and javelin took place in the stadium.

Domitian's stadium was stripped of its marbles in 356 by Constantinus II on a visit to Rome *(pp 105, 130)* and by 5C it was in ruins.

It came to life again during the Renaissance when it developed into one of the most beautiful sights in Rome under the Popes. In 1477 the market from the foot of the Capitol was moved here and other attractions were added to bring in the crowds, such as the *Cuccagna,* a greasy pole which strong men tried to climb, or puppet shows. In 1869 the market moved away to the Campo dei Fiori and now the market stalls appear in the Piazza Navona only at Christmas and Epiphany for the fair of the *Befana* (the Italian equivalent of Father Christmas).

The Fountains. — At the centre of the square stands the **fountain of the Four Rivers** ★★★ (Fontana dei Fiumi) created by Bernini for Pope Innocent X who wanted to provide his palace (Palazzo Pamphili) with worthy surroundings. The brilliant Baroque architect contrived a pile of rockwork hollowed out into grottoes on top of which he erected an obelisk; the rigidity and symmetry of the latter contrasts strikingly with the fluid lines of the base; the wind seems to tear at the trees and the marble statues seem to gesticulate. They were carved from the master's designs by some of his pupils and represent four rivers symbolising the four quarters of the world: the Danube for Europe, the Nile for Africa (the veiled head indicated that the source was unknown), the Ganges for Asia and the Plate for America. The obelisk, a Roman work dating from Domitian's reign, was recovered by Innocent X from the Via Appia where it lay. The fountain was completed in 1651. To illustrate the rivalry between Bernini and Borromini, who designed the façade of St Agnes' Church, a Roman legend explains that the statues of the Nile and the Plate, their arms raised in a defensive gesture, are trying to protect themselves from the façade which is about to collapse. In fact the façade was built several years after the fountain.

The **fountain of the Moor** (E) was built at the end of 16C. In 1653 at Innocent X's request it was renovated by Bernini: he designed the central figure of the Moor and one of his pupils was responsible for its vigorous interpretation. The statues on the rim of the basin and the tritons date from 19C. The **fountain of Neptune** (F) was also built at the end of 16C. The statue of Neptune at the centre and those around him date from 19C.

Sant'Agnese in Agone. — According to tradition a small oratory was built in 8C on the site where St Agnes was throught to have been martyred. In 1652 Pope Innocent X commissioned Girolamo Rainaldi and his son Carlo to rebuild the church as a family chapel attached to his palace. From 1653 to 1657 Borromini took charge of the work. The church was completed at the end of the century by a group of architects. Borromini was responsible for part of the dome and for the façade which demonstrates his taste for contrasting convex and concave lines, particularly in the campaniles.

The **interior** ★ is captivating: the deep recesses in the pillars supporting the dome transform the Greek cross plan into an octagon. The altars are adorned with beautiful 'marble pictures' by Bernini's pupils. The decorations in stucco, gilt and painting are far from the spirit of Borromini's sober interiors and were added at the end of the century.

Palazzo Pamphili. — This was the Pamphili residence; it was enlarged between 1644 and 1650 by Girolamo Rainaldi when Giovanni Battista Pamphili became Pope Innocent X.

Distance: 4 km — 2 1/2 miles. Time: about 4 1/2 hours. Start: Piazza Colonna

The walk covers the northern part of the Campus Martius which was mostly reserved for the colossal tombs belonging to the imperial families and the funeral pyres (ustrina) where the bodies were burnt, whereas the southern part was more elegant and contained theatres, porticoes, amphitheatres and sports facilities.

Like the other districts of the city through which the pilgrims passed on their way to the Vatican, this one was raised out of its mediaeval misery under Sixtus IV (1471-84). In his thirteen years on the papal throne he changed the face of Rome, using the money from the sale of indulgences to pay for his projects. Early in 16C Leo X cleared the way for the Via Leonina (now Via di Ripetta) to run straight from the Porta del Popolo, through which foreigners from the north entered the city, to the Mausoleum of Augustus.

Some of the streets round St Augustine's Church and the Via Scrofa have not changed much since the Renaissance while the palaces in the Piazza Colonna and Piazza di Monteci-torio have since 1870 become banks or newspaper offices or department stores. At the same period the old river port of the Ripetta was destroyed; it had been built in 1706, a set of curving riverside steps, of which Piranesi has left some attractive engravings; it was one of the most famous 'views' in Rome.

TOUR

Piazza Colonna ★. — It is one of the most crowded places in Rome, being at the junction of the two main shopping streets (Via del Corso and Via del Tritone).

The **column ★** at the centre of the square was probably erected between 176 and 193 in honour of **Marcus Aurelius** (161-80), who preferred philosophy to war but was forced to campaign on the banks of the Danube. He died at the front of the plague. His victories were short-lived and did not contain the barbarian thrust. Just as Trajan's column illustrated that Emperor's exploits against the Dacians *(p 130),* so Marcus Aurelius' column depicts the significant episodes in his wars with a series of low relief carvings arranged in a spiral. The carving was done by a group of sculptors and even the designs were probably the work of several artists. In order to make the work more visible the scenes are larger and in higher relief than those on Trajan's column but the quality of the craftsmanship has suffered.

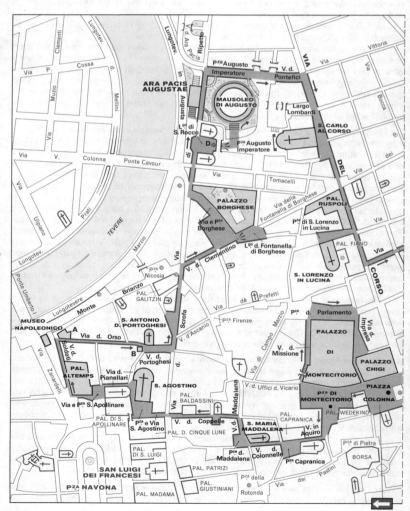

The overall appearance is spoiled by the lack of entasis two thirds of the way up the shaft which would have avoided the impression of concavity.

In 1589 Pope Sixtus V had the statue of the Emperor on the top of the column replaced with a statue of St Paul. He also restored the base and added an inscription wrongly attributing the column to Antoninus Pius, Marcus Aurelius' predecessor.

Palazzo Chigi. — The building was begun in 1562 to designs by Giacomo della Porta; it was continued by Carlo Maderna according to the severe concepts of the Counter-Reformation; it was completed in 1630 in the Baroque era. In 1659 it was bought by Pope Alexander VII for his family, after whom it is named. Since 1917, when it was acquired by the State, the Palazzo Chigi has been involved in politics: Ministry of Foreign Affairs after the First World War, in the Fascist period it housed the Head of the Government; now it belongs to the Presidency of the Council of Ministers.

Piazza di Montecitorio. — The Egyptian obelisk which dates from 6C BC was erected in the square in 1792 by Pope Pius VI and surmounted by a bronze ball bearing his coat of arms. It was brought from Heliopolis to Rome in 10 BC by Augustus and served as the pointer for his huge solar clock.

Palazzo di Montecitorio. — It stands on the site of the funeral pyres belonging to the Antonine family for the cremation of their dead. It was begun by Bernini in 1650, taken over by one of his pupils and completed in 1697 by Carlo Fontana. Little remains of Bernini's Baroque fantasies: the rustic effect, reminiscent of rockeries, of the rough hewn stones framing some of the windows and the impression of enhanced size conveyed by the slightly convex façade which is surmounted by a clock tower. Since 1870 the palace has housed the Chamber of Deputies. The square is therefore full of comings and goings and solemn greetings; even the cafés with their regular patrons keep the same hours as the Montecitorio.

To the rear (Piazza del Parlamento) the building was extended and provided with a majestic new façade (1903-25).

Take Via in Aquiro to Piazza Capranica and then Via delle Colonelle to reach the heart of papal Rome.

St Mary Magdalen (Santa Maria Maddalena). — In 15C an oratory and a hospice were built here. In 1586 St Camillus of Lellis, the founder of the Ministers of the Sick, a nursing order, moved in.

The church was rebuilt in 17C by Carlo Fontana who was succeeded by followers of Bernini.

The façade was erected later in 1735 by Giuseppe Sardi; his contorted lines and abundant decoration are an exaggeration of Borromini's style.

The **interior ★** is a rare example of the Rococo in Rome. The elaborate plan, also suggesting Borromini's influence, gives the church a majestic appearance despite its small size: an elliptical nave with recesses for altars set at an angle and a short transept covered by a dome. The rich decoration in stucco, gold and marble and the frescoes on the dome and in the apse which is bathed in a clear light lend the church the charm of an old fashioned drawing room.

The relics of St Camillus are venerated at the altar in the south transept beneath the Glory of St Camillus painted by Sebastian Conca. In the passage south of the chancel is a 15C wooden statue of Mary Magdalen. The sumptuous organ dates from 18C as do the attractive furnishings in the Sacristy.

Take Via della Maddalena turning left into Via delle Coppelle to reach Piazza Sant'Agostino.

St Augustine's Church ★ (Sant'Agostino). — The church, which is dedicated to St Augustine of Hippo, was built between 1479 and 1483 owing to the generosity of Cardinal d'Estouteville, Archbishop of Rouen in France.

The broad travertine façade, with its roses, was one of the first to be built in Rome according to the concepts of the Renaissance. The two orders are linked by large loose scrolls; the powerful moulding adds character to their ornamental effect.

The interior, which was decorated according to contemporary taste by Luigi Vanvitelli in 1760, has been cluttered by 19C additions which rob it of its soaring elegance, now only faintly perceptible in the nave.

The surviving features of the Renaissance building are the Latin cross plan with apsidal chapels in the transept and side aisles and the dome, one of the earliest in Rome, which rises directly above the transept crossing without a drum.

The church contains several fine works of art: near the main door is the much loved **Madonna del Parto ★** (1521) by **Jacopo Sansovino;** he took great interest in antique sculpture (filmy draperies and proud bearing) during his visits to Rome and was also influenced by the vigour of Michelangelo's work.

On the altar in the righthand transept chapel is a painting by Guercino (1591-1666). The side panels are illustrations of scenes from the life of St Augustine by Lanfranco (1582-1647).

The third pillar on the left in the nave bears a fresco painting by Raphael (1512) of the **prophet Isaiah ★**, which owes much to Michelangelo's work in the Sistine Chapel.

The first chapel on the left contains **Caravaggio's Madonna of the Pilgrims ★★★** (1605): the artist's contemporaries did not always recognise the force of his art, which was opposed to Mannerism and was a major influence in the development of painting. They criticised him for his rough pilgrims, inspired by ordinary people, and for the ugliness of the man's feet. Even the Virgin, for all her gentleness, is nursing her bonny baby in a very realistic manner.

Take Via dei Pianellari which leads into Piazza Sant'Apollinare.

Palazzo Altemps. — The palace was begun in about 1480 for Girolamo Riario, Sixtus IV's nephew. In 1568 it was acquired by Cardinal Marco Sittico Altemps who had it rebuilt by Martino Longhi the Elder. In 1725 it was the residence of Cardinal de Polignac, the French Ambassador. It now belongs to the Holy See.

Napoleon Museum (Museo Napoleonico). — *Open 9 am to 2 pm (1 pm Sunday and holidays) and 5 to 8 pm Tuesday and Thursday. Closed Monday. 500 L.*

The museum was founded in 1927 by Giuseppe Primoli, a descendant of Lucien Bonaparte, and contains many souvenirs of the Napoleonic presence in Rome. Lucien lived in the Via dei Condotti, Pauline had her villa near to the Porta Pia *(p 122),* while Napoleon's mother died in her palace in the Via del Corso *(p 101).*

The museum contains a collection of portraits of the Emperor and his family as well as some of their possessions. Rooms IV and V are devoted to Napoleon's son, who was declared King of Rome at his birth in 1811. Room VI, which is devoted to Pauline, Napoleon's sister, contains the couch on which she posed for Canova *(p 175).* Room IX deals with the reigns of Pius VI and Pius VII which were both interrupted by quarrels with Napoleon; the first pope died a prisoner in Valence while the second did not return to Rome until 1814 after 5 years captivity in Fontainebleau *(p 156).*

Albergo dell'Orso (A). — From the Middle Ages to the Renaissance the Via dell'Orso and the Via Monte Brianzo consisted almost entirely of inns. The hostelry at the sign of the Bear was set up in a fine 15C building *(restored).*

Take Via dell'Orso which becomes Via dei Portoghesi.

Various craftsmen still have businesses in these charming quiet streets.

Monkey Tower (B). — The building on the corner of Via dei Portoghesi and Via dei Pianellari incorporates a 15C tower. It has been immortalised by the American novelist, Nathaniel Hawthorne (1804-64), with the following story.

The family living in the house owned a very facetious monkey. One day it climbed to the top of the tower carrying the new-born baby. The father was terrified, not knowing what to do and fearful that the animal would let its precious burden fall. After praying to the Virgin for her to intercede he decided to whistle to the monkey to bring it back. The monkey came down by the drainpipe holding the child in its arms and they both returned safe and sound. Since then at the top of the tower a little light burns continuously before an image of the Virgin.

Sant'Antonio dei Portoghesi. — The Portuguese national church, which was built in 17C, has an attractive Rococo façade; the interior is gorgeously decorated with gold, stucco, marble and paintings. The first chapel on the right contains a funeral monument by Canova (1806-08). In the first chapel on the left above the altar is a fine painting by Antoniazzo Romano (15C) depicting the Virgin between St Francis and St Anthony.

Turn left into Via della Scrofa and then bear right into Via del Clementino.

At the far end of this street the Church of the Trinità dei Monti is visible.

Palazzo Borghese. — The palace was built at the end of 16C and the façade overlooking the Piazza Borghese demonstrates the dignity and austerity of the Counter-Reformation. The palace was acquired by Cardinal Camillo Borghese who became Pope in 1605 as Paul V. The courtyard *(entrance in Largo della Fontanella di Borghese)* with its loggias, statues, fountains and rockeries is a beautiful evocation of the luxurious life of the noble families in 17C.

Paul V gave the palace to his brothers who commissioned Flaminio Ponzio, the architect (1560-1613), to extend it towards the Tiber. He it was who designed the picturesque front in the Via di Ripetta which used to overlook the Ripetta riverside port *(p 164).*

Botticella Fountain (D). — It was built in 1774 at the expense of the Ripetta watermen's association. There is a fine view of the apse and dome of San Carlo al Corso *(p 168).*

Augustus' Mausoleum. — The ruins of the mausoleum are now surrounded by the modern buildings of the Piazza Augusto Imperatore which was laid out in 1940.

Augustus' Mausoleum was one of the most sacred monuments in antiquity. It was built between 28 and 23 BC and, like Hadrian's mausoleum, the Castel S Angelo, it took the form of an Etruscan tumulus tomb. On a rectangular base stood a cylindrical section surmounted by a conical hillock of earth *(tumulus)* planted with cypress trees. On the south side flanking the entrance stood two obelisks, Roman imitations of Egyptian models, which now stand in the Piazza dell'Esquilino and the Piazza del Quirinale. The funeral chamber in the middle of the mausoleum was reserved for the Emperor; round it was a series of chambers for the other members of the Julio-Claudian family.

In the Middle Ages the mausoleum was converted into a fortress by the Colonna family; Gregory IX (1227-41) dismantled it and stripped it of its blocks of travertine; in 1936 the concert hall which it then contained was closed and the remains were restored.

Augustus' Altar of Peace ★★ **(Ara Pacis Augustae).** — *Reconstructed in a modern building between Augustus' Mausoleum and the Lungotevere in Augusta. Open 9 am to 1.50 pm (1 pm Sunday in summer); also 4 to 7 pm Tuesday and Thursday from 1 April to 30 September. Closed Monday, 1 January, Easter, 21 April, 1 May, 15 August, Christmas. 500 L.*

The monumental altar was erected by the Senate and inaugurated in 9 BC in honour of the Peace which Augustus established throughout the Roman world and in the capital where the concentration of power in one person put an end to twenty years of civil war. The Ara Pacis originally stood in the Campus Martius beside the Via Flaminia (now Via del Corso) about where the Palazzo Fiano stands today. In 1970, to celebrate Rome's centenary as the capital of modern Italy, the monument was opened to the public. It had been reconstructed from excavated fragments assembled from various museums and modern reproductions of the pieces which were missing entirely. The altar was the major work of the Augustan 'golden age' and marks the apogee of Roman art. It consists of the altar itself standing within a marble enclosure decorated with low relief carvings. There were two entrances to the enclosure in opposite walls: the entrance facing the Campus Martius was the main one used by the Pontifex Maximus and his suite of priests and Vestals; the rear entrance was used by the *camilli,* who were the priests' young assistants, by the men who performed the sacrifice and by the animals to be sacrificed.

External decoration of the enclosure. — On the outside of the enclosure the lower part is decorated with scrolls of acanthus leaves and swans, a faithful representation carved with great skill and variety. Two panels flank the main entrance: Aeneas making a sacrifice *(right)* and Faustulus the shepherd finding Romulus and Remus (*left* — a few fragments). These two scenes illustrate the legendary founding of Rome and glorify Augustus who claimed to be descended from Aeneas.

The east side facing Via di Ripetta shows a procession of people including the Emperor and his family, some of whom have been identified: at the head Augustus (incomplete figure); Agrippa, his son-in-law, is probably the tall figure following the four priests *(flamines)* and a sacrificer (the symbolic axe on his shoulder); Antonia has turned to speak to her husband Drusus, Augustus' grandson. The human touch is not omitted: the young couple is cautioned to be

(After photo by Gab. Fot. Naz., Rome)

Altar of Peace: imperial procession

quiet by an old woman standing between them with a finger to her lips. The two children behind Drusus are shown with natural simplicity.

The rear entrance is flanked by two panels: the personification of Rome triumphant (*right* — mostly missing) seated on a pile of weapons, dominating the world; the personification of the fruitful Earth *(left)* accompanied by two figures symbolising wind and water. The latter scene is full of the realism characteristic of Roman art: a sheep is grazing at the goddess' feet while the two children play on her lap. Both scenes reflect the glory of Augustus, author of the Roman peace and token of the earth's fertility. The side facing the river shows a procession composed of members of the various priestly colleges.

The procession shown on the Ara Pacis represents the procession which took place on inauguration day.

Internal decoration. — The lower half is decorated with broad vertical flutes which represent the temporary wooden palissade which surrounded the altar on the day of its consecration; the upper half is covered with garlands of fruit and flowers and the heads of the cattle which were sacrificed on that day; the vessels between the garlands were used for pouring a liquid on to the altar. The altar itself, which is flanked by winged lions, is decorated with a frieze of clear cut small figures.

On the outside of the modern building facing Via di Ripetta is a reproduction of the *Res Gestae,* the text drawn up by Augustus of the acts accomplished in his reign; it also contained his Will. The original, which has been lost, was engraved on bronze plaques at the entrance to his mausoleum but a copy of it was found in the Temple of Augustus in Ankara (formerly Ancyra in Asia Minor).

Take Via dei Pontefici out of the square and turn right into Via del Corso (p 98).

San Carlo al Corso. — In 1471 the Lombard community in Rome was given a small church in the Corso by Sixtus IV. They rebuilt it and dedicated it to St Ambrose who was Bishop of Milan in 4C. In 1610 they wanted to enlarge the building in honour of Charles Borromeo, Archbishop of Milan who had just been canonised. The full name of the church is therefore Sant'Ambrogio e San Carlo al Corso. Construction began in 1612. The majestic interior is in the shape of a Latin cross with an ambulatory, a rarity in Rome, more usually found in northern churches. The heart of St Charles Borromeo now rests in the chapel behind the high altar. The **dome★** is the work of Pietro da Cortona (1668). The Apotheosis of St Ambrose and St Charles, on the high altar, is one of the best works of Carlo Maratta (1685-90), restored in 19C. The handsomely carved 15C tabernacle on the pillar to the left probably comes from St Ambrose' sanctuary.

Palazzo Ruspoli. — This 16C palace is now a bank. After the downfall of Napoleon, in 1825 it became the refuge of Hortense de Beauharnais, ex-Queen of Holland, under the name of the Duchess of St Leu. "A flirt and a gossip, sentimental and romantic, Hortense was a pretty woman with forget-me-not eyes" (M Andrieux). Her salon became the centre of attraction for every pleasure-loving member of society. Her son, Prince Charles Louis Napoleon, the future Napoleon III, brought this sumptuous life to an end when he was implicated in a scheme to declare a republic in Rome and was expelled from the Papal States together with the Duchess of St Leu.

Turn right into Piazza di San Lorenzo in Lucina.

San Lorenzo in Lucina. — The Church of St Lawrence was built in 12C on the site of a *titulus* in the house of a woman called Lucina. Three features from the mediaeval church remain: the bell tower, the porch and the two lions flanking the door. Inside is a monument *(against the pillar between the 2nd and 3rd chapels on the right)* erected by Chateaubriand, the French ambassador, to commemorate Nicolas Poussin who spent many years in Rome. The fourth chapel on the right contains a bust *(back lefthand corner)* of Dr. Gabriele Fonseca, by Bernini, a late and rather theatrical work (1668).

Return to Via del Corso and then turn left into Via della Vite which is lined with smart shops.

Palazzo di Propaganda Fide. — This imposing building, the property of the Holy See, houses the Congregation for the Evangelisation of Peoples, which originated in the institution of the Congregation for the Propagation of the Faith by Gregory XV in 1622. It was Urban VIII (1623-44) who began construction of the building by inviting his protégé, Bernini to design the façade overlooking Spanish Square *(p 99).* The result is unexpectedly sober for this brilliant Baroque architect. On Innocent X's accession Bernini fell into disgrace. The new pope wished to give his reign a new look and he turned to Borromini — the only architect able to compete with Bernini — whom he commissioned to design the façade overlooking the Via di Propaganda. With Borromini a touch of fantasy was introduced: in the cornices and in the elaborate pediments over the windows.

Borromini also designed the little **Church of the Three Magi** (1666) inside the palace *(on the left immediately inside the door in the Via di Propaganda).*

Sant'Andrea delle Fratte. — St Andrew's Church, which originated in 12C, stands in the Via di Capo Le Case (end of the houses) which in the Middle Ages was the northeastern limit of the city. Its name recalls the thickets *(fratte)* which used to abound in the vicinity. Early in 17C the rebuilding of the church was begun; the work was completed by Borromini. From higher up the street there is a view of the **campanile★** and the dome which he treated as precious objects, abandoning the traditional form and giving full expression to the eccentric products of his fertile imagination: the dome, which would normally soar into the sky, is imprisoned in a space circumscribed by convex and concave surfaces.

The façade dates from 19C. Inside at the entrance to the chancel are two statues of **angels★** presenting the instruments of the Passion. When Bernini sculpted them in 1669, his art was very close to the extreme delicacy characteristic of the Rococo period. They were designed to accompany the other statues commissioned by Clement IX for the St Angelo Bridge but the Pope found them too beautiful to be exposed to the elements. They remained with Bernini's family until 1729 when they were placed in the church.

Take Via della Mercede.

The **Piazza San Silvestro** is dominated by the façade of the Central Post Office which was established in 19C in the monastery of the Church of San Silvestro in Capite. Every bus route and taxi fare seems to end in this square, which with its church and the post office, its café and its newspaper stall, is an excellent place for observing the Roman way of life.

Santa Maria in Via. — A miracle led to the foundation of St Mary's Church: an image of the Virgin, painted on a tile, fell into a well; the well overflowed and the image re-appeared. Many pilgrims still come to drink the water of the famous well and to venerate the 'Madonna of the Well' *(Madonna del Pozzo).* The late 16C Baroque façade is by Carlo Rainaldi.

Galleria Colonna. — This arcade was built in 1923 linking the Via di Santa Maria in Via with the Via del Corso and the Piazza Colonna.

VILLA BORGHESE

Distance: 3.5 km — 2 miles. Time: about 4 hours. Start: Viale delle Belle Arti.

This walk explores Rome's largest public park, which borders on the elegant Parioli district and contains two museums, an art gallery and various national academies of art in a setting of lakes and lawns and groves of trees.

When Cardinal Camillo Borghese acceded to the papal throne in 1605 he made generous gifts to his family. To his nephew Scipione Caffarelli he gave his name. On becoming a cardinal Scipione Borghese started to build a private house, a little palace *(palazzina)* set in magnificent gardens. Two men were employed on the plans: the architect Flaminio Ponzio and the landscape gardener Domenico Savino da Montepulciano.

The section of the Aurelianic Wall (Mura Aureliane) from the Porta del Popolo to the Porta Pinciana, which marks the southwest boundary of the Villa Borghese, follows such an irregular line that the Romans call it the crooked wall **(Muro Torto)** and tell many legends about it. When the Goths led by Witigis besieged Rome in 6C, they failed to take advantage of a breach in the Muro Torto and the Romans concluded that the area must be protected by St Peter. Imagination ran riot in the Middle Ages when the vicinity was used as a cemetery where people denied a Christian burial were interred.

TOUR

Via Flaminia. — This modern artery follows the line of the ancient Flaminian Way which was constructed in 220 BC by the Consul Flaminius who died in the battle of Lake Trasimene against Hannibal. It ran almost straight for 314 km — 195 miles from the city centre *(p 98)* along the via del Corso to Rimini on the Adriatic.

Pius IV's Palazzina. — The little palace was built by Pius IV (1559-65) who offered it to his nephew Cardinal Charles Borromeo. The slightly concave façade exhibits the mannered style typical of late Renaissance works. Since 1929 the building has housed the Italian Government Embassy to the Holy See.

Sant'Andrea. — St Andrew's Church was built in 16C by Vignola for Julius III. It is an unusual little building, with a clear cut silhouette, stressed by heavy dentilated cornices, an elliptical dome resting on a solid base and plain brick walls.

■ VILLA GIULIA NATIONAL MUSEUM ★★★

Open 9 am to 2 pm (1 pm Sunday and holidays). Closed Monday, 1 January, 25 April, 1 May, 1st Sunday in June, 15 August, Christmas. 1 000 L.

The museum is devoted to **Etruscan civilisation.** The exceptional interest of the collection is enhanced by its charming situation in Julius III's country villa.

Villa Giulia ★. — Julius III's reign (1550-55) was contemporary with the Council of Trent but the Pope did not therefore lose his taste for the cultivated life of a Renaissance prince. In 1551 he invited Vignola to design a summer villa for him. The plain and sober façade is typical of Vignola who also studied and wrote about architectural theory. The first courtyard is framed by a semi-circular portico with tunnel vaulting.

Beyond in the main courtyard is a charming Mannerist construction designed by Bartolomeo Ammannati who collaborated on the Villa Giulia from 1552: a little loggia, perfectly proportioned, opens on to horse-shoe steps descending to a *nymphaeum* adorned with cariatids, rockeries and false grottoes. Several pieces of Roman sculpture are on display.

In the past the public was permitted to enjoy the tranquillity of this villa and to gather the fruit and flowers. When the poet Joachim du Bellay was visiting Rome as secretary to his cousin the French ambassador Jean du Bellay, he disapproved severely of the Pope for leading a life of pleasure to the detriment of affairs of state. When Julius III raised a young man of 17, who led a troop of performing monkeys, to be a Cardinal, du Bellay did not omit to poke fun at the new Jupiter and his Ganymede.

The courtyard is laid out in pleasant gardens bordered by the modern galleries of the museum. To the right of the *nymphaeum* an Etruscan temple has been reconstructed.

The Etruscans. — No one knows where they originated but they arrived in the Italian peninsula towards the end of 8C BC and settled between the Arno and the Tiber (an area covering Tuscany and parts of Umbria and Latium). More advanced than their neighbours, they governed Rome from the end of 7C BC *(p 37)* and established a veritable 'empire' stretching from Corsica to the shores of the Adriatic and from Capua to Bologna. Decline set in at the end of 6C BC and Rome, now free of their domination, began to expand and attacked their cities; in 1C BC the Etruscans became Roman citizens.

Traces of Etruscan civilisation have mostly disappeared but some have survived in their tombs which contained objects once the property of the dead person from which it is possible to deduce the character of their society. Until 18C Etruscan art was thought to be a derivative of Greek art without any aesthetic value. The re-evaluation of the canons of Greek art, the elegant stylization of Etruscan works and their expressive quality have aroused a very lively interest in Etruscan art which has an unusual affinity with modern forms.

Ground Floor *(plan p 170)*

Italic civilisations. — *Room 2.* The Italic civilisations at the time of the Etruscans' appearance are represented by funeral urns shaped like huts, such as the Latins built, and clay urns characteristic of the Villanovan civilisation, which is named after the village of Villanova near Bologna and developed around the year 1000 BC in the Po valley, Tuscany and the north of Latium where the Etruscans later settled.

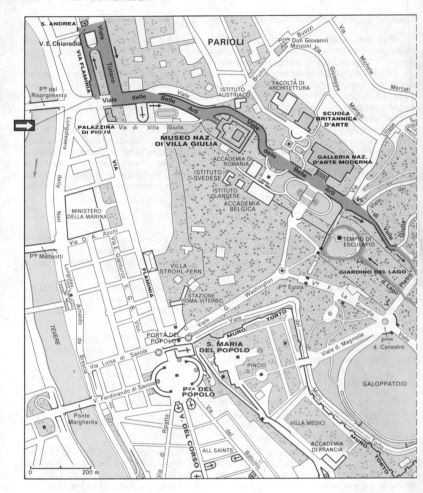

Etruscan tomb. — *Beneath room 5.* This is a reconstruction of a tomb dating from 6C BC, with two funeral chambers, similar to the tomb found in the necropolis at Cerveteri to the northwest of Rome.

Bisenzio Tombs. — *Room 6.* Among the objects found in the tombs in this city are two small pieces of bronze (**1**) which illustrate early Etruscan art (late 8 to early 7C BC): a miniature chariot and a covered vessel decorated with figures in the round. These objects were used for domestic decoration before being buried beside their owners.

Veii Sculptures★★★. — *Room 7.* The statue of a goddess with a child (**2**), which probably represents Apollo and his mother Leto, and the statue of Apollo (**3**) were sculpted at the end of 6C BC when Etruscan art was at its zenith. Set up as they were originally on the roof ridge of a temple, they give an idea of how they would have looked silhouetted against the sky. They are made of terracotta and are strikingly realistic and animated. The other sculptures include a fine head of Hermes (**4**) and several antefixae in the shape of Gorgon heads which masked the ends of the roof beams and the painted pediments (**5**). These sculptures all come from the same temple and may be the work of Vulca, the only Etruscan sculptor known by name; his reputation was such that the king of Rome sent for him in 509 BC to do the statues for the Temple of Jupiter on the Capitol.

Terracotta sarcophagus★★★ (**6**). — *Room 9.* This is one of the masterpieces of Etruscan terracotta sculpture. It dates from the end of 6C and comes from Cerveteri. It expresses the Etruscan belief in the afterlife. The husband and wife, reclining as if at a banquet, seem to be pursuing their life in the beyond. The artist has given the figures individual faces as if they were portraits.

(After photo by Gab. Fot. Naz., Rome)

Villa Giulia National Museum:
terracotta sarcophagus

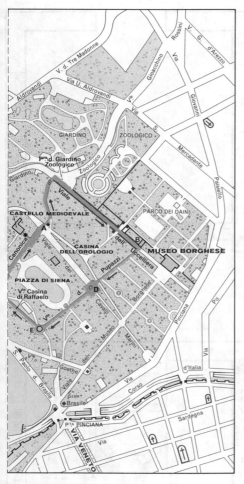

First floor

The rooms in the north gallery of the museum are chiefly devoted to small **bronze objects ★**, both useful and decorative. Bronze was one of the main Etruscan exports which contributed largely to their wealth; they fashioned it with great creative skill: rudimentary **clasps** dating from 8 to 6C BC, **mirrors** very finely etched on the back with elegant scenes from family life or mythology, statuettes with astonishingly modern forms. The Etruscans' liking for bronze is explained by the rich copper deposits in Etruria and the island of Elba which belonged to them. The tin may have been imported from Great Britain or from the neighbouring islands.

Room 15 contains a famous **wine pitcher ★★** (7) which was found at Veii; it is one of the most beautiful examples of Greek art from the middle of 7C BC. This is the proto-Corinthian period when the ceramics produced in Corinth, an important port on the sea routes to the East, were decorated with subjects treated in miniature in bands of delicate silhouettes. On the upper part two groups of warriors marching into battle against one another can still be seen. The incision work shows each detail clearly. The lower part is covered with figures and hunting scenes.

The same display cabinet shows two *bucchero* **vases ★** dating from 6C BC; the technique for producing this particular type of Etruscan ceramic, which is black, is not well understood. One of the vases bears the Etruscan alphabet, the other a long inscription. The Etruscan alphabet has been deciphered but the meaning of their language is still unknown.

Castellani Collection ★. — *Room 19.* The collection traces the evolution of Greek and Etruscan ceramics from 8C BC to the Roman era. The Etruscans imported a considerable amount of Greek pottery, so much in fact that it could be said that the finest Greek vases have been found in Etruscan tombs.

The exhibits are displayed in show cases numbered from 1 to 12.

Case 1. — The elongated vases, which date from 7 and 6C BC and come from eastern Greece, are imitations of Egyptian alabaster vessels. They were used by athletes for the perfumed oil with which they massaged their bodies; hence the flat lip.

Case 2. — Several *bucchero* vases dating from 7 and 6C BC.

Case 3. — The two water pitchers which date from between 530 and 520 belong to the Caere *hydriae,* so called because this type of water pot was found in a necropolis in Cerveteri (ancient Caere). The decoration of picturesque mythological scenes includes the Abduction of Europa by Zeus on one and on the other Hercules in his lion skin leading Cerberus against Eurystheus who is hiding in a large jar in terror.

Case 4. — Beautiful wine bowl made in Sparta in about 570 *(stile laconico)* and decorated with lotus flowers, an eastern motif.

Cases 5 to 8. — From 540 to 530 BC Attic cermaic art was transformed by the change from black to red figure technique. Henceforth artists signed their work; two amphora (Case 5) are signed by Nicosthenes.

Case 8 contains two vases by Cleophrades; one is decorated with a very realistic painting of Hercules and the Nemean lion.

Cases 9 and 10. — From the beginning of 5C to about 480 BC the red figure technique made Athens the capital of Attic vase painting. Articles produced during this period can be identified by the fact that the face is shown in profile while the eye is drawn full face. The quality of the work is remarkable; the detail within the outline of the body and garments is done with a fine brush. Macron, who painted for the potter Hieron, was a specialist in beautiful female figures: a cup *(case 9)* painted by him shows some Maenads dancing, some young men and a figure of Dionysius in the bottom of the bowl.

Cases 11 and 12. — Here the style is different. At the end of 4C BC Hellenistic production experimented with other techniques, not only in Athens but in Magna Graeca (southern Italy), in Apulia and in the Faliscan region (round Città Castellana): the artist has decorated the black varnished surface of the vases with flowers, fronds and elaborate decorations painted in white, yellow and dark red. The ceramics from Egnatia in Apulia belong to this period.

The raised decoration on some pieces is the result of a desire to produce a cheap imitation of metal vessels.

Castellani Collection of Jewellery★. — *Ask at the ticket office on the ground floor.* This stunning collection of over a thousand pieces assembled by the Castellani family of jewellers consists of antique jewellery dating from 8C BC to 7C AD, of copies or of arrangements of antique jewels.

Rooms I to IV. — They contain Etruscan pieces found during the excavations at Cerveteri, Veii, Vulci etc.

At the far end of the semi-circular corridor two flights of steps lead down to the first floor of the south wing of the museum.

Tombs from Capena and the Faliscan region. — *Rooms 24 to 28.* A showcase (8) in **Room 25** contains a plate decorated with an elephant accompanied by its calf and guided by some archers perched on the elephants' back in a sort of tower. This example of the ceramic art of Egnatia was found at Capena (an Etruscan town north of Rome) and dates from the early 3C BC. It is evidence of the impression made on the Etruscans by the elephants in Pyrrhus' army which appeared in 280 BC during the war between Rome and Tarentum.

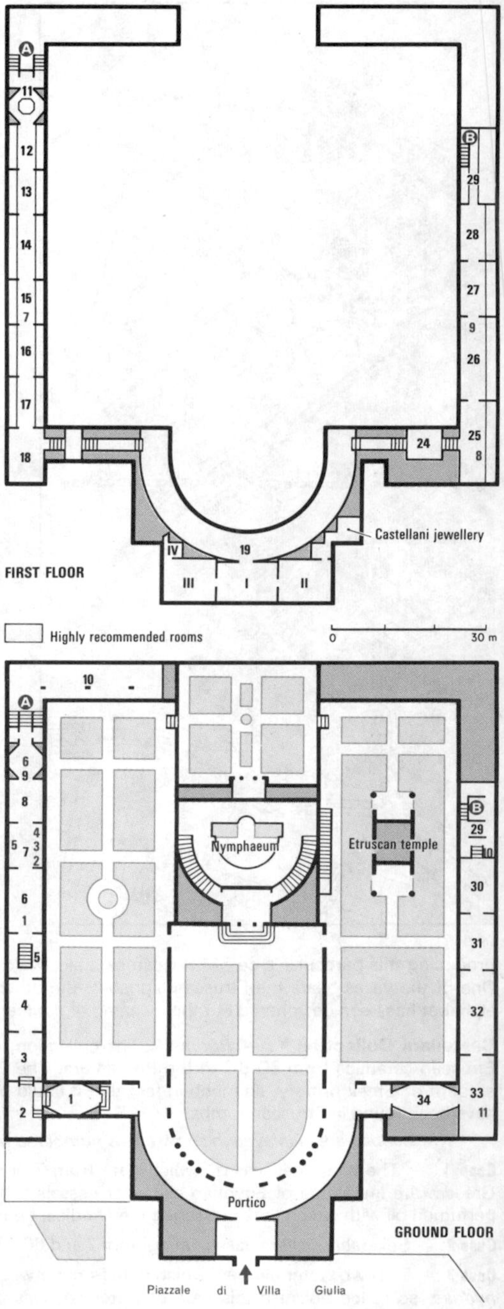

The exhibits in **Room 26** are drawn in particular from

FIRST FLOOR

Castellani jewellery

☐ Highly recommended rooms

0   30 m

Nymphaeum   Etruscan temple

Portico

GROUND FLOOR

Piazzale di Villa Giulia

VILLA GIULIA NATIONAL MUSEUM

Falerii Veteres, the capital of the Faliscans (who were attached to the Confederation of Etruscan Cities); the site is now occupied by Città Castellana. The city was always in a state of rebellion and was finally destroyed in 241 BC.

The wine bowl (9) dates from about the middle of 4C BC; it shows Aurora and Cephalus in their chariot and Peleus abducting Thetis; round the neck a deer and a bull are being attacked by griffins.

Ground floor

Temples of Falerii Veteres★. — *Room 29, split level.* The architecture of these buildings is known to us from plans left by Vitruvius, a Roman architect and theorist (1C BC). The room contains partial reconstructions of pediments, examples of antefixae and acroteria (decorative elements, often in terracotta, which beginning in 4C were placed on the peak and at either end of the pediments). The **bust of Apollo★** (10) *(illustration opposite page)* shows late Greek Classical influence.

'Barberini' and 'Bernardini' Tombs. — *Room 33.* These very rich tombs, situated near Palestrina (ancient Praeneste) were full of articles dating from mid 7C BC. Trading relations between the Etruscans and the Phoenicians are responsible for preserving the magnificent carved **ivory pieces.**

The Etruscans were expert goldsmiths and worked in this metal from 7C BC using the filigrane technique; they perfected the granulation technique, splitting the gold into granules only a few tenths of a millimetre in diameter. The **jewellery** on display includes some beautiful brooches decorated with small figures in the round.

Ficoroni Cists ★★★ (11). — The cists were marriage coffers; they were also sometimes used for toilet or religious articles. Some magnificent examples were produced by the Etruscans between 4 and 2C BC. Their manufacture was a speciality of Praeneste where the largest known example was found in 18C; it is called the Ficoroni cist after its owner. It stands on feline feet which are attached to the body by carved plaques; it is decorated with fine engravings of the Argonauts

(After photo by Gab. Fot. Naz., Rome)

Villa Giulia National Museum: bust of Apollo

arriving among the Bebryces, with Pollux tying King Amycos to a tree. On the lid are hunting scenes and three statues in the round — the one in the centre represents Dionysius.

> *At Cerveteri (51 km — 32 miles) and Tarquinia (97 km — 60 miles) northwest of Rome there are several Etruscan tombs on their original sites (described in the Michelin Green Guide Italy)*

British School. — *Not open to the public.* It was founded in 1901 as a school of archaeology analogous to the one in Athens. The present Classical style building was designed by **Sir Edwin Lutyens** in 1912 on the site of the British Pavilion at the International Exhibition of Fine Arts held in Rome in 1911. In this year the school was reconstituted with scholarships funded by the Royal Commissioners of the Great Exhibition of 1851. It has since been enlarged to provide studios and accommodation for the staff and 24 resident post-graduate students in various fields: painting, sculpture, art history, architecture, archaeology (Classical and mediaeval) and Classical studies (history and letters).

At the foot of the steps is a statue of the Danish sculptor Thorwaldsen (1770-1844), who worked in Rome from 1797 to 1838, receiving many honours and commissions.

■ **NATIONAL GALLERY OF MODERN ART ★**

Open 9 am to 5 pm (1 pm Sunday and holidays). Closed Monday, 1 January, 25 April, 1 May, 15 August, Christmas. 2 000 L.

The gallery, which was built in 1911, houses mainly Italian painting and sculpture from 19C to the present day. Some rooms are reserved for temporary exhibitions of contemporary art, for lectures and slide shows.

After passing through the barrier in the entrance hall bear left.

Neo-Classical works *(Rooms I-III)* including **Canova** are followed by the Romantics, in particular **Francesco Hayez** (1791-1882); in the Sicilian Vespers *(Room IV)* he has confined himself to a conventional setting.

The painters of the **Neapolitan School** *(Rooms V-VI)* provided Italian painting with a direct link with the Barbizon School of landscape painters in France.

The Macchiaioli. — These artists, who were contemporaries of the French impressionists, took their name from their technique of painting nature as a collection of spots or patches of colour (*macchia* means spot) with light shed upon them. This section is being reorganised but the most representative of the group are hung in Rooms VII-VIII: Telemaco **Signorini** (1835-1902), Giovanni **Fattori** (1825-1908) who became the greatest exponent of the style, Silvestro **Lega** (1826-95) and Adriano **Cecioni** (1836-86).

Domenico Morelli (1826-1901). — *Rooms XI, XII and XIII.* These rooms are devoted to the very varied output of this theorist of the Neapolitan School: portraits, religious subjects, oriental scenes, historical events such as "Tasso reading *The Liberation of Jerusalem* to Eleonora d'Este" in two contrasting versions.

The Scapigliati. — *Room XVI.* The *Scapigliature* movement began in Milan between 1860 and 1870 and brought together artists with extravagant ideas and manners (*scapigliato* means dishevelled). Tranquilo **Cremona** (1837-78) the dominating influence in the group is characterised by his indistinct contours where form seems to dissolve beneath the effects of light. There are also several works by Antonio **Fontanesi** (1818-82) a member of the Piedmont School; he was acquainted with the French landscape painters of the Barbizon school, especially Corot.

Medardo Rosso (1858-1928). — *Room XVII.* A great artist of the late 19C who transposed the luminosity of the Impressionists into his sculpture. In Paris he had known Rodin. This room also contains works by Courbet, Monet, Degas and Van Gogh.

The Divisionists. — *Room XVIII.* Divisionism was based on the juxtaposition of primary and complementary colours so as to obtain a more intense luminosity. Giovanni Segantini (1858-99) was their leader but his freshness of style owes more to his sense of poetry than to pure science.

Room XXII/XXXIV. — This room contains the work of some foreign artists: two sculptures by Rodin and "The Three Ages" a masterpiece by Klimt.

Room XXVI. — Although a Roman by birth, Antonio Mancini studied in Naples; here are examples of his early and later portraits.

Gaetano Previati (1852-1920). — *Room XXX.* This painter was a Divisionist and visionary who sought to fuse materialism and spiritualism.

Room XXXV. — The Veranda is devoted to the sculpture of Vincenzo Gemito, a product of the Southern Italian School; the collection covers all his varied phases from 1873 to 1928 and includes his most important works.

The Futurists. — *Rooms XXXVIII-XL.* In 1910 a year after the launch of Futurism by Marinetti, artists such as **Bracioni, Balla** and **Severini** began to follow the Futurist theories in Milan. They wanted to replace the old values with the cult of dynamism and speed. The sculptures are by Arturo Martini who greatly influenced the development of sculpture at the beginning of 20C. These rooms also contain works by foreign artists: Modigliani, Kees Van Dongen, Braque, Kandinsky, Mondrian.

Giacomo Manzù. — *Room XLII.* He adopted Medardo Rosso's technique of achieving luminosity to express his melancholy.

This room gives access to an outdoor display of 20C sculpture in the garden.

Surrealism. — *Room LIII.* Foreign contemporaries in the Surrealist movement: Miro, Ernst.

Giuseppe Capogrossi. — *Room LIV.* He was one of the leading artists of the Roman School between 1930 and the Second World War.

Alberto Burri. — *Room LV.* His original style has produced collages, works composed of a variety of materials etc.

Lucio Fontana. — *Room LVI.* He was a versatile artist who expressed his talent in ceramics, painting, decorating, drawing and sculpture.

Room LVII. — Works by Henry Moore, Alberto Giacometti, Arnaldo Pomodoro, Jackson Pollock.

Ettore Colla. — *Room LVIII.* In 1951 Colla joined the group called "Origin" and began to produce his metal 'figures' made from salvaged scrap iron.

Room LIX. — Works by Italian and Spanish artists of the 'informal' schools expressing revolt and protest: Umberto Mastroianni, Antonio Tapies, Emilio Vedova.

Visual and Kinetic Art. — *Rooms LXI, LXII and LXIII.* These rooms contain new types of art form in which the distinction between sculpture and painting no longer exists and in which electric impulses are used to produce light and movement.

Pino Pascali. — *Room LXIV.* The influence of American Pop Art is apparent in the work of this promising young artist who died young.

■ WALK IN THE BORGHESE GARDENS ★★

This walk wanders through a romantic landscape of lakes, trees and flower gardens set with imitation antique sculpture.

Take Viale di Valle Giulia and then the first path on the right which leads to Viale Pietro Canonica; turn left.

The little **castle** *(castello medioevale)* is an imitation of a mediaeval fortress. It used to be the house and studio of the sculptor Pietro Canonica (1869-1959) and has been converted into a museum.

The **Temple of Antoninus and Faustina (A)** was built in the late 18C.
Continue along the path as far as Viale dell' Uccelliera; turn right.

The building topped by a wrought iron cage (**B**) is a 17C aviary. The Viale dell' Uccelliera (Aviary Avenue) leads to the Borghese Gallery *(see below)*.
Turn right into the Viale dei Pupazzi.

The **Sea horse Fountain (D)** was commissioned in 1791 by Prince Marcantonio Borghese who renovated the gardens.

The **Piazza di Siena** further on is named after the native town of the Borghese. Set among umbrella pines, it is sometimes used for international equestrian events. On the northeast side stands the **Casina dell' Orologio,** built in the late 18C.

The Viale dei Pupazzi leads to the **Temple of Diana (E)**, modelled on an ancient building. From there an avenue runs north to the **Lake Garden** (Giardino del Lago), one of the most popular corners of the park; it was created by the architect, Asprucci, who worked on the enlargement of the Borghese Gardens at the end of 18C; the waters of the lake reflect the columns of the little Temple of Aesculapius, another imitation of an ancient building.

BORGHESE GALLERY ★★★

The Borghese Gallery is not described in this walk but on page 175, as it is open only in the morning.

Distance: 3 km — 2 miles. Time: about 3 1/2 hours. Start: Porta Pinciana.

This walk, which starts in the Borghese Gardens *(plan p 170)*, includes the most elegant and sophisticated districts of modern Rome. The route from the Borghese Gallery to the Church of Santa Maria della Vittoria passes some of Bernini's most beautiful and famous works of art.

Porta Pinciana. — The gateway in the wall which Aurelian built round Rome in 3C was fortified in 6C by Belisarius, the Emperor Justinian's great general, who strove to re-gain the western territories of the Roman empire. He captured Rome in 537 and expelled the Ostrogoths and Pope Silverius.

Cross Piazzale Brasile.

The main entrance to the Borghese Gardens is flanked by pillars bearing the eagle and the dragon from the Borghese coat of arms.

Bear right into Viale del Museo Borghese.

■ BORGHESE GALLERY ★★★ (Museo Borghese)

Open 9 am to 2 pm (1 pm Sundays and holidays). Closed Monday, 1 January, Easter, 25 April, 1 May, 15 August, Christmas. 2 000 L.

This little palace *(palazzina)* was designed in 1613 by a Dutchman, Jan Van Santen (called Vasanzio in Italian), for Cardinal Scipione Borghese. It is a delightful example of a rich prelate's house.

In the late 18C when Prince Marcantonio arranged for the gardens to be restored, the southwest façade (the present front entrance) was considered too ornate and stripped of some of its decoration and the steps were altered. Early this century the balustrade bounding the forecourt (but not the statues which were classed as works of art) was acquired by Lord Astor and removed to Cliveden.

Between 1801 and 1809 the Borghese collection was greatly depleted; Prince Camillo, Pauline Bonaparte's husband, sold over two hundred sculptures which went to swell the collection in the Louvre in Paris. In 1891 the paintings which had hung in the Borghese Palace *(p 166)* were moved to the *palazzina;* this led to the official distinction between the 'Borghese Museum' comprising the collection of sculpture on the ground floor and the 'Borghese Gallery' comprising the paintings on the first floor. Its silvan setting in the Borghese Gardens, its elegant late 18C décor and its outstanding collections make this museum-cum-gallery one of the most agreeable in Rome.

The **main hall** is decorated with antique statues (originals and copies), paintings and reliefs and provides a good idea of neo-Classical taste. The pieces of 3C mosaic, set into the floor, were discovered on a property belonging to the Borghese family near Tusculum.

Ground floor

Room 1. — The statue of **Pauline Bonaparte ★★★** as Venus by Canova dominates the room. Enthusiasm for the artist together with the celebrity of the model, the 'idol of high society', meant that the sculpture was accepted as a masterpiece.

Works by Bernini ★★★. — The artist was 21 when he sculpted **David** *(Room II)*. Whereas Michelangelo, working during the Renaissance, chose to present the calm and victorious hero, Bernini has captured the moment of most intense effort: the movement of the body in action and the facial expression make the statue a masterpiece of Baroque sculpture.

In his **Apollo and Daphne** *(Room III)* Bernini shows the metamorphosis of Daphne from nymph to laurel bush coinciding with Apollo's attempt to seize her and thus fulfils the intentions of Baroque art in an incomparably graceful composition.

The **Rape of Proserpina** *(Room IV)* is one of Bernini's youthful works, probably done in collaboration with his father, Pietro Bernini. Although the statue of Pluto, God of the Underworld, shows traces of the academic style, the supple modelling of Proserpina foreshadows Bernini's works of genius. The sumptuous room in which the sculpture is displayed is called the Emperors' Room owing to the 18 busts sculpted in porphyry and alabaster in 17C.

The group of **Aeneas carrying Anchises** *(Room VI)*, in which the figures are rather stiff with set expressions, was for a long time attributed to Bernini alone but his father's collaboration is now recognised. **Truth** is a fairly emphatic work which Bernini began in 1645; when he fell from grace on Innocent X's accession to the papal throne he intended to recommend himself with a representation of 'Truth being unveiled by Time'; the second statue was never executed.

(After photo by Gab. Fot. Naz., Rome)

Bernini: the Rape of Proserpina

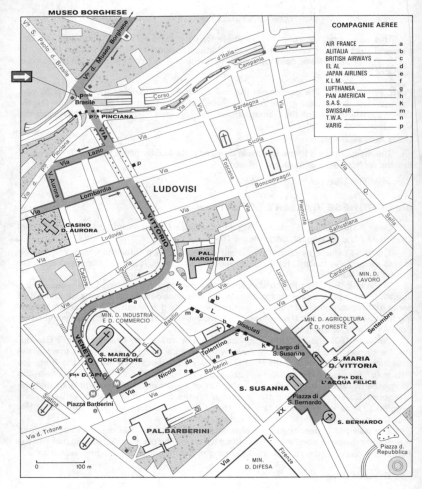

First floor

(Access to stairs in Room IV — plan p 177)

Room IX. — The Crucifixion with St Jerome and St Christopher (**1**) by **Pinturicchio** (1454-1513) reflects the artist's liking for miniatures which characterised the art of 15C Primitives. The portrait of a man (**2**) by **Raphael** (1483-1520), a work of admirable vigour, still shows signs of 15C art: full face presentation, indistinguishable background. The portrait of a Lady with a Unicorn (**3**), spoiled by being changed into a St Catherine but restored in 1935, is a fine example of the nobility of Raphael's art: the delicacy of the necklace and pendant.

The attribution of the Virgin and Child with St John and Angels (**4**) to **Botticelli** is disputed; the painting is thought to be too sentimental.

In the Virgin and Child with St Jean the Baptist (**5**) by **Lorenzo di Credi** (1459-1537) and in the Holy Family (**6**) by **Fra Bartolomeo** (1475-1527) the influence of Leonardo da Vinci and the Renaissance is quite marked: in the delicacy of the Virgin's expression in the one and in the indistinct outline of the background landscape in the other.

The **Deposition ★★★** (**7**) by **Raphael** was painted while the artist was in Florence before coming to Rome.

Room X. — In his painting of the Virgin and Child with St John the Baptist (**8**) **Andrea del Sarto** (1486-1531) was influenced by Michelangelo's drawing and by Leonardo da Vinci's *sfumato* technique. Venus (**9**) by **Lucas Cranach** (1472-1553) is one of the rare works by a northern artist in Cardinal Borghese's collection. The portrait of a man (**10**) by **Dürer** shows remarkable psychological insight.

Room XI. — The Holy Conversation (Virgin and Child and saints) (**11**) and the portrait of a man (**12**) are examples of the very varied work of the Venetian **Lorenzo Lotto** (c1480-1556).

The Holy Conversation (**13**) by **Palma the Elder** (1480-1528) is remarkable for its colours and for the keenly observed portrait of the pious devotee *(left)*.

In Tobias and the Angel (**14**) by **Girolamo Savoldo** (1480-1548) there are signs of Baroque painting in the powerful figures and the bold effects of light.

Room XIII. — The panels of the door are painted with attractive 18C landscapes. The **Crucifixion ★** (**15**) **in low relief** is a composition by Guglielmo della Porta, in wax on a slate base framed in ebony and precious stones.

Room XIV. — After the insipid Mannerist style, two currents brought about the transition to Baroque painting. In Bologna a style based on tradition developed round the Carraccis which **Domeni-chino** (1581-1641) helped to propagate; his painting of **Diana the huntress** ★★★ (16) demonstrates the Bologna expertise very well (the detail of the trees and the bird hit by arrows).

In contrast there was **Caravaggio** (1573-1610), who drew his inspiration from

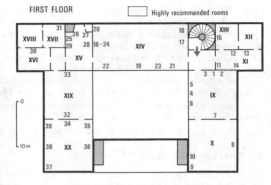

FIRST FLOOR   ☐ Highly recommended rooms

nature and boldly used the effect of light to reveal his figures; he began a veritable revolution in painting. The **Madonna dei Palafrenieri** ★★★ (17) — the Virgin and Child and St Anne — was intended for an altar in St Peter's Basilica but the realism of the three figures was too great: St Anne was compared by the art critic Bernard Berenson to a *ciociara*, i.e. a peasant woman from the hills between Rome and Cassino. Three other admirable works by Caravaggio are a sorrowful David showing Goliath's head (18), a sad St John the Baptist (19) and St Jerome (20).

This room also contains some fine **sculptures by Bernini:** two busts of Cardinal Scipione Borghese; the second (21) was executed because there was a vein in the marble in the first one (22) on the Cardinal's forehead. Young Jupiter with the goat Amalthea (23) was probably the artist's first work (c1615). Sixty years later in 1673 he made a terracotta model for an equestrian statue of Louis XIV (24) for Versailles; after all sorts of intrigues the commission went to Girardon; Bernini altered his statue to represent Marcus Curtius *(p 43).*

Room XV. — Bernini was not only a sculptor but also a brilliant painter: one of his portraits (25) is worthy of comparison with Velazquez; one of himself (26) and another of a man who has been recognised as his young brother (27) are worthy of attention.

The portrait of Monsignor Merlini (28) by **Andrea Sacchi** (1599-1661) shows a taste for sober nobility unusual in the Baroque period. The Deposition (29) by **Rubens** was executed early in 17C during the artist's visit to Rome.

Room XVI. — Most of the works are by **Jacopo Bassano** (1516-1592); he enjoyed painting country scenes and interiors which he used even in his religious works (the Last Supper — 30); he was a Venetian and used exceptional colour effects.

Room XVII. — Late Renaissance works including a painting of St Stephen Martyr (31) in the soft style of **Francesco Francia** (1450-1517).

Room XIX. — The outstanding painting here is **Danaë** ★★★ (32) by **Correggio** (c1489-1534) which illustrates the myth of Zeus visiting Danaë as a shower of gold. The use of oils has produced very subtle colour tones. Contemporary with Bassano and Correggio, **Dosso Dossi** (c1489-1542) demonstrates his great talent as a colorist in Circe the Sorceress (33).

Room XX. — The **Portrait of a man** ★★★ (34) by **Antonello de Messine** (1430-79), with its powerfully expressive look, its precision (garment folds) and the delicate modelling of the face, is a masterpiece. In the Virgin and Child (35) by the Venetian **Giovanni Bellini** (c1429-1516) the firm line of the figures is bathed in a beautiful luminosity. **Sacred and Profane Love** ★★★ (36) by **Titian** (c1490-1576) shows the young artist's search for an ideal of beauty. When he painted The Education of Love (37) at 88 his art had been utterly renewed. As well as Titian in 16C Venice there was **Veronese;** St John the Baptist preaching (38) and St Anthony of Padua preaching to the fish (39) (when the citizens of Rimini had refused to listen to him) demonstrate Veronese' attraction to the narrative picture.

Return to Porta Pinciana.

■ VIA VITTORIO VENETO ★★

This avenue which was opened after 1879 is named after a commune in the Veneto (Venetia) which took the name of King Victor Emmanuel II in 1866 and in 1918 was the site of a battle in which Italian troops were victorious against the Austro-Hungarians. The Via Veneto, as it is often called, runs through the heart of the beautiful **Ludovisi district,** which was divided into building lots in 1883 when Prince Ludovisi sold up his magnificent 17C property. Its luxury hotels, boutiques and elegant cafes have made it a meeting place for the smart set — rich tourists and those who like the sophisticated life. It is also the address of several ministries and the large international airlines.

Turn right into Via Lazio, left into Via Aurora and right again into Via Lombardia.

Aurora Casino ★. — *Open Sunday 9 to 11 am.* The Aurora Casino is the only extant building of the Ludovisi estate. Just as Cardinal Scipione Borghese, Paul V's nephew, had his casino decorated by Guido Reni *(p 156),* so Cardinal Ludovico Ludovisi, Gregory XV's nephew, invited Guercino to decorate his. Both artists, who were pupils of the Carracci, chose the subject of Aurora.

Return along Via Lombardia to Via Vittorio Veneto.

Palazzo Margherita. — Designed by G Koch in 1886, it was the residence of Margaret of Savoy, King Humbert I's wife; it is now the embassy of the United States of America.

Santa Maria della Concezione. — The church was built in 1624 in the austere style imposed by the Counter-Reformation. In the pavement at the entrance to the chancel lies the tomb stone of Cardinal Antonio Barberini, who founded the church, with the inscription *Hic jacet pulvis, cinis et nihil* (Here lies dust, ashes and nothing).

Below the church *(access on the right of the front steps)* there is a most unusual gallery curiously 'decorated' with the bones and skulls of Capucine friars.

Bees Fountain (Fontana delle Api). — This fountain was designed by Bernini (1644) using the bees of the Barberini coat of arms as the motif.

Turn left into Via San Nicola da Tolentino then right into Via Bissolati.

■ SANTA SUZANNA ★★

A Christian sanctuary was probably established here in 4C in the house of Pope Caius where St Suzanna was thought to have been martyred. Rebuilt by Leo III in 9C and restored at the end of 15C by Sixtus IV, the church assumed its present appearance in the late 16C.

Façade ★★★. — This beautifully proportioned masterpiece was designed by Carlo Maderna and finished in 1603. It is derived from the Counter-Reformation style typified by the façade of the Gesù Church *(p 109)* but the use of semi-engaged columns and the effect of perspective, created by recesses and pediments which relieve the austerity, give it an individual distinction.

The two storeys are harmoniously linked by the repetition of the two superimposed pediments and the elegant lateral scrolls.

Interior. — The decoration is typical of the Roman Mannerist style (late 15C): the walls of the nave are covered with paintings made to look like tapestries and executed by Baldassarre Croce (1558-1628); they illustrate the story of the biblical Suzanna. The scenes in the chancel depict the history of St Suzanna and of other martyrs whose relics are kept in the church; they were painted by Cesare Nebbia (1536-1614) and Paris Nogari (1558-1628). The wreathed columns framing the paintings in the nave were probably added in 17C after Bernini had designed the baldaquin in St Peter's (1624).

■ SANTA MARIA DELLA VITTORIA ★★

Carlo Maderna was commissioned to design the church in 1608. The original dedication was to St Paul but this was changed in 1622 to St Mary of the Victory after an image of the Virgin, whose miraculous intervention had delivered the battle of the White Mountain near Prague (1620) to the Catholics, had been carried to the church with great pomp.

Façade. — Although the façade was built some twenty years after that of Sta Suzanna, between 1624 and 1626, it is not so daring; with its flat pilasters in place of columns, it is closer to the Counter-Reformation style. It was designed by Giovanni Battista Soria for Cardinal Scipione Borghese.

Interior ★★★. — Maderno's plan is based on the Gesù Church; a nave, a broad shallow transept and a dome over the crossing. The simple lines of the design enhance the elegant decoration of the cornice; during 17C a very rich Baroque décor was applied throughout; the vault, originally white and coffered, and the dome were painted with *trompe-l'œil* frescoes of the Virgin triumphing against heresy and entering into heaven; the walls were faced with multicoloured marble, their warm tones mingling with the gilded stucco and the white cherubs. The decoration of the organ is by one of Bernini's pupils.

The apse was entirely rebuilt after being destroyed in 1833 by a fire in which the sacred image of the Virgin also disappeared.

The Baroque decoration culminates in the Cornaro Chapel *(left transept)* which was designed by Bernini in 1652 like a theatre décor: eight members of the Cornaro family, as if in boxes at the theatre, gaze at the **Ecstasy of St Theresa of Avila ★★★**. Marble has never been made to look so supple nor to express so accurately the texture of rough cloth (the Carmelite habit), of light veiling (the angel's garment) and the delicacy of human flesh. This presentation of divine love must be appreciated in conjunction with St Theresa's own description of her ecstasy when God sent his Seraph to pierce her heart with an arrow: "The pain was so sharp that I cried aloud but at the same time I experienced such delight that I wished it would last for ever".

The chapel in the right transept was created late in 17C to complement the Cornaro Chapel.

The paintings in the chapels include the life of St Francis by Domenichino *(second chapel on the right)* and the Trinity by Guercino *(third chapel on the left)*.

Acqua Felice Fountain. — This huge fountain was designed in 1587 by Domenico Fontana. It is supplied by an aqueduct built by Sixtus V from near Colonna on the Via Casilina and bears the Pope's Christian name: Felice Peretti.

It is dominated by the colossal statue of Moses; it was sculpted by Prospero Bresciano who was no doubt inspired by Michelangelo's Moses *(p 132)*; his disappointment was so great when he saw the finished work that he died.

San Bernardo alle Terme. — St Bernard's Church was created late in 16C in a rotonda, formerly the southwest corner of Diocletian's baths *(plan p 118)*. The handsome coffered dome, similar to the one in the Pantheon, lends dignity to the interior.

Distance: 2.5 km — 1 1/2 mile. Time: about 4 1/2 hours. Start: Piazza di Porta Capena.

This walk is centred on the Old Appian Way which, between the Porta Capena and the Porta San Sebastiano, is called Via delle Terme di Caracalla and Via di Porta San Sebastiano. The road is pleasantly shaded by trees and bordered by parks and gardens which lend a rural touch.

The **Porta Capena** is a gate in the defensive wall built by Servius Tullius in 6C BC which was rebuilt at the end of 4C BC after its weakness had been made apparent by the invading Gauls. It was here, according to Livy, that in the reign of Tullus Hostilius (672-40 BC) the last of the Horatii, who had defeated the Curiatii of Alba, slew his sister with his sword because she had dared to weep for her fiancé, one of the Curiatii; ''Let that be the fate of any Roman who mourns the enemy'' *(p 212).*

An **obelisk,** brought back from Axum, a religious town in Ethiopia, in 1937, marks the beginning of the Via delle Terme di Caracalla, which is flanked by umbrella pines and flowering laurels.

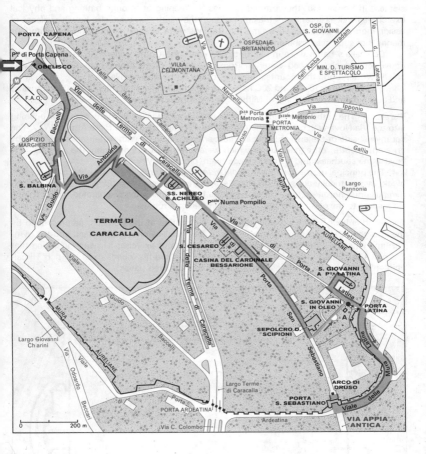

Follow Via delle Terme di Caracalla and then turn right into Viale Guido Baccelli.

On the right stands the building of the F A O (Food and Agriculture Organisation), an agency of the United Nations, which employs over 3 000 people of all nationalities. It studies food production, control of plant and animal diseases and experimentation with new strains.

Santa Balbina. — *Usual entrance by the northwest door via the courtyard of the Ospizio Santa Margherita.*

In 1927 the church underwent a thorough restoration which returned it to its mediaeval simplicity. It was probably a 4C house converted to a place of worship. A pitched roof covers a single nave punctuated by recessed chapels and lit by high barred windows.

On the right of the entrance is Cardinal Surdi's **tomb ★,** bearing a recumbent Gothic figure and decorated with multicoloured marble inlay in the Cosmati style (1295).

In the fourth chapel on the right the low relief showing Mary and John the Baptist standing by the Cross is a fine sculpture by Mino del Reame (15C); it came from the mediaeval church of St Peter in the Vatican.

The third chapel contains the remains of some 13C frescoes.

The *Schola contorum* where the choristers stood has been reconstructed in front of the high altar.

Behind the high altar is the **episcopal chair ★,** a fine piece of Cosmati work (13C). The frescoes in the apse are 17C.

Turn left into Via Antonina, then right.

Baths of Caracalla ★. — *Open 9 am to one hour before sunset (1 pm Sunday). Closed 1 January, 25 April, 1 May, 1st Sunday in June, 15 August, Christmas. 2 000 L.*

Four sets of baths had already been built — by Agripppa, by Nero on the Campus Martius, by Titus near the Golden House and by Trajan on the Aventine — when the Emperor Antoninus Caracalla began the largest baths (212 AD) that Rome had ever seen; they covered over 11 hectares - 25 acres; only Diocletian's baths were more extensive *(p 117).* They were finished by Elagabalus and Alexander Severus (222-35 AD), the last two emperors of the Severan dynasty.

The sober exterior concealed a contrastingly rich interior: floors paved with marble and mosaic, walls covered with mosaic and gilded stucco work; the white marble capitals and cornices contrasting with the multicoloured marble, porphyry and granite of the columns. The huge building, with its massive walls and bold vaulting rising to 30 m - 98 ft, was much admired; it offered facilities for 1 600 bathers. The Romans used the baths daily, early in the afternoon at the end of a day's work. The poorest people were not excluded, although they had fewer slaves than the rich to assist them with their ablutions. Baths were an important element in Roman life; they offered facilities for keeping fit through bathing and physical exercise as well as libraries for the cultivation of the mind; they were also however places of assignation and by Caracalla's time the Romans were already denouncing the notorious manners of such establishments.

Caracalla's baths were in use until 537 when the Goths under Witigis damaged the aqueducts which supplied water to Rome. Shelley's poem Prometheus Unbound "was chiefly written upon the mountainous ruins of the Baths of Caracalla".

Excavations in 16, 19 and 20C have uncovered magnificent statues, vases and mosaics and also a *mithraeum* (temple of Mithras) in the northeast corner.

The plan. — The baths consisted of a central block enclosed by a wall with gateways opening into the Via Nova which runs at the foot of the Aventine parallel with the Appian Way. The southwest side of the enclosure was almost entirely taken up with water tanks screened by an amphitheatre, on either side of which were two pavilions containing the libraries. The bays in the southeast and northwest sides were probably gymnasiums.

The principal rooms *(caldarium, tepidarium, frigidarium)* were at the heart of the central block; symmetrically arranged on either side were the secondary rooms (changing rooms, gymnasiums, hot air baths). On entering the building the bathers separated, some to one side, some to the other, only to meet again in the main rooms.

Tour. — It is best, where possible, to follow the routine of the Romans, as prescribed by their doctors. The changing rooms (traces of fine mosaics on the floor) lead into the gymnasiums where the bathers indulged in various forms of exercise; it is such a setting that Petronius described in his *Satyricon* when Encolpius and his friends meet the rich Trimalchio, a 'bald old man… who played ball with his long haired slaves…'.

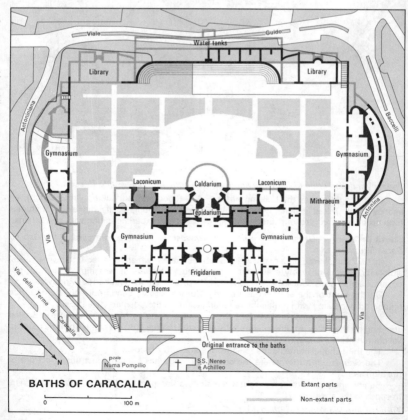

BATHS OF CARACALLA

0   100 m

━━━ Extant parts

▬▬▬ Non-extant parts

Perspiring after the exercise, the bather went on into an oval room heated to a very high temperature *(laconicum)*; the dry heat induced greater perspiration. The heating system was very efficient; hot air from huge stoves in the basement circulated beneath the floors, which were supported on little brick pillars, and spread into ducts in the walls.

Next the bather passed into the *caldarium* for a very hot bath after which he scraped his skin to remove all impurities. The *caldarium* was a huge circular room, 34 m - 112 ft across, covered by a dome; some of the supporting pillars can still be seen. *(In summer operas are staged among the ruins of the caldarium)*. Bathers from both sides of the building met in the *caldarium*. From here they went on into the *tepidarium* for a cooler bath before plunging into the bracing water of the cold bath *(frigidarium)*.

A variety of archaeological fragments has been uncovered in these rooms, particularly some fine mosaics from the northeast gymnasium.

After bathing Trimalchio, who followed the latest fashion, went off in his litter to carouse. Less wealthy or more serious Romans stayed to talk to their friends, to walk in the gardens or to read in the libraries until the baths closed. The following day they would all be back again.

Santi Nereo ed Achilleo. — There was a little church here in 4C called *Titulus Fasciolae*. Its presence on this site is explained by the legend of the bandage *(fasciola)* which had been bound round St Peter's leg to cover the sores caused by the chains which had held him in the Mamertine prison *(p 39)*; when Peter fled from Rome in fear of the fate which awaited him there, the bandage fell from his leg on this spot which was venerated as a place of worship. A little further on along the Appian Way came St Peter's meeting with Christ and his question "Domine, quo vadis?" *(p 143)*.

The church was completely rebuilt by Leo III (795-816) and later restored by Sixtus IV (1471-84). In 1596 the incumbent appointed to the church was Clement VIII's confessor, Cardinal Baronius, who had a great devotion to St Nereus and St Achilleus. He had their relics transferred from Domitilla's Catacombs *(p 145)* and converted the church into a handsome sanctuary for them. He retained the basilical plan, with its pitched roof and the octagonal pillars dating from the 15C restoration which divided the nave and aisles. He transferred the high altar from the crypt of St Paul Without the Walls, decorated it with Cosmati work and crowned it with an attractive baldaquin.

The lefthand reading desk *(ambo)* stands on a porphyry base which came from the Baths of Caracalla. Baronius commissioned Pomarancio to paint the walls but the mosaic on the chancel arch dates from the reign of Leo III and shows Byzantine influence. The mosaic has been much restored and is eclipsed by the painting in the apse. On the back of the bishop's throne, which is adorned with beautiful mediaeval lions, Baronius had engraved a passage from the sermon given by St Gregory over the martyrs' tomb.

Cross Piazzale Numa Pompilio and take Via di Porta San Sebastiano.

San Cesareo. — *To visit apply to the Sacristan at no 4.*
Little is known of the church's history before 1600 when Clement VIII entrusted its restoration to Cardinal Baronius. The latter followed contemporary taste in the coffered ceiling bearing the arms of Clement VIII and in the paintings by Cavaliere d'Arpino on the upper walls of the nave. Elsewhere he tried to reproduce the decoration of a mediaeval church: the marble facing on the chancel screen, the pulpit, the altar and the bishop's throne were composed of rich Cosmati fragments; the apse and chancel arch are decorated with mosaics from drawings by Cavaliere d'Arpino.

There is some Renaissance work: the two angels drawing back the curtains before the confessio *(below the altar)* and the pretty little fresco of the Madonna and Child *(above the throne)*.

Beneath the church is the floor of a 2C bath house *(apply to the Sacristan)* paved with a marine mosaic in black and white.

Cardinal Bessarion's House ★. — *Open 9 am to 1 pm and 3 to 6 pm; 10 am to 4 pm in winter; 9 am to 1 pm on Sundays. Closed Monday and holidays. 500 L.*
This handsome house, surrounded by gardens and furnished with fine Renaissance pieces, belonged to Cardinal John Bessarion, the humanist scholar *(c1402-72)*. In 1439 he attended the Council of Florence and was one of the authors of the union between the Greek and Roman churches. Pope Nicholas V, who started the Vatican library, invited him to translate Aristotle.

Scipio Tomb ★ (Sepolcro degli Scipioni). — *9 Via di Porta San Sebastiano. Open 9 am to 2 pm (1 pm Sundays); also 4 to 7 pm Tuesdays, Thursdays and Saturdays from 1 April to 30 September. Closed Mondays, 1 January, 21 April, Easter, 1 May, 15 August, Christmas and Polling Days. 500 L.*
Before the construction of the Aurelianic Wall (Mura Aureliane) this site was beyond the town boundary and could therefore, according to Roman custom, be used as a burial ground.

The Scipios belonged to one of the greatest patrician families which died out at the end of the Republic. As members of the Cornelia clan *(gens)* the men all bore the name Cornelius Scipio, preceded by their own individual name (often abbreviated to an initial letter) and sometimes followed by a nickname.

The Scipio family tomb was discovered in 1614 and restored in 1926. The funeral inscriptions constitute a remarkable document on the Republican period and on the infancy of Latin literature. Their concentration on the dead man's public spiritedness and his moral rectitude reveal the mentality of those days when Roman civilisation was being forged.

The tomb is hollowed out of a low hill. It consists of passages roughly arranged in a square. The sarcophagi, carved in a single block of stone or composed of separate panels assembled together, are placed in the passages or in recesses made in the walls. The tomb was probably full by the middle of the 2C BC so that an annexe *(to the right of the original square)* was excavated. It was at this period that the entrance façade was constructed in the northwest corner.

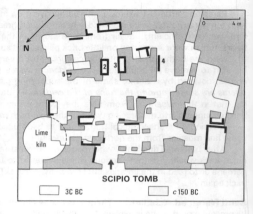

SCIPIO TOMB

☐ 3C BC   ☐ *c* 150 BC

Tour. — The first person to be buried here was L Cornelius Scipio Barbatus; Consul in 298 BC he fought against the Etruscans. His sarcophagus (1) — the original is in the Vatican museum *(p 83)* — bears a description of his exploits.

Of his son's sarcophagus (2), only a few fragments and the inscription remain.

Opposite is a fine inscription (3) dedicated to a young man of the Scipio family who died at the age of 20; his courage made up for his lack of years.

In the next passage, lay Scipio Africanus' son, P Cornelius Scipio (4); as Augur in 190 BC he interpreted the auspices; he was also a priest of Jupiter *(Flamen Dialis)*, one of the highest religious offices. In all about thirty people were buried in the tomb.

The inscription (5) to be found in a small recess in the later part of the tomb refers to the burial of a member of the Cornelius Lentulus family which inherited the tomb during the Empire and buried some of its dead there.

In the northwest corner of the tomb a lime kiln was constructed in the Middle Ages for converting marble fragments into chalk.

Colombarium. — *Below ground in front of the Scipio tomb.* The colombarium was a type of communal tomb which became popular at the beginning of the Empire. It consisted of a chamber fitted with rows of recesses in which the cinerary urns were placed. The wealthy families built them for the ashes of their slaves and freedmen.

Nearby are the remains of a three-storey house which was built in 3C on top of the Scipio tomb without regard for the site's venerable connections.

Pomponius Hylas' Columbarium (A). — *Guided tour; apply to the Keeper of the Scipio tomb. 500 L.*

Part way down the ancient stair which leads into the chamber is a recess decorated with a mosaic which contained the urns of one C Pomponius Hylas and his wife. The *columbarium* itself is decorated with stucco work and fine paintings and probably dates from the Julio-Claudian period (31-68 AD).

Oratory of San Giovanni in Oleo. — This small octagonal building was built in the Renaissance style in 1509 by Benoit Adam, a Frenchman and member of the Rota (Roman Catholic ecclesiastical court); over the door he placed his arms and his motto ''Au plaisir de Dieu'' (at God's pleasure). The oratory commemorates an event in the martyrdom of St John the Evangelist, which took place during the reign of Domitian; St John was supposed to have emerged unscathed from a cauldron of boiling oil.

St John at the Latin Gate (San Giovanni a Porta Latina). — This charming site ★ is created by the church and its campanile framing the peaceful forecourt with its well in the shade of a cedar tree.

The beautifully simple interior is decorated with 12C frescoes; although much damaged, they are a fine example of Romanesque painting.

Latin Gate (Porta Latina). — This gate in the Aurelianic Wall (Mura Aureliane) was restored by Honorius (5C) and again by Belisarius (6C). The key stone bears a Greek cross on the town side and the Chi Rho on the outside.

Turn right outside the gate into Viale delle Mura Latine which skirts the city wall.

St Sebastian's Gate ★ (Porta San Sebastiano). — This is without doubt the most spectacular of the gates of Rome with its base of tall marble blocks supporting crenelated towers. It is the ancient Porta Appia which Aurelian (271-175 BC) constructed when he built his defensive wall; it has been strengthened several times particularly by the Emperor Honorius who carried out fortifying work along the full length of the wall between 401 and 402 in the face of invasion by the Goths.

Arch of Drusus. — This arch was not raised in honour of Drusus (39-8 BC), the younger brother of the Emperor Tiberius, but dates from 2C AD. Caracalla (211-17 AD) used it to support the aqueduct which carried water to his baths.

*The **Maps** **Red Guides** and **Green Guides** are complementary publications.*
Use them together.

Access: *By bus or underground — consult a transport plan (see p 30); By car — take Via Cristoforo Colombo, see plan in the Michelin Red Guide Italia (hotels and restaurants).*
Time: *allow about 3 1/2 hours.*

The three letters E U R, which stand for *Esposizione Universale di Rome,* are the name of a new district to the south of Rome.

Its origins go back to 1937 when the Government conceived a grandiose project for a universal exhibition to be held in 1942 (the district was also called E42). It was to be the first step in the expansion of Rome along the motorway built in 1928 to link Rome and Ostia.

The contract was given to the architect Marcello Piacentini. The first buildings began to go up in 1939 but on 10 June of the following year Italy entered the war on the side of the Germans and in 1941 work stopped. The bombing of Rome on 19 July 1943 and the fall of the Fascist government meant the abandonment of the scheme.

Two events — Holy Year in 1950 and the Olympic Games in 1960 — brought it to the fore once again: in 1950 the Via Cristoforo Colombo was opened linking Rome and the E U R. The underground, which runs from Statione Termini to the new district in less than a quarter of an hour, stimulated the building of an administrative and cultural centre, a business forum and residential accommodation.

The **Sports Palace,** by Marcello Piacentini and Pier Luigi Nervi, and the cycle race track were built for the Olympic Games.

Inspired by an obsession with size, the colossal white buildings of the actual E U R mean that it looks very much like the scheme proposed by the Fascists.

There are several museums in the E U R; apart from the Museum of Roman Civilisation *(p 184),* it is worth mentioning the **Luigi Pigorini Museum** of Ethnography and Prehistory *(open 9 am to 2 pm (1 pm Sundays and holidays); also Saturdays 2 to 6.30 pm only; closed Mondays, 1 January, 25 April, Easter, 1 May, 1st Sunday in June, 15 August, Christmas; 1 000 L)* and the **Museo dell' Alto Medioevo** (Mediaeval Museum) which contains exhibits covering the 5 to 11C as well as plans of Classical and Christian Rome *(open 9 am to 2 pm (1 pm Sundays and holidays); closed Mondays and in August; 1 000 L.*

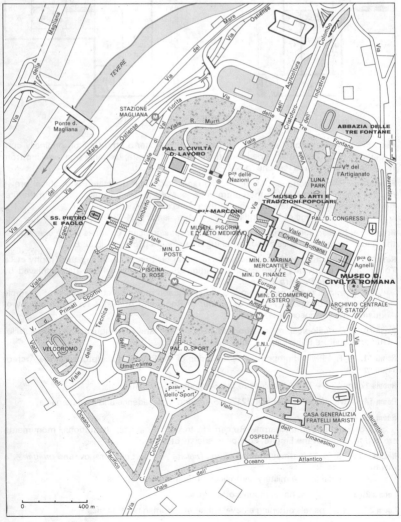

■ MUSEUM OF ROMAN CIVILIZATION ★★ (Museo della Civiltà Romana)

Open 9 am to 2 pm; Tuesdays and Thursdays also 5 to 8 pm (3.30 to 6.30 pm from 1 November to 30 April). Closed Mondays, 1 January, Easter, 21 April, 1 May, 2 and 29 June, 15 August, Christmas. 1 000 L.

This huge museum is housed in two buildings linked by a portico and illustrates, by means of reproductions, the history of ancient Rome from the origins of the city to the end of the Empire. It traces the development of a peasant people who founded an empire which has influenced the history of the whole world for more than a thousand years.

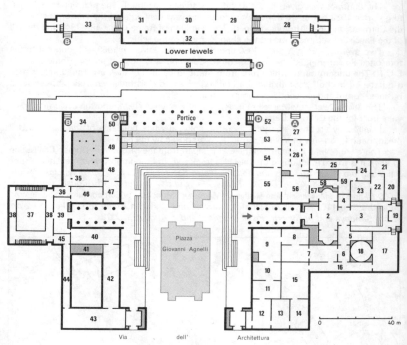

MUSEUM OF ROMAN CIVILIZATION

Room 5. — Origins: model of a temple dedicated to Jupiter on the Capitol, originally constructed in 6C BC and maintained until the end of the Empire; example of a dwelling from Romulus' village on the Palatine *(p 50)*.

Room 7. — Roman conquest of the Mediterranean: column decorated with ships' prows *(rostra)* which was erected in the Forum in honour of the Consul Duilius; he won the first Roman naval victory by defeating the Carthaginians at Mylae in 260 BC.

Model of the siege of Numantia by Scipio Aemilianus (134-33 BC).

Room 8. — Caesar: reconstructions of the two most significant episodes in the war against the Gauls: the siege of Alesia and the taking of Avaricum (Bourges) in 52 BC.

Room 9. — Augustus: several monuments raised in his honour including the Trophy at La Turbie in the south of France commemorating the union of Gaul and Italy achieved by Augustus, the Ara Pacis *(p 167)* etc.

The entrance to the next room is a reconstruction of the porch *(pronaos)* of a temple built by the inhabitants of Ankara in honour of Rome and Augustus on which a copy of Augustus' will was inscribed *(p 168)*.

Room 10. — Genealogical tree and portrait gallery of the family of Augustus and of the Julio-Claudian emperors (Tiberius, Caligula, Claudius, Nero).

Room 11. — The Flavian emperors: reproduction of the low relief sculptures on the Arch of Titus *(p 46)*.

Rooms 12 and 13. — The Antonines to the Severans (96-235 AD).

Room 14. — Macrinus to Justinian (217-565): period of decadence and megalomania.

Room 15. — Christianity.

Subsequent rooms illustrate Roman life in all its aspects: institutions, monuments erected throughout the Empire, economy, society etc.

Rooms 16 to 19. — The army: engines of war *(balista* — a sort of crossbow and *onager* — a mechanical catapult).

Reconstruction of a military camp accommodating two legions.

Rooms 20 and 21. — The navy: models of war galleys.

Room 22. — Two panels outlining a naval career and Roman naval tactics.

Room 25. — Reconstruction of a triumph: the victorious general, robed like Jupiter and riding in a chariot, proceeding to the Capitol, accompanied by his soldiers and his booty.

Rooms 26 and 27. — The major monuments in the imperial provinces and in Italy which Augustus divided into 11 regions.

Rooms 28 to 33 display models of the major building and construction works.

Room 29. — Architecture of baths, aqueducts, nymphaea and cisterns.

Room 30. — Leisure: theatres, amphitheatres, circuses, gymnasia.

Room 31. — Public life: the forum, temples, basilicas.

Room 32. — Several large scale exhibits: the amphitheatre in Nîmes, Domitian's stadium (now the Piazza Navona, *p 163*), the acropolis at Baalbek etc.

Room 33. — Roads and means of communication.

Room 37. — Huge model ★★ of Rome at the time of Constantine (306-37) constructed by the architect Italo Gismondi in 1937 on the scale 1/250.

Room 40. — Housing: from imperial palaces (built by Hadrian at Tivoli and by Diocletian in Split) to private houses and flats.

Room 43. — Religion: from the early days of Rome's existence to the introduction of oriental cults.

Reconstruction of part of a temple in Rome and of a temple to Augustus in Athens. Reconstruction of a Roman calendar.

Room 46. — Law: legislative texts (the Twelve Tables published in 451 BC containing the principles of law, knowledge of which was a patrician privilege).

Room 47. — Reconstruction of a small library.

Rooms 48 to 50. — Music, literature, science and medecine.

Room 51. — Reconstruction of the low relief sculpture from Trajan's Column *(p 130)*.

Room 59. — Reconstruction of several low relief sculptures from Marcus Aurelius' Column *(p 164)*.

■ ADDITIONAL SIGHTS

Folk Museum (Museo delle Arti e Tradizioni Popolari). — *Closed for restoration.*

The museum is in the **Piazza Marconi** where a huge obelisk in marble (sculpture finished in 1950) has been raised to the glory of the Italian physician Guglielmo Marconi (1874-1937), inventor of wireless telegraphy.

The museum records the folklore and daily life of the regions of Italy.

Palazzo della Civiltà del Lavoro ★. — The building which is one of the most characteristic of the E U R was designed in 1938 by three architects: Guerrini, La Padula and Romano. Devoid of capital or cornice to delight the eye, its stark mass is accentuated by the rows of superimposed arches.

The ground floor arcade contains allegorical statues representing the various arts, symbols of the grandeur of Rome. The building houses several organisations connected with the improvement of working conditions.

Sts Peter and Paul ★ (SS. Petro e Paolo). — This spectacular travertine church was built between 1937 and 1941 on the highest point in the E U R. Set among shrubs and flowers its white mass dominates the whole district. The principal architect was Arnaldo Foschini. At the top of the steps stand two large statues of St Peter and St Paul. The Greek cross plan is stressed by the clean angles and sober lines. The dome, covered in little tiles overlapping like fish scales, rests on a drum pierced by oculi.

The main door, designed by Giovanni Prini (1877-1958), is made of bronze, ornamented with low reliefs illustrating the lives of St Peter and St Paul.

From the surrounding terrace, flanked by two porticos, there is a view of the suburbs of Rome.

To appreciate the full charm of Rome you must be willing to walk.

Twenty eight centuries of history and art are not revealed without some mental and physical effort: identifying the different styles which have intermingled over the years taxes the mind; tireless feet are indispensable as the only means of acquiring an intimate knowledge of "the most beautiful city in the world", even though it is very often accompanied by the bustle and noise of a modern capital aggravated by the inhabitants' passion for the motor car.

Distance: 2 km — 1 mile. Time: about 3 hours. Start: Piazza Sonnino.

Trastevere (from *trans Tiberim* meaning over the Tiber) was not originally part of Rome; it was the beginning of Etruscan country.

From the time of the Republic it was inhabited mainly by Jews and Syrians and was incorporated into Rome by Augustus as the fourteenth administrative district. Not far from the present San Cosimato hospital, Augustus created a naumachy, a vast pool where naval warfare spectacles were mounted; there were temples dotted here and there but Trastevere was above all a popular district inhabited by artisans and small traders attracted by the proximity of the docks to the south of Tiber Island.

Few public buildings were situated here but rather utilitarian services such as a 2C fire station near the Via dei Genovesi of which traces were discovered in 19C. Among the religious buildings is a Syrian sanctuary, traces of which were found under the Villa Sciarra near the Via Emilio Dandolo.

The whole of Trastevere was enclosed in 3C by a section of the Aurelianic wall (Mura Aureliane) in which were three gates: the Porta Settimiana to the north, the Porta Aurelia (now Porta S. Pancrazio) *(plan p 190)* to the west and to the south the Porta Portuensis (further south than the present Porta Portese).

In the Middle Ages however some powerful Roman families had palaces in Trastevere and the tradition persisted under the Renaissance *(p 191)* and into 18C *(p 190)*.

Trastevere has never lost its popular character. Throughout the centuries the inhabitants have kept their reputation of stout fellows ready to lend their strength and courage to a revolutionary cause. The district has sometimes been decried but Stendhal thought it superb; it was, he said, "full of energy".

Poets who celebrated Rome in the local dialect have always found a response there. The exploits of the Trasteverians, who defied the inhabitants of the St Mary Major district with catapults, have been the subject of several sonnets in Roman folklore. Even nowadays the cafés of Trastevere re-enact the comic efforts of Meo Patacca in his dogged defence of his district against Marco Pepe.

All along the noisy Viale di Trastevere, the side streets are packed with stalls and costers' barrows beneath the benign watch of madonnas lit up by small lanterns.

On summer evenings the quiet squares are transformed into happy family groups eating out in the open air: a charming aspect of the Roman way of life.

On Sundays the Porta Portese and the neighbouring streets become a huge flea market where the pickpockets have a field day; even if one does not pick up a great bargain, it is well worth going to see the spectacle.

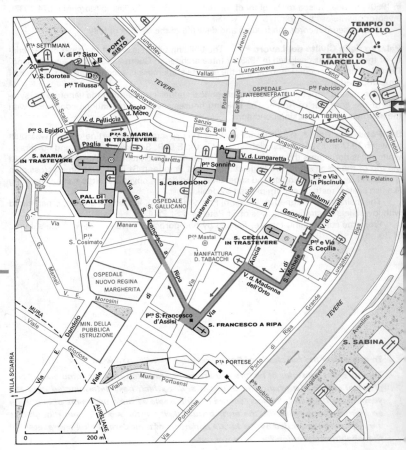

TOUR

Anguillara Tower (A). — The 13C tower, flanking a small palace of the same name, recalls one of the most powerful Roman families; as warlords or magistrates, outlaws and forgers or clerics, the Anguillara were at the forefront of events from the Middle Ages to the Renaissance.

The palace, built in 15C and restored in 19C, is now used for the study of Dante.

San Crisogono. — The Church of St Chrysogonus, which was started in 5C, bears witness to the many people who have tended it over the centuries.

The **belfry,** which was erected when the church was almost entirely rebuilt in 12C, was altered in 16C by the addition of a spire. The **east front** is the work of Giovanni Battista Soria who was commissioned by Cardinal Scipione Borghese, the incumbent in 17C, to bring the mediaeval building up to date.

Interior ★. — Only the basilical plan of a nave and two ailes has survived from 12C; the floor is 13C work by Roman marble masons. The overall effect — half Mannerist, half Baroque — was acquired in 17C from G B Soria who retained the ancient pillars refashioning their capitals in stucco, opened up great windows in the nave to let in more light and installed a fine coffered ceiling of complex design, showing the arms of Cardinal Borghese. Two monolithic porphyry columns support the chancel arch.

The baldaquin over the high altar is also the work of Soria.

The fine wood carving in the chancel dates from 1863.

The mosaic in the apse, showing the Virgin and Child with St James and St Chrysogonus, comes from the Cavallini school (late 13C).

Underground church. — *Access down awkward iron steps. Apply to the Sacristan.*

6 m - 20 ft below floor level archaeologists have discovered traces of the 5C building which was altered by Gregory III in 8C and then abandoned in 12C when the present church was built.

Here is the lower part of the apse (probably partially 5C) below which Gregory III hollowed out a confessio in 8C; it is similar in design to the confessio in St Peter's in the Vatican (6C) and follows the curve of the apse before drawing in on each side into a horse shoe shape, thus creating a semicircular corridor; it is divided in two by a straight passage at the end of which (towards the nave) is a relic chamber. The apse still bears traces of 8C paintings as does the straight passage in the confessio. There are 10C paintings on the walls of the semicircular corridor.

From Piazza Sonnino, take Via della Lungaretta as far as Piazza in Piscinula; then take Via dei Salumi and Via dei Vascellari to reach Piazza Santa Cecilia.

St Cecilia in Trastevere ★ (Santa Cecilia in Trastevere). — A sanctuary dedicated to St Cecilia existed in a private house on this site in 5C. Pope Pascal I (817-24) replaced it with a church which was much altered in 16, 18 and 19C.

The church is preceded by a courtyard planted with flowerbeds round a large antique tank. A fine 12C campanile flanks the façade which was remodelled in 18C but the 12C porch with its ancient columns and mosaic frieze was preserved.

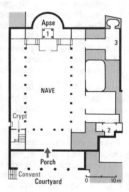

The interior has lost its overall mediaeval appearance although it still retains the **mosaic** with which the apse was adorned by Pascal I in 9C: the Byzantine influence absorbed by Roman workers in mosaic in earlier centuries is evident in the way the figures are presented: on Christ's right — St Paul, St Agatha and Pascal I with a blue halo since he was still alive; on the left — St Peter, St Valerian and St Cecilia; the lively postures and the beautiful colours are also typically Roman.

The **baldaquin (1)** over the high altar is by Arnolfo di Cambio (1293); it is eight years later than a similar work by the same artist for St Paul Without the Walls *(p 140)* and shows a growing heaviness of style and the influence of Classical works; in the left back corner is an equestrian statue of a saint reminiscent of the statue of Marcus Aurelius in the Piazza del Campidoglio.

St Cecilia's Statue ★. — *Below the altar.* This fine sculpture by Stefano Maderno (1599) recalls the history and legend of St Cecilia. Pascal I (817-24) who was desperately searching all the Christian cemeteries for the remains of St Cecilia, was guided by a dream. He found the saint's corpse lying beside her husband St Valerian in a catacomb on the Old Appian Way *(p 145).* He had them transferred immediately to a place beneath the altar. Seven centuries later, during the reign of Clement VIII, Cardinal Sfondrati undertook alterations to the chancel; during the work the sarcophagi came to light and St Cecilia's body was discovered in the posture in which Maderna has represented it.

The Cardinal also wanted to restore the little room (2) venerated as the site of St Cecilia's martyrdom. This work disclosed several pipes against the wall which were identified as belonging to the steam bath in which Cecilia was condemned to suffocate; she was saved by a miraculous dew only to be beheaded so inefficiently that she lingered in agony for three days.

The Cardinal commissioned Guido Reni to paint the Decapitation of the Saint; the picture stands on the altar.

Cardinal Rampolla's Tomb (3). — This dramatic exercise in perspective (1929) commemorates the Cardinal whose generosity made it possible to open up the crypt.

Crypt. — *Open 9 am to 12 noon and 4 to 7 pm (6 pm from mid-September to May). 1 000 L.*
The crypt was created from 1899 to 1901 in the Byzantine style. The excavations uncovered the remains of several ancient houses among which was the first sanctuary dedicated to St Cecilia. Also visible are a room containing 7 grain silos and another in which are exhibited sarcophagi and inscriptions: a low relief representing Minerva (2C BC) in a little recess and a column also from the Republican period.

Behind the grating in the confessio *(beneath the apse)* are several sarcophagi including those of St Cecilia and St Valerian.

The Last Judgment by Pietro Cavallini ★★★. — *Open Sunday 12 noon. Closed in August. Ring the bell of the Benedictine Convent in the courtyard.*
This masterpiece of Roman mediaeval painting by Pietro Cavallini (*c*1293) was formerly on the inside wall of the façade of the church but was badly damaged in 16C. All that remains is the figure of Christ in judgment surrounded by angels with magnificent outspread wings, flanked by Mary and John the Baptist, hands raised beseechingly; below are the Apostles and angels blowing trumpets.

Note the perfect distribution of light and shade, the individual expression on each face and the subtle harmony of the colours.

Take Via di San Michele, turn right into Via della Madonna dell'Orto, then left into Via Anicia, as far as Piazza S. Francesco d'Assisi.

San Francesco a Ripa. — The Church of St Francis was rebuilt in 1682 to replace the earlier church of the Franciscan order. The fourth chapel in the lefthand aisle contains a **statue of Blessed Ludovica Albertoni ★★** by Bernini; she was a member of the Franciscan Tertiaries (1474-1533) and is buried beneath the altar. Bernini shows her suffering and in this, one of his later works (1674), the marble perfectly expresses the final agony of a saintly life.

Take Via di S. Francesco a Ripa to reach Piazza Santa Maria in Trastevere.

The **Piazza Santa Maria in Trastevere ★** is probably the most charming corner of Trastevere and full of local colour. The fountain at the centre was remodelled by Bernini in 1659.

On the left is the fine 17C façade of the **Palazzo di San Callisto.**

Basilica of St Mary in Trastevere ★. — On this spot in 38 BC a fountain of oil, *fons olei*, flowed for a whole day. Christians later interpreted this miracle as a sign of the grace which Christ would spread throughout the world. Pope Calixtus (217-22) built the first sanctuary but it was the energetic Julius I (337-52) who constructed a proper basilica. The building was altered in 9C by Gregory IV to provide a crypt in which he laid the saintly remains of Calixtus, Pope Cornelius and Calepodius.

The present basilica dates from 12C; it was built about 1140 during a brief period of calm in the troubled reign of Innocent II who was beset by the anti popes, Anacletus II and Victor IV. Despite St Bernard's assistance, when Innocent II died, Rome was in the hands of revolutionaries who had proclaimed a republic. His successors restored and embellished the church on many occasions right up to 19C.

Façade. — The belfry is 12C; a small recess at the top is decorated with a mosaic of the Virgin and Child to whom the basilica is dedicated. The Virgin and Child are also celebrated in the mosaic on the façade (12-13C) which shows a procession of women approaching from both sides.

The statues of the saints on the balustrade over the porch were erected from 17 to 18C. The re-opening of the three windows in the façade and the addition of the paintings took place under Pius IX in 19C.

The porch, which was restored early in 18C, shelters several fragments, some from the buildings which preceded the present one. Two 15C frescoes (1) (one rather damaged) depict the Annunciation. The door frames are made of friezes dating from the time of the Empire.

Interior. — The basilical plan of Pope Innocent II's 12C church is still visible. As in all mediaeval Roman buildings, the columns dividing the nave from the aisles were taken from ancient monuments; all are crowned with their Classical capitals in either the Ionic or the Corinthian orders; the figures of some Egyptian divinities were removed in 19C by Pope Pius IX.

The cornice is composed of an assortment of ancient fragments.

The Virgin appears again on the ceiling in a fine painting of the Assumption by Domenichino (17C) *(ask the Sacristan to turn on the light).*

Chancel mosaics ★★. — The mosaics on the chancel arch (the prophets Isaiah and Jeremiah and the symbols of the Evangelists) date from 12C; so do those in the semi dome of the apse: to the right of Christ and the Virgin are St Callistus, St Lawrence and Pope Innocent II offering his church to Mary;

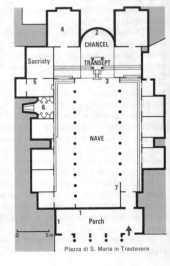

Piazza di S. Maria in Trastevere

on the left are St Peter, St Cornelius, St Julius and St Calepodius. During the Romanesque period mosaic art was still influenced by the Byzantine style: the Virgin is adorned with gold like an Empress, the group of figures betrays a certain oriental rigidity and loses some of its expressive force in the multitude of detail (the Virgin's dress). At the top is a representation of Paradise with the hand of God placing a crown on Christ's head; at the bottom are lambs, symbols of the Apostles, coming from the cities of Jerusalem and Bethlehem and facing the Lamb of God.

The mosaics between the windows and at the base of the chancel arch are a masterpiece by **Pietro Cavallini** (late 13C) representing scenes from the life of the Virgin (her birth, the Annunciation, the Nativity, the Epiphany, the Presentation in the Temple and the Dormition). The medallion above the throne shows the Virgin and Child between St Peter and St Paul with Cardinal Stefaneschi, who commissioned the work, on a smaller scale.

The bishop's throne (2) standing in the apse is made of marble (12C).

An inscription (3) before the chancel marks the site of the *fons olei (p 188)*.

Altemps Chapel (4). — The stucco and frescoes of this chapel are in the style of the Counter-Reformation which developed after the Council of Trent (late 16C).

Transept. — The fine coffered ceiling is late 16C work. The central low relief in gilded and painted wood illustrates the Assumption.

The **Sacristy** lobby contains two very fine old mosaics (5).

The **Avila Chapel** (6) with its dome is the exuberant creation of Antonio Gherardi (late 17C); the *trompe-l'œil* has been used to create a Baroque effect.

Among the treasures of this church is the charming tabernacle (7) by Mino da Fiesole (late 15C).

Continue to Piazza Trilussa.

The narrow streets leading to the square contain a charm quite foreign to the bustle of a capital city.

The Piazza Trilussa commemorates Carlo Alberto Salustri who wrote poetry in the Roman dialect under the pseudonym **Trilussa** (1871-1950); in his racy and mildly satirical style he highlights the popular spirit of the Roman people describing their lives in a long and colourful story. A monument (B) was set up in his honour in 1954.

Nearby is a colossal fountain (D) installed by Paul V in 1612 at the beginning of the Via Giulia and transferred here in 19C when the Tiber embankments were built.

Opposite is the **Sistine Bridge (ponte Sisto)** named after Sixtus IV (1471-84) who had it built (modernised in 19C).

Take Via di Ponte Sisto and then Via S. Dorotea.

According to local tradition the house before the corner (no 20) with the charmingly decorated window on the second floor was the home of La Fornarina, Raphael's mistress, whom he immortalised in his famous painting *(p 154).*

(After photo by Gab. Fot. Naz., Rome)
Raphael: La Fornarina

Distance: 2 km — 1 mile. Time: about 4 hours. Start: Porta Settimiana.

One of the oldest legends in Roman mythology maintains that the **Janiculum** Hill (Monte Gianicolo) was the site of the city founded by the God Janus, whence its name, who had several children, one of whom, Tiber, gave his name to the river.

For many years the Janiculum was a country district. It was not until 17C that Urban VIII constructed a defensive wall with bastions on the line of the presentday Viale delle Mura Aurelie and Viale delle Mura Gianicolensi.

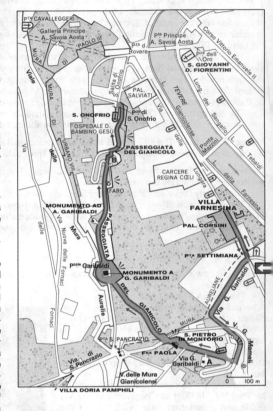

From Mucius Scaevola to Garibaldi. — The Janiculum seems to have inspired many of the heroic acts, legendary or true, which have shaped the history of Rome.

The oldest goes back to 6C BC when the town had broken free of the Etruscan kings and was being besieged by Lars Porsena. Mucius, a young Roman noble, infiltrated the enemy camp on the Janiculum in order to kill their chief. Unfortunately he was mistaken and killed one of the chief's aides; he was immediately arrested. To prove to Lars Porsena that life was of little account to a Roman defending his country, he put his right hand on a burning brasier. Porsena was so struck by such bravery that he let him go. Mucius was henceforth nicknamed Scaevola, left-handed.

In his footsteps came Cloelia, a young woman who, according to Livy, showed a courage 'without precedent among women'. Held hostage in Porsena's camp, she escaped with her companions and made them swim the Tiber to reach Rome.

In 1849 the Janiculum was the scene of one of the battles in the struggle for Italian unity. Garibaldi defended it valiantly in the name of the Roman republic against the French troops commanded by General Oudinot; on 4th July the papal government was re-established after a month of bloody combat, particularly in the Villa Pamphili.

Porta Settimiana. — One of the gates in the Aurelianic wall (Mura Aureliane), it was repaired by Alexander VI (1492-1503) and reinforced with merlons.

■ PALAZZO CORSINI

The palace was built in 15C by the Riario, nephews of Sixtus IV, and passed in 18C to Cardinal Corsini, nephew of Clement XII, who had it rebuilt by F Fuga. Now it houses an art gallery and the Academia dei Lincei, a learned society of scholars and men of letters.

French interlude. — On 31 August 1797 the Ambassador of the Directory, Joseph Bonaparte, accompanied by the young General Léonard Duphot, settled in the Palazzo Corsini. On 28 December a riot broke out in front of the palace led by a few revolutionaries who called for the intervention of the French against the papal government. Shots were fired and General Duphot was killed.

On 10 February 1798 General Berthier besieged Rome and drove out Pius VI who died in exile in Valence in France. Until 29 September 1799 Rome took its cue from the French Republic.

National Art Gallery★. — *Open 9 am to 2 pm (1 pm Sundays and holidays). Closed Mondays. 1 000 L.*

Rooms 1 and 2. — Devoted to foreign painters: Madonna and Child by Murillo; St Sebastian by Rubens; Rest on the Flight into Egypt by Van Dyck.

Room 4. — The **Portrait of Beatrice Cenci★** by Guido Reni (1575-1642) is a remarkable work showing great subtlety.

Room 5. — The **Portrait of Bernini★** by Baciccia (1639-1709) is one of the rare surviving portraits by this artist; he was responsible for the frescoes in the Gesù Church *(p 110)* and is famous chiefly for his talent as an interior decorator.

Room 6. — An inscription commemorates Queen Christina of Sweden who died in this room on 19 April 1689.

Room 8. — The **Narcissus** ★ shows the novel style of Caravaggio (1573-1610) who was a contemporary of Guido Reni and Guercino. Dispensing with background he painted his figures in close-up using light to stress a detail (in this picture the person's knee). Although his unruly life prevented him from having any pupils, his powerful style had considerable influence on the painters of his period, including the painters of *bambocciata* who congregated round **Pieter van Laer**, nicknamed *Il Bamboccio.*

In his Madonna and Child **Gentileschi** followed Caravaggio's style so closely as to be confused with him.

■ VILLA FARNESINA ★★

The villa in its garden setting was built from 1508-11 for Agostino Chigi (1465-1520) the great banker. Known as the Magnificent, he entertained in sumptuous style, including Pope Leo X among his guests.

The villa is designed as a country house with two projecting wings. For the construction and the décor he commissioned the best Renaissance artists: Baldassarre Peruzzi, architect and painter, Raphael with his usual following of Giulio Romano, Francesco Penni, Giovanni da Udine, Sebastiano del Piombo, Sodoma.

The friendship linking all these men is enshrined in the Farnesina Villa: Agostini Chigi was Raphael's most ardent patron and Leo X had a sincere affection for him. None of them saw the sack of the city which brought the Roman Renaissance to an end. Raphael died aged 37 on Good Friday 1520; a few days later came Chigi's death; the following year Leo X succumbed to a 'slight fever'.

Later in 16C the villa was sold to Cardinal Alessandro Farnese and assumed the name of its new owner.

Interior. — *Open 9 am to 1 pm. Closed Sundays and holidays.*

The collection of paintings to be seen in this house is one of the gems of the Renaissance. On the ceiling of the **gallery** along the garden front is a fresco, depicting the legend of Cupid and Psyche (in the centre the Council of the gods and the marriage of Cupid and Psyche), painted by Raphael assisted by Giulio Romano, Francesco Penni and Giovanni da Udine. Finished in 1520 these paintings contain elements which were to become characteristic of the Mannerist style (a series of scenes as in a tapestry framed by garlands).

At the eastern end of the gallery is the **Galatea** room (1511) where Nereus' sea maiden has been painted by Raphael riding in a shell drawn by Dolphins *(right of the entrance).* The monstrous Polyphemous as well as the scenes from Ovid's Metamorphoses *(in the lunettes)* are by Sebastiano del Piombo. The Constellations on the ceiling are the work of B Peruzzi. The young man's head painted in grisaille *(left of the entrance)* is probably by S del Piombo but tradition attributes it to Michelangelo who wanted to show Raphael that his figures were too small.

On the **first floor** the **salon** is decorated with landscapes in *trompe-l'œil* by Peruzzi and his assistants; views of Rome are revealed between the painted columns.

In the next room, formerly a bedroom, the **Marriage of Roxana and Alexander** is by Sodoma (1477-1549). Dismissed from his work in the Vatican by Julius II in favour of Raphael *(p 84)* Sodoma was commissioned by Agostino Chigi to decorate this room, probably in 1509. In a Renaissance setting Alexander extends the crown to Roxana against a cloud of cherubs. The merit of this pleasant painting lies in the beauty of the figures and the harmony and balance of the composition.

These qualities are lacking in the other scenes: Alexander and Darius' mother, Vulcan and three little angels *(on either side of the chimney piece),* the battle scene. To the left of the entrance are Alexander and Bucephalus (late 16C).

Return to the Porta Settimiana and turn right into Via Garibaldi; after crossing Via G Mameli, turn right up the steps to San Pietro in Montorio.

■ SAN PIETRO IN MONTORIO ★

This church which has a commanding view of Rome was built in Sixtus IV's reign at the end of 15C by Ferdinand II of Spain and dedicated to St Peter who, according to a 15C legend, was crucified on the site.

The simple façade is typical of the Renaissance as is the interior, which consists of a nave flanked by apsidal chapels. The chancel was damaged in the siege of 1849 and has been restored.

Several Renaissance works have survived, particularly the **Flagellation** ★ *(first chapel on the right),* a fresco by Sebastiano del Piombo, clearly influenced by the monumental art of Michelangelo.

The ceiling in the next chapel was painted by Baldassarre Peruzzi (1481-1536). The pale fresco of the Virgin, by Pomarancio (1552-1626), and the two transept chapels were added at the Counter-Reformation. In the righthand chapel the allegorical figures on the tombs and the cherubs on the balustrade are by Bartolomeo Ammanati, a pupil of Michelangelo. Beatrice Cenci *(p 116)* is buried beneath the high altar.

The fourth chapel on the left with its multitude of statues is typical of the Counter-Reformation.

Bernini designed the second chapel on the left in the Baroque period; his pupils were responsible for the sculptures.

The "tempietto" ★. — *Access from outside the church through the iron gates on the right, from inside the church through the fourth chapel on the right.*

This charming miniature temple was one of Bramante's first works on his arrival in Rome in 1499.

Despite its small scale the construction has all the grandeur and rigorous conformity of a Classical building. Perfectly proportioned, it is surrounded by a portico supported on Doric columns and surmounted by a dome.

Behind the building in a little chapel is a small cavity said to have held St Peter's cross.

View ★★★ **of Rome.** — *From the open space in front of the church.* The view extends from Monte Mario *(left)* and Castel Sant' Angelo right across the city with its various roofs and domes: to the right of the monument to Victor Emmanuel II and the Capitol are the arches of the Basilica of Maxentius in the Forum; further right again beyond the green expanse of the Palatine is the façade of St John Lateran spiked with statues.

(After photo by Gab. Fot. Naz., Rome)

Bramante: Tempietto

Return to Via Garibaldi.

On the left is a **monument (A)** set up in 1941 to those who died to ensure that Rome was not excluded when Italy was unified.

Pauline Fountain (Fontana Paola). — This fountain was commissioned by Pope Paul V; its shape — a commorative arch — shows the nascent taste for Baroque pomp.

Either make a detour uphill to Porta San Pancrazio and the road of the same name which leads to the Villa Doria Pamphili — 1 km - 1/2 mile — 3/4 hr on foot Rtn. or turn right into Passegiata del Gianicolo.

Villa Doria Pamphili. — A vast public park surrounds a 17C country house *(casino)* which is decorated with statues and low relief sculptures and set among terraces.

■ **THE JANICULUM WALK (Passeggiata del Gianicolo)**

This road winds along the crest of the hill beneath the umbrella pines; it is lined by busts of Garibaldi's men and has some of the finest **views** ★★★ of Rome.

Giuseppe Garibaldi Monument. — In Emilio Gallori's grandiose work (1895) the hero is shown on horseback, gazing towards the Vatican, the object of his revolutionary struggles.

From here there is a **view** of Rome from Villa Medici to St John Lateran; in the distance are the Alban Hills. The midday cannon is fired daily from below the parapet.

Anita Garibaldi Monument. — Garibaldi's wife is shown as an amazon as she appeared at her husband's side. After the 1849 retreat they tried to reach Venice which was fighting the Austrians but Anita fell ill and died near Ravenna. This monument was erected in 1932.

Further on near the lighthouse there is a fine **view** over the whole of the city of Rome.

Further on go down the steps on the right which cut off the hairpin bend of the Passeggiata.

The old tree stump **(B)** is all that remains of the oak tree beneath which Tasso *(see below)* used to sit and reflect on all his misfortunes *(inscription)*.

View of Rome. — *From the square in front of the Ospedale del Bambino Gesù (Hospital of the Infant Jesus).* To the left is the drum of Castel Sant'Angelo surmounted by its angel and the white mass of the Law Courts; just below the Janiculum across the river is the dome of San Giovanni dei Fiorentini; in the background on the edge of the park is the Villa Medici with its two towers and the dome of San Carlo al Corso; slightly to the right are the two belfries of the Trinità dei Monti; then the Quirinal Palace behind the shallow dome of the Pantheon; next, nearer the river is the high dome of Sant'Andrea delle Valle with the lower dome of the Gesù Church behind it; in the background is the Militia Tower; before it rises the monument to Victor Emmanuel II and the flat façade of Santa Maria d'Aracoeli.

Sant'Onofrio. — *Open mornings only.* This church has retained the appearance and atmosphere of a hermitage which it received from its founder, a monk of the order of the Hermits of St Jerome, in 1434. It was here that Tasso (1544-1595) came to die, pursued to the end, even to madness, by his religious doubts; his poem *The Liberation of Jerusalem* is a masterpiece of Italian Renaissance poetry. Chateaubriand too would have liked to finish his days here; on the outside wall of the church overlooking the grave is a long quotation from his Memories from beyond the grave. On the right of the main door beneath the arcade are frescoes by Domenichino illustrating the life of St Jerome (1605). The attractive frescoes in the **apse** ★ were probably painted by Baldassarro Peruzzi assisted by Pinturicchio.

The graceful cloisters were built in 15C.

Distance: 2.5 km - 1 1/2 mile. Time: about 3 1/2 hours. Start: Piazzale Romolo e Remo.

The **Aventine** is the southernmost of the seven hills of Rome; about 40 m - 131 ft high, it has two peaks separated by a gully down which runs the Viale Aventino. Throughout the ancient Roman Republican period it was a popular district, inhabited particularly by merchants who traded among the quays and warehouses on the banks of the Tiber. Many religious shrines were built; among the oldest are the Temples to Diana, Ceres and Minerva, situated between the Via di S. Melania and the Via di S. Domenico.

During the Empire the Aventine became a residential area. Trajan lived there before becoming Emperor and his friend Lucinius Sura built his own private baths there *(northwest of Santa Prisca church);* the Emperor Decius also built a bath house there in 242. So much luxury aroused the envy of the Visigoths; in 410 under their leader Alaric they proceeded to the sack of Rome which lasted three days. The Aventine was utterly devastated.

Nowadays it is a residential district, quiet and green, with many religious houses.

Southwest of the Aventine, near the river, is the **Monte Testaccio,** topped by a cross; it is an artificial mound of potsherds thrown out of the riverside warehouses in antiquity.

A plebeian stronghold. — After the expulsion of the last king (509 BC) the establishment of the new institutions of the Republic was marked by a struggle between the patricians and the plebeians. In 5C BC the plebeians, weary of fighting, which brought them only misery, withdrew to the Aventine as a protest. Menenius Agrippa, who was sent to reason with them, told them the parable of the human body and its members: since their effort benefited only the body, the members decided to stop work; the result was the death of the whole body including the members. As a result of the crisis two tribunes were elected from among the plebeians to protect them against the consuls.

Death of a tribune. — The plebeian tribune Caius Gracchus and his brother Tiberius (the Gracchi) were among the group of Roman citizens who shaped the history of the Republic. Continuing the work begun by Tiberius (assassinated in 133 BC), Caius proposed reforms in the ownership of land confiscated by Rome from subject peoples, which was administered by the Senate and cornered by the wealthiest. He made a last stand on the Aventine against some soldiers recruited by one of the Consuls. When he could hold out no longer, he fled but was overtaken and killed at the foot of the Janiculum in 121 BC.

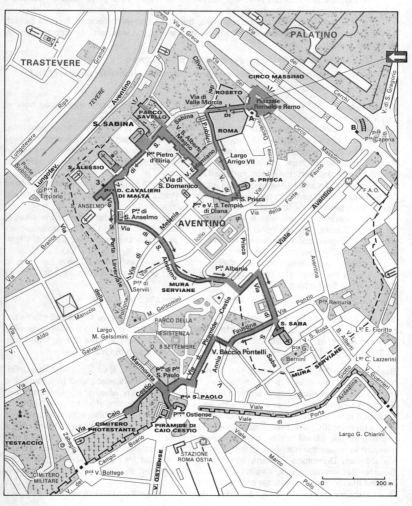

TOUR

There is a fine **view**★ from the Piazzale Romolo e Remo over the ruins of the concave façade of Flavian's Palace on the Palatine.

At the centre of the Piazzale stands a **monument to Giuseppe Mazzini (A)** (1805-72), a writer and politician, who proclaimed a republic in Rome in 1849; papal power was re-instated by the French general, Oudinot *(p 190).*

"Circus Maximus". — The Great Circus, laid out in the valley between the Palatine and the Aventine (the Murcia Valley) and now transformed into a long esplanade, was the largest in Rome. It was used exclusively for two-, three- and four-horse chariot *(biga, triga* or *quadriga)* races which drew larger crowds than any other spectacle.

The track, over 500 m - 550 yds long, was bordered by banks of seats; the stand at the northwest end was reserved for the magistrates in charge of the spectacle; beneath it were the stalls; at the southeast end stood an archway. From 4C BC the arena was divided in two down its length by a central reservation, called the *spina,* which linked the two conical turning posts *(metae)* round which the chariots raced.

In the Augustan era the Circus Maximus became very magnificent. In 10 BC an obelisk (now in the Piazza del Popolo) more than 23 m - 75 ft high, was erected on the *spina* and a splendid stand was built below Flavian's Palace for the Emperor and his family. The Circus Maximus could accommodate 150 000 spectators.

The Emperors continued to make improvements: Claudius (41-54) replaced the wooden turning posts with new ones in bronze gilt and substituted marble for tufa in the stables; after the fire in 64 his successor Nero extended the circus to 600 m - 656 yds long and 200 m - 219 yds wide; Domitian (81-96) and Trajan (98-117) increased the number of stands and the capacity of the circus grew to 250 000 places.

The major events took place during the September games which went back to 6C BC. During the Empire the games became pure entertainment, offered by the Emperor to the people, and a passion for racing often led the Emperors to the worst excesses: Vitellius (68-69) who championed the 'Blues' (there were four stables each distinguished by a different colour) quite simply had his favourite charioteer's rivals put to death; Caracalla (211-217) dealt out the same fate to the 'Greens'.

The circus was still in use in 4C and Constantinus II set up a second obelisk (now in the Piazza di San Giovanni in Laterano).

The few remains which can be seen near the Porta Capena belong to Trajan's period. The little tower (**B**) at this end dates from the Middle Ages; it was part of a fortress built by the noble Frangipani family.

Take Via di Valle Murcia on the right of the Mazzini monument.

The road is bordered by the **Rome Rose Garden** (Roseto di Roma) *(in flower in May).*

Turn left into Clivo dei Publicii.

Santa Prisca. — The church was reconstructed in 17 and 18C but its origin goes back to 2C; it is one of the very first places of Christian worship in Rome.

Various touching legends are connected with the name of the holy woman venerated here. Prisca is said to be the first woman to have suffered martyrdom in Rome: she was baptised by Peter himself but denounced to the imperial authorities and martyred by execution on the road to Ostia. In 13C a Classical capital was set up as a font *(south aisle)* and inscribed with the 'fact' that Peter had used it.

According to another legend Prisca was the wife of Aquila whose memory is recalled by St Paul in his Epistle to the Romans: "Greet Prisca and Aquila, my helpers in Christ Jesus, who have for my life laid down their own necks...".

Excavations have uncovered a **Mithraeum** *(access from the south aisle of the church, 10 am to 12 noon, Mondays and Fridays; 500 L)* dating from the end of 2C. Contemporary with it is a neighbouring twin-nave building which may have been an earlier place of Christian worship above which the present church was built.

Traces of even older buildings, dating from the late 1 and early 2C have been found nearby; they may belong to Trajan's residence (98-117) or to the house of his friend, Licinius Sura, next to the baths he had built.

Take Via del Tempio di Diana, Via Eufemiano and then Via S A Magno.

Savello Park. — In 10C fortifications were built to defend the hill; in 13C they became the stronghold of the Savelli family. From the northwest side high up above the river there is a pleasant **view**★ of Rome: from the Janiculum, St Peter's dome and the Monte Mario with its TV mast round to the monument to Victor Emmanuel II and the Militia Tower.

Santa Sabina ★★. — The church was built in 5C by Bishop Peter of Illyria who had officiated as priest to a *titulus (p 17)* on his site. From the first it was dedicated to Sabina; the legend about this saint, which arose in 6C, does not say clearly whether she lived and died on the Aventine or whether her remains were brought back here after her martyrdom in Umbria under Hadrian (117-138). The building has undergone many alterations: a campanile was added in 10C; the crenellations were removed in 17C. In 13C Pope Honorius III, a member of the Savelli family, gave the church to St Dominic who built the cloisters and convent to house the members of his order. In 16C the enterprising Sixtus V (1585-90) and his architect Domenico Fontana transformed the interior into a typical example of the Counter-Reformation style; this together with subsequent Baroque additions completely effaced the mediaeval character of the church.

Extensive restoration work has revived its earlier appearance in all its glory.

Exterior. — In 15C a portico was added to the door in the side wall. The narthex on the west front was one side of a four-sided portico surrounding an **atrium** which disappeared in 13C when the convent was built.

Opening into the nave is a very beautiful **door**★★ made of cypress wood; it belonged to the original church and dates from 5C. The two leaves are divided into panels, eighteen of which are decorated with the original low relief carvings illustrating scenes from the Old and New Testaments. High up on the left is a representation of the Crucifixion, the oldest example of a representation of this scene in a public place.

Interior★★. — The well-proportioned interior with light streaming through the clerestory windows reflects the vigorous expansion of the flourishing early Christian church.

The basilical plan (the two side chapels added in 16 and 17C have been retained) consists of a nave and two aisles separated by two rows of columns with Corinthian capitals directly supporting a very light arcade (no architrave). The overhead windows have been restored to their original appearance.

The mosaic above the entrance, the only one left of many mosaics which extended along both sides of the nave between the arches and the windows, bears an inscription in gold lettering commemorating the construction of the church by Peter of Illyria during the reign of Pope Celestine I (422-32); the female figures on either side are allegories of the church of the Jews ('Ecclesia ex circumcisione') converted by St Peter and the church of the Gentiles ('Ecclesia ex gentibus') converted by St Paul.

Nave: the frieze of tessellated marble above and between the arches dates from 5C; the mosaic tomb on the floor in front of the *schola cantorum* (the space reserved for the choristers in front of the chancel) belongs to a Master General of the Dominican Order who died in 1300.

Chancel: the rich marble décor *(schola cantorum, presbyterium, ambones)* dating from 9C and destroyed by Sixtus V has been reconstructed from fragments of the original; the ambones and the paschal candlestick are reconstructions. The Mannerist mosaic in the apse by Taddeo Zuccari (retouched in 19 and 20C) replaced the original 16C mosaic which depicted the saints who were venerated in the church.

South aisle: the upper part of a Classical column, discovered during excavations underneath the church, may have belonged to the 3/4C house, the *titulus* of the early church.

At the east end of the aisle is a chapel dedicated to the Virgin in 15C by Cardinal Poggio del Monte di Auxia; his attractive tomb recalls the funeral art of Lombardy at the time of the Renaissance which was introduced to Rome by Andrea Bregno.

North aisle: the 17C Baroque chapel dedicated to St Catherine of Siena has been preserved; its multi-coloured marbles, frescoes and painted dome clash with the serenity of the rest of the church.

In the monks' garden *(apply to the Sacristan),* perfumed by jasmine and geraniums and shaded by orange and lemon trees, is a sculpture of the Last Supper (1974) by Gismondi.

St Alexis' (Sant'Alessio). — This is a church for those who are interested in legends. On the left immediately inside the door is St Alexis' staircase: the son of a patrician family, St Alexis set out for the Holy Land as a mendicant, returning to Rome to die, but his family did not recognise him and he spent his last days beneath the staircase of his father's house. The legend of the 'Beggar beneath the stairs' was one of the main themes of the mystery plays in 15C.

Continue along the road to Piazza dei Cavalieri di Malta.

This charming **square** was designed by Piranesi in 18C.

The door into the Priory of the Knights of Malta (Villa del Priorato di Malta, no 3) is famous for the view through the keyhole which reveals the dome of St Peter's at the end of a well clipped avenue of trees.

Take Via di Porta Lavernale and turn left into Via di S. Anselmo.

On the right just before the Via di S Anselmo reaches the Piazza Albania is a section of the **Servian Wall** (Mura Serviane) which surrounded Rome in 6C BC; this part of the wall was probably rebuilt in 1C BC.

Cross Piazza Albania and take Via di S. Saba.

The San Saba district occupies one of the peaks of the Aventine; its elegant mansions interspersed with open spaces, dating from early this century, have made it a model of town planning for many years.

St Sabas★ **(San Saba).** — When the monks of the Great Laura in Palestine, a religious community founded by St Sabas in 5C, were dispersed in 7C by the Persians and then by the Arabs, many of them took refuge in Rome in a building inhabited a century earlier by St Sylvia, the mother of St Gregory the Great. Towards the end of 10C the monks from the east constructed the present church on top of their smaller 7C oratory. Over the centuries the building was subject to various alterations but was restored from 1911. Excavations below floor level have revealed traces of the early oratory and of a building from the Imperial era which may have been the headquarters of a fire brigade formed by Augustus.

A flight of steps and a porch lead into a courtyard.

Façade. — The portico is contemporary with the church but the columns have been replaced with thick pillars. In 15C a single storey surmounted by a loggia was built on top of the portico by Cardinal Piccolomini, nephew of Pius II; later the floor of the loggia was lowered, the original windows were filled in and replaced by the five existing openings. The campanile on the left dates from 11C.

The main door was attractively decorated in 1205 by one of the Cosmati at the invitation of the Cluniac monks who had succeeded the original community.

Interior. — The basilical plan, with a nave and two aisles each ending in an apse, has been conserved. The lack of uniformity between the pillars (bases, shafts and capitals) is typical of mediaeval buildings in which material from a variety of sources was used. An unusual feature is the additional aisle on the east side of the church; it probably linked the church to the monastery of the eastern monks. It was the Cluniac monks who rebuilt the convent in a new position in 13C thus exposing the additional aisle on the exterior of the church; it contains vestiges of 13C paintings.

The paving was part of the refurbishing carried out by the Cosmati, as is a section of chancel screen, now placed against the wall in the west (right) aisle. In the frieze at the top of the righthand central pillar is a small sculpted head with black stones for eyes; both it and its inscription are an enigma.

During the Counter-Reformation (16C) the paintings in the apse were executed for Gregory XIII; the paintings above the episcopal throne date from 14C.

The Annunciation above the apse dates from 15C.

Turn left into Via Annia Faustina and then right into Via Baccio Pontelli and descend the steps into Via della Piramide Cestia.

St Paul's Gate ★ (Porta San Paolo). — This gate is an interesting example of the alterations that have been made to the Aurelianic Wall (Mura Aureliane) (270-75); in Aurelian's day the gate consisted of two arches flanked by two semi-circular towers on the outside. Maxentius (306-12) raised the towers, extended them towards the inside and linked them to an inner gate also consisting of two arches. Honorius, Emperor in the West (395-423), replaced the two outer arches with the present single arch and added the crenellations to the towers. The gate has been restored on subsequent occasions, particularly in 15C and 18C.

Known in antiquity as the Porta Ostiensis, the gate opened into the Via Ostiense which led to St Paul's Basilica from which the gate took its present name in the Middle Ages.

Via Ostiensis. — The road dates from 4C BC; it was one of the most important commercial arteries in antiquity. Starting in the Forum Boarium, it followed the line of the Lungotevere Aventino and the Via della Marmorata, passed through the wall by a gate situated slightly to the west of the Porta Ostiensis and then more or less followed the route of the present Via Ostiense as far as Ostia, thus linking the salt marshes of the Tiber estuary to Rome.

The road continued to be used in the Christian era since it led to the site of St Paul's martyrdom (Tre Fontane) *(p 142)* and to his tomb in St Paul's Basilica *(p 140).*

Caius Cestius' Pyramid ★. — Caius Cestius, praetor and tribune of the people, who died in 12 BC, devised the most original mausoleum in Rome. The marble covered pyramid testifies to the grandeur of the Augustan era when a simple citizen could erect a tomb worthy of a Pharaoh. Nowadays the white silhouette is one of the most famous sights in Rome.

Take Via della Marmorata and then turn left into Via Caio Cestio.

Protestant Cemetery. — It is also known locally as the Testaccio Cemetery after the mound which is visible at the end of the road *(p 193);* this is a better name as it is in fact a cemetery for non-Roman Catholics both foreign and Italian and includes the graves of members of the Orthodox Church. Between the neat box hedges in the shade of pines and cypress trees many famous people are buried: at the eastern end of the gravel path — John Keats and his faithful friend Joseph Severn, Axel Munthe the author of San Michele; at the foot of the last tower in the Aurelianic Wall — Shelley's tombstone on which Byron had some verses of Shakespeare engraved; half way down the slope in the main cemetery between two tall cypress trees — a tombstone bearing a bronze medallion which marks the grave of Goethe's son who died in Rome in 1830 (the son's name is not given).

Monuments, Museums, Churches:
Most museums close at 2 pm and churches are generally closed between 12 noon and 4 pm.

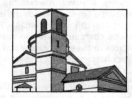

The visitor is very likely to meet the signs "Chiuso per restauri" and "Chiuso per mancanza di personale";
in both cases the place is closed (for restoration or for lack of staff).

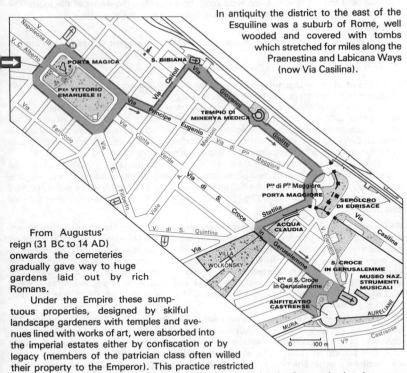

Distance: 2 km - 1 mile. Time: about 2 1/2 hours. Start: Piazza Vittorio Emanuele II.

In antiquity the district to the east of the Esquiline was a suburb of Rome, well wooded and covered with tombs which stretched for miles along the Praenestina and Labicana Ways (now Via Casilina).

From Augustus' reign (31 BC to 14 AD) onwards the cemeteries gradually gave way to huge gardens laid out by rich Romans.

Under the Empire these sumptuous properties, designed by skilful landscape gardeners with temples and avenues lined with works of art, were absorbed into the imperial estates either by confiscation or by legacy (members of the patrician class often willed their property to the Emperor). This practice restricted development to the east and aggravated the problem of lack of space in the city centre which was becoming overcrowded with huge prestigious buildings. In 3C the district was enclosed by the Aurelianic wall (Mura Aureliane). It remained untouched by the building projects of the Popes in the Renaissance and Baroque periods and was not developed until 19C when Rome had become the capital of Italy.

Piazza 'Vittorio'. — The square is usually thronged with people attending the large market held there. It was laid out in the late 19C by Gaetano Koch and other architects with arcades at pavement level as in Turin *(p 121).*

In the north corner of the square are the ruins of a huge 3C fountain which was adorned with the 'trophies of Marius' *(p 56).* The adjacent **Magic Gate** (Porta Magica) continues to excite speculation; the signs inscribed round the doorway (bricked up) have never been deciphered.

Leave the square by Via Principe Eugenio before turning left into Via Cairoli.

Santa Bibiana. — The church was rebuilt in 17C and was one of Bernini's first architectural projects. His **statue** ★ of St Bibiana (or Viviana) *(inside above the altar)* is also one of his early works; note the pictorial effect of the left hand gathering up the folds of the garment.

Continue down Via Giolitti.

Temple of Minerva Medica. — The beautiful circular building, originally covered by a dome, dates from 4C; it was probably a *nymphaeum* in one of the patrician gardens.

Porta Maggiore ★. — The gate was built in 1C AD to carry the Claudian aqueduct across the Praenestina and Labicana Ways where it entered the city. The use of huge roughly hewn blocks of travertine (even for the supports) is an innovation typical of the Claudian era. The upper section which carried the water channels is inscribed with details of the work ordered by Claudius and also by Vespasian (71 AD) and Titus (81 AD) who both carried out restoration work.

In 3C the gate was incorporated in the Aurelianic Wall (Mura Aureliane). When Honorius (395-423) restored the fortifications a bastion was added on the outside; its demolition in 19C revealed the tomb of Marcus Vergilius Eurysaces *(see below).*

Claudian Aqueduct (Acqua Claudia). — Aqueducts are without doubt the most remarkable public works in Roman architecture. This one, which was begun by Caligula in 38 AD and completed by Claudius in 52 AD, is the most impressive. Starting in the mountains near Subiaco it reached Rome after 68 km - 42 miles of which 15 km - 9 miles were above ground. From Porta Maggiore Nero (54-68 AD) built a branch channel, traces of which remain in the gardens of the Villa Wolkonsky, in the Piazza della Navicella and at the eastern end of the Via di San Paolo della Croce (Dolabella's Arch) *(p 138).* This aqueduct was extended by Domitian as far as the Palatine to supply his palace with water.

Tomb of Marcus Vergilius Eurysaces ★ (Sepolcro di Eurisacce). — Eurysaces was a baker who lived in Rome at the end of the Republic. As supplier to the army he probably grew rich during the civil wars of this period and built an enormous tomb in travertine (dating from *c*30 BC) designed to commemorate his trade.

The cylindrical motifs, some vertical and some horizontal, recall the receptacles in which the flour was kept. The inscription separating them identifies the owner of the tomb. The low relief frieze round the top illustrates the different steps in breadmaking.

Go west along Via Statilia.

On the left among acacias and umbrella pines are the elegant arches of the Claudian aqueduct.

Turn left into Via di S. Croce in Gerusalemme.

Museum of Musical Instruments ★. — *Open 9 am to 1.30 pm (12.30 pm Sundays; 7 pm Tuesdays and Thursdays). Closed Mondays. 1 000 L.*

This charming museum displays a very varied collection of instruments dating from antiquity to 19C. Antique whistles, horns and handbells are succeeded by exotic instruments such as beautiful inlaid mandolins; tambourines and ocarinas evoke provincial folk dances. Every sort of instrument is here: mechanical, portable, military, religious and domestic, adorned with fine paintings or inlaid with mother-of-pearl and ivory.

The 17C Barberini harp *(room 11),* which is named after the famous family which owned it and decorated with sumptuous gilt sculptures, is one of the museum's most valuable items. Two rare instruments are the 17C upright harpsichord *(room 13)* with a prettily painted lid and the pianoforte, built in 1722 by Bartolomeo Cristofori, one of the instrument's inventors *(room 15).*

St Cross in Jerusalem ★ (Santa Croce in Gerusalemme). — In this church, originally known simply as Jerusalem, the legend of the Holy Cross is closely linked with history. Here stood the **Sessorian Palace** where Constantine's mother, Helen, lived; it was built in 3C and remained an imperial palace until 6C. In 4C Helen went on a pilgrimage to Jerusalem as was the custom at that time. She returned in 329 bearing a fragment of the true cross which she kept in the palace. The same year she died. A legend then developed according to which it was she herself who had found the true cross. The cult of the Holy Cross was not introduced to Rome until 7C.

History of the church. — In memory of his mother, the Emperor Constantine (or perhaps his sons) converted part of the Sessorian Palace into a church to house the precious relic. It consisted of one large chamber with an apse where the services were held and of a smaller room (the present St Helen's Chapel) where the relic was kept. In 12C Pope Lucius II (1144-45) divided the larger chamber into three and built a campanile without altering the outside walls. He raised the level of the floor in the church but not in the chapel, perhaps because according to tradition the floor of the chapel was composed of soil brought back from Calvary. The chapel was isolated from the church and had a separate entrance until the Renaissance when it was linked to the church by two stairways one on each side of the apse. The church acquired its present appearance in 18C.

Tour. — The 12C campanile is flanked by a lively façade and oval vestibule in the 18C style consistent with the principles dear to Borromini.

The nave vault was refashioned in 18C; the impressive baldaquin over the altar is of the same period.

The apse has conserved the mark of the Renaissance; it is decorated with an attractive fresco by Antoniazzo Romano (late 15C) illustrating the legend of the discovery of the cross by St Helen.

St Helen's chapel *(access by one of the sets of steps beside the chancel)* is decorated with beautiful **mosaics ★**, designed by Baldassarre Peruzzi and, perhaps, by Melozzo da Forli *(time switch on outer pillar of the central arch).* The statue above the altar is a Roman work originally representing Juno but converted into St Helen.

The Chapel of the Relics *(access by a flight of steps from the north aisle)* houses the relics of the Passion; it is visited by thousands of pilgrims who come to venerate the exhibits: the crosspiece from the cross of the penitent robber who was crucified beside Christ *(at the foot of the steps, opposite the entrance);* fragments of the True Cross *(behind the altar);* the 'title' of the Cross, i.e. the superscription discovered at the end of 15C walled up in a cavity at the top of the chancel arch; two thorns from the Crown; St Thomas's finger; fragments of the scourging column, of the Bethlehem grotto and of St Sepulchre; a nail used in the Crucifixion.

On leaving the church bear left; on the left through the opening in the Aurelianic Wall are the remains of the Amphitheatrum Castrense.

Amphitheatrum Castrense. — Its name comes from the Latin word *'castrum'* which in 4C meant an imperial residence. This amphitheatre, like the Sessorian Palace *(see above),* was probably part of the imperial properties in this district. It must have been of great importance since the Aurelianic Wall made a detour in order to enclose it. Built entirely of red brick and dating from the end of the Severian dynasty (3C), it originally consisted of three storeys, of which only the first is well preserved.

This district lies outside the walls between the Via Salaria and the Via Nomentana. It is called "African" because many of the streets are named after the countries which made up the Italian empire and its development took place during the Fascist era (1926).

The monotonous streets, lined with large blocks of comfortable flats, give way in the **Piazza Mincio** to extravagantly decorated buildings in a mixture of Renaissance, Baroque and Egyptian styles, which were designed between 1922 and 1926 by the architect, Gino Coppede.

The sights in this district are described in alphabetical order and shown on the adjacent plan. To reach the African district, consult a transport plan (p 30).

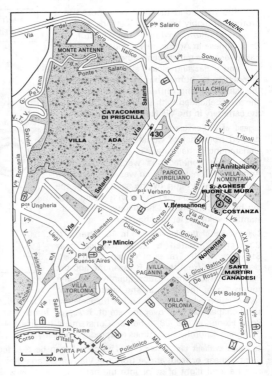

Holy Martyrs of Canada
(Santi Martiri Canadesi). — The church was built in 1955 as the national Canadian church and is dedicated to Jesuit missionaries who set out in 17 and 18C to convert the Indians and were murdered by the Iroquois. The single nave rises in great arches in the shape of a parabola which is repeated throughout the church: in the windows and in the baldaquin which is adorned with low reliefs in ceramic and crowned by a Crucifix. The confessionals on the left are decorated with mosaics. The grouping of the organ pipes over the main door is impressive in its stark simplicity.

Priscilla's Catacombs ★.
— *No 430 Via Salaria. Guided tour (1/2 hr) 8.30 to 12 noon and 2.30 to 6 pm (5 pm 1 October to 30 April). Closed Mondays, 1 January, Easter, Christmas. 2 000 L.*

The catacombs developed out of a private underground chamber *(hypogeum)* beneath the house of the Acilii, a noble family to which Priscilla belonged. Excavations in this chamber have uncovered inscriptions mentioning Priscilla and a certain Acilius Glabrio, who was mentioned by Suetonius; he was condemned to death in 91 AD by Domitian for the same offence as Domitilla's husband, Flavius Clemens *(p 145).* The family was converted to Christianity and allowed the Christian community to create underground galleries in which to bury their dead. During 3C two storeys of galleries developed round the *hypogeum.* In 4C St Sylvester's Basilica, in which several popes are buried, was built by Pope Sylvester (314-35) over the Christian graves.

The **Chapel of the Taking of the Veil** is named after a scene painted on the far wall and originally interpreted as showing a young virgin taking the veil in the presence of the Virgin Mary; nowadays it is thought to represent three episodes in the dead woman's life: marriage, worship, motherhood.

The **Chapel of the Virgin and Child** contains the earliest representation of the Virgin *(on the ceiling)* who is holding the Christ child on her knees while another figure points to a star. The scene is thought to be an illustration of a passage from Isaiah, Chap 7 ("Behold, a virgin shall conceive, and bear a son…").

The **Greek Chapel** (in which there are Greek inscriptions) consists of two chambers separated by an arch. Over the arch in the inner room is a painting of a banquet at which one of the figures at the table is breaking bread; on the table are a chalice and a plate of fish; at the sides are seven baskets of bread which could be an allusion to the miracle of the feeding of the multitude.

The presence of all these items has led to the painting being interpreted as a representation of the Eucharist. Archaeologists give its date as 2C on account of the hairstyle of one of the women seated at the table, a style made fashionable by Faustina, the wife of the Emperor Antoninus Pius (138-61).

St Agnes Without the Walls ★ and St Constance ★ (Sant Agnese fuori le Mura e Santa Costanza).
— The history of these two churches begins with the death of Agnes, a young girl of 12 who was martyred under Diocletian (284-305).

Legend of St Agnes. — Both St Ambrose and Damasus, writing at a period soon after the Diocletian persecution, mention the martyrdom of Agnes. The 6C legend was therefore founded on a basis of truth: Agnes refused to marry the son of the Praetor declaring that she had vowed her soul to God.

She was condemned to be exposed in a brothel, probably beneath the stands in Domitian's stadium, where the church of Sant'Agnese in Agone now stands (p 163); her nakedness was miraculously covered by her long hair and a dazzling cloak; she was then condemned to be burned but escaped unscathed, the flames turning on her executioners; finally she was beheaded with a sword and buried in the cemetery in the Via Nomentana.

Legend of St Constance. — The saint's name is derived from that of Constantia, the Emperor Constantine's daughter or grand-daughter. Such great benefactions were attributed to Agnes that Constantia, who was suffering from leprosy spent a night by the saint's tomb; the young martyr appeared to her in a dream, urging her to convert to Christianity; when Constantia awoke the leprosy had gone.

Construction of the churches. — In 4C (after 337) Constantia erected a huge basilica near St Agnes' tomb. Traces of the apse still exist, clearly visible from the Via Bressanone and the Piazza Annibaliano. Subsequently, to the southwest of the basilica, she built a circular construction which was to be her mausoleum and has become St Constance' Church. A small chapel was built over the site of St Agnes' tomb itself; it was rebuilt and enlarged by Pope Honorius (625-38) whereas Constantia's basilica fell into ruin. This chapel is now St Agnes' Church, many times restored, particularly in 19C.

St Agnes Without the Walls ★. — The church can be reached from below from the Via di Saint'Agnese or from above from the Via Nomentana through the convent courtyard and down a long flight of steps into the narthex; the steps which were restored in 16C were already part of the 7C construction. The walls are covered with fragments from the catacombs, in particular (almost at the bottom on the right going down) a low relief of St Agnes praying, which decorated her tomb, and an inscription to the glory of her martyrdom, which was commissioned by Pope Damasus (366-84) and runs to 10 lines, the first of which is:

FAMA REFERT SANCTOS DUDUM RETULISSE PARENTES.

Despite the addition of 19C paintings above the chancel arch, between the high windows and over the arcades in the nave, the interior still gives some idea of its 7C appearance; it was designed like a basilica with a nave and two aisles and galleries.

The ceiling and baldaquin are 17C. It was during the restoration undertaken by Paul V (1605-21) that the bones of St Agnes were discovered next to another body, probably that of Emerentiana, who continued to pray by St Agnes' body when the other Christians fled from the stones thrown by pagans. Paul V arranged for her bones to be placed in a shrine beneath the altar.

The statue of St Agnes on the altar is a curious work by the French sculptor, Nicolas Cordier (1567-1612) who used the torso of an old alabaster statue of Isis. On the left of the altar is a very fine antique candelabra made of marble.

The **mosaic ★** in the apse was part of the 7C building; it shows St Agnes with Pope Symmachus (498-514) who restored the early chapel and Pope Honorius who is offering the church he built. The work is typical of Roman art under Byzantine influence: Agnes is dressed like a Byzantine empress; the colours are muted and repetitive (same for all three robes); the vertical lines are very clear, in perfect accord with the lines of the vault.

Catacombs. — Guided tour with commentary. Closed mornings Sundays and holidays. 1 000 L. A cemetery was already in existence when St Agnes' remains were buried here. The oldest part on the north side of the church dates back to 2C. After St Agnes' burial the graves spread round behind the apse and down between the church and the mausoleum.

St Constance' ★. — The Emperor Constantine's daughters, Helen and Constantia, were buried in this circular building which dates from 4C. It was probably converted into a church in 13C. The outline of an oval vestibule can still be traced in front of the entrance. The rotunda itself is covered by a dome resting on a drum which is supported on a ring of twinned columns linked by elegant arches. The surrounding barrel-vaulted gallery is still adorned with its original 4C **mosaic ★**, which is an example of the artistic renewal which followed in the wake of Constantine's reign; the vault is divided into panels and covered with a variety of motifs against a light background: floral and geometric, portraits in medallions, vine tendrils entwined with harvest scenes. The mosaics in the side recesses have Christian themes: God handing down the Law to Moses (or according to another interpretation, St Peter receiving the keys) and Christ giving the New Law (the Gospel) to St Peter and St Paul.

In the recess opposite the entrance is a copy of Constantine's sarcophagus (p 81).

Villa Ada. — This vast public park contains the site of the Monte Antenne which is closely connected with the founding of Rome; here stood the Sabine city of the Antemnates who, according to Livy, were conquered by Romulus after attacking the Romans in retaliation for the rape of the Sabine women.

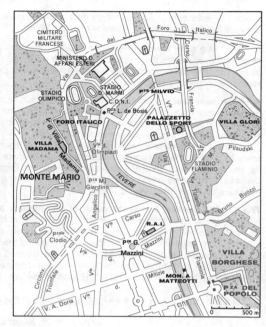

The modern districts bordering the Tiber to the north and northwest of Rome are not particularly interesting for walking so the sights are described in alphabetical order. To reach them, consult the adjacent plan and a public transport map (p 30).

Foro Italico. — The huge sports centre was created by the Fascist government (1929-37). Once the seat of the Academy of Physical Education, it is now occupied by the Italian National Olympic Committee (C O N I). There are tennis courts, a fencing school and swimming pool but the most important facilities are the Olympic Stadium and the Marble Stadium (stadio di Marmi). The opening ceremony of the 1960 Olympic Games was held in the former (capacity: 100 000 spectators) and the latter (capacity: 10 000 spectators) is decorated with 60 statues of athletes and groups of wrestlers in bronze (on the podium).

The road from the Piazza L. de Bosis with its great obelisk to the Piazzale del Foro Italico is paved with mosaics bearing inscriptions to the glory of the 'Duce'.

Matteotti Monument. — This elegant monument in bronze gilt was designed by Iorio Vivarelli and erected by the Tiber in 1974. Its symbol — a young shoot bursting from the earth — commemorates the socialist MP, Giacomo Matteotti who was assassinated in June 1924 for denouncing the illegality of the Fascist regime.

Milvian Bridge (Ponte Milvio or Molle). — There has been a bridge here since 2C BC; it has frequently been restored and rebuilt, particularly in 15 and 19C when it was enlarged and a fortified gate was added.

It was near here that the famous battle took place on 28 October 312 between Constantine and Maxentius, rival pretenders to the imperial throne. On the eve of the battle Constantine had a vision which resulted in his victory. Christ appeared to him and told him to mark his soldiers' shields with a Christian symbol. The alternative tradition that a cross appeared in the sky with the legend. "You will conquer in this sign" is less reliable. Certain historians consider this to be the date of Constantine's conversion to Christianity.

Monte Mario. — The natural beauty of this little hill makes it a popular place among Romans for taking a walk. It offers a fairly extensive **view** ★ of the Tiber and Rome which is particularly interesting at night when the city monuments are floodlit.

Palazzetto dello Sport. — This concave structure was designed by Annibale Vitellozzi and Pier Luigi Nervi for the 1960 Olympics. It is composed of prefabricated concrete sections supported on a ring of distinctive piers which gives the impression of a lightweight construction.

R.A.I. (Radio and TV Centre). — Situated in the new district which has grown up round the Piazza Mazzini and distinguished by a magnificent statue of a rearing horse in bronze by Francesco Messina, this building is one of the many successful modern constructions in Rome.

Villa Glori. — The steep slopes of this pleasant public park are dedicated to the memory of those who died for their country: one of the Cairoli brothers *(p 100)* fell in combat here.

Villa Madama ★. — *For permission to visit apply to the Ufficio Cerimoniale at the Foreign Office (Ufficio Informazioni, Ministero degli Affari Esteri) behind the Olympic Sports Centre; proof of identity essential. Closed Sundays.*

Walk up the Via di Villa Madama.

This Renaissance villa, which has an enchanting **position** ★ on the slopes of Monte Mario, was restored in 1925 to be used by the government for the entertainment of foreign visitors. It was built in 1515 by Cardinal Giulio de' Medici, the future Clement VII, to plans by Raphael and completed by Sangallo the Younger. Like the Palazzo Madama *(p 107)* it passed to Madam Margaret of Austria and was named after her. The main entrance is set in the centre of the semi-circular south front. The north front contains a magnificent deep loggia decorated with stucco work and grotesques by Giovanni da Udine and Giulio Romano, Raphael's pupils, and overlooking a beautiful formal garden (9 ha - 22 acres).

31 km - 20 miles east of Rome. Access by bus leaving from Via Gaeta opposite the station or by car leaving Rome by Via Tiburtina (map pp 34-35).

Tivoli is a small town on the lower slopes of the chalky Apennines (Monti Simbruini) where the river Aniene plunges in cascades into the Roman plain before joining the Tiber. Its main commercial enterprises are the travertine quarries, paper mills, hydro-electric power stations and chemical industries.

A Greek seer and a Roman sybil. — Tivoli, Tibur in antiquity, is said to have been founded earlier than Rome by Tiburtus, grandson of the Greek seer Amphiaraos whom Zeus caused to be swallowed up in the earth outside Thebes. Tibur came under Roman control in 4C BC and became a holiday resort under the Empire.

Several centuries later, according to a mediaeval legend, two great prophecies were made by a Sybil. When Augustus asked her whether there would be anyone greater than he, she sent him a vision of the Virgin and Child on the Capitol in Rome and added that on the child's birthday a spring of oil would bubble up from the ground; this is supposed to have taken place in Trastevere *(p 188)*.

The Tivoli Rebellion or the downfall of an emperor and a pope. — In 1001 Tivoli rebelled against the German Emperor Otto III, who was in Italy with Pope Sylvester II. The Romans who had no love for their neighbours in Tivoli, made common cause with the Emperor. The Pope intervened and the Emperor spared the town and the rebels but, when the Pope and the Emperor returned to Rome, the Romans reproached them for their leniency; both had to flee the mob. The following year Otto died and Sylvester the year after. Tivoli retained its independence until 1816 when it was attached to the Papal States.

■ **HADRIAN'S VILLA** ★★★ **(Villa Adriana)** *(plan p 203)*

4,5 km - 3 miles west of Tivoli, alight from the bus at the stop (Fermata) called "Bivio Villa Adriana". There is a walk of 1.5 km - 1 mile south from the bus stop to the Villa.

Open 9 am to one hour before sunset. Closed Mondays, 1 January, 25 April, 1 May, 15 August, Christmas. 3 000 L.

The 5 km - 8 mile perimeter enclosed an estate consisting of vast gardens adorned with works of art, an imperial palace, baths, libraries and theatres. It was probably the richest building project in antiquity and was designed entirely by Hadrian. He had visited every part of the Roman empire and it was on his return from the Oriental provinces in 126 AD that he began work on his villa. He was very knowledgeable about art and architecture and he tried to recreate the works and sites he had visited during his travels. In 134 the villa was almost finished; Hadrian was 58. Ill and griefstricken at the death of his young favourite Antinoüs, he died in Baiae in 138. His remains were buried in his huge mausoleum in Rome *(p 93)*. The Emperors who succeeded him probably continued to come to Tivoli. It was here that Zenobia, Queen of Palmyra, ended her days as Aurelian's prisoner.

Then the Villa fell into ruin. From 15 to 19C the site was explored; over 300 works were recovered which now enrich museums and private collections in Rome, London, Berlin, Dresden, Stockholm and Leningrad. Since 1870 the site has belonged to the Italian Government which has organised its excavation. The vegetation has been cleared from the ruins revealing magnificent vaults, columns, stucco work and mosaics.

The present entrance is probably not the one used in Hadrian's day. The design of the Villa is so unusual that archaeologists have not been able to identify the buildings or their uses with any certainty. Before exploring the site it is adviseable to study a model of the villa which is displayed in a room next to the bar.

Poikile ★★. — This was the name of a portico in Athens which Hadrian wished to reproduce. Only the north wall remains through which the visitor enters the excavation site itself. Notice the latticework effect created by small blocks of tufa set on their edges to form a diaper pattern; Hadrian's Villa is one of the last examples of this technique which fell into disuse in 2C. The horizontal grooves in the wall were filled with bricks which disappeared when the villa was plundered for its materials, in particular for the Villa d'Este in Tivoli.

The Poikile was built in the shape of a large rectangle with slightly curved ends and lined with a portico; it was sited so that one side was always in the shade.

The apsidal chamber called the **philosophers' room** (1) was perhaps a reading room.

Maritime Theatre ★★★. — The circular construction consists of a portico and a central building surrounded by a canal which was spanned by small swing bridges. It was obviously an ideal retreat for the misanthropic Hadrian.

Bear south.

The flat area enclosed between sections of high wall was at first thought to be a stadium but has since been identified as a *nymphaeum*. Among the ruins is a *cryptoporticus* part of a whole network of underground passages which made it possible to walk from one end of the villa to another without coming up above ground level. The columns *(to the west)* belonged to a building comprising three semi-circular rooms round a courtyard (2).

Baths ★★. — First come the Small Baths and then the Great Baths. They both show the high architectural standards attained in the villa: rectangular rooms with concave walls, octagonal rooms with alternate concave and convex walls, circular rooms with recesses alternating with doors. The most impressive room is in the Great Baths; it has an apse and the remains of some superb vaulting.

The tall building, called the **Praetorium,** was probably a storehouse.

Museum. — It contains the results of the most recent excavations: Roman copies of the Amazon by Phidias and Polyclitus; copies of the Cariatids from the Erechtheion on the Acropolis in Athens. These statues adorned the sides of the Canopus.

There are more ruins belonging to the villa to the west of the museum in a large olive grove but it is private property.

Canopus ★★★. — It was his visit to Egypt that gave Hadrian the idea of constructing a souvenir of the town of Canope with its famous Temple of Serapis. The route to Canope from Alexandria consisted of a canal lined with temples and gardens. Hadrian had part of his estate landscaped to look like the Egyptian site and completed the effect with a canal down the centre and a copy of the Temple of Serapis at the southern end. He combined the cult of Serapis with the cult of Antinoüs, his young favourite who had been drowned in the Nile.

On leaving the Canopus bear right between the Great Baths and the Praetorium, climb to the upper level and continue towards the Nymphaeum before bearing right.

The path circumscribes a large **fish pond** surrounded by a portico (Quadriportico con peschiera) (3).

Imperial Palace. — The complex extended from the Piazza d'Oro to the Libraries.

Piazza d'Oro ★★. — The rectangular area was surrounded

HADRIAN'S VILLA

0   100 m

⟶ Sightseeing route

CANOPUS

Praetorium

Museum

GREAT BATHS

4

Piazza d'Oro

SMALL BATHS

5

3

6

7

IMPERIAL PALACE

9

8

Nymphaeum

2

Library Court

POIKILE

10

MARITIME THEATRE

13

12

11

Bar

P

Vale of Tempe

14

Theatre

N

TIVOLI / ROME

by a double portico; the Piazza was an aesthetic caprice serving no useful purpose. On the far side are traces of an octagonal chamber (4): each of the eight sides, which are alternatively concave and convex, was preceded by a small portico (one of which has been reconstructed). On the opposite side is a chamber (5) covered by a dome and flanked by two smaller chambers: the one on the left contains traces of a fine black and white mosaic pavement.

Doric Pillared Hall ★★ (6). — It takes its name from the surrounding portico which was composed of pilasters with Doric bases and capitals supporting a Doric architrave (partial reconstruction in one corner). Opposite stood the **firemen's barracks** *(Caserma dei vigili)* (7).

Adjoining the Pillared Hall *(north side)* is a huge section of curved wall which may have been part of a summer **dining room** *(triclinio estivo)* (8); the oval basins further east mark the site of a **nymphaeum** *(ninfeo di palazzo)* (9). These buildings overlook a courtyard which is separated by a *cryptoporticus* from the **library court**; the east side of the latter court is composed of a complex of ten rooms ranged down both sides of a corridor; this was an infirmary (10); each of the rooms held three beds; the **floor ★** is paved with fine mosaics. The library courtyard offers a pleasant **view ★** over the countryside.

Libraries. — The ruins of the library buildings are on the north side of the courtyard; according to custom there was both a Greek library (11) and a Latin library (12).

Next to the libraries *(east side)* is a group of rooms paved with mosaic which belonged to a **dining room** *(triclinio imperiale)* (13).

Terrace of Tempe. — A grove of trees hangs on the slope above a valley which Hadrian called his Vale of Tempe after the Greek beauty spot in Thessaly. The path runs through the trees past a **circular temple** (14) (reconstructed) which contained a statue of the goddess Venus and was thus attributed to her. Further along *(left)* is the site of a **theatre**.

Proceed to Tivoli; town plan in the Michelin Red Guide Italia (hotels and restaurants).

The **Rocca Pia**, a fortress built by Pius II (1458-64), dominates the Largo Garibaldi.

■ VILLA D'ESTE ★★★

In 1550 Cardinal Ippolito II d'Este, who had been raised to great honours by François I of France but had fallen into disgrace when the king's son Henri II succeeded to the throne, decided to retire to Tivoli, where he immediately began to convert the former Benedictine convent into a pleasant country seat. The Neapolitan architect, Pirro Ligorio, was invited to prepare plans. The simple architecture of the villa contrasts with the elaborate gardens which descend in a series of terraces covering 3 ha - 7 1/2 acres on the western slope of the hill. The statues, pools and fountains enhance the natural beauty with all the grace of the Mannerist style. Many distinguished guests visited the Villa, including Pius IV and Gregory XIII and after the Cardinal's death, Paul IV, Paul V, Pius IX and writers and artists: Benvenuto Cellini, Titian and Tasso, and Liszt. In 1759 when the avenues were overgrown with brambles and the fountains silent, Fragonard and Hubert Robert, who were staying at the French Academy in Rome, came to spend the summer in Tivoli with their patron the Abbé de Saint Non; there is scarcely a corner of the gardens where they did not set up their easels nor a perspective that escaped their brushes.

St Mary Major (Santa Maria Maggiore). — This is the old abbey church belonging to the Benedictine convent. It has an attractive Gothic façade and a 17C bell tower. Inside are two 15C triptychs *(in the chancel):* above the one on the left is a painting of the Virgin by Jacopo Torriti, who also worked in mosaic at the end of 13C.

House and gardens ★★★. — *Open 9 am to 7.30 pm (5 pm November to March). Closed Mondays, 1 January, 25 April, 1 May, 1st Sunday in June, 15 August, Christmas. 4 000 L. The gardens are floodlit after dark from 1 April to 31 October. Route shown on plan below.*

The entrance is in the courtyard, formerly the convent cloister.

The **Old Apartment** (Vecchio Appartamento) on the first floor of the Villa now houses a small picture gallery; notice the ceiling frescoes in the Throne room *(Room 4),* the frieze of allegorical figures with the Este eagles and the arms of Ippolito II in the library *(Room 5),* the painted wooden ceiling by the Flemish artist Flaminio Bolinger in the Cardinal's bedroom *(Room 6)* and finally the elaborately decorated Chapel with a fresco by Livio Agresti over the altar.

Return to the courtyard and descend to the ground floor.

Central Hall. — The decorations in the Mannerist style were painted by pupils of Girolamo Muziano and Federico Zuccari. The fountain which is decorated with mosaics faces a wall panel showing the gardens in 16C. On the ceiling is a fresco of the Banquet of the Gods.

Leading out of this room is a series of four rooms in the west wing. The mythological paintings in the first room are attributed to Muziano and Luigi Karcher: the Labours of Hercules around a fresco of the Synod of the Gods *(ceiling).* Federico Zuccari and his school painted the allegorical frescoes in the next room, known as the Philosopher's Hall, and also the frescoes in the third room called the Glory of Este. In the Hall of the Hunt Tempesta's frescoes show hunting trophies and scenes of hunts in the country round Tivoli.

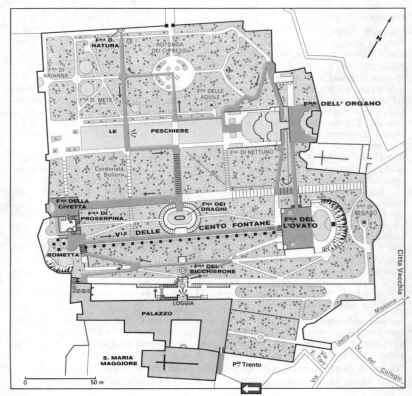

From the balcony of the Central Hall there is a pleasant **view ★** of the gardens and Tivoli itself.

Double flights of steps lead down to the upper garden walk.

Bicchierone Fountain. — The huge moss covered beaker which overflows into a shell-shaped basin is often attributed to Bernini.

Rometta Fountain. — 'Mini Rome' is an attempt by the Cardinal to reproduce some of the well known monuments of Classical Rome: a pool bearing a boat (Tiber Island) surmounted by an obelisk; higher up next to some artificial ruins an allegorical statue of Rome and the she-wolf.

Avenue of a Hundred Fountains ★★★ (Viale delle Cento fontane). — This is one of the most charming spots in the gardens. One side of the straight walk is lined by fountains of water spouting from small boats, obelisks, animal heads, eagles and lilies which recall the Este coat of arms.

Oval Fountain ★★★ (fontana dell' Ovato). — On the upper terrace is the statue of the Sybil flanked by allegorical figures of rivers. Round the edge of the basin, half covered in moss, are statues of naiads pouring the water of the river Aniene from their water pots. An attractive ceramic decoration adorns the front rim of the oval basin.

Organ Fountain ★★★ (fontana dell' Organo). — It used to play music on a water-powered organ concealed in the upper part of the fountain. This ingenious mechanism was invented by a Frenchman, Claude Venard, in 16C. After seeing and hearing the fountain Montaigne, the French writer and philosopher, wrote in his journal that "the organ music is made by water falling into a cave with such power that the air is forced out through the organ pipes while another stream of water turns a toothed wheel which operates the keyboard; one can also hear the distorted sound of trumpets".

Fishponds (le Peschiere). — The three basins were fishponds which supplied the Cardinal's table on fast days. There is a fine **view ★★** of the water spouts and the Organ Fountain.

Nature Fountain (fontana della Natura). — The statue is of Diana of Ephesus, goddess of fertility.

The gate in the wall *(right)* was originally the main entrance to the Villa and opens into the road which drops down into the valley below.

Dragon Fountain (fontana dei Draghi). — It was created in honour of Pope Gregory XIII who visited the Villa in September 1572 shortly before the Cardinal's death; the dragons recall the coat of arms of the Buoncompagni family to which the Pope belonged.

Owl Fountain (fontana della Civetta). — It is more commonly known as the **Bird Fountain** on account of the hydraulic mechanism, originally concealed in a recess, which used to produce bird song; periodically an owl appeared and uttered a mournful screech. Several times restored, the fountain is now silent.

On the left is the **Fountain of Proserpina** who was abducted by Pluto; it has been modernised.

From the Villa d'Este it is possible to walk down to the Villa Gregoriana through the streets of the old town (città vecchia).

The town is agreeably lively and some traces of the past still remain.

The **Cathedral,** rebuilt in 17C and flanked by a 12C Romanesque campanile, contains a fine group of carved wooden figures depicting the **Deposition ★** (13C).

■ VILLA GREGORIANA ★

Open 10 am to 7 pm (9.30 am to 6.30 pm in winter). 750 L.

A tangle of paths winds down the steeply wooded slopes to the river Aniene where it cascades through the ravine.

Take the path downhill from the entrance and bear right to the **Great Cascade ★★** (Grande Cascata).

There is a terrace overlooking the waterfall from above. Take the path which zigzags down to a viewpoint near the foot of the fall (Veduta inferiore della Cascata) where the river plunges into the ravine throwing up a fine spray.

Return to the last junction and take the path marked "Grotte di Nettuno e Sirena, cascata Bernine" which starts with a short flight of steps and winds down into the valley bottom to the **Siren's Cave** where the Aniene plunges out of sight into a cavern with a great roar.

Return to the sign marked "Grotto di Nettuno et tempio di Vesta" and take the path leading up the opposite side of the valley. Ignoring the righthand turning to "Tempio di Vesta e Sibilla", bear left towards "Grotta di Nettuno". After the tunnelled section bear left downhill. In **Neptune's Cave** the water bursts from the rock face which has been eroded into eerie configurations.

Return to the beginning of the tunnelled section but bear left up the path which climbs the slope overlooking the ravine and its many little waterfalls.

Next to the park gates which lead into the town stand the ruins of two temples.

Sybil's Temple. — *Access via Ristorante Sibilla.* It is also known as the Temple of Vesta as shrines dedicated to this goddess were usually round. This elegant Corinthian structure dates from the late Republic. Next to it stands a contemporary building in the Ionic style, also supposed by some to be dedicated to the Sybil. Both temples were built of travertine.

24 km - 15 miles southwest of Rome. Access: by car along Via del Mare (plan in the Michelin Red Guide Italia — hotels and restaurants); by underground train (B line) leaving from Stazione Termini or from Porta San Paolo (alight at Ostia Antica).

The long grey sandy beach at **Ostia Lido** is the nearest to Rome and the most popular.

■ OSTIA ANTICA ★★

There is nothing to see of the mediaeval village of Ostia except the 15C **castle** built by Cardinal Giuliano della Rovere (Julius II) to protect Rome from attack by sea.

The main interest of a visit to Ostia Antica lies in the vast area of ruins which once constituted the principal port of Rome.

HISTORICAL NOTES

Ostia, at the mouth of the Tiber, takes its name from the Latin word *ostium* meaning mouth. According to Virgil, Aeneus disembarked here. Livy says that it was Ancus Martius (640-616 BC), the fourth king of Rome after Romulus, who 'extended his dominion to the sea, founded Ostia at the mouth of the Tiber and established salt pans all around'. Archae-ologists, however, place the founding of Ostia in 4C BC while also admitting that an earlier village of salt extractors may have existed. Ostia's development has reflected that of Rome: it was a military port when Rome embarked on her conquest of the Mediterranean shores and a commercial port when the victorious city established an organised system of trade.

Military port. — Roman control of the mouth of the Tiber, set at *c*335 BC, corresponds with her expansion in the Mediterranean; several years earlier (in 338 BC) the Romans had won their first naval victory at Antium. During the war against Pyrrhus (278 BC) the fleet sent by Carthage to assist the Romans docked in Ostia. During the Punic wars (264-41 and 218-01) Ostia served as an arsenal; Scipio's army embarked here for Spain (217 BC) to prevent reinforcements reaching Hannibal who had already crossed the Alps and defeated Flaminius at Lake Trasimene; two years later about thirty ships set sail from Ostia for Tar-entum which was planning an alliance with Hannibal; in 211 BC P Cornelius Scipio took ship for Spain in order to avenge the defeat of his ancestors; barely 25 years old and excep-tionally invested with proconsular power, he covered himself with glory.

Commercial port. — At first there was simply a castle *(castrum)* to protect the port from pirates but by 1C BC Ostia had become a real town. In 79 BC Sulla built a rampart round three sides using the Tiber to protect the fourth side. (The last bend in the river was then further east than it is now so that the river flowed in a straight course along the north side of the town: *p 208*.) Rome imported food from her numerous overseas provinces. A cargo of wheat from Sardinia was unloaded in Ostia as early as 212 BC. It was essential that the cargoes should be protected. The efforts of Pompey in 67 BC and of Agrippa from 63 to 12 BC had rid the sea of pirates. Only the problem of entering port remained: frequent strong winds restricted access to the summer months and the adjacent coastline consisted of dunes, lagoons and shallows. As a result the merchant ships usually docked in the Nea-politan ports and the goods had to be carried overland to the capital.

Claudian Port. — In antiquity the shoreline ran parallel to the west side of the excavated site *(plan p 209)*. Claudius' engineers avoided the mouth of the Tiber itself because of the pres-ence of a sand bar created by the currents. Instead they sited the harbour on the right bank of the river, north of the town of Ostia and the Fiumicino branch of the Tiber (roughly corresponding to the site of the Leonardo da Vinci international airport). The harbour cov-ered about 70 ha - 173 acres and was protected by two incurving breakwaters, with an artificial island in the harbour entrance between the ends of the breakwaters. Since the entrance faced northwest the harbour was sheltered from the strongest winds such as the Libeccio (from the southwest) and the Scirocco (from the southeast).

Trajan's Port. — When the Claudian harbour became too small, Trajan (98-117) built a second harbour inland. It was hexagonal in shape, covered 30 ha - 74 acres and was lined with docks and warehouses. It was joined to the Claudian harbour by a broad channel and to the Tiber by a canal, the Fossa Trajana.

Decline and excavation of Ostia Antica and the Isola Sacra. — Like Rome, Ostia began to decline in 4C. The harbours silted up, the alluvium deposited by the Tiber extended the shoreline seawards and malaria depopulated the town. Ostia suffered the fate of all Roman ruins and was pillaged for its materials. Regular excavations have been undertaken since 1909; the western sectors of the town were excavated from 1938 to 1942.

Between the town and the harbour the **necropolis of Trajan's Port** was discovered on the Sacred Island (Isola Sacra) which had been created by digging the Fiumicino channel; since the days of antiquity the land has advanced several miles towards the sea.

Life in Ostia. — Ostia was a very busy commercial town and under the Empire its popula-tion rose to 100 000. Its main streets were lined with shops; administrative buildings clus-tered round the forum; warehouses and industrial premises were concentrated near the Tiber; the residential districts extended towards the seashore.

It was a cosmopolitan town, which welcomed a variety of foreign religions; several of their places of worship have been discovered: the oriental cults of the Great Mother (Cybele), of Isis and Serapis, of Jupiter Dolichenus and particularly of Mithras.

Christianity too had its adherents; Minucius Felix, a Christian writer, chose the sea baths at Ostia during the harvest holiday as the setting for his conversation with Octavius Januarius, another Christian, and Caecilius, a pagan whom they were trying to convert.

In 387 St Augustine's mother, Monica, died in Ostia on her way home to Africa.

Ostia dwelling houses. — Their discovery has added to our knowledge of the houses of the lower paid in the ancient world.

The most common dwelling in this densely populated town was the **insula**, a block of flats to let, several storeys high; the wealthier citizen lived in a **domus**, a detached house with a courtyard and garden. All the buildings were of brick and probably unrendered. Some have elegant entrances framed by a triangular pediment resting on two pillars. Here and there a porch or a balcony adds interest to the street front. Sometimes the brickwork is finished with a decorative effect; **opus reticulatum** is frequently used: small squares of dark tufa and lighter limestone are laid on edge to form a diaper pattern; this technique was practised from 1C BC to 2C AD; after 1C AD the corners were sometimes reinforced with courses of brick. Another technique used in Ostia, particularly in 2C AD, is **opus testaceum**: pyramid shaped bricks are laid very regularly on their sides — point inwards, flat bottom outwards; to strengthen the structure courses of ordinary rectangular bricks were inserted every so often between the bands of triangular patterning.

TOUR OF THE EXCAVATIONS

Open 9 am to 6 pm (4 pm 1 October to 1 March). Closed Mondays, 1 January, 25 April, 1 May, 1st Sunday in June, 15 August, Christmas. 2 000 L. About 4 hours.

A tour of this extensive ruined site usually means a pleasant tree-lined walk.

On the left inside the entrance but outside the town limits is the **Via delle Tombe** reserved for burials of various types: sarcophagus, columbarium or chapel.

Rome Gate. — This was the main entrance to the town and led into the **decumanus maximus**, the east-west axis of all Roman towns; in Ostia it was paved with large slabs and lined with porticoed buildings and warehouses *(horrea)*. From the outer side of the gate the broad and busy Via Ostiense carried traffic to Rome.

Piazzale della Vittoria. — The small square took its name from a **statue of Minerva Victoria** (1C) (1), a copy of an original Greek work. The statue probably adorned the town gate.

Neptune Baths. — This 2C building has a terrace *(steps up from main street)* with a view of the fine **mosaics** ★★ which depict the marriage of Neptune and Amphitrite (2).

Via dei Vigili. — The construction of this street in 2C meant the demolition of earlier buildings which contained a **mosaic** ★ (3) showing the heads of figures symbolising the Winds and four provinces (Sicily, Egypt, Africa, Spain). At the end of the street stand the **firemen's barracks** built in 2C; on the far side of the courtyard is the Augusteum (for the cult of the Emperor) (4); the floor mosaic shows a bull being sacrificed.

Take Via della Palestra.

Via della Fontana. — This well preserved street still contains its public fountain (5). On the corner with the Decumanus Maximus stood Fortunatus' tavern; the mosaic floor bears the inscription: *"Dicit Fortunatus: Vinum cratera quot sitis bibe"* (Fortunatus says: Drink wine from the bowl to quench your thirst) (6).

Hortensius' Warehouses ★. — These grand 1C warehouses *(horrea)*, built round a pillared courtyard and lined with shops, are a striking example of *opus reticulatum*. On the right of the entrance is a small shrine dedicated by Hortensius (floor mosaic).

Theatre. — Ostia was probably provided with a theatre under Augustus. It has been much restored. The three fine masks (7) come from the stage.

Piazzale delle Corporazioni ★★★. — Under the portico in the square were the offices of the 70 trading corporations; set into the mosaic pavement are their emblems showing in which commodity they traded and their country of origin: grain assessors, caulkers, ropemakers, ship builders and fitters, from Alexandria, Arles, Narbonne, Carthage etc.

The **temple** (8) in the centre of the square (only the podium and two columns remain) is sometimes attributed to Ceres and sometimes to the *Annona Augusta*, i.e. the imperial corn supply which was worshipped like a god (Ostia was a centre for the *Annona*, the office responsible for organising the distribution of corn among the people of Rome *(p 151)*.

Apuleius' House. — A house with a pillared *atrium* and mosaic floors.

Seven Spheres Mithraeum. — This is one of the best preserved of the many temples dedicated to Mithras which have been found in Ostia. One can still see the two benches for the initiates and a relief showing the sacrifice of the bull.

Return to the Decumanus Maximus.

Via dei Molini. — The street is named after some mill stones which were found in one of the buildings (9). Opposite are the ruins of several warehouses *(horrea)* where goods were stored.

Return to the beginning of the block and turn right into Via di Diana.

Piazza dei Lari (10). — In the square *(left)* there is an altar dedicated to the Lares. Here also are traces of a primitive fortress *(castrum)* made of huge blocks of tufa.

Diana's House ★ **(Casa di Diana).** — Facing on to the square is a striking example of an *insula* (block of flats) with rooms and passages arranged round an internal courtyard; note the fine corbel in the side street (Via dei Balconi).

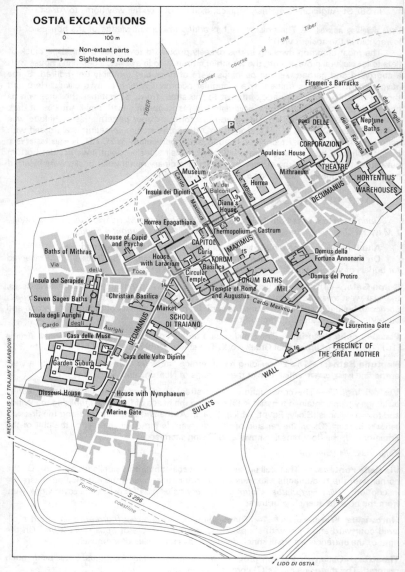

OSTIA EXCAVATIONS

0   100 m

—— Non-extant parts
▷▶ Sightseeing route

"Thermopolium" ★ . — This building was a bar with a marble counter and display stands below paintings of the fruit and vegetables which were on sale. Its name, which is derived from a Greek word, means 'hot drinks for sale'.

Insula dei Dipinti. — Block containing several dwellings grouped round a garden.

At the end of the Via dei Dipinti on the right an oil store (11) was found with huge jars half buried in the ground.

Museum ★ . — *Open 9 am to 1 pm. Same ticket as for the excavations.*

The museum displays the articles found at Ostia in a clear and well lit presentation. The first rooms *(I to IV)* are devoted to crafts illustrated by low reliefs and to the oriental religious cults, which were particularly flourishing in a town such as Ostia with so many overseas contacts; the group showing Mithras about to sacrifice the bull, which is remarkable for its size, indicates the strength of the cult which had some fifteen shrines in Ostia.

Room VIII contains not only a fine 1C BC statue of a hero in repose (Cartilius Poplicola is written on the base) but also a series of **portraits** ★ , particularly of the Antonines: the quality of expression and of detail indicates the high standard of 2C Roman portraiture. The decline which set in 3C is evident *(Room X)*.

Rooms XI and XII contain examples of the rich interior decoration found in Ostia: walls covered with mosaics *(opus sectile: p 22)*, paintings and frescoes from 1C to 4C.

Take Via del Capitolium which opens into **Cardo Maximus**, an important street at right angles to the Decumanus.

Capitol and Forum ★★ . — The **Capitol** was the largest temple in Ostia, built in 2C and dedicated to the Capitoline trio: Jupiter, Juno and Minerva. Although the marble facing is missing from the walls, the brick remains are impressive, as are the steps leading up to the *pronaos;* in front of the steps is a partial reconstruction of the altar.

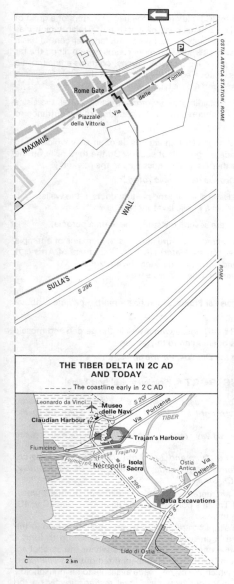

THE TIBER DELTA IN 2C AD AND TODAY

- - - - The coastline early in 2 C AD

The **forum** was enlarged in 2C; the few pillars still standing belonged to the surrounding portico. At the far end stands the **Temple of Rome and Augustus** (1C), a grandiose building once faced with marble, which indicates the loyalty of Ostia, the first Roman colony, to the government in Rome.

As in all Roman towns, the forum in Ostia had a **basilica**, a covered building where the citizens could meet, and a senate house (**curia**) where the municipal council met.

Circular Temple. — It was built beside the basilica and was probably dedicated to the cult of the Emperors in 3C.

House with Lararium ★ (Casa del Larario). — The building consists of shops ranged round an internal court. The recess decorated in attractive red and ocre bricks housed the statues of the Lares.

Continue along the Decumanus before turning right into Via Epagathiana.

Epagathiana Warehouses ★. — This huge complex of warehouses built near the Tiber in 2C has a fine doorway with columns and a pediment. It belonged to two rich freedmen — Epagathus and Epaphroditus.

House of Cupid and Psyche ★★. — Like most of the buildings facing the seashore, this was a private house (4C). Fine remains of mosaic and marble floors and of a *nymphaeum* decorated with niches, arcades and columns.

Turn left into Via del Tempio d'Ercole and then right into Via della Foce.

Baths of Mithras. — An arcade leads into the 2C building. Inside is a flight of steps descending to the underground hypocaust (heating system) and traces of a *frigidarium* (pool and columns with Corinthian capitals). Traces of floor mosaics.

Return to Via della Foce.

Serapis Insula ★. — The two blocks of dwellings were built in 2C with porticos round a courtyard and a bath house in between. Traces of stucco work on a doorway.

Seven Sages Baths ★. — The baths are part of a complex. There is a handsome mosaic floor in the large circular room and one of the communicating rooms is roofed with a dome decorated with mosaics on a white ground.

Charioteers' Insula (Insula degli Aurighi). — At the centre of this block of dwellings is an attractive court with a portico; some rooms still have traces of paintings.

Take Cardo degli Aurighi and then Via delle Volte Dipinte.

Casa delle Volte Dipinte; casa delle Muse; casa delle Pareti Gialle. — *Apply to the Keeper of the Museum to visit these houses.* 2C residential houses with traces of mosaics and paintings.

Garden Suburb. — Example of a 2C residential complex with blocks of dwellings surrounded by gardens and fountains (there are remains of several fountains, one containing mosaic).

Dioscuri House. — It was built in 4C in one of the garden suburb blocks. The rooms are paved with beautiful multi-coloured mosaics, one of which shows the Dioscuri *(p 44)*.

House with Nymphaeum. — Incorporated in 4C into a 2C building; one of the rooms is screened by three arches supported on slim columns with capitals.

Marine Gate. — This gate in Sulla's walls gave access to the seashore. A few huge blocks of tufa remain. Inside the gate *(left)* was a tavern (12) and outside *(right)* a tomb (13).

The Decumanus came to an end outside the gate in a large colonnaded square.

Schola di Traiano. — This impressive 2 to 3C building was the head-quarters of a guild of merchants. On the left of the entrance is a plaster copy of a statue of Trajan which was found in the building, hence its name. Next comes a court with a rectangular central basin surrounded by brick columns. The basin was altered when more rooms were built on the far side of the court in 3C. The central room, preceded by two columns, contains a fine mosaic floor. During excavations a 2C house was discovered on the east side of the court furnished with a *nymphaeum* (paintings and mosaics) and a peristyle.

Christian Basilica. — In this 4C Christian building, a row of columns separates the aisles which end in apses; an inscription on the architrave of a colonnade marks the entrance to what has been identified as the baptistry.

Market. — There were two fishmongers' shops (**14**) on either side of an alley which led to a pillared podium standing on the west side of the market square. On the third pillar on the left it says in Latin: "Read and know that there is a lot of gossiping in the market".

Take Via del Pomerio and then turn left into Via del Tempio rotondo.

Forum Baths ★. — The largest baths in Ostia showing the heating ducts in the walls.
Adjacent to the north side of the baths is a public lavatory (**15**).

Mill. — On the left of the Cardo Maximus are several millstones beneath a pergola.

Precinct of the Great Mother. — This sacred enclosure contains the remains of a temple dedicated to Cybele (the Great Mother — *Magna Mater*) (**16**). The Sanctuary of Attis (**17**) has a statue of the goddess in the apse and two fauns flanking the entrance.
The Cardo Maximus ends at the **Laurentina Gate** in Sulla's wall.

Turn left into Via Semita dei Cippi.

On the right in this street is the **Domus del Protiro** which has a marble pediment above the door, an exception in Ostia.

Domus della Fortuna Annonaria. — 3 to 4C house with a well in the garden and mosaic floors; one of the rooms has three arches opening on to the garden.

Take Via del Mitreo dei Serpenti to rejoin the Decumanus Maximus.

■ **NECROPOLIS OF TRAJAN'S PORT ★** (Sepolcreto dell' Isola Sacra)

5 km - 2 miles north of the excavations. Access by car: take S 296 (towards Leonardo da Vinci airport near Fiumicino) then turn right into Via Cima Cristallo. Entrance to the necropolis on the left of the access road.
Access by bus: take bus 02 from the railway station, alight at the stop (fermata) called Necropoli.
Open 1 April to 30 September, 9 am to 1 pm and 2 to 7 pm; 1 October to 31 March, 9 am to 12 noon and 2 pm to 1 hour before sunset; Sundays closes 1 pm. Closed Monday, 1 January, 25 April, 1 May, 15 August, Christmas.

Isolated and silent the necropolis is an impressive place, studded with umbrella pines, cypresses and laurels. The inhabitants of Trajan's port buried their dead here from 2C to 4C. Ostia had its own graveyards outside the town.

There are tombs of every sort. The simplest are marked by an amphora buried in the ground or by several amphorae arranged in an oval or by a row of tiles set up to form a ridge. Other tombs built of brick comprise one or more chambers where the sarcophagi were placed. Sometimes there is a court in front of the chambers fitted out as a *columbarium* (with recesses for the cinerary urns) which the owner made available to his household.

The majority of the tombs have a low door beneath a lintel resting directly on the uprights; the inscription gave the name of the dead person with sometimes a low relief sculpture depicting his occupation in life.

■ **ROMAN SHIP MUSEUM** (Museo delle Navi)

Access by car: continue along S 296. Access by bus: take bus 02 into Fiumicino and then take an airport bus asking to be put down at the entrance to the airport. From Rome take the airport bus from Statione Termini (Via Giovanni Giolitti) asking to be put down at the entrance to the airport.
Open 10 am to 1 pm. Closed Monday, 1 January.

The museum, a modern building on the site of Claudius' Port *(p 206)*, houses the Roman remains which were uncovered during the building of the airport in the late 50s. On display are the hulls of five **vessels**: two large and one small shallow draft cargo barges, drawn by oxen, for transporting goods from the port up the Tiber to Rome; a sea-going sailing boat; a fishing boat, propelled by oars, with a central wooden keep for live fish; and smaller articles: pottery, fishing floats, rope, nails, wooden pegs, needles, money. There are two electronic wall **panels** which show, at the touch of a button, the pattern of imports in the Roman Empire from 1 to 4C AD and the position of all the Roman boats which have been excavated. A low relief sculpture *(copy)* shows the boat which transported Caligula's obelisk, now in St Peter's Square. The boat was sunk deliberately to provide a foundation for the lighthouse at the harbour mouth; it stood 50 m - 164 ft high and the light could be seen up to 30 km - 18 miles out to sea.

Northwest of the museum are remains of the harbour mole where the lighthouse stood; northeast was the customs house; other related buildings have been excavated to the southeast *(across the road)*.

CASTELLI ROMANI

Castelli Romani, "Roman fortresses", is the name given in the Middle Ages to the region southeast of Rome. While anarchy reigned in Rome, the noble families sought refuge in the outlying villages building themselves castles. Thirteen villages were fortified in this way: Frascati, Grottaferrata, Marino, Castel Gandolfo, Albano, Ariccia, Genzano, Nemi, Rocca di Papa, Rocca Priora, Monte Compatri, Monte Porzio Catone, Colonna.

Nowadays the Romans readily leave the capital for the 'Castelli' where they find fresh air, extensive views, clear skies and little country inns with pleasant arbours.

Historical and geographical notes. — The 'Castelli' are situated in the **Alban Hills** *(Colli Albani)* which are volcanic in origin. They form a circle, the circumference of which is the edge of an immense burnt out crater, pockmarked with secondary craters which have now turned into lakes.

Meadows and sweet chestnut trees spread up the hillsides, while the lower slopes are covered with olive groves and vineyards which produce the famous Castelli wine. In the valleys the volcanic soil is particularly suited to the cultivation of early vegetables.

The history of the Alban Hills is linked to that of Rome. Cicero, the Emperors Tiberius, Nero and Galba had country houses there and Cato the Censor was born near Camaldoli in 234 BC.

■ ROUND TOUR STARTING FROM ROME★★

Distance: 122 km - 76 miles. Time: a whole day. Map below.

Leave Rome by Via Tuscolana (S 215).

On the outskirts of Rome the Via Tuscolana passes **Cinecittà,** the Italian Hollywood.

Frascati★. — This was the favourite resort of the affluent youth of ancient Rome. From the main square there is an extensive view downhill as far as Rome and uphill to the terraces of the Villa Aldobrandini.

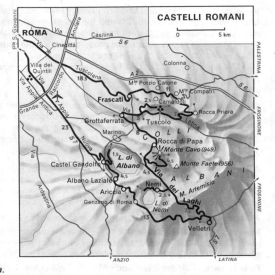

Frascati has gained a reputation for its white wine and for its 16 and 17C villas, particularly the **Villa Aldobrandini★** set high on the hillside above its terraces, clipped avenues, fountains and rockeries *(park only open 9 am to 1 pm, Monday to Friday; apply for permission to the Tourist Office (Azienda di Soggiorno e Turismo), 1 Piazza Marconi, Tel: 942.03.31 — closed Saturday and Sunday.*

Take S 216 bearing right after 6 km - 3 miles for Rocca Priora.

The road offers a good view of **Monte Compatri** and **Monte Porzio Catone** as it climbs up to **Rocca Priora** which clings to the northern rim of the huge crater in the Alban Hills.

Descend to Via Latina (S 215); turn right; after 4 km - 2 1/2 miles turn right again to Tuscolo.

Tuscolo. — It was in his villa in ancient Tusculum that Cicero set his series of philosophical treatises known as the Tusculanes.

The city was once the fief of the Counts of Tusculum; from 10 to 12C this powerful family owned most of the Castelli and extended its power as far as Rome, also providing several of the popes. Tusculum was completely destroyed in 1191 in an engagement with the Romans and was never rebuilt. A few traces survive: up the slope to the left near the large cross which is now half hidden in the trees on what was once the citadel are the ruins of a small theatre with the remains of a water cistern at the back.

Return to Via Latina and turn right.

Grottaferrata. — In 1004 a monastery was founded in the ruins of a Roman villa by Greek monks from Calabria. The **abbey★,** which is served by Roman Catholics of the oriental rite, looks like a fortress, being surrounded by ramparts and a moat which were added in 15C. It stands at the lower end of the main street which runs down through the town centre.

In the narthex *(on the left)* is an attractive marble font (10C). The doorway into the church is in the Byzantine style decorated with representations of animals and leaves; the carved wooden doors are 11C; above them is an 11C mosaic. The interior was remodelled in 18C but the chancel arch is still decorated with a late 12C mosaic representing the Apostles at Whitsuntide. St Nilus' chapel *(right)* has a 17C coffered ceiling and is adorned with frescoes (1608-10) painted by Domenichino. In the right aisle is the *crypta ferrata,* a room in the Roman villa which was converted to a place of Christian worship in 5C.

Take S 218 to Rocca di Papa.

Rocca di Papa. — The village fans out on a picturesque **site** ★ on the slopes of Monte Cavo facing the Alban lakes and hills. It lies at the heart of hunting country and is a favourite spot among those who appreciate hare and rabbit dishes *(coniglio alla cacciatora)*.

Continue along S 218 bearing left to Monte Cavo.

Monte Cavo. — Alt. 949 m - 3 114 ft. *Toll road: 500 L.* On the way up there are glimpses of huge stones which paved the ancient Sacred Way leading to the Temple of Jupiter on the top of Monte Cavo. Here in 5C BC the representatives of the cities of the Latin League, including Rome, used to meet. In 4C BC, however, Rome defeated the other cities in the League and embarked on her conquest of the peninsula.

The Temple of Jupiter became a convent which has, in its turn, been converted into a hotel and restaurant. There is a fine **view** ★ from the terrace of the Apennines, the Castelli Romani, Lake Albano and Lake Nemi, Rome and the surrounding countryside.

Rejoin S 218; turn left into Via dei Laghi; after 3.5 km - 2 miles turn right to Nemi.

Nemi. — The village occupies a charming **site** ★★ in a natural amphitheatre on the steep slopes of a crater now filled by Lake Nemi. One tower of the Ruspoli castle still stands, the only trace of the mediaeval *castello.* In June delicious wild strawberries are served in Nemi.

Lake Nemi. — The road down to the lake passes through fields of daisies, poppies and strawberries. The lake is called Diana's mirror because the sacred wood next to the Temple of Diana is reflected in it. In 1929 the level of the water was lowered by 9 m - 30 ft so that two boats from the reign of Caligula (37-41 AD) could be recovered. They were burned during the war and only a few charred remains are housed in the museum *(closed).*

Rejoin Via dei Laghi (S 217).

Via dei Laghi ★. — A beautiful road winding between oak and sweet chestnut woods.

Velletri. — The town has been prominently involved in Italian history: it resisted Joachim Murat, was captured by Fra Diavolo the Calabrian brigand chief, was fought over by the troops of Garibaldi and Naples and was damaged by bombardments during the Second World War. It is now a prosperous modern town on the south facing slope of a crater in the Alban Hills at the centre of a wine producing region.

The imposing 14C **Torre del Trivio** rises from the main square, Piazza Cairoli.

Descend to the Cathedral at the bottom of the town.

Cathedral Chapter Museum. — *Open June to September from 9.30 am to 1 pm. Closed Mondays and holidays. 700 L. Entrance in the portico to the left of the cathedral door.*

It contains several fine paintings on wood (Madonna and Child by Gentile da Fabriano, 15C), 12 and 13C parchments, one illustrating the story of Christ's Passion with text in English, and other religious treasures (14C chasuble belonging to Benedict XI etc.).

Take S 7 to Ariccia.

Ariccia. — The main square, with its two fountains, was given its present appearance in 1664 by Bernini: the palace on the right *(north side)* of the road became the property of the Chigi banking family in 17C; the Church of the Assumption on the left *(south side)* is elegantly flanked by two porticos (the circular interior, capped by a dome, is worth a visit).

Albano Laziale. — It takes its name from Domitian's villa, Villa Albana.

Tomb of the Horatii and the Curiatii ★. — *At the entrance to the town on the left below the road.* The tomb, which is made of huge blocks of peperine, with truncated cones at the corners, dates in fact only from the last days of the Republic *(see below).*

Porta Pretoria. — *At the lower end of Via A. Saffi in Via Alcide de Gasperi.* These ruins were once the entrance gate to a fortress built by Septimius Severus (193-211).

Santa Maria della Roṭonda ★. — *At the end of an alley at right angles to Via Aurelio Saffi.* The church is a converted *nymphaeum* belonging to Domitian's villa. It was been restored to its original brick appearance. Bold 13C Romanesque campanile.

Villa communale ★. — *Piazza Mazzini.* The huge public garden contains traces of a villa which belonged to Pompey (106-48 BC).

Castel Gandolfo. — On the edge of a crater now filled by Lake Albano stands Castel Gandolfo, famous worldwide as the summer residence of the Pope.

Alba Longa. — The site of ancient Alba Longa has been identified as that of Castel Gandolfo. It was the oldest town in Latium founded, according to legend, *c*1150 BC. Its rivalry with Rome led to the famous battle between the Horatii and the Curiatii. Tired of fighting a costly war, the two cities decided to settle their differences by single combat between three Roman brothers, the Horatii, and three Alban brothers, the Curiatii. At the first encounter two of the Horatii were killed, the three Curiatii were wounded; the last of the Horatii pretended to take flight in order to separate his adversaries and then turning defeated them one by one. On returning to Rome, Horatius met his sister Camilla at the Capena Gate *(p 179)* mourning her lover, one of the Curiatii, and cursing Rome, the "sole object of her resentment". He killed her, was put on trial but acquitted.

Papal Villa. — *Not open.* The entrance is in the main square. The Holy See acquired the 'Castello' Gandolfo at the end of 16C. In 1628 Urban VIII commissioned Maderno to design a villa on the site of Domitian's earlier villa (81-96 AD) which had extended as far as Albano Laziale. The Vatican observatory *(Specola Vaticana)* was established here in Pius XI's reign.

Lake Albano ★. — There is a good **view** ★ of its enclosed site from a terrace at the entrance to the village; there is a road down to the lakeside.

Return to Rome along Via Appia Nuova.

INDEX